M000188746

SENECA INDIAN MYTHS

Collected by
Jeremiah Curtin

DOVER PUBLICATIONS, INC.
Mineola, New York

Published in Canada by General Publishing Company, Ltd., 30
Lesmill Road, Don Mills, Toronto, Ontario.

Bibliographical Note

This Dover edition, first published in 2001, is an unabridged
republication of the edition published by E.P. Dutton & Company,
New York, in 1922.

Library of Congress Cataloging-in-Publication Data

Seneca Indian myths / collected by Jeremiah Curtin.
    p. cm.
    Originally published: New York : E.P. Dutton, c1922.
    ISBN 0-486-41602-X (pbk.)
    1. Seneca Indians—Folklore. 2. Seneca mythology. 3. Tales—
New York (State) I. Curtin, Jeremiah, 1835–1906.

E99.S3 S237 2001
398.2'089'9755—dc21

                                     2001022026

Manufactured in the United States of America
Dover Publications, Inc., 31 East 2nd Street, Mineola, N.Y. 11501

NOTE

The Indian myths here presented, in their original form as dictated to Mr. Curtin by aged Indians of the Seneca people, were collected by him while acting as an agent of the Bureau of Ethnology of the Smithsonian Institute, and are now published with the permission and approval of that body.

Mr. Curtin considered the collection of the ideas of primitive peoples as indispensible to the study of the development of the human mind. From college days, though living abroad and occupied with affairs connected with his diplomatic position, he spent his leisure time studying philology and mythology; and when, many years later, in 1883, he was offered a position in the Bureau of Ethnology, he was very glad to enter the field as an active worker.

His teacher in the Seneca language was Sim Logan, a Seneca Indian, who was in Washington in government employ and was willing to add to his earnings by acting as Mr. Curtin's tutor. At the end of four months Mr. Curtin had acquired considerable knowledge of Seneca, which he found one of the most interesting of Indian languages. In September of that year Logan left for his home near Versailles, N. Y., and a few days later Mr. Curtin went to Versailles to begin work in the field.

He remained there till late in December and it was during this time that he collected most of the myths in the present volume. He appointed a time and place, and when the Indians assembled he told them why he had come to the Reservation; that the Bureau of Ethnology wished to preserve their traditions and myths and that this could only be done by writing them down. A young man called Two Guns, immediately advised the people to have nothing to do with Mr. Curtin, as he was there to get hold of their Seneca religion and store it away as a curiosity. He had

considerable influence, and Mr. Curtin might have been unable to get any of their traditions had not Solomon O'Beal,
a wise old "pagan," stood firmly by him and for the Insti-
tution that wished to collect and save the folk-lore of the
Senecas. O'Beal was a son of Corn Planter, a descendant
of Handsome Lake, "the great teacher." He was highly
respected by the old Indians of the tribe and after he had
told Mr. Curtin all the traditions and myths stored in his
mind, each man was willing to add what he knew. It was
only the old who possessed any knowledge of Seneca mythology—middle aged and young men had "thrown it away."
If the myths in this book had not been collected at that
time they would have been lost.

Before Mr. Curtin left the Reservation he had so far
won the esteem and confidence of the Senecas that they
wished to adopt him into the tribe and give him an Indian name. He was glad that they were friendly, and was
willing to become one of them. A Council was called, and
an 'old man performed the ceremony of adoption; afterward announcing to those present that the old men of the
trible had given their new member the name of HI-WE-SAS
(Seeker of Knowledge).

How the Indians obtained the traditions of "the first
people" is recounted in the story entitled, *The Origin of
Stories*.

Mr. Curtin was again in Versailles in May, 1888, and
on that occasion met with no opposition, for he was now
a member of the tribe. At this time however, he found
very few myths that he considered of value, for in 1883
they had given him the best of all they had. Nevertheless he obtained much information regarding their old-time
customs and ceremonies. For instance: On May 2nd of
that same year he was present at an Indian funeral feast
given by George White for his wife, ten days after her
death. It was the last time her spirit would enter the
house and eat—she ate "the spiritual part of the food."
A large quantity of food was placed on a table in the living room. After a time an old man arose and eulogized
the dead woman; then he divided her clothing among her
intimate friends—the relatives retained no part of it.
Later he divided the food, none of which was eaten in

the house or left there. The Indians who participated in this funeral feast were all "pagans."

A week after the funeral feast Mr. Curtin gave a "Kettle feast" to the Indians of New Town—the "pagan" Indians. It was their annual spring festival after the planting season was over. Mr. Curtin simply paid for the uncooked food. Three fires were lighted outside the "Long House" and a huge kettle was hung over each fire. In one kettle was hulled corn; in the second beef was cooked, in the third pork soup and brown beans. When each person had partaken abundantly of the corn and soup, dancing began. The dances were all of a religious nature— dances in honor of the Great Spirit, who gives the blessed Springtime.

Mr. Curtin left Versailles on June 1st of that year and was never able to return there.

It is perhaps hardly necessary to emphasize the extraordinary interest and value to students of folklore and primitive beliefs of the material so tirelessly and carefully collected here by Mr. Curtin, or to stress the fact that if the collecting of it had been delayed a few years the opportunity to gather it would have been lost forever.

As a matter of fact, the knowledge here brought together of the early Seneca traditions has, as far as the Indians are concerned, entirely vanished from the earth, and is only preserved in these records left behind him by Mr. Curtin.

G. M. A.

CONTENTS

CONTENTS

CONTENTS

SENECA INDIAN MYTHS

SKAGÉDI AND THE MAN-EATER

[Told by Andrew Fox]

Characters

SKAGÉDI (*Half of anything*) ....The Half Man
ONGWEIAS ....Man-eater

SKAGÉDI lived on a hill and a man-eater lived at the foot of the same hill. The man-eater had a little kettle and a piece of chestnut. One day he scraped some of the chestnut into the kettle and taking a stick whipped the kettle till it was of the size he wanted and was full of chestnut pudding. Then he called for someone to come and eat with him.

He began to sing and dance; when he reached the end of the house, he struck his mallet against a post, and sang, "If a man-eater comes, I will kill him."

SKAGÉDI heard the song and the call, and he thought, "I am hungry, maybe I had better go down to that man's house and get something to eat. He will not kill me, for I am not a man-eater. If he calls again, I will go." He stood waiting uncertain what to do.

Soon the man-eater sang, "I wish SKAGÉDI would come and help me eat this pudding."

"Now is my time," thought SKAGÉDI, "I will go."

He sang "HE-GĀH-YA" and jumped. Again he sang, "HE-GĀH-YA" and jumped; this was the way he traveled, he jumped by singing. At the first jump he went over the hill, then he said to himself, "This is too risksome; that man is dangerous." Again he heard the song, "if a man-

8

eater comes, I will kill him," and he said, "I think I had better go home, he may kill me."

SKAGÉDI turned around, and singing, "HE-GĀH-YA" jumped, but he didn't go where he wanted to. He came down near the man-eater's house. Hearing the man-eater's song he was frightened and singing in a whisper, "HE-GĀH-YA," he jumped, but again he didn't go where he intended; he came down in front of the man-eater's house—the man-eater's song was drawing him there. He heard the mallet strike the wall, and singing, "HE-GĀH-YA" to get away he jumped and came down at the door. The man-eater opened the door and said, "Come in!"

SKAGÉDI was terribly frightened; singing "HE-GĀH-YA" in a low whisper he jumped to get away, but he went straight into the house.

"I am not going to kill you," said the man-eater, "I want you to eat some of my pudding."

SKAGÉDI ate a good while, then stopped.

"You must eat all of the pudding I have given you," said the man-eater. "That is my rule."

SKAGÉDI ate more of the pudding and then wanted to stop, but the man-eater said, "Hurry, I must go away, eat quickly."

SKAGÉDI finished the pudding.

"The next time I invite you," said the man-eater, "if you start you must come, not start and try to turn back."

SKAGÉDI was so full of pudding that it was night before he got home; he could jump only a few feet at a time.

The man-eater had always gone South to hunt for game, but now he went North. After a while he came to an opening in the forest, and, in the middle of the opening, he saw a house.

"I have never seen that house," thought he. "I will go and find out who lives there."

In the house was a very old man. "Hello!" said the man-eater, "I have come to visit you."

"I have never seen you before," said the old man.

"No. What are you doing here?"

"I have lived here always, I am a betting man."

"What game do you play?"

"I play hide-and-seek, and bet heads."

"Oh, that is the way you bet! I am alone in the world, but I don't want to have my head cut off. Can I come to life afterwards?"

"No, you will stay dead."

"Well, I will go and talk with my uncle about this. I will come back."

By his "uncle" the man-eater meant SKAGÉDI. He went home, made a pudding, struck the kettle twice and had enough for two, then he went to the post of the house, beat time on it with the mallet, and sang, "I want my uncle to come and help me eat this pudding."

SKAGÉDI heard the song and said to himself, "I am hungry, I will go." He sang "HE-GĀH-YA," took a short jump and was outside of the door. Turning in the direction of the man-eater's house he sang, "HE-GĀH-YA," jumped and was down the hill. Then he listened and wondered if the man-eater really called him. Again he heard the song, then he said, "Oh, he means me!" He sang "HE-GĀH-YA," jumped and was near the man-eater's house. Then he heard the blows of the mallet and was so frightened that he sang "HE-GĀH-YA" in a whisper and jumped to get away, but he didn't go as he wanted to; he came down at the door of the man-eater's house.

"Come in," said the man-eater. "Yesterday I went toward the North. I had never been in that direction before, but I have killed everybody in the South so I thought I would find out who lived in the North. I came to a house in an opening. In the house was a very old man, who said that he lived by betting. The man who loses the game loses his head also. He asked me to play. I told him I didn't know the game, but I would ask you if you knew anything about it."

"I know the game," said SKAGÉDI. "My father was a great player, but at last he lost his head."

"If you will help me," said the man-eater. "I will help you. When you are hungry you can always come here and get something to eat; I will never harm you."

"I will tell you what to do," said SKAGÉDI. "The old man will hide first and you will have three chances to find him. Begin inside the house, but for your last chance say, 'I have found you, you are up behind the sun.' Then it will be your turn to hide. Go under the back of the old man's breech-clout. If he finds you it will be a tie. Then he will go in at one end of the log on the fire and out at one end of the house, I don't know which end. That is your chance."

SKAGÉDI ate his pudding and went home.

The next morning the man-eater hit the post and sang, "Now I must be strong and kill the old man who bets heads."

He went to the house in the opening and called out, "Hello, my friend!"

The old man looked up, and said, "Oh, you have come again. Will you play a game with me?"

"I will play."

"What do you do at home?"

"I hunt."

"Do you find enough game?"

"Yes, I go in every direction and kill everybody I find."

"You kill animals?"

"I do not, I kill men and witches."

"That is my way of living," said the old man. "Now we will have a little sport. We will play hide-and-seek. If you find me and I find you it will be a tie, then we will have a foot-race, or we will pitch quoits to decide the game. I will hide first. Stand here and cover your head with a blanket, when I say One^n! throw off the blanket and hunt for me."

The man-eater waited a while, when he heard, far away, "One^n;" he took off the blanket and found himself alone. He hit the fire with a mallet, and said, "You are under the fire"—No answer. He waited, then called out, "You are up behind the sun."

The old man came down, and said, "Now it is your turn to hide," and he threw the blanket over his own head.

The man-eater made himself small, crawled under the old man's breech-slout, then said, and his voice seemed far away, "One^n."

The old man looked everywhere. "You are behind that big star up there," said he. No answer. He went out and around the house and finding a crack in the house struck it, and said, "You are in here." No answer. Then he went into the house and taking his pipe, made of a wild-cat's head, said, "I will smoke. Maybe the smoke will tell me where to find that man."

He drew a long whiff, the smoke went toward the corner of the house where the corn pounder was. The old man struck the pounder and called out, "You are in the pounder." His three chances were gone.

The man came from the back of the breech-clout. The old man felt him move, and clapping his hand to his thigh said, "You were here!"

"I was."

"That was sport. Let's play again," said the old man.

"I have played long enough," said the man-eater, and, catching the old man by the hair he cut off his head. Then he thought he would look around and see what the man had been doing.

At the edge of the woods he found a great many bones. He stacked the bones up, then going to a tree gave it a push and called out, "Get up or the tree will fall on you!" Men sprang up and ran for their lives. All the people in the world heard the tree fall and knew that some one had killed the old man.

The man-eater burned up the old man's house and his body, then he carried the head home and put it up at the end of his house.

The next morning he thought, "Now I will make a pudding for my uncle."

He scraped a little chestnut into a kettle, struck the kettle with a switch and straightway the kettle was large and was full of pudding. Then he struck the post with his mallet and sang for SKAGÉDI to come.

SKAGÉDI heard the song, and said, "My nephew has killed the betting man." He sang "HE-GÄH-YA" and with two jumps was at the house.

"What luck did you have?" asked he.

The man-eater showed the head, and said, "This is my luck!"

"Well, nephew," said SKAGÉDI, "that would have been your head if I hadn't helped you."

"I know it, and I will always help you and give you

a plenty to eat. Will I have more trouble if I go farther North? Have you been in the North?"

"I have been all over the world; two long jumps will take me anywhere. If you have trouble I will help you."

SKAGÉDI went home and the next morning the man-eater went North again. He passed the house he had burned and went on till he came to an opening and saw a woman standing on a log that was lying on the ground. The woman had great eyes and was looking around in every direction; if she saw anything, even a bird or a mouse, she called out, "I have caught you, I think you are a man!" When the man-eater saw her, he dodged behind a tree. If the bird or animal she called to were a man, her words made him take his own form, then she squeezed his heart and killed him.

The man-eater had never seen such a woman. He thought, "That is a dangerous woman, I will go home," and he crept away. The next morning he sang and danced and his steps shook the world and frightened everybody.

SKAGÉDI said, "My nephew has come!"

The man-eater cooked a bit of the chestnut he had stolen from people in the South and when he had switched the kettle and made it large, he said, "Now I will sing for my uncle. I want to ask him about the woman who stands on a log."

SKAGÉDI heard the song and, singing "HE-GĀH-YA" he made a jump and was over the trees and down the hill. Then with a whispered song and a short jump he was in the man-eater's house.

While he was eating, his nephew said, "Off in the North there is a woman who stands on a log and says to every mouse or bird or living creature she sees, 'I have caught you, I think you are a man.' I have never seen such a woman, I want to talk to her."

"I know that woman," said SKAGÉDI. "She caught my brother. If she sees you first, she will catch you and squeeze your heart. If you are weak, she will kill you; if you are very strong you may come home, but you will be sick."

"I want to kill that woman," said the man-eater.

"Well," said SKAGÉDI, "I will help you if you will promise to stop killing people. It is wrong to kill people and eat them."

"I was brought up on such flesh," said the man-eater. "I couldn't live on game as you do. I will try, but I don't want to starve."

"You must come and eat of my kind of food," said SKAGÉDI. He went home and cooked fat deer meat, then he sang, "The man-eater must come and eat! the man-eater must come and eat."

The man-eater heard the song and started. When he came into the house SKAGÉDI placed deer meat before him, and said, "You must eat it all, that is my rule."

He ate the meat and went home. For a time he was sick, then he felt better and was hungry. He tried to eat some of his own kind of meat but the first bite made him sick. He thought he would go and ask SKAGÉDI what he could do to get well. He was so weak that he was a long time getting to the house on the hill.

SKAGÉDI said, "Try my meat," and he gave him bear meat. He ate it and felt stronger.

"I will come to-morrow and eat more of your kind of meat," said he. "If it doesn't make me sick, I will hunt deer and bears hereafter and let men alone."

The next morning he took a mouthful of his own food. It made him sick. "I will eat no more of this kind of meat," said he, and he went to SKAGÉDI, and said, "Hereafter I will eat your kind of food. Now tell me about the woman."

SKAGÉDI said, "When you come to the opening you must call a mole, go inside of it and tell it to take you to the log. When the mole gets to the log, jump out and say to the woman, 'I have caught you!'"

The man-eater went home, took down the heads stuck up around the house and, pushing them along with a stick, for he was afraid of getting sick if he touched them, he got them far away from the place. Then he went off and killed a deer, came home, cleaned up his kettle, cooked the deer meat and ate it with relish.

The next day the man-eater went to the opening and found the woman standing on the log watching for a fly, a bird, a mouse or any living thing so that she could sing out, "I have caught you! I think you are a man."

He called a mole and told it to carry him under the ground and come up near where the woman stood. He made himself small, went into the mole and when it was right at the log, he sprang out and called, "I have caught you!" That minute he took hold of the woman's heart and squeezed it. She screamed and begged him not to kill her.

"You must go home," said the man, "and on the way you must sing, 'We will have a dance, we will have a dance!' "

The woman started and as she traveled she sang, "We will have a dance." Her sisters heard the song and said to one another, "Our sister has been beaten, she is sick."

The mother sent the youngest sister to tell an old medicine man to come and cure her daughter. He asked what the woman's song was and when told he said, "You must notify all the people in the world and have a great dance for your sister."

The dance was called and food made ready. The woman came and danced, but all at once she fell to the ground and died.

The man-eater saw a great many bones around the log where the woman had stood. After working a long time he got the bones into a pile, then going to a nearby tree he called out, "Get up or the tree will fall on you!"

Men and women sprang up and started to run, but he called them back and sent them to their homes.

SKAGÉDI's father and mother and his brother were in the crowd, so was the man-eater's wife. When SKAGÉDI saw his relatives he was glad.

The man-eater never ate human flesh again.

GEHA AIDS A DESERTED BOY

[Told by John Jimison]

Characters

GÉHA ....Wind

NYAGWAIHE ....The Ancient of Bears

IN a cabin at the edge of a village lived a grandmother
and her grandson. The grandmother was old and the
grandson was young and they were so poor that they ate
scraps given them by their neighbors.

Once, when a hunting party was starting off, the little
boy followed it. The hunters traveled five days, then
camped and built a bark hut.

The boy was too young to hunt; he went out with the
men but never killed anything. They called him OTHWÉN-
SAWÉNHDE from the part of a deer they threw out for him
to eat—"the small liver by the side of the large one."

When the hunters were ready to start for home, they
agreed to leave the boy, not letting him know that they were
going; they wanted to travel fast.

One day when he came back to the hut, the boy found
only the pile of hair left from the skins they had dressed.
The men had taken everything and gone. The child
didn't know the way home.

That night he slept on the pile of hair; the next morning
he found the chin bone of a deer and getting out the
marrow ate it. When it was night again, he heard somebody coming; the door opened, and a man said, "Well,
OTHWÉNSAWÉNHDE, you think you are going to die, but

16

you are not. Get your knife and put it on the stump outside the door, and in the morning go and bring it in. You
must hunt, to-morrow." The stranger, who was GÉHA
(Wind), went away.

The boy had an old basswood knife; he carried it out
and put it on the stump. Early in the morning he went
to the stump and there he found a new knife. He took his
bow and arrow and knife and went into the woods. He
saw a deer, ran after it, overtook it and killed it with his
knife. Then he threw his bow and arrow away and afterward when hunting used his knife. He killed large game
and had plenty of meat.

One night he heard somebody coming, then a man
pushed open the door, and said, calling him by name,
"I am here to tell you that NYAGWAIHE is coming to kill
you. To-night put your knife on the stump outside, get
it in the morning and go to the top of the tall elm tree
at the end of the hut; hide in the branches and wait.
NYAGWAIHE will climb the tree and look over into the hut
to see if you are there. When he is coming down backwards, stick your knife into a small white spot in his
right hind foot; he will fall to the ground, dead. Then
pile up wood around the body and burn it."

GÉHA went out.

The boy put his knife on the stump and in the morning
the old knife was gone and a larger and longer knife was
in its place. He picked up the knife and climbing the
tree hid in the branches. Just at daybreak he heard a
terrible roar, and right away NYAGWAIHE was climbing
the tree. When he got to the top, he looked into the
smoke-hole of the hut, and said, "There is a fire; the boy
must be there," and he started down the tree.

The boy saw the white spot and stuck his knife into it;
NYAGWAIHE fell to the ground, dead.

That night, just as the boy was going to sleep, he
heard somebody coming. GÉHA opened the door, and said,
"I came to tell you that those hunters who left you here
are starving. Ten days from now they will come back
to the hut. You must be kind to them. Don't feel proud
or boast of your swiftness. You felt proud, that is why
NYAGWAIHE came to destroy you.

"Don't say that there is no one who can outrun you. When they come tell them to help themselves to the meat you have dried. When they are ready to go home, go with them; tell every man to take as much meat as he can carry. Put your knife on the stump."

GÉHA went away. The boy put his knife, which was made of basswood, on the stump. In the morning the knife was shorter and smaller.

During the next nine days the boy killed many deer. The tenth day he stayed in the hut, watching and listening. At midday the hunters came. When they saw how much meat the boy had, they asked forgiveness. He told them to eat as much meat as they wanted, then take as much home as each man could carry.

They took half of the meat. The boy packed up the other half, shook it till it was as light a pack as any one of the men was carrying, then started on behind them.

When they got back to the village, the boy went to his grandmother's house and threw down his pack. That minute it came to its natural size.

"Oh," cried his grandmother, "I am happy now. The hunters said you were lost in the woods. But you are back and have brought plenty of meat."

"Go, grandmother," said the boy, "and ask all the women to come and get as much meat as they can carry away."

The women came and carried away many loads of meat, but the meat in the house wasn't diminished. There seemed to be as much as before any was taken.

Now a chief in the East challenged the chief of the village to run a race; whichever side was beaten all the men on that side would lose their lives.

The chief called the people together to decide on a runner. The boy said, "I will run with the man you choose and you can decide which is the better runner."

The chief was pleased. He chose a man and the two stood apart. Other men also volunteered to run. The chief raised his hand, then dropped it, and the runners started, that minute the boy was out of sight, then off at the end of the opening a small dark object was seen. The other runner was only half way across the opening

when the boy was back at the starting place. Then he
began to boast that nobody could outrun him; he forgot
GÉHA's warning.

There was a valley that went across the world; that
valley was to be the race course. At the edge of the
world was a rock that stood up like the trunk of a huge
tree. The rock was white flint and it shone brightly;
there was no other rock like it. The runner who reached
the rock was to bring back a chip of it.

The runner for the challenging chief was tall and thin.
At midday the sign was given and the runners started—
the boy ran on the ground, his opponent ran in the air.

The boy used his full power and soon came back with
a piece of the stone in his hand. After a long time the
other runner came—the challenging chief and his men
lost their heads.

The boy was proud and boastful. That night, just as
he was falling asleep, he heard somebody coming. The
door opened and a man said, "Come out, I want to talk
to you."

He went out.

"I challenge you to a foot race," said the man. "You
must wager the heads of all the people of the village,
except yourself, against my head. I have no people. We
will start at daylight and run till the sun reaches the
middle of the Blue."

"Very well," said the boy.

The man disappeared. The boy told his grandmother
what had happened and she started off to notify the people
that their heads had been put up as a wager. While she
was gone GÉHA came to the boy, and said, "I warned you
not to boast and told you what would happen if you did.
Now you must do your best or you will be beaten. You
must help yourself. I am going home."

The people assembled and the challenger came. Just
as the sun rose, word was given and the runners started.
As the challenger ran he threw up so much dirt that the
boy was thrown back, and he fell. The people couldn't
see the runner; but off in the distance was a NYAGWAIHE.

As the boy fell, GÉHA was there, and said, "Get up
and start! Help yourself and I'll help you."

The boy ran to the first knoll, looked but didn't see his opponent, reached the second knoll and saw him on a knoll far ahead, then saw him on the fourth knoll.

Now a Whirlwind took the boy up and, like a flash of lightning, put him at the runner's heels. He called out, "Hurry, or I'll overtake you!"

The runner used all his strength and soon was out of sight.

Again a Whirlwind picked up the boy and put him at the heels of his opponent. He shot twice and called out, "Do your best or I'll beat you!"

The runner couldn't get out of sight, he was losing strength.

Again a Whirlwind came and as it picked the boy up a voice said, out of the cloud, "This is the last time I'll help you."

Whirlwind put the boy down at his opponent's heels; the runner, now in his real form, the form of a NYAG-WAIHE, said, "You have overtaken me and won the race."

Exactly at midday the boy cut off the Bear's head, and taking it started for home. When over three hills he was tired; he hung the head on the limb of a tree and taking the tongue went on. He went over two other hills and was tired; he hung the tongue on the limb of a tree and went on over other hills and knolls. When he reached home and told the people that he had killed his opponent, they said,

"We will go and see the body."

"You'll find it over the tenth hill. I tried to bring back the head, but seven hills from here I was tired and I hung it on the limb of a tree. I took the tongue, but when I came to the fifth hill I was tired and I hung the tongue on the limb of a tree."

It took a long time for the people to get to the first hill. When they had traveled five Summers and five Winters, they came to a hill. On the top of the hill was a tree, and on the tree was the tongue of the NYAGWAIHE. The ground around the tree was trampled down; thousands of wild beasts had been there and tried to get the tongue, the men looked at it and went on.

When they had traveled two more Summers and two

more Winters they came to the seventh hill and found a skull, all that was left of the head.   The ground around the tree was trampled down: thousands of wild beasts had been there and tried to get the head.

They traveled three Summers and three Winters, then reached the tenth hill.   For a great distance around the ground had been made bare and hard by the trampling of wild beasts.

The place where NYAGWAIHE fell had become a deer-lick, not a bone or a trace of the body was left.

The men were ten years going home.   The boy aided by GÉHA had made the journey between sunrise and mid-day.

THE ADVENTURES OF WOLF-MARKED

[Told by John Jimison]

Characters

OTHAIONI HOYA′DA ....Wolf-Marked
HAQGEEAH ....Ragged or Shabby Man
OTSOON ....Turkey

A BROTHER and sister lived together. The brother
loved his sister so well that he did not want her
to work; he did all the work himself. Each morning when
he was starting off to hunt he said to her. "You mustn't
go out," and he fastened the door. When he came home
in the evening he cooked and after they had eaten he said
to his sister, "Lie down and sleep, I am going to a council."

The sister never knew when her brother came home,
but when she wakened in the morning he was cooking.
The girl didn't like to be fastened in, she said nothing, but
all the time she was thinking how she could get out of the
house.

At last a night came when her brother started off forgetting to fasten the door, then she determined to follow
him to the council. She found his tracks and after following them a long distance came to a house; she pushed
the skin door aside and went in.

An old man sat by a fire making a wooden ladle. He
looked up, and said, "Thank you, my niece, I have waited
a long time for you to come."

"I have come to get you to do something for me,"
said the girl.

"I expected that you would ask me to do something for you. There they are, take your choice," and he pointed to a pile of ladles.

"It isn't a ladle that I want."

"What is it then? Any one who wishes for something asks for it."

"I want you to destroy my brother. He keeps me fastened into the house."

"I can't do that; your brother has great power. Perhaps my brother who lives near here can; he has greater power than I have."

The girl went on. She soon came to an opening and in the opening was a house. She went to the house and looking through a crack saw an old man making bark bowls.

"Come in!" called the old man. "I have been expecting you."

"I have come to get you to do something for me," said the girl.

"There they are, take your choice," said the old man pointing to a pile of bowls.

"I don't want a bowl."

"What do you want?"

"I want you to destroy my brother."

"I can't destroy him, but I can make him go a long way off."

"Do that," said the girl.

"This is what you must do," said the old man. "When you get home begin to help about the cooking. To-morrow morning, just as the sun comes up, look toward the South till you see me. I shall come in the form of a white turkey. When you see me, call to your brother, 'Oh, catch that turkey! I want it for a pet.' He will say, 'I have never heard of any one's having a turkey for a pet.' Then say, 'Kill it for me.' Stand just back of the door and as he draws to shoot push the door, hit the arrow and make it glance off, then your brother's courage will appear, he will say, 'I have never been outrun,' and he will chase me."

The next morning the girl insisted on helping her brother cook. Just at sunrise she saw a turkey coming from the South. When it was near the cabin she called out, "Oh, brother, catch that white turkey! I want it for a pet."

"Who ever heard of having a turkey for a pet?" asked he.

"Well, kill it for me."

The man fixed an arrow in his bow and as he let it fly, the girl shut the door so quickly that it hit the arrow and sent it away from the turkey—then off ran the man to catch the bird.

The two ran till midday, the turkey always a little ahead. Then the turkey called out, "Let us rest. Mark where you stop and I will mark where I stop." After resting a while they started again and ran till dark, then the turkey called out, "Let us rest till morning."

The man lay down at the foot of a tree; the turkey roosted in a hemlock not far away. Early the next morning they started; rested at midday, and when the sun went down they stopped for the night.

For ten days they ran, then the man began to gain on the turkey. The eleventh day they were running along the edge of a precipice when the turkey turned, ran around the man and pushed him over the cliff, saying, "This is the kind of man I am, I cannot be overcome."

At the bottom of the cliff was a swift river. The man struck the water and floated down till he came to a fish dam made by the women of the river. He lodged in the dam. Soon two girls came to the river to see if they had caught many fish. One said to the other, "Look! there is a dead man in the dam. Run and tell mother to come!"

The old woman came and the three pulled the man out of the water. On each side of this man's body was the mark of a wolf.

"It is the Wolf-Marked man," said the mother. "He has never been overpowered before."

They carried the man to the house and began to work over him; in a short time he opened his eyes, but he could not speak. By motions he made the girls understand that he wanted to smoke. One of the girls looked around for a pipe, then he motioned for his pouch. She found a pipe in the pouch and was about to light it when he motioned her to give it to him. He put the pipe between his lips and drawing twice or three times lighted it.

The smoke gave him strength and soon he said, "Hang skin blankets around me."

The old woman said, "From now on you will be my son, and these girls will be your sisters."

The women took great care of Wolf-Marked, and he was soon as well as ever.

One day steps were heard outside, the door was kicked open and a man came in. "I've come to give you some pudding," said he, as he threw down a lot of nasty bark. He went off and the women swept out the bark.

"Have you a bow and arrows?" asked Wolf-Marked.

The old woman gave him a bow and arrows. He dusted the bow and straightened the arrows, then stringing an arrow and saying to it, "Go and kill a bear," he shot it through the smoke hole. Soon a noise was heard outside. The women went to the door and found a bear lying dead on the ground. They skinned it and cutting up the meat put it where it would dry.

The next morning a man kicked the door open and was about to throw down a bundle of nasty bark when he saw the meat, and, knowing there must be a man around, he turned and ran off. Soon afterward Wolf-Marked said, "A man is coming to visit me. When he gets here let him come inside the skin blankets."—He had always stayed behind the blankets the women hung up when he first came.

The next morning when the dew was getting off the grass, the women saw a man coming; he was unkempt and shabby. When he reached the house, the mother told him to go behind the skins. The women heard the two men talking; toward night Shabby Man came out and went away.

In a few days the same man came again. This time he brought news: the chief's daughters were to marry but their husbands must be men who possessed powerful spirits. Spirits that could take any form they liked, walk around a fire and scatter wampum beads.

"Will you try?" asked Shabby Man.

"No," said Wolf-Marked.

That night Shabby Man went to the chief's house. All
the powerful men were there. When they saw Shabby
Man they pushed him out, but he looked through a crack
and saw what was going on.

The power of the first man who tried was in a fisher
pouch. He called the pouch to life and sent it around the
fire. It went half way, then dropped down, a pouch again.

The second man's power was in a mink pouch. The
pouch became a live mink, took wampum beads from a
nearby pile and scattered them till a little more than
half way around the fire, then the mink dropped down,
a pouch again. Each man tried his power, but the power
died before it got around the fire.

After a while, the chief said to the people, "Go home
now, but come again to-morrow night."

The next day Shabby Man urged Wolf-Marked to go to
the chief's house and try his power. At last Wolf-Marked
said, "I will go to-morrow night."

Shabby Man went to the chief's house. Again he was
thrown out and again he looked in through a crack. The
men cheered one another; Shabby Man cheered too. Soon
he saw that as each man tried, all of the others blew
against his power to prevent its getting around the fire;
Shabby Man blew too.

After a while the chief said, "Go home now; we will
try again to-morrow."

That night when Wolf-Marked was walking around outside thinking what he could use to show his power, he
heard a noise and then a voice said to him in a whisper,
"I have come to help you. Here is a pouch. You will
find another pouch inside of this one. Your friend will
use the mud turtle pouch; the fawn pouch is yours, but
you must not go to the chief's house. Let the old woman
and Shabby Man go. Inside the pouches are little pieces
of medicine for the woman and Shabby Man to put in
their mouths when they blow. When they are in the
chief's house they must sit side by side. The woman will
take the mud turtle pouch, shake it till it grows large and
comes to life, then Shabby Man will set it down and tell
it to go around the fire and not to let anything stop it.
When the turtle gets around, the woman must put the

fawn pouch down, bring it to life and tell it to go around the fire. When the turtle and fawn have won Shabby Man must take one of the chief's daughters and go to his own home; the other daughter must come to you.''

Wolf-Marked took the pouches and thanked his friend.

The next morning, just at daylight, Shabby Man came and asked, ''Are you ready?''

''I am ready,'' answered Wolf-Marked.

''Well, let us try our power and see if we are going to succeed.''

''We will succeed,'' said Wolf-Marked.

''Let us try so as to get used to doing it,'' urged Shabby Man.

''There is no need of trying,'' said the other.

Shabby Man urged a long time, then he went off but he soon came back and began again, urged till he was tired, went off and again came back to tease Wolf-Marked to try his power. All day he kept going and coming back to urge again. At dark he said, ''We must start now or we will not get seats.''

''Wait a while,'' answered his friend. ''They will give us seats when we get there.''

After dark Wolf-Marked said to the old woman, ''Mother, I want you to go with this man to the chief's house.''

Shabby Man was disappointed. ''Won't you go?'' asked he.

''No, my mother will go in my place.''

''You had better go, we may fail.''

''You will not fail,'' said Wolf-Marked.

On the road Shabby Man said, ''Let us hurry!'' And he went ahead and waited. When the woman overtook him, he again urged her to walk fast. At last they were there.

When the people saw Shabby Man and the woman they wanted to throw them out, but the chief said, ''Let them stay.''

When Shabby Man's turn came he put the piece of medicine in his mouth; the woman put down the turtle pouch and urged the turtle on. The people began to call for a close of the meeting. Shabby Man insisted on trying and said, ''O chief, give us a chance!''

The chief said to the people, "Sit down and give them a chance."

They did all they could to obstruct the turtle, but it came around to the starting point. Shabby Man picked it up and gave it to the woman. She shook it and made it small. It was again a pouch.

Shabby Man got up and took his place by the chief's daughter.

The people said, "Now we will go home," but the woman insisted on having a chance. They got up to go, but she cried at the top of her voice, "Come back, and let me try. If I succeed I have some one to marry the chief's daughter."

The chief said, "Sit down and let the woman try."

She got the fawn skin pouch out and shook it. It became a live fawn. She put it down and told it to run around the fire. It was around in a flash.

The chief said, "This is the end. What I required has been accomplished."

Everyone went home, with Shabby Man went the chief's elder daughter.

The next morning men came to Wolf-Marked, and said, "The chief has sent for you to come and claim his daughter."

"She must come to me," said the young man, "and Shabby Man and his wife must come too."

The three came, and Wolf-Marked was the husband of the chief's younger daughter.

The men hunted and killed plenty of game; the women took care of the skins, and cooked. Some time passed. The men of the village were jealous of Wolf-Marked and they plotted against him. They put up a long pole, and said, "Whoever can lodge a ball on the top of the pole will win, we have a man who can do it. We will challenge Wolf-Marked and he will lose. The wager will be seven heads."

As the woman and her daughters sat in the house, they saw a man coming on a run; the door flew open and in he came. When he saw Wolf-Marked he said, "I have come to challenge you to lodge a ball on the top of a pole, the wager is seven heads on each side."

"Very well," said Wolf-Marked. "That is the game I amuse myself with." When the runner left, the old woman began to cry and lament. "Don't cry," said Wolf-Marked. "Nothing will happen to us." She only cried the harder, and wailed that he would surely lose, and then the seven members of the family would be destroyed. But after a time he was able to quiet her.

That night when Wolf-Marked was standing outside and thinking about the challenge, thinking that maybe he would lose, he heard a whisper and a voice said, "When you were challenged you said, 'That is the game I amuse myself with.' This will come true. Don't use their ball and don't begin the game. Here is the ball you are to use, and here is a piece of medicine for you to put in your mouth when you go to the place; with it in your mouth blow against their ball."

The next morning, when it was time to go, Shabby Man said, "I am sick, I can't go. Couldn't you bet three against three, the old woman and her two daughters on our side?"

"No," said Wolf-Marked, "We have agreed seven against seven. We must all go."

When they reached the place, they saw a long pole standing in the center of an opening. Seven men were standing near the pole; they were the wager on the chief's side. Now Wolf-Marked and his wife, the mother and her two daughters and Shabby Man and his wife stood together as the wager on Wolf-Marked's side. Stuck into the pole was a great flint knife with which to cut off their heads.

The chief asked Wolf-Marked to begin the game. When he refused a man on the chief's side picked up the ball, rubbed it a long time, then threw it into the air. It came down, hit the top of the pole and bounded back and went up again. Wolf-Marked was blowing against it, and he had the medicine in his mouth. At last he said in his mind, "Let the ball fall." It came to the ground, then the chief gave it to Wolf-Marked, and said, "Now it is your turn."

"I have a ball of my own," said Wolf-Marked, and he refused to take the chief's ball. He said to his own ball, "Be faithful. Don't fall, stick to the pole."

He rubbed the ball in his hands, then threw it up, the whiz was heard, and right away the ball was out of sight. After a long time they heard it strike the sky, and it made a pleasant sound, a sound that was heard by all of the people in the world. It came down, hit the pole and bounded back to the sky. Three times it went to the sky. The third time it hit, the sound was very faint. Many times it went up, but a little lower every time.

Each man on the chief's side was wishing with all his power that the ball would fall to the ground. The seven of Wolf-Marked's party were wishing it to stay on the pole. There was great excitement.

The ball struck the top of the pole and stayed there.

"You have won the game," said the chief.

"That is what I expected. I knew that we would win," said Shabby Man. And straightway he cut off the seven heads, the chief's wager.

Wolf-Marked and his friends went home and were happy, but the men of the village were still plotting. After a good deal of talk one of the men said, "This is what we will do: I am the swiftest runner in the world. I have never been beaten. Challenge Wolf-Marked to run a race with me. We will run around the lake, and the wager will be seven heads."

A man went to Wolf-Marked and notified him of the race and its conditions.

"That is the game I like best," said he. "I have never been beaten; I can outrun anyone."

When the old woman heard of the challenge, she cried and lamented.

"Stop crying," said Wolf-Marked. "Nothing will happen to us."

When everyone in the house was asleep, Wolf-Marked went outside and stood thinking what he could do to win. All at once he heard a whisper and a voice said, "Come here!"

He went toward the voice and listened, soon the voice said, "You are going to run a race. You said that you liked the game; you will not be disappointed this time. When the runner finds that you are winning, he will throw back a buffalo horn. It will stick in your foot, pull it out and throw it at him as hard as you can. You will win."

The next morning Wolf-Marked said to his family, "Get ready!"

"I am sick," said Shabby Man, "I can't go."

"You must go," said Wolf-Marked. "The wager is seven heads, we must all be there."

When they reached the place, they saw a crowd of people, and seven men standing a little to one side; they were the chief's wager.

The chief said, "Each runner must take hold of a long pole and run against that hickory tree over there, bend the tree down drawing the pole across it. When the pole comes off from the top and the tree springs back, drop the pole and run." The pole was of red willow.

The runners started exactly at midday, the chief's runner holding one end of the pole, Wolf-Marked the other. They had to pull hard to bend the tree over. Just as they got the pole near the top, the chief's runner let go of his end and Wolf-Marked was thrown far back beyond the crowd of people. He sprang up and saying, "I have never been beaten!" he gave a whoop and ran. His opponent was out of sight. People shouted with joy.

Shabby Man rolled on the ground, and cried, "Oh, we are beaten! We are beaten! If he had only said that the wager would be one head, and that his own!"

When Wolf-Marked got out of sight, he called a mole, and said, "You see that man running. Get ahead of him!"

Wolf-Marked went into the mole; the mole went under the ground and came out ahead of the runner, who wasn't going very fast for he thought Wolf-Marked was far behind.

After a while he saw a track and thought, "Can he be ahead?" then he ran swiftly, but didn't see anyone. Looking again at the tracks he said in his mind, "He is ahead!" and taking a buffalo horn out of his pouch he told it to go to the young man and stick in his foot; and he threw it. The horn overtook Wolf-Marked and as one of his feet came up it went into it, and he fell to the ground. He tried to pull the horn out, but couldn't. As the chief's runner passed he called out, "Get up! I never before saw a man sit down when he was running a race."

Just then Wolf-Marked's whispering friend said to him, "Pull the horn out, throw it, and say, 'Go fast and enter the runner's foot so deep that he can't get you out.' "

Wolf-Marked threw the horn and ran on. He hadn't gone far when he saw his opponent sitting on the ground trying to get the horn out of his foot. "Stop and help me," begged he.

"I didn't say that when you sent the horn into my foot," said Wolf-Marked, and he ran on.

All the people were watching to see which runner was ahead. The chief's party said, "We might as well begin to cut off those heads, we will cut off six, then take Wolf-Marked's when he comes."

A man seized a flint knife and ran to Shabby Man, but the chief called to him, "Wait till the runners get here."

At last they saw one runner, then the crowd shouted, "Our man is coming! Our man is coming!"

When the runner came a little nearer, people began to feel uneasy; they were not quite sure that it was their man—then they saw that it was Wolf-Marked.

Shabby Man looked up, he had been sitting with his head down, thinking that right away he was going to lose his life. Then he called out, "Just as I told you! I knew Wolf-Marked would win."

When the runner came near, he called to his friend, "Why don't you take the wager?"

Up jumped Shabby Man, and soon seven heads were lying on the ground.

Twin boys were born to Wolf-Marked and they were marked exactly as he was. When the first one was born, the father picked him up and threw him over the skin enclosure where he himself had stayed when he first came to the old woman's cabin, and as he threw the child, he said, "This, my first son, must grow to be a powerful man." When the second child was born, he threw it over the enclosure, and said, "This, my second son must grow to be a powerful man."

Nobody paid any attention to the children. After a

time talking was heard, then a voice said, "Father, we want a club and a ball to play with."

Wolf-Marked threw in a ball and a club. Some days passed, then one of the boys called out, "Father, we are tired of the club and ball, we want a bow and arrows." He gave them a bow and made them red willow arrows.

For a time they were satisfied, then one called out, "Father we want to go for our aunt!"

"Very well. When you start go in the direction the sun goes, and don't let anything stop you."

The boys started. They went through a wide valley and climbed a hill at the end of the valley. They were walking along quietly when the younger brother called out, "Stop brother, and look at this."

"No," answered the elder brother, "our father told us not to stop."

The younger brother thought, "Yes, our father told us not to let anything stop us," and he hurried on.

They had traveled a number of days when the younger boy asked, "Brother, what would frighten you most?"

"Our father told us not to be frightened by anything," answered the elder boy. "What would you be afraid of?"

"Of Big Head (Whirlwind)."

That minute the boys heard a great noise. From the southwest came a terrible roar. The elder brother kept on; the younger was frightened, but when Big Head was near he said to himself, "I won't be afraid."

That minute the roar and wind ceased.

At last the brothers came to a trail and saw foot-prints all going in one direction. The trail ran north and south, the foot-prints pointed north, some were very large, others were small.

The elder brother glanced at the tracks and went on, the younger stopped and looking at the tracks said, "Let us follow them and find out what is going on."

"Our father told us not to stop," answered his brother.

"It won't take long; we can come right back," urged the younger. The elder brother yielded and they followed the foot-prints; they had not gone far when a man of enormous size came along, seized the boys and, tucking one under each arm, walked off. Soon he came to a village and going into a hut at the edge of it said to men sitting around, "I have brought game. We will notify the people."

The boys were taken to the long house in the center of the village. Two large kettles were brought and made ready. As people came in they went up and looked the game over. When the chief came he looked also, but what he saw frightened him. Right away he said, "Free these boys; they are the sons of the Wolf-Marked Man. If we harm them he will destroy us; he is the most powerful man in the world."

The people of this village were all Frost (or Ice) people.

They liberated the boys and the two traveled on till they came to a beautiful country.

"I think that our aunt is near here," said the younger boy.

"Oh, no," said the elder, "she must be far away yet."

The younger brother insisted that his aunt was near and he began to look around. The elder stopped and watched him.

The boy came to a hollow tree and in the opening saw the body of a woman.

"Come here, brother," called he, "I have found our aunt."

He struck the woman with his arrow; she didn't move, then he struck her twice with his bow, and said, "Your brother has sent for you."

The woman moved and roused up a little; her face was covered with scabs and sores and she was frightful to look at. The younger boy rubbed her with saliva; the scabs fell off, and she was well. Then the boys saw that she was a fine-looking woman.

"Now we will go home," said the younger brother, and the three started.

Wolf-Marked had forgiven his sister for trying to destroy him; he was glad to see her. After this they all lived together happily.

OKTEONDO^n AND HIS UNCLE, THE PLANTER

OR

WINTER DELAYING SPRING

[Told by John Armstrong]

***

Characters

OKTEONDO^n .... Roots, or the Rooted One
HAIENTHWÛS .... Planter
WADYO^{n}YO^{n}DYES,
        Wild Duck People (Wild Duck is T'o^{n}we)
HÓTHO .... Cold Weather

***

OKTEONDO^n lived in the woods with his uncle HAIENTHWÛS. The young man lay fastened under the roots of an elm tree which grew through his uncle's bark house. When very small, his uncle had hidden him there so nobody could carry him off. There were persons in the South who came North to steal the boys of the Wampum people.

One day, while the uncle was planting corn, he heard his nephew sing in a loud voice, "I am rising, I am rising."

The old man dropped his planting stick, and saying, "No, nephew, you are in too great a hurry," he ran home, and, finding that the boy had raised his head, he pushed him back, and said, "I will tell you when it is time to rise. As soon as you get up, women, who float around in a canoe, will come from the South and carry you away."

The next day the old man went out to plant corn and

a second time his nephew began to sing and to try to get up. He ran home so fast that he lost his seed corn by the way and when he came to the house he found the tree leaning over. He put his nephew back, but the tree could not be fixed as firmly as before.

On the third day HAIENTHWÛS went to finish his planting, but the minute he began to drop seed he heard the song, "I am rising! I am rising!" He ran towards home but while running he heard an awful crash, and he knew the tree had fallen; when he reached the house OKTEONDO^n was sitting on the ground.

The old man didn't go back to his planting; he stayed at home to look after his nephew.

Early the next morning they heard women singing and soon a beautiful young woman came in; one of the Wild Duck sisters.

She put down a basket near the old man, and said, "Here is the marriage bread," and going to OKTEONDO^n she said, "I have come to take you home with me."

"Very well," answered the young man, and he was starting to go when his uncle stopped him, and said, "You must not go yet, you have friends coming, men whom these sisters have stolen. You must wait for them."

The women went away and the old man began to cook. He put over the fire a kettle with hominy (snow) in it. When the hominy was ready, three young men came in. HAIENTHWÛS invited them to eat and when they had eaten, he put clothing in a bundle and said to his nephew, "If your friends are in need of things, you will find them in this bundle."

The young man put on snowshoes, told his friends to walk in his tracks; and they started. The three young men found that walking in OKTEONDO^n's tracks was like walking on solid ground.

Toward night the young man saw a smoke and going near it found four fires and four young women. Each woman had her own fire.

"We will make our fires near theirs," said the young man.

When the fires were burning, he went boldly up to where the four sisters had their fires. Over each fire a kettle of hominy was boiling. He walked through the fires from the first one to the last, and threw the kettles over. Three of the sisters were angry, but the youngest sister laughed.

OKTEONDO^n went back to his friends, and said, "I am going to hunt now," and he started off. Very near his fire he saw bear marks on a tree. He struck the tree, and said: "You who are in here, come out."

A bear came out; he killed it and carried the meat to the camp. Then he said, "I will bring my uncle's kettle," and going behind a tree he brought back a big kettle.

When the meat was cooked, the friends sat down and ate, and when all had eaten enough OKTEONDO^n said, "We will go to where our wives are, but we must not take any of this meat to them, if we do we will have bad luck."

When they came to the women, they found they had hominy cooked and were cooling it; they sat with their backs to the men, facing the direction they were traveling in. The youngest sister, whom OKTEONDO^n claimed as his wife, asked him to come and eat; the other sisters said nothing.

HÓTHO (Cold), one of the three friends, was naked; he had a hole through his hip and in that hole he carried a mallet; he chose the eldest of the Wild Duck sisters.

The women kept their canoe on one side of the first fire and when they undressed they put their clothes in the canoe.

The next morning the men went back to their fires, but one of them had lost his leggings and moccasins; his wife had stolen them.

The sisters warmed up the cold hominy and ate it. After eating they sat in their canoe and sailed away through the air.

OKTEONDO^n opened the bundle his uncle had given him, took out leggings and moccasins and gave them to the man whose wife had stolen his clothes.

When the men had eaten and were ready, they started off, following the canoe, the trail of which they saw in the air.

Towards evening the young man saw a smoke and when some distance from it, he said, "We will stay here."

Again he went to where the sisters were camped, walked

through their fires and spilled their hominy. Then he went back to his friends and started off to hunt for game; but this time he had to go far, for the woman who had stolen the leggings and moccasins had long arms. She had stretched them out over the country, made a circle with them and told the game to go outside that circle. OKTEON-DO^n had to go outside the circle too, before he could find a bear. When he had the bear, he went back to camp and said to the three men, "You have tired me with your folly. I told you not to take even one bite of our meat to those women. You disobeyed me."

He got a kettle as before, cooked some of the bear meat and they all ate heartily, then they went over to where the women were camped. Each woman was sitting with a dish of hot hominy on her knees, cooling it. Their faces were turned in the direction in which they were traveling.

The youngest sister asked OKTEONDO^n to eat. The young man grew angrier and angrier and in the night, when all were asleep, he said to a great tree that stood near the canoe the women traveled in, "I want you to bend down to me." The tree bent down to him and he fastened the canoe among its topmost branches, then he said, "I want you to stand straight." The tree stood erect. Then he said, "I want you to be covered with ice." The tree was covered with ice.

OKTEONDO^n did this because he was angry at the woman who had stolen the leggings and moccasins of one of his companions, and had driven the game away and made him go so far to hunt for a bear.

Early the next morning the young men went back to their own camp.

When the women couldn't find their canoe they ran around looking for it, ran for a good while. At last they saw it in the top of the tree. The eldest sister said, "I will try to get it down." She spat on her hands and feet, rubbed the spittle in and right away long nails, like bear claws, grew out on her fingers and toes. She began to climb, went half way up the tree, then lost her grip and came down, her claws scratching the ice as she slipped.

Now the sisters talked together and said that OKTEONDO^n, and no one else, had done this. They asked him about it and he said, "I put your canoe on the tree because you made me angry."

When they promised not to steal again, he told the tree to bend down. The tree bent to the ground and OKTEONDO^n took off the canoe and gave it to the sisters, who dressed themselves, took their food out of the canoe, cooked hominy, ate it and then sat in the canoe and continued their journey.

All day the four men followed the trail of the canoe. Towards evening they saw a smoke in the distance, but when they drew near they found a great lake covered with smooth ice.

In the middle of the lake the four sisters were camped. OKTEONDO^n said to his friends, "We will camp on the ice too." And getting a handful of dry leaves and hemlock boughs he said to the men, "Follow in my steps, and be sure to put your feet in my tracks."

When near the sisters' camp, he said, "We will camp here." He put down his handful of boughs and leaves and it became a great pile. He said, "I want a fire!" And there was a fire. He scattered a handful of hemlock boughs on the other side of the fire, and said, "Here will be our house and beds." And straightway a house of hemlock boughs covered their fire, and in the house was a place for each one of the four men to sleep.

The home of the sisters was on the edge of the lake, but they camped in the middle of it, on the ice, to see how the men would act and what power they had.

In the morning OKTEONDO^n saw that the banks of the lake were black with people.

The sisters went to their home on the land and their mother asked, "Which of your husbands has the most power?"

They answered "OKTEONDO^n."

Now OKTEONDO^n said to the three men, "We will go to the women, but you must not look at the people."

The four started, from their camp on the ice, for the shore. When they had gone a short distance three of them heard a voice singing, "We are raining bones. We are raining bones." They heard the song a second time, and nearer, then they heard a rustling noise and a mass of dry bones swept past them on the ice. OKTEONDO[n] said, "One of us has looked up and he has turned to bones."

At that moment all the people on the shore disappeared except an old woman who was walking back and forth singing, "OKTEONDO[n] is my son-in-law. OKTEONDO[n] is my son-in-law."

When the young man and his two friends came to the shore, the old woman went home and they followed her and went to her house. When there she said, "I will see if my daughters are getting you something to eat. You must wait here till I come back." Her house was of ice.

While she was gone, OKTEONDO[n] took a small bundle of sticks and said, "Let them burn." Straightway the pile of sticks became large and there was a great fire. Then he said to the two men, "The old woman will bring food, but you mustn't eat it. I will eat it for it won't hurt me." He made a hole in the ice, took a reed and put it through himself into the hole.

The old woman came, and said, "Son-in-law, I have brought you a little to eat. It is the rule to eat only a little after a long journey."

The young man took the bark bowl and ate all the food. It ran through the reed into the ground. The food was hominy (snow) and bloodsuckers (clouds).

Soon she came with a second bowl, and said, "I have brought more for you. This is hominy cooked with maple sugar." (It was wild flint, a weed that floats on water.)

When the old woman's house was getting full of holes from the heat of the fire, she said, "Whu! My son-in-law has spoiled my house. We'll go to my daughters' house."

OKTEONDO[n]'s wife said to him, "My mother will try to kill you; she doesn't care about the other men for she knows what power they have and that she can kill them whenever she wants to."

Towards night the old woman said, "Whu! I think it's going to be cold to-night, I will get logs and make a great fire to keep my back warm." She brought logs from the woods and made a hot fire.

OKTEONDO[n]'s wife said, "My mother will say to-night, 'I dreamed that my son-in-law must go hunting and kill SKADA'GÉA. [In-the-Mist, a bird] and he must come back before the door that he slams behind him stops shaking. If he doesn't, something bad will happen.' "

When night came, all lay down to sleep. In the middle of the night the old woman began to groan terribly, she rolled out of her place and into the fire with such force that she pushed the fire-brands and coals about the house.

OKTEONDO^n jumped up, took the corn-pounder, struck her and called out, "Well, Mother-in-law, what are you doing?"

The old woman sat up, and said, "Oh, I have had a dream. I dreamt that you, my son-in-law, must kill In-the-Mist and bring him in here before the door, that you slam behind you when going out, stops trembling. If you fail to do this, something bad will happen."

"Go to sleep, Mother-in-law," said the young man, "we will see to that in the morning."

The old woman lay down again and slept.

The next morning OKTEONDO^n was ready. He took hairs from his wife's head and tied them together till he had a long cord. Then he tied one end of the cord to the door and giving the other end to his wife told her to jerk it and keep the door trembling till he came back from shooting In-the-Mist.

OKTEONDO^n started and before he had gone far from the house he saw In-the-Mist sitting on a cloud. He let go his arrow, and the bird fell to the ground.

The old woman was very angry when she saw that the door didn't stop trembling after OKTEONDO^n had slammed it in going out. She pushed the door to, but her daughter kept it moving, unknown to her.

When OKTEONDO^n went in and threw the bird on the ground saying, "Here is a feast for you!" she said, "O, my son-in-law, you must give me one of the wings for a fan, my old one is worn out."

"No," said the young man. "You cannot have a wing," and he threw the bird on the fire.

HÓTHO, OKTEONDO^n's friend, hung a kettle over the fire and filled it with water. As soon as the feathers were burned off the bird OKTEONDO^n cut it up and put the pieces in the kettle. When cooked he took out the meat and skimmed every drop of fat from the broth.

"Now," said the old woman, "you must invite all the best men of the village to come and eat."

"I'll invite whom I please," said OKTEONDO^n. He went out and shouted, "I invite you all, O Whirlwinds (DAGWANOE^{n}YENTS), to a feast."

Soon the guests began to come, one after another. When all were present, OKTEONDO^n said, "I have invited you to a feast at which everything must be consumed. You must eat the meat, drink the broth, chew up and swallow the bones."

They finished everything, left neither a drop of broth nor a bit of bone. When they were through eating, they laughed and said, "The flesh of the old woman's husband made a good meal."

The woman was raving. She took a pounder and struck the guests. They flew up through the smoke-hole and off as fast as they could. One of them made a great rent in the side of the house as he rushed through.

When she had driven the guests out and the house was clear, the old woman said, "I think the night is going to be cold, I must go for wood."

She brought wood, made a great fire, and said, "Now I will warm my back." Then she went to sleep with her back to the fire.

OKTEONDO^n's wife said, "My mother will dream again to-night, and will say, 'I dreamed that my son-in-law was to kill the white beaver and bring it here before the door, that he slams when going out, stops moving. If he doesn't get back before the door stops moving, something bad will happen.'"

Late in the night the young man heard his mother-in-law groaning. She rolled around, threw the wood from its place on the fire and scattered the coals.

He jumped up, took the corn-pounder, hit the old woman on the head, and said, "You must be dreaming about me, Mother-in-law."

"Yes, I was dreaming about you, and I am afraid something bad may happen, but you are powerful. The dream says that my son-in-law is to kill the white beaver, and if the door that he slams behind him stops trembling before he comes back, something bad will happen."

"Go to sleep, Mother-in-law, that is nothing."

In the morning the young man fastened the cord made of his wife's hair to the door and told her to keep the door moving while he was gone. Then he went out and running to a knoll where there was a butter-nut tree, he took a nut from the tree and hurried to the lake. He threw the nut into the water, and said, "You who live in this lake, come out."

The water rose up and rushed after him till he reached the knoll where the butter-nut tree was, there it stopped. OKTEONDO^n saw the white beaver looking out of the water. He drew his bow, killed the beaver, seized the body and hurried home.

When he reached the door, the old woman was trying to hold it still and was repeating every word that had power to stop it.

When the young man threw the beaver into the house, she said, "My son-in-law, you must make me a pouch of this skin."

"Oh, no! I'll do what I like with it," said he, and he threw the beaver into the fire. HÓTHO put on a kettle, prepared everything and when the water was boiling, he put the beaver into the kettle and cooked it. Then the old woman said, "Son-in-law, I want you to invite all the chief men of this place to the feast."

"I will invite such men as I like," said OKTEONDO^n.

When the beaver was cooked, he took out the pieces of meat and cooled them, then going outside he called loudly, "I invite all you Whirlwinds to come to a feast."

They came and when all were there OKTEONDO^n said, "You must eat everything to the end. Here is meat, broth and bones. You must eat all, and lick the bowls."

They ate the meat, swallowed the fat and drank the broth, then the crunching of bones could be heard. Last of all they licked the bark bowls.

When they had finished and were satisfied, they began to laugh. "Hi; hi; hi!" said they. "The flesh of the old woman's brother has made us a good meal."

The old woman was terribly angry. She ran at them with the corn-pounder and drove them out of the house.

After the feast OKTEONDO^n's wife said, "There is one

more trial, the worst of all. My mother will say to-night, 'I dreamed that my son-in-law was killed and skinned and I made a pouch of his skin.' "

Okteondo[n] said, "When she kills and skins me and puts my flesh in a bowl, take the bowl and place it on the top of the house."

Towards night the old woman said, "The sky is clear, we will have a cold night, I must get logs and make a big fire."

She made a great fire and in the night began to groan and throw the logs and fire about. Okteondo[n] jumped up, struck her on the head with the corn-pounder, and said, "Mother-in-law, what is the trouble, what are you dreaming about?"

"I dreamed that I killed you and made a pouch of your skin."

"Go to sleep, we will see to that in the morning."

The next morning the young man said, "Now, Mother-in-law, I am ready."

The old woman put a large piece of bark on the ground and told him to lie on it. He lay down, she struck him on the head and killed him. Then she took off his skin, leaving his hands and feet on the skin, and cutting up the flesh put it into a bark bowl. As soon as Okteondo[n]'s wife saw her put in the last piece, she took the bowl and placed it on the top of the house.

The old woman sewed up the skin in the form of a pouch and distended it by blowing. Then she hung it over the fire and poked the fire to make it blaze. The pouch swayed to and fro over the fire and the old woman sang, "Oh, what a nice pouch have I, no woman living has such a pouch!"

Each time she punched the fire, the pouch swayed more quickly to and fro. At last it began to sing, "Oh, if the wind were out of me!" She poked and poked the fire and the pouch swayed faster and faster. "What a beautiful pouch I have," said she, "it even sings."

After a while the pouch made a noise: "Sho!" and went out through the smoke-hole.

As it went the old woman cried, "Oh, I've lost my pouch, I've lost my pouch! It has run away from me!"

She hurried to the door, but in going out she met her son-in-law coming in alive and well.

That night OKTEONDO^n had a dream; he groaned and rolled around till the old woman got up and hit him with the corn-pounder, saying, "Wake up!"

"I had a dream," said he.

"What was it?" asked the old woman.

"I dreamed that I must kill the Ancient of Bears and have a feast and invite all the people in the village."

The· next morning the young man killed the Ancient of Bears.

HÓTHO got the kettle ready and when the flesh of the bear was cooked OKTEONDO^n said to his wife and the two friends, who had come with him from his uncle's place, "You must go out of the house."

They went out and the new company came in: the old woman and her other daughters and the people of the place. OKTEONDO^n said, "Here is flesh, fat, and bones. You must eat all that is placed before you and clean the bowls."

The chief of the people said, "We have everything here before us. Now eat."

OKTEONDO^n went out and ran around the house; while running he said, "Let this house become stone, and the ground under it be stone, so that the greatest wizard couldn't get out, and let the house become red hot."

While the people were eating and drinking and saying, "Ho, ho, this is a great feast," the house began to grow hot. Someone spoke up so loudly that he was heard outside, and said, "Let us get out of here as quickly as we can. Something is wrong."

They all tried to get out, but couldn't. One jumped up to where the smoke-hole had been, and those outside heard him knock his head against solid stone and fall back. Another said, "I will go out through the ground."

After a while the voices and screams inside the house died down; and all was quiet.

The house cracked open, the heads of the people burst, one after another, and out of them came screech owls, horned owls, and gray and red foxes, and all rushed out of sight.

The people of the old woman's village were man-eaters. The sisters sailed around everywhere in their canoe, deceiving men and luring them to that village to be devoured. All the sisters, except OKTEONDO^n's wife were burned up with the old woman and the man-eaters.

The young man and his wife went to the lake shore where they found a great pile of bones; they gathered them up, put them under a large hickory tree, then pushed the tree and called out, "Rise up, or the tree will fall on you!"

At this call the bones sprang up living men, and each man went to his own home.

"We will go home too," said the young man to his wife, and they went to the house of his uncle, HAIENTHWÛS.

When OKTEONDO^n went away his uncle hung up a belt, and said, "The deeper you are in trouble the nearer this belt will come to the ground, if you die it will touch the ground."

The belt had touched the ground and the old man had mourned, but now it was up again.

While his nephew was away, many persons had come to the door pretending to be OKTEONDO^n and had deceived the old man. Now when his nephew knocked, he said, "Put your arm through the hole in the door." He did so. The old man tied it there firmly, then said, "Now, I have got you!" and he opened the door to strike whoever was outside, but seeing OKTEONDO^n and his wife he said, "Oh, my nephew, wait a minute till I clean up a bit." He brushed away the ashes and then he welcomed his nephew.

The narrator said that this story described winter trying to delay spring.

A BATTLE BETWEEN FROST AND WHIRLWIND

[Told by Peter White]

Characters

DAGWANOE^{n}YENT GOWA .... Whirlwind or Cyclone
GÉNO^{n}SKWA .... Frost and Cold
HADIQSADO^n GÉNO^{n}SKWA GANYUDAI,
    The Grave of Frost, or the so-called Stone Coats

DAGWANOE^{n}YENT (Whirlwind), an old woman, the oldest of all her people, lived in the forest with her two grandchildren, a boy and a girl.

One day when the grandmother was out digging roots a GÉNO^{n}SKWA (Frost and Great Cold) woman came to the cabin, picked up the little girl and, after speaking kindly, telling her she was a nice little thing, swallowed her.

Then she began to talk to the boy. Sitting down by him, she said, "Get on to my back and I will carry you to where your grandmother is digging roots."

The boy did as GÉNO^{n}SKWA told him to, but he was frightened, and he clung to her so tightly that he became fastened to her back, and couldn't get off, though he tried hard.

GÉNO^{n}SKWA started off, but in a different direction from where the boy's grandmother was. When the boy told her she was going the wrong way, she said, "No, I am not, we will soon come to where she is at work."

The woman went far into the forest and the boy began to cry for his grandmother. He cried so hard and loud

47

that GÉNO[n]SKWA told him to get off of her back. She didn't like to hear him cry, and she thought it was best to eat him at once.

He couldn't get off and she couldn't put her hands around to pull him off, nor turn her head to bite him.

When the boy saw that she couldn't harm him if he stayed where he was, he clung all the tighter and stopped trying to get away.

When the grandmother came home and found that the boy and girl were not in the cabin, she was frightened and began to search for them. After a while she came upon the tracks of the GÉNO[n]SKWA woman and then she knew who had stolen the children and she followed the tracks, thinking she would soon overtake the thief.

The woman was tired of the boy and tried in every way to free herself of him. She rubbed him against hickory trees and against rocks. He said, "Oh, I like that, rub harder." She stopped then and traveled on.

The grandmother followed in the form of a Whirlwind. GÉNO[n]SKWA said to the boy, "Your grandmother is coming. She will kill us both. Get off of my back."

The boy kept still, didn't answer. The woman looked around for a hiding place and found one in a deep ravine. She dug a hole, went into it and covered herself with the earth that slipped down from above. When she heard Whirlwind coming nearer and nearer she asked the boy, "Can you hear your grandmother coming?"

He didn't answer.

When Whirlwind rushed over the place where the woman lay, the boy shouted to her. She heard him and, changing her course, came straight to where they were. When she asked the boy if he was there, the woman told him to keep still, but he called out, "I am here!"

Whirlwind blew the earth from the hiding place and shouted, "DAGWANOE[n]YENT, get off of GÉNO[n]SKWA's back!" That instant the boy slipped off and went among the rocks. The old woman hurled stones at the GÉNO[n]SKWA, tore off her clothes and killed her. Then she took her grandson and started for home.

On the way, she said to him, "Never let yourself be treated in that manner again. Never let anyone abuse you. You can conquer everybody if you use your power, for you are of the Whirlwind family.''

The old woman stayed at home for a time, caring for her grandson.

Meanwhile some of the Géno^{n}skwa woman's people found her trail and followed it till they came to where her body was. They asked who had killed her and her spirit answered, "Whirlwind killed me." Right away the Géno^{n}skwa men decided to kill old woman Whirlwind.

Whirlwind, out on one of her journeys, discovered their plans. She went home and said to her grandson, "We must get your sister out of Géno^{n}skwa's stomach, she is sitting there and crying for me."

They set out and when they reached the place where the body lay, the old grandmother built a fire and began to burn tobacco, saying, "This is what we like! This is what we like!" She burned half a pouchful and pushed the smoke toward the body, repeating, "This is what we like." Then she called, "My grandchild, come out of Géno^{n}skwa's body!"

When the girl didn't come, the old woman said to her grandson, "We must have people come and help us. We have many relatives, uncles, aunts, and cousins, we will call them." Then she called each relative by name, and one after another they came. They built a fire at Géno^{n}skwa's head, and burned tobacco, as they walked around the fire each threw in tobacco, saying, "Ne vonoes, ne vonoes" (This is what we like).

When the last one had thrown in tobacco, the girl, panting for breath, came out and asked, "How long have I been here?" She was very weak. They gave her tobacco smoke and she inhaled it till she gained strength, then all the Whirlwinds went home.

When the old woman and her grandchildren had been at home some time a Géno^{n}skwa woman came to the cabin, she talked pleasantly, found out there were only three persons there and left thinking it would be a small task to kill them.

After the woman had gone, Whirlwind said to her grandchildren, "We are in trouble now. A great number of those people will come against us. They have assembled somewhere nearby. When the struggle begins I don't know that we will be able to come home again." She went out and called, "DAGWANOE^{n}YENT GOWA! DAGWANOE^{n}YENT GOWA!"

The girl asked, "Grandmother, what are you doing?"

"I am calling our relatives," answered the old woman.

The Whirlwinds came, one by one, when all were there, the old woman said, "Each one of you must have a big round stone to strike with."

They had just picked up the stones when the GÉNO^{n}S-KWAS began to come; there were thousands and thousands of them.

The Whirlwinds were frightened when they saw how strong the enemy was. The old woman said, "We must separate and fight singly. Keep the stones in your hands. Be firm and have faith that you will kill one man with each blow you strike."

The Whirlwinds went in different directions; the GÉNO^{n}SKWAS chased them.

The Whirlwinds struck whenever they had the chance and kept retreating, they went up a high mountain, fighting as they went. The old woman said, "When we all reach the top we will go down a short distance on the other side. When the GÉNO^{n}SKWAS come to the top we will strike them on the east and on the west, some of us will get behind them and drive them over the mountain and into the deep ravine on the other side, they will die there for a river runs through the ravine and they cannot cross it."

The GÉNO^{n}SKWAS came to the top of the mountain and seeing nothing of the Whirlwinds, thought they had escaped. They stood and listened. Soon they heard wind on each side of them. The sound grew louder and louder and right away the DAGWANOE^{n}YENTS struck them on both sides and, uniting in the rear, struck them from behind. So fierce was the attack and power of the Whirlwinds that they tore out all the trees by their roots, swept the earth from the top of the mountain and hurled trees and earth into the ravine and river below. The GÉNO^{n}SKWAS were piled up, like rocks, in the river and along the banks.

The Whirlwinds were dancing and rejoicing on the top

of the mountain when the old woman said, "We have hurled our enemies into the ravine, now we will finish them. Half of you go along the ridges east of the river and the other half go along the western ridges and blow all the trees and rocks and earth into the ravine."

They went, and when they came together again they had stripped the mountain spurs naked and filled up the ravine. The river had no outlet; it became a great lake and ever after was called, "The grave of the Génoⁿs-kwas."

HÓTHO CONQUERS SHAGODYOWEG GOWA

Characters

HÓTHO .... Cold Weather (Winter)
SHAGODYOWEG GOWA,
　The Great One who protects us (Wind People)
　(The sisters personify Spring)

A MOTHER and her two daughters lived in an opening in the woods. When the daughters became women the mother said, "You must marry. Make twenty loaves of green corn bread, tie up the bread in husks and go to the house of two brothers, who live not far from here. Their house has a partition; you, my elder daughter, go in at the first door and say to the man, 'This is marriage bread, I have come here to be your wife.' You, my younger daughter, go in at the other door and say to the man, 'This is marriage bread, I have come here to be your wife.' The brothers will take your bread and tell you to stay.

"Before you come to the house a trail branches off. Be sure to keep the straight trail."

The sisters started. When they came to the branch trail they mistook it for the straight one and followed it till they came to a bark house. Looking in through a crack they saw a number of men, SHAGODYOWEG GOWAS, and were so frightened that they ran toward home.

The men followed. When they were near, one of the sisters threw down her basket of bread. The men stopped, ate the bread, then followed again. The second sister put down her basket.

Piece by piece the sisters threw off their clothes, the pursuers stopped and examined each piece. In this way the girls kept a little ahead and finally reached home.

"You didn't do as I told you," said the mother, "you must try again."

They made bread and the next morning started again. This time they reached the right house. The elder sister went in at the first door and placing her basket of bread before the man said, "I have come here to be your wife." He ate the bread, and thanked her.

The younger sister went in at the second door, placed her basket in front of the man, and said, "I have come here to be your wife." He ate the bread, and thanked her.

In the morning one of the brothers called, through the partition, to the other, "I am up."

"So am I," answered the other.

"We are eating."

"So are we."

"I am going to hunt."

"So am I."

Before starting, each brother said to his wife, "You must stay in the house ten days. If you don't, our brother, SHAGODYOWEG GOWA, may come and carry you away."

For nine days the sisters stayed indoors, then the younger said, "It is bright and pleasant, let us sit outside a little while."

The elder sister consented and they sat down near the house, but they hadn't been there long when SHAGODYOWEG came. The sisters didn't see him as he was and when he asked them to come and eat with him they went.

When the men came home and didn't find their wives they knew that their brother had captured them. The elder brother went to SHAGODYOWEG, and said, "I have come to ask you to give us our wives; watch over them, but let them stay with us."

At last he consented and the women went home with their husbands.

HÓTHO (Cold Weather) was a brother of these men and lived not far away. HÓTHO always went naked, his only weapon was a hatchet that he carried in a hole in his hip. It is Hótho who, in winter, makes the trees crack with such a loud noise; he is striking them with his hatchet.

The two brothers went to Hótho and asked him to protect their wives.

Some time after this, the two again went hunting. Shagodyoweg gowa came to the house and said to the sisters, "Come and eat with me. You can eat and be back in a little while."

Not seeing him as he was they went. He took them to his house in the forest and shut them up. The younger sister escaped but had not gone far when her brother-in-law found it out and followed, screaming as he ran.

The woman was terribly frightened and ran straight to Hótho. He said to her, "Go home, I will meet my brother."

They met and began a terrible battle. Shagodyoweg gowa fought with his rattle; Hótho with his hatchet. As they went toward the East, fighting, they tore up all the trees and bushes. But at last Hótho conquered his brother and made him promise not to steal the sisters again.

SUMMER KILLS AUTUMN AND IS HERSELF KILLED BY WINTER

[Told by John Armstrong]

Characters

DAGWANOEⁿYENT, Whirlwind or Cyclone, always represented as an immense head

SHAGODIÄQDANE .... The Woman in the South

DOⁿWEⁿWA

SHAGODYOWEG GOWA, God of the Air (Wind People)

THERE was a man called Doⁿweⁿwa. This man wouldn't let anyone come into his house. He had two nephews old enough to hunt small game: birds, squirrels and coons. The boys lived in a house near their uncle's and each morning he called to them, saying, "Up, boys! or the game will be gone." The boys jumped up and were off.

One day the younger boy heard something making a noise. He listened and listened and at last found that the noise came from the ground. He ran to his brother, and said, "Come and help me dig. I hear a noise down in the ground."

The brother went to the place with him and they began to dig with sharp sticks. When they got down some distance they found a hollow and in it a little child.

"This is the best luck we've had yet," said the elder

55

boy. "This will be our brother, but I'm afraid our uncle will find out about him; if he does he'll kill him and eat him."

"We'll try to save him, we'll fix it so our uncle won't find him," said the younger boy.

They carried the child home. That night the uncle woke up, stretched himself, and said, "I think my nephews have found game, I hear it breathing. I'll go and ask them." He stuck his head in at their door, and asked, "Well, boys, have you any game?"

"No," answered the younger brother.

"I hear it breathing."

"How can you tell? There are two of us here."

"I hear three breathing."

"If you know there are three, you may as well kill us."

"Our people don't allow a man to kill his nephews."

"Well, you'll not kill our brother," said the younger nephew. "If you kill him you must kill us."

The old man went home, but came back and stuck his head in again. "You might as well give me that boy," said he.

"If you kill him, you'll kill us," answered the elder nephew.

When the old man found that his nephews wouldn't give him the child, he promised not to harm it.

All went well for a time, then the younger brother said, "I think we had better go away and leave our uncle."

"We can't leave him," said the elder.

"Why can't we?"

"He would follow us."

"We can try to get away. We are not safe here."

They gathered dry sticks and piled them up near the house. Then one morning they set the sticks on fire and running around on the house top they jumped into the smoke, and it carried them up and away. After a while they came to the ground and hid under a big stone.

That night Doⁿweⁿwa thought the boys were very quiet. He went to their house, stuck his head in and found that they were gone.

"Oh, my poor nephews!" said he. "They think they can get away from me."

He tracked them to the top of the house and found that they jumped into the blaze and went off in the smoke. Then he went straight to the stone where they were and struck the stone with a *dadishe* (sort of cane). The stone split open and he found the three boys.

"Come out, boys," said he, "we'll go home. You should stay at home, not try to go away from me."

When the boys were back in their own house the second brother asked, "Haven't we any relatives except this old man?"

"We have," said the elder brother. "We have another uncle worse looking and crosser than this one, and we have aunts."

"Can't we go and see our uncle?"

"We can, but we must ask this uncle how to go."

The younger brother went to the old man, struck him with a mallet, and said, "I want you to tell me how I can go and see my uncle in the East?"

"You have no uncle in the East."

"Yes, I have."

"You have no uncle there, or if you have he is very cross. He is HATDEDASES (Whirlwind maker). He'll kill us all if he comes here. But you can go and see him if you are able to draw a bow that I will make for you."

The old man made a strong bow and a big double-headed arrow and told his nephews to try it. The elder brother took the bow first and couldn't bend it; the younger brother bent it easily. Then the uncle gave him the arrow, and said, pointing to a great hickory tree, "Shoot that." He shot and the arrow split the tree.

Then the old man said, "That will do. You may go and try to see your Uncle DAGWANOEᴺYENT (or HATDEDASES). If he sees you before you shoot him, he'll say 'Ogongahgeni,' and fly off. If you succeed in shooting him before he sees you, pick up the arrow and shoot again then he'll ask you what you want, and you'll answer 'I want you to come and live with us. We'll give you plenty of rocks and hickory sticks to eat, and make you a nest to lie in.'"

The boy started and after traveling a long distance came to a place where he heard a great noise; cracking and gnawing. He called his medicine mole and told it to make a trail under the ground to the place the noise came from and he would follow in the trail.

DAGWANOEⁿYENT stopped gnawing and listened; the mole stopped. The old man gnawed again; mole went on. A second time the old man stopped and listened; mole stopped. And so it went on till mole was straight in front of DAGWANOEⁿYENT. Then he made a hole and the boy came to the top of the ground, drew his bow and hit his uncle in the middle of the forehead; the arrow rebounded, he caught it and shot again. The third time he shot DAGWANOEⁿYENT called out, "I give up, what do you want?"

"I want you to come and live with us, we'll give you plenty of rocks and hickory sticks to eat and a good nest to live in. If you don't come, I'll shoot you again."

DAGWANOEⁿYENT said, "Go and fix the nest, and gather rocks and sticks for me to eat, and I'll come."

The boy went home and he and his brother and uncle put up a strong platform and on top of it they made a nest. When all was ready the old man came and settled on the nest.

Once when the two boys were out hunting the younger boy heard a noise off in the South. While he stood listening, a False Face ran toward him. The boy was frightened; he darted around trees and tried to get away. At last, when he was getting tired, he called loudly, "*Hak-noseⁿ Doⁿweⁿwa gadjionegaqdianh* (Doⁿweⁿwa, if you don't come, I shall be killed)."

That minute Doⁿweⁿwa was there, and saying, "I'll save you," he struck False Face with his *oⁿwe* and killed him.

Now the old man told his nephews never to go toward the South, that in the South there were bad women, who would kill them.

After a time the elder nephew thought he would go toward the South and see if anything would happen to him. When he had traveled a long distance, he heard some one singing, and, going toward the voice, through the dense woods, he came to an opening, and at the farther end of the opening saw the singer. Her song said, "A young boy is coming for me. He has no power; he can't come where I am."

When the boy heard this he was angry, and said, "She isn't strong enough to keep me back, I'll go there and pound her."

He doubled up his fist and ran toward the woman. She didn't look up, kept on singing. When he came to where she was sitting, he struck her a heavy blow, but instead of falling over, she said, "Ha! ha! who touches me?" That minute the boy fell to the ground dead.

The woman straightened out the body and talked to it, saying, "Poor boy, you thought you could kill me, now you are dead." She pushed the body a little to one side and kept on singing.

When the boy didn't come home, his brother went to hunt for him. He tracked him till he came to where he had stood and listened to the singing. He heard the same song and looking across the opening saw the woman and his brother's body. He was angry and doubling up his fist he ran across the opening and struck the woman a heavy blow on her head.

"Ha, ha! Who touches me?" growled she. That minute the boy fell to the ground, dead. She straightened out the body and kept on singing.

The third boy, the boy the brothers had dug out of the ground, went to look for the other two and was killed as they had been.

That night Do^{n}wE^{n}wA wondered why he heard no breathing at the other house, wondered if the boys had run away again. Going to the house he stuck his head in and seeing no one, said, "They can't get away from me, I'll find them, wherever they are."

The next morning he went toward the South till he came to the place where the boys stood and listened to the woman's song. When he saw the woman and the three bodies he said, "You've killed my nephews, now I'll kill you!" And running to the woman he gave her a terrible blow and before she had a chance to say anything he gave her a second and a third blow; but then she got a chance to call out, "Ha! ha! who touches me?" and that instant the old man grew weak and died.

Now Dagwanoe{n}yent missed his brother and nephews. "My brother," said he, "thinks that he has great power, but he hasn't, maybe he has been killed by that woman in the South, I'll go and find him."

He followed the tracks of his nephews and brother till he came to the clearing and saw the woman sitting on the ground singing. He flew at her and struck such a heavy blow that she had no chance to speak, he hit her a second and third blow then his hair began to fall out,— his strength was in his long hair—but he kept striking. The woman had no chance to speak and at last he killed her. Then he called to his brother and nephews, "Get up, you ought to be ashamed to lie there."

The four came to life and went home. They lived on quietly for a while, then the younger brother said that he was going to travel around the world and see what he could find, and he started off toward the East. After traveling some distance, he saw a hut and going into it found an old blind man, and began to torment him.

The old man said, "My brothers will come soon and then you'll stop abusing me."

The boy thought he would go before the other men came. He spent the night under a tree and the next day he traveled till nearly sundown, then came to a house. There was an old man in the house, who said, "I'm glad you have come; I want to gamble with plum stones."

"What will you bet?" asked the boy.

"I always bet heads. If you beat me, you'll cut off my head; if I beat, I'll cut off your head."

The old man had a stone bowl and some plum stones. The boy threw first, and lost, then the old man threw and lost, but in the end the boy won, and cut off the old man's head; then he went on. Soon he saw a wasp's nest hanging from the limb of a tree. He stopped up the hole in the nest, and cutting off the limb carried it along with him in a bundle. He hadn't gone far when he saw a great many people coming toward him. He wanted to pass them but they caught hold of him, and said "You are only a boy. We are going to kill you."

"You must wait a while," said the boy. "When anyone is going to be killed it is the custom to let him do

something first.'' He put down his bundle, and said,
''Tear it open if you want to.''

They snatched up the bundle and tore it open. The
wasps flew at them, and in the excitement they forgot the
boy, who ran off as fast as he could, and this time he ran
toward home. When he came in sight of his uncle's house
things looked strange; he didn't see DAGWANOEⁿYENT'S
nest. Then he found that his uncles and brothers were
gone. He searched for tracks and finding none he began
to mourn and he mourned till at last he changed to a red
fox.

The woman in the South was Summer, the boys Autumn
and old Cyclone, who at last conquered her was Winter.

GÉHA, THE FRIEND OF A DESERTED BOY

Character

GÉHA ....Wind

A PARTY of Senecas went hunting. When they had killed many deer and were ready to go home, they didn't know what to do with a little boy whose father and mother had died while they had been in the forest.

The hunters had so much meat they couldn't carry the boy and he couldn't walk so far. At last they decided to leave him in the cabin, leaving plenty of wood and meat.

The child cried bitterly and begged to go, but they left him.

When the hunters reached home and the report went around that the child had been left in the woods, every one thought it would die.

After some days the chief sent a man to see if the child was alive.

As soon as the messenger was outside of the village, he changed himself into a bear.

The little boy kept a fire, cooked meat, and lived. One cold night he began to cry; the meat was almost gone and the wood was burned up. While crying he heard some one come to the door. After making a noise, as if shaking off snow, a man said, "Little boy, you think you are going to die, you are not. I am going to take care of you. The chief has sent a man to see if you are alive, but he will not be here for a long time. I will be your friend. When you want me think of me and I will come."

The man went away and the boy fell asleep. In the morning he found a pile of wood at the door, and on a low limb of a tree hung a piece of deer meat. Now he was happy; he built a fire and cooked some of the meat.

The next night the man came again; he stopped at the door, and shook his feet, as if shaking off snow, but he didn't go in. He called to the boy, and said, "The man who is coming won't help you; he has taken the form of a bear. He will be here at midday, to-morrow. In the morning you will find, between the roots of the old stump near the door, a rusty knife. Sharpen it and kill the bear. When you hear him coming, run to the spring where the tall hemlock stands, and climb the tree; the bear will follow you. Slip down on the other side and as he is coming down stab him in the forefoot."

The boy did as the voice told him. When he had killed the bear, he went back to the cabin. The next night the stranger came to the door, and said, "My friend, men are coming for you. Go home with them, they will be good to you. The chief will adopt you and you will become the swiftest runner living, but don't be proud and boast of your power. I am your friend but you will never see me. I am the one who is called GÉHA (Wind). If you are in trouble think of me and I will help you. When the men come they will ask about the messenger the chief sent, you will say, 'I haven't seen a man, but one morning a strong wind went through the woods.'"

The next day four men came with food for the boy. They saw that he had wood and meat, but no bow or arrow. He went home with the men and the chief had him brought to his own house, for the child's relatives were all dead.

The chief said, "You will be my grandson and live with me." When they gave the boy a bow and arrows, he asked for a club.

"What do you want of a club?" asked the chief.

"To kill deer."

The chief had a club made for him. He chased deer, overtook them, hit them on the head and killed them. He killed birds before they could fly away. GÉHA had told him he would be the swiftest runner living and he always had that in mind. When he saw boys running he laughed, and thought, "That running is nothing. I can run faster than any boy living."

One night some one struck on the door near the boy's bed and a man called out, "Who is in here?"

"I am," answered the boy.

"Well, I challenge you to run a race with me. You think you are the swiftest runner in the world. We will start from the second mountain and run from sunrise till sundown."

In the morning the boy asked the chief, whom he called "Grandfather," if in the night he had heard some one talking outside.

"I did not," answered the chief.

"Well, a man came and challenged me to run a race."

"I don't think it was a man," said the chief; "it must have been a beast and I am afraid you will get killed."

"I've been challenged, and I must go," said the boy. "I must be ready the third morning from this."

He made ten pairs of moccasins, put flint in his arrows, and parched corn to eat. On the third morning he started. When near the appointed place he saw a dark mass. At first he didn't know what it was, but when daylight came he saw it was a great bear.

When the sun appeared, the bear said, "Now, we'll start."

He leaped across the valley and on to the first mountain; where he struck the ground sank. He leaped from mountain to mountain, but the boy had to run through the valleys.

At midday the bear was ahead and the boy thought, "I am lost. I wish my friend Géha would come."

That minute Géha came as a whirlwind and carried the boy far ahead of the bear. As Géha traveled he threw down trees and that delayed the bear for it had to jump over them.

At last the bear's strength gave out and he called to the boy that he might have his life.

The boy killed the bear, then he burned tobacco to his friend Géha and asked to be taken home.

Géha carried him in a whirlwind and put him down in front of the chief's house.

"I have come, Grandfather," said the boy, "I have killed a bear. You must send men to bring it home."

The chief sent eight men. They were twenty days going and twenty returning, the boy wasn't half a day, for Géha had carried him over the woods and under the clouds.

WHIRLWIND AND PANTHER

Characters

DAGWANOEⁿYENT ....Cyclone or Whirlwind

HEⁿES ....Panther

ONCE, in a Seneca village, a party of men was preparing to go on a hunting expedition. In that village was a young man whom people thought was foolish, not strong of mind. He knew that hunters were getting ready for an expedition and he went to one and another and asked to go with them, but no one would let him go.

After the hunters started a young woman took pity on the young man, went to him, and said, "Let us marry and go hunting." He was willing. They started off together and after going some distance camped in the forest. The man couldn't find any big game, but he killed squirrels and small game. He made traps to catch deer and put them down where he thought deer would come.

One morning, when the young man went to look at his traps, he heard some one crying; the sound came nearer and nearer. Soon he saw a woman and two little boys. The woman was crying.

As she came up she said to the young man, "Help me, or we will be killed. One of my little boys stole a feather and pulled it to bits and we are going to be killed for it. I want you to shoot the hawk on that tree over there and when the person comes whose feather my little boy took, throw the hawk at him and call out, 'Here is your feather!' "

The man killed the hawk and no sooner had he done

66

so than he heard a terrible roar and noise, and trees began to fall. A man came and stood on a close-by tree. This man had enormous eyes and long hair, and that was all there was of him—just a great head without a body. The young man threw the hawk at him, and said, "Here is your feather." The Head caught it, said, "Thank you," and was satisfied.

The woman was a panther and the children were her cubs, but to the young man she appeared to be a real woman. She told him that she lived among the rocks and that the Head (Whirlwind) was her neighbor. While he was away from home, her little boy went to his cabin, found his feathers and spoiled one of them. When Whirlwind came home he was angry and chased her.

She told the young man that she knew he was poor, that no man would hunt with him, and she said, "Hereafter I will help you and you will get more game than any of the hunters, I do this because you saved me and my boys."

After that the young man killed more game than any other hunter in the village.

A BIRD IN SEARCH OF A MATE

[Told by Peter White]

A YOUNG woman lived alone on the bank of a large river. One day she thought, "I am old enough to have a husband. It is lonely here by myself."

She oiled her hair, painted her face red, put on her best clothes and went to a spring. She dipped up a bucket of water and looking in it said, "I am nice enough for any man."

Then she started off along the bank of the river that ran through a forest. Toward midday she came to a place where she saw signs of people living near, and, seating herself on a log she began to sing, "I wonder if any man around here wants a wife. I wonder if any man around here wants a wife."

Soon some one far off in the forest answered, "I want a wife. I want a wife."

Then the woman sang back, "What will we live on? What will we live on when we live together?"

And he sang, "We will live on moss."

And she, singing, answered, "I couldn't live on moss. I am too good for such coarse food; I'm a nice looking girl."

Again she traveled along the bank of the river. It was near sunset when the young woman came to a place where she saw signs of people living near. She seated herself on a log and sang, "I wonder if any man around here wants a wife. I wonder if any man around here wants a wife."

Some one, not far off, answered, singing, "I want a wife. I want a wife."

Then she sang, "What will we live on? What will we live on? What will we live on when we live together?"

And he, singing, answered, "We will live on hawthorn berries and roots."

She sang, "I cannot live on hawthorn berries and roots. I am too good for such food; I'm a nice looking girl."

The young woman traveled on till dusk then, seeing signs of some one having been along a short time before, she seated herself on a log and sang, "I wonder if any man around here wants a wife. I wonder if any man around here wants a wife."

Close by some one sang, "I want a wife. I want a wife."

And she, singing, asked, "What will we live on? What will we live on when we live together?"

And he sang back, "When we live together we will live on seeds."

Singing, she answered, "That is the food I like; seeds are nice and soft."

The singer, hearing her answer, was pleased. He came and sat on a log by her side, and, singing, asked, "Did you understand my song when you asked what we would live on when we lived together?"

She, singing, answered, "Yes, seeds. I love seeds, they are sweet and soft."

Then the two flew off along the bank of the river, and ever since have lived happily together—The first birds of Spring.

The first man to answer the young woman's call was a deer—the second was a bear; the third was a bird like herself.

THE ORIGIN OF STORIES

[Told by Henry Jacob]

"This happened long ago, in the time of our forefathers."

IN a Seneca village lived a boy whose father and mother died when he was only a few weeks old. The little boy was cared for by a woman, who had known his parents. She gave him the name of POYESHAO^n (Orphan).

The boy grew to be a healthy, active little fellow. When he was old enough, his foster mother gave him a bow and arrows, and said, "It is time for you to learn to hunt. To-morrow morning go to the woods and kill all the birds you can find."

Taking cobs of dry corn the woman shelled off the kernels and parched them in hot ashes; and the next morning she gave the boy some of the corn for his breakfast and rolled up some in a piece of buckskin and told him to take it with him, for he would be gone all day and would get hungry.

POYESHAO^n started off and was very successful. At noon he sat down and rested and ate some of the parched corn, then he hunted till the middle of the afternoon. When he began to work toward home he had a good string of birds.

The next morning POYESHAO^n's foster mother gave him parched corn for breakfast and while he was eating she told him that he must do his best when hunting, for if he became a good hunter he would always be prosperous.

The boy took his bow and arrows and little bundle of parched corn and went to the woods; again he found plenty of birds. At midday he ate his corn and thought over what his foster mother had told him. In his mind he said,

"I'll do just as my mother tells me, then some time I'll be able to hunt big game."

Poyeshao[n] hunted till toward evening, then went home with a larger string of birds than he had the previous day. His foster mother thanked him, and said, "Now you have begun to help me get food."

Early the next morning the boy's breakfast was ready and as soon as he had eaten it he took his little bundle of parched corn and started off. He went farther into the woods and at night came home with a larger string of birds than he had the second day. His foster mother praised and thanked him.

Each day the boy brought home more birds than the previous day. On the ninth day he killed so many that he brought them home on his back. His foster mother tied the birds in little bundles of three or four and distributed them among her neighbors.

The tenth day the boy started off, as usual, and, as each day he had gone farther for game than on the preceding day, so now he went deeper into the woods than ever. About midday the sinew that held the feathers to his arrow loosened. Looking around for a place where he could sit down while he took the sinew off and wound it on again, he saw a small opening and near the center of the opening a high, smooth, flat-topped, round stone. He went to the stone, sprang up on to it and sat down. He unwound the sinew and put it in his mouth to soften, then he arranged the arrow feathers and was about to fasten them to the arrow when a voice, right there near him, asked, "Shall I tell you stories?"

Poyeshao[n] looked up expecting to see a man, not seeing any one he looked behind the stone and around it, then he again began to tie the feathers to his arrow.

"Shall I tell you stories?" asked a voice right there by him.

The boy looked in every direction, but saw no one. Then he made up his mind to watch and find out who was trying to fool him. He stopped work and listened and when the voice again asked, "Shall I tell you stories?" he found that it came from the stone, then he asked, "What is that? What does it mean to tell stories?"

"It is telling what happened a long time ago. If you will give me your birds, I'll tell you stories."

"You may have the birds."

As soon as the boy promised to give the birds, the stone began telling what happened long ago. When one story was told, another was begun. The boy sat, with his head down, and listened. Toward night the stone said, "We will rest now. Come again to-morrow. If anyone asks about your birds, say that you have killed so many that they are getting scarce and you have to go a long way to find one."

While going home the boy killed five or six birds. When his foster mother asked why he had so few birds, he said that they were scarce; that he had to go far for them.

The next morning POYESHAO^n started off with his bow and arrows and little bundle of parched corn, but he forgot to hunt for birds, he was thinking of the stories the stone had told him. When a bird lighted near him he shot it, but he kept straight on toward the opening in the woods. When he got there he put his birds on the stone, and called out, "I've come! Here are birds. Now tell me stories."

The stone told story after story. Toward night it said, "Now we must rest till to-morrow."

On the way home the boy looked for birds, but it was late and he found only a few.

That night the foster mother told her neighbors that when POYESHAO^n first began to hunt he had brought home a great many birds. but now he brought only four or five after being in the woods from morning till night. She said there was something strange about it, either he threw the birds away or gave them to some animal, or maybe he idled time away, didn't hunt. She hired a boy to follow POYESHAO^n and find out what he was doing.

The next morning the boy took his bow and arrows and followed POYESHAO^n, keeping out of his sight and sometimes shooting a bird. POYESHAO^n killed a good many birds; then, about the middle of the forenoon, he suddenly started off toward the East, running as fast as he could. The boy followed till he came to an opening in the woods and saw POYESHAO^n climb up and sit down on a large round stone; he crept nearer and heard talking. When he couldn't see the person to whom POYESHAO^n was talking he went up to the boy, and asked, "What are you doing here?"

"Hearing stories."

"What are stories?"

"Telling about things that happened long ago. Put your birds on this stone, and say, 'I've come to hear stories.'"

The boy did as told and straightway the stone began. The boys listened till the sun went down, then the stone said, "We will rest now. Come again to-morrow."

On the way home POYESHAO^n killed three or four birds.

When the woman asked the boy she had sent why POYESHAO^n killed so few birds, he said, "I followed him for a while, then I spoke to him, and after that we hunted together till it was time to come home. We couldn't find many birds."

The next morning the elder boy said, "I'm going with POYESHAO^n to hunt, it's sport." The two started off together. By the middle of the forenoon each boy had a long string of birds. They hurried to the opening, put the birds on the stone, and said, "We have come. Here are the birds! Tell us stories."

They sat on the stone and listened to stories till late in the afternoon, then the stone said, "We'll rest now till to-morrow."

On the way home the boys shot every bird they could find, but it was late and they didn't find many.

Several days went by in this way, then the foster mother said, "Those boys kill more birds than they bring home," and she hired two men to follow them.

The next morning, when POYESHAO^n and his friend started for the woods the two men followed. When the boys had a large number of birds they stopped hunting and hurried to the opening. The men followed and, hiding behind trees, saw them put the birds on a large round stone, then jump up and sit there, with their heads down, listening to a man's voice; every little while they said, "$\hat{U}^n$!"

"Let's go there and find out who is talking to those

boys," said one man to the other. They walked quickly to the stone, and asked, "What are you doing, boys?"

The boys were startled, but POYESHAO^n said, "You must promise not to tell anyone."

They promised, then POYESHAO^n said, "Jump up and sit on the stone."

The men seated themselves on the stone, then the boy said, "Go on with the story, we are listening."

The four sat with their heads down and the stone began to tell stories. When it was almost night the stone said, "To-morrow all the people in your village must come and listen to my stories. Tell the chief to send every man, and have each man bring something to eat. You must clean the brush away so the people can sit on the ground near me."

That night POYESHAO^n told the chief about the story-telling stone, and gave him the stone's message. The chief sent a runner to give the message to each family in the village.

Early the next morning every one in the village was ready to start. POYESHAO^n went ahead and the crowd followed. When they came to the opening each man put what he had brought, meat or bread, on the stone; the brush was cleared away, and every one sat down.

When all was quiet the stone said, "Now I will tell you stories of what happened long ago. There was a world before this. The things that I am going to tell about happened in that world. Some of you will remember every word that I say, some will remember a part of the words, and some will forget them all—I think this will be the way, but each man must do the best he can. Hereafter you must tell these stories to one another—Now listen."

Each man bent his head and listened to every word the stone said. Once in a while the boys said "Û^n!" When the sun was almost down the stone said, "We'll rest now. Come to-morrow and bring meat and bread."

The next morning when the people gathered around the stone they found that the meat and bread they had left there the day before was gone. They put the food they had brought on the stone, then sat in a circle and waited.

When all was quiet the stone began. Again it told stories till the sun was almost down, then it said, "Come to-morrow. To-morrow I will finish the stories of what happened long ago."

Early in the morning the people of the village gathered around the stone and, when all was quiet, the stone began to tell stories, and it told till late in the afternoon, then it said, "I have finished! You must keep these stories as long as the world lasts; tell them to your children and grandchildren generation after generation. One person will remember them better than another. When you go to a man or a woman to ask for one of these stories carry something to pay for it, bread or meat, or whatever you have. I know all that happened in the world before this; I have told it to you. When you visit one another, you must tell these things, and keep them up always. I have finished."

And so it has been. From the Stone came all the knowledge the Senecas have of the world before this.

THE MAN-EATING WIFE, THE LITTLE OLD WOMAN AND THE MORNING STAR

[Told by John Armstrong]

Characters

GAᴺDEWITHA .... Morning Star
ONGWEIAS .... Man-eater

A MAN and a woman lived by themselves in a clearing in the forest. The man hunted; the woman raised beans and corn.

One day, when the woman sat in front of the fire baking an ash cake, a large spark flew out and burned her. She rubbed the spot with her finger, and when it began to blister she wet her finger in her mouth and rubbed the blister; in this way she got the taste of her own flesh, and she liked it.

She took a flint knife, cut out the burnt piece of flesh and ate it. The taste was so agreeable that she took a coal of fire, burned another place on her arm, cut out the flesh and ate it. The desire grew upon her and she kept burning and eating herself till she had eaten all the flesh she could reach on her arms and legs.

The man had a dog that was wise and was his friend. The dog sat by the fire and watched the woman. When she was about half through eating herself, she said to him, "You had better go and tell your friend to run away and to take you with him. If he doesn't hurry off, I shall eat both of you."

The dog ran as fast as he could and when he came to

where the man was hunting, he told him what had happened, that his wife had become a ONGWEIAS (Man-eater) and was going to eat herself and then eat them.

The man and the dog started off. The dog's legs were short, he couldn't run fast, so the man put him in a hollow tree and commanded him to become punk. The dog was willing, for he wanted his master to save himself.

The man went on as fast as he could till he came to a river with high banks. By the river sat an old man.

"Grandfather," said the man, "I am in great trouble. Put me across the river; save me, my wife is following me, she wants to kill and eat me."

"I know she is following you," said the old man, "but she is still a long way off. I will put you across but first you must bring me a basketful of fish from my fish pond."

The man went for the fish. The pond was enclosed. On the bank was a basket with a handle. The man caught a large number of fish, filled the basket and carried it to the old man, who cooked the fish and then said, "Sit down and eat with me."

They ate together, then the old man said, "Now you must bring me a basketful of groundnuts."

The man ran to the old man's garden, dug up the groundnuts as quickly as possible and carried them to him. After he had cooked and eaten the nuts, he said, "Now I will put you across the river."

He lay down at the edge of the water and, leaning on his elbows, stretched his neck to the opposite bank, and called out, "Walk across on my neck, but be careful, I am not as strong as I used to be."

The man walked over carefully, then the old man bade him good-bye, saying, "Far off in the West you will come to a large bark house; that house belongs to your three aunts; they will help you."

After the women sent the dog away, she took a stick, and pushing the marrow out of her bones, ate it. She filled her bones with pebbles and the pebbles rattled as she moved. Every little while she stopped eating and danced and when she heard the stones rattle in her legs and arms, she said, "Oh, that sounds good!"

The woman devoured everything in the cabin, meat,

bread, skins, everything that could be eaten, and when there was nothing left she started off to find her husband.

She came upon his tracks and followed them. Once in a while she stopped and danced and listened with delight to the rattle of the pebbles in her bones; then she went on again.

When she came to the bank of the river and saw the old ferryman she screamed to him, "Old man, come and put me across the river; I am following my husband. Be quick!"

The fisherman turned slowly toward her, and said, "I can't put you across. There is no crossing for a woman who is chasing her husband to catch and eat him."

But the woman urged and begged till at last the old man said, ".I'll put you across, but first you must bring me a basketful of fish, and dig me a basketful of ground-nuts."

She brought the fish and the nuts, but when they were cooked she wouldn't eat with the old man. She would eat nothing now but human flesh.

After the old man had eaten the fish and the nuts he stretched his neck across the river but in the form of a horse's neck, very narrow and arching. The woman was angry, and asked, "How do you think I am going to walk on that?"

"You can do as you like," answered he, "I am old. I can't make my neck flat; it would break. As it is you must walk carefully."

No matter how the woman raged, she had to stay where she was or cross on the arched neck. At last she started, picking her steps and scolding as she went.

The water was deep and full of terrible creatures. When the woman reached the middle of the river the old man, angry because she scolded, jerked his neck. She fell into the water and that minute was seized and devoured all except her stomach; that floated down the river and past the house of the three aunts.

The woman's life was in her stomach.

The aunts were watching, for their nephew had been at the house and they had promised to help him; they caught the stomach, chopped it up and killed it.

The husband hurried on till he came to a forest where he found a young woman gathering sticks.

"Where are you going?" asked the woman.

"I am going on till I find pleasant people to live with."

"Stay here and be my husband," said the woman, "we can live happily if you can manage my Grandmother, who is a little old woman and is very troublesome."

The woman was good-looking, pleasant and young; the man was glad to go home with her.

When they came to the cabin the little old woman was sitting outside, she was not half as tall as an ordinary person and was very thick. As soon as she saw them she called out, "Oh, you have brought a husband! Give him something to eat."

"Ask him in, Grandmother," said the young woman.

The old woman said, "Come in!" They followed her into the cabin and sat down, then she picked up a club and began to beat her granddaughter, saying, "You want a husband, do you?"

She struck and struck and the woman endured the blows without saying a word.

The next morning the old woman said to her grandson, "We must go to the island and hunt." They went— The island was low and in the center of a deep lake. They landed and drew up the canoe, then the old woman said, pointing in a direction away from the landing, "Take your place over there, I will drive the game toward you."

When the man had gone some distance he turned and saw that the old woman was in the canoe and paddling off as fast as she could go. He called to her, but she didn't answer. He stayed all day on the island; there was no way of escape. After a while he noticed water marks very high up on the trees and then he knew that at times the island was almost under water.

When night came the water began to rise; the man climbed the tallest tree he could find; the water kept rising and he kept climbing.

About half way between midnight and morning, when all the smaller trees were covered, the man was at the very top of the high tree and around was a crowd of creatures waiting to devour him.

All at once the man saw the Morning Star shining brightly. Then he remembered that in his youth the Morning Star had promised him, in a dream, to help him in time of trouble or peril, and he thought, "If the Morning Star will hurry the day and make light come quickly, the water will go down and I will be saved." And he called out, "Oh, Morning Star, hurry on the day; Oh Morning Star, hurry on the day! When I was young you promised to help me if I were ever in great peril."

The Morning Star lived in a beautiful house and had a small boy as servant, hearing the voice he called to the boy, "Who is that shouting on the island?"

"Oh," said the boy, "that is the husband of the little old woman's Granddaughter. He says that when he was young you promised in a dream, to help him."

"Yes, I did promise," said Morning Star. "Let day come right away!"

Day came immediately and the water on the island went down at once.

When the ground was dry the man slipped down from the tree and going to the landing place buried himself in the sand, leaving only his nostrils and eyes exposed.

Early in the forenoon the little old woman came in a canoe and pulling it up on the beach, she said to herself, "The flesh of my granddaughter's husband is eaten up, but maybe his bones are left; they are young and full of nice marrow. I'll find them and eat the marrow." And she began to search for the bones. When she was far enough away, the man crawled out of the sand, sprang into the canoe, pushed out, and paddled away.

When he was some distance from the island the old woman turned, and seeing him, cried out, "Come back, my Grandson, come back! I'll never play another trick on you. I will love you."

"Oh, no!" called the man, "You'll not play another trick on me," and he hurried on.

When night came and the water began to rise the old woman climbed the tall pine tree. Half way between midnight and morning, when the water was near the top of the tree, and the creatures in the water were waiting to eat her, she screamed out to the Morning Star, ''When I was young, you promised to help me if ever I were in distress. Help me now.''

The Morning Star heard the voice and called to his boy, ''Is that man on the island yet?''

''Oh, no!'' answered the boy. ''He got off yesterday; that is the little old woman herself. She says that, when she was young, you promised in a dream that if ever she were in trouble you would help her.''

''Oh, no!'' said the Morning Star. ''I never had any conversation with that old woman, I never made her any promise.''

The Morning Star went to sleep and let day come at its own time. The water rose till it reached the top of the pine tree, then the creatures of the lake seized the little old woman and ate her up.

The man went home to his wife and they lived happily ever after.

TWO YOUNG MEN WHO WENT TO "THE BLUE"

SPEAKER AND DEFINER

Characters

HÁWENIYO ....Great Spirit (The Sun)
HADENTHENI ....Speaker
HANIGONGE^{n}DATHA ....Definer
NYAGWAIHE GOWA ....The Ancient of Bears
GADJIQSA ....Husk False Faces
GÉNO^{n}SKWA ....Frost and Cold

IN a village, in olden times, lived two young men who were such great friends that they cared for no one else, on that account everybody disliked and shunned them. They could find no home to live in so they said to each other, "Since everybody dislikes us the sooner we go away from the village the better," and they started toward the South.

When night overtook them they looked around for a dry place, where leaves had fallen, for they wanted to sleep comfortably.

At first the friends had only evergreen and roots to eat, but afterward they made bows and arrows and killed birds and small game.

When they were out of the forest, they came to an opening where there was swampy ground, but they traveled on. Once in a while one said to the other, "I am afraid we will never get across the swamp"; but the other said encouraging words, and they went on.

One day the two young men came to a tall hemlock tree. "Climb up and look around. See if there is a house in sight," said one to the other.

The limbs of the hemlock came almost to the ground and the young man climbed up easily. When he reached the top of the tree and looked off, he saw a beautiful trail leading from the tree into the air. He called to his companion, "Throw down our bows and arrows and come up here and see what a splendid trail I have found."

The other climbed the tree and looking at the trail, said, "Let us find out where it leads to."

They looked in every direction, but saw no forest or trees on any side.

It had always been necessary that whatever the two friends undertook they should be of one mind. They were now of one mind and they started off together.

The trail from the tree seemed as solid as if upon the ground, and extended as far as eye could see.

The young men traveled along the trail and never knew they were going up till they had reached another world. It seemed pleasant there, but the leader said, "Don't stop here, let us go on and see where the trail ends."

Along the trail there was plenty of game, but the young men paid no heed to it. After a time they came to a bark-house out of which smoke was rising. One of the young men said, "It is customary for travelers to stop at any house near a trail and find out who is living there. Let us look in here."

The elder went first. The house was of bark with bark suspended for a door. They pushed the door open and saw an old man sitting inside; he saluted the young men, and said, "I know the trouble you have undergone, I know that people dislike you. I have called you and you have come from the lower world, you often spoke of the world above. I caused you to follow the trail that leads up here. Come into my house, but you cannot stay long for I must go elsewhere."

The man, who seemed to be about middle age, said, "People down in your world often speak of a brother whose home is in 'the Blue.' I am that brother. I am he who makes light (the sun. HÁWENIYO commands me, says I must give light to the world. This is my resting place and I can stay here but a short time. When you come this way again you must stop. I am always here at midday. I go under the earth and come out in the East. When you come to the next house you must go in and speak to the woman who lives there," said the man as he started off toward the West.

The two young men traveled on till they came to a second bark house, then the leader said, "We must stop here for our friend told us to."

The house looked exactly like the first one. The young men went inside and saw an old woman sewing skins together. They said to her, "We have come, Grandmother."

"I am glad," said she. "It was your brother who sent you here. Now you must eat, for it is a long time that you are without food."

In one part of the house they saw a bark bowl full of boiled squash, evidently just from the kettle. They sat down and the old woman gave each of them half of a squash and a quarter of a loaf of Indian bread, saying, "This will be enough for both."

"No," said one of the young men, "there is no more here than I can eat."

"It is enough," said the woman, "when you come back, stop and I will give you more. I am the woman whom people down below call the 'Moon.' Be on your guard; the trail is full of danger, you must be brave. Don't look at anything outside of your path for an enemy is there. Don't heed anything you see or hear; if you do you are lost. After a while you will pass the dangerous part and come to a house where you can stop."

As the friends traveled on they saw all kinds of fruit and game. It called to them "Stop! Come and eat, I am good!"

But they remembered the old woman's words and paid no heed. Each fruit had words of its own with which it begged the young men to come and eat of it. After a while the fruit stopped calling, and the friends thought, "Maybe we are out of trouble now and will soon come to the house where the old woman told us to stop."

But they came to a second place. The first fruit was

full of witchcraft. If they had eaten of it, they would have died, but at the second place they ate of the fruit and were refreshed. After a while, they saw a house in the distance and one said to the other, "We are coming to a place where we may be in danger, we may have no mind of our own. We wanted to come and now that we are here we must endure what we meet."

They talked in this way till they came to the house. In the house they found a man who called himself their uncle and said, "I am glad that your brother has sent you. You are going to a large assembly, but you cannot join it unless I change you."

One of the young men was frightened. He asked, "Why should we be changed? We are men, we have come thus far in our own form."

"You have come here in your own form, but now you must be made ready to enter the assembly of this world."

The other young man looked steadfastly at his uncle and was not frightened or discouraged.

The old man went to another part of the house and brought out a long wide strip of bark, set it up slanting, and said, "The first that came shall be transformed first," and he called to the young man to come and lie on the bark. He did so; then the old man asked, "Are you ready?"

"I am ready."

The uncle blew through his hand on to the young man's head, and bones and flesh separated and fell into two heaps.

The other nephew looked on, saw how the uncle took every joint, separated the parts, wiped and put the bones aside, and he thought, "My luck is hard. I am alone here; my friend is gone."

After the bones had been cleaned the old man put them in place again, then, saying, "Be ready!" he blew through his hands on to the skull of the skeleton. The force of the blowing sent the skeleton a long distance, but again it was a man. This was the way in which each man had to be purified.

The second nephew did not want to be treated in the

same manner. He did not go forward willingly, but when the uncle was ready he gave the word and the young man could not hold back. He lay on the bark and was treated as his friend had been treated, while the friend in his turn looked on. Because he had been unwilling, his body was more difficult to purify.

The old man washed and wiped each bone. He took more uncleanness from this nephew than from the first. After he had put the bones in place, and said, "Be ready!" he blew on the skull with such force that the skeleton shot off a long distance, but it became a beautiful young man.

Then the old man said, "You are purified. Now I will try your power."

They went outside and stood in the opening. A deer was feeding on the grass. The uncle said to one of the young men, "Catch that deer." To the deer he called out, "Be on your guard, my nephew is going to kill you!"

The deer sprang off, but had made only a few bounds when the young man was at its side. The uncle saw how he caught the deer, and, knowing that he was fit for any race, he said, "You are ready now."

Then he told the second nephew to catch the deer, calling out to the deer, "Be on your guard, my nephew is going to kill you!"

The deer sprang away, but the young man overtook it and brought it to the old man, who said, "You also are ready. You can go to the assembly and see what you can accomplish."

The young men started. They had not gone far when they saw a man coming toward them. There was a little hollow ahead. They saw him go down into this hollow and come up, walking very fast. As the three men met, the stranger said, "You have come, brothers. Your elder brother wanted you to come. Now you must go with me to the great assembly. He who has charge of the assembly is the same who made the world from which you have come. As you could not go to the assembly alone I have been sent to conduct you."

The stranger turned and the young men followed him at what seemed to them incredible speed. Soon they heard the noise as of a multitude of voices and the sound grew louder and louder. The stranger said, "It is the sound of mirth and it comes from the assembly."

When they approached there seemed to be an immense settlement and the stranger said to one of the young men, "Your sister's house is off at the end, and your brothers' are there too. You cannot go into their houses for you did not die before you came here. You must pass through the same that they have to enter their homes."

As the young men went along, they felt a great desire to go into the houses, but they knew they could not. As they walked they inhaled the odor of beautiful flowers that grew along the path.

After a while the guide pointed to a long house, and said, "That is where HÁWENIYO lives, he who made the world below and allowed you to come here. We will sit down by the door and afterward go in."

The long house was built with low walls and hung inside with green boughs that gave out a delightful odor. As the air moved, a strong perfume came from the flowers and herbs that were inside the house. As the young men entered, they saw a great many people, who had come to praise HÁWENIYO and have the Green Corn dance. These people did not notice that two men were there in human flesh—for the two had been purified.

A man came out of the crowd and proclaimed what things had to be done. The guide said, "This is the one whom you call HÁWENIYO. It is here that those who are good in the lower world come when they die. When you reach home you will tell your people what you have seen. Now I will go back with you."

The three started. When they came to the place where he had met them, the guide left them and the young men went on alone. They traveled very swiftly, calling at each place where they had stopped when coming, but only to return thanks.

When they reached Sun's house, Sun said, "You are going home. I caused you to come hither. You have been ten days traveling, but what we call a day here is a year in the lower world."

When the young men got back to the lower world they were about thirty years old. The ten years they had been gone seemed no longer than going in the morning and coming back in the evening.

Sun took them to the hemlock tree where the trail began. They found that their bows, which they had left on the ground, were covered with moss. Sun reached for the bows and arrows, took them in his hands, rapped off the moss, and they were as new as if just made. He said, "Long ago the people moved from the village where you were born."

It was twelve looks [1] from the hemlock tree to where the village had been. When they came to the end of twelve looks Sun said, "Here is where the village was." Clearings and little hillocks where corn had been were to be seen, but grass was growing everywhere.

Sun said, "You will find your people twelve looks farther on. When you come to the first house ask the old man you will find there, if years ago he heard of two young men who disappeared from his village. If he gives you no information, go to the next house, you will find an old woman there, ask her the same question. Now we will part."

Sun turned back and the young men went forward. After a time they came to an opening in the woods and saw a village. They entered the first house and called the old man sitting there "Grandfather" and one asked, "Do you remember that once two young men were lost from the village where you were living?"

The old man held his head down, as if thinking, then raised it and said, "Why do you ask the question? Two young men did disappear. It was said that they were lost, but it was never known in what way."

"How long ago did this happen?"

"At the time they were lost the village was forsaken. It was ten years ago. The old chief told the young men that they must not stay any longer in that place; their children or grandchildren might disappear in the same way the two friends had. But," said the old man, "there is a woman in the next house, who can tell you more than I can."

[1] In olden times distance was measured by "looks": as far as one could see.

They went to the second house and said to the woman they found there, "How do you do, Grandmother, we have come to talk with you." Their first question was, "Why did your people desert the old village?"

"Two young men disappeared," replied the old woman. "The place was blamed for it; people thought it must be inhabited by some evil thing which took off their children."

The young men thought they had done as Sun instructed them to do, so they said, "We are the two who were lost. We have returned."

"Where have you been?" asked the old woman.

"We cannot tell you alone, but let an assembly be called and we will speak of all we have seen. Notify the people that there will be dancing, then they will come. There was nothing but mirth where we were."

The old woman said, "It is the duty of the man who lives in that house yonder to notify the people of such gatherings. I will go and tell him."

"Very well," said the young man, "the account of our journey is important, none of our people will ever see what we have seen and return to tell about it."

The old woman told the messenger that two men had come to the village with important news and a meeting of the people must be called.

The messenger started and when he came to a certain spot he called out, "*Gowe! Gowe!*" and continued to call till he reached the end of the village.

The people assembled and the chief went to the old woman's cabin and said to the two strangers, "Let your work be done."

When the young men came to the assembly, people looked at them with curiosity, for they seemed to be a different kind of people. They did not recognize them.

The chief said, "These men are here with a message. Whence they have come no one knows, for we know of no other people living in the world but ourselves."

The chief sat down and one of the young men rose, and said, "Listen!"—He was the first one purified, he had been first in all things afterward and was now the first to speak—"I want to ask you a question. Did you, while living in your old village lose two young men?"

A woman rose up, and said, "I will answer that question. Two young men, despised and shunned by all, disappeared and have not been seen since." And she sat down.

Then the old man whom the two friends had visited rose, but he couldn't say much.

The last man purified stood up, and said, "We are the two who disappeared, nobody cared for us and we were grieved. We have been to the other world, have been in the Southern world, and have returned to you. A guide came with us to our starting place. Your own wickedness caused you to leave your village and homes. You are like animals in the forest; when their young are old enough, they desert them. As soon as we were large enough, you deserted us. The birds build homes for their young, but soon leave them. You will see that whenever the young bird meets its mother it flutters its wings, but the mother passes it by. We, like the young bird, were happy to meet you, but you didn't want to see us. When we went away we were young; we are now men. What is your opinion? Will it be customary hereafter to desert homeless children?"

(The two wanted to be received into the gens [clan].)

The young man's companion listened to his speech and then said, "Let this be a starting point. Whenever a poor family are rearing children, never forsake them. When parents die, care for their fatherless and motherless children."

The two friends told how they had visited the long house in "the Blue" and seen HÁWENIYO; how they had been directed to describe to their people in the lower world all they had seen. Then they told the people they must learn the dance that HÁWENIYO wished them to know, the Green Corn dance.

One of the young men sang the song he had heard in the world above; the other taught the people how to dance to the song. He said to them, "Let it be that whatever we saw done up there will be done here." The people adopted the rules laid down for them at this time, and their religion was formed.

The friend, who was last to be purified, became HADEN-

THENI (Speaker), the first to be purified became HANIGON-GEⁿDATHA (Definer), to explain the meaning of everything touching HÁWENIYO.

After a time, the two young men said, "Let us continue our journey." They went on. They found many villages and spoke to the people. This is why the Indians are religious to-day. Those men were good in all things and the people followed their example.

They traveled till they had finished their work in the North, then they said, "We have spoken peace to all the tribes of the North, now we will return to our birthplace."

After they had been at home a while, they said, "Let us travel South from the hemlock tree and let our food be the game we kill."

When they had traveled a few days they camped and began to hunt, going in different directions in quest of game. During one of those expeditions, the Speaker saw a man dodging around the trees. As he approached the dodger stopped, and said, "Grandson, I am glad to see you. I have been sent to tell you that you and others are in great danger. This is all I can say, but come with me to my chief, he will answer your questions."

The Speaker followed the stranger for he wanted to find out if there were really people living near.

The two soon came to a high cliff and the stranger said, "We live down there."

Looking closely the young man saw an almost invisible trail. They followed the trail to the bottom of the ravine and came to an opening in the rocks. When about to enter the stranger said, "Leave your bow and arrows, as you do when you go into other houses."

They went through the first opening and into a second. In the second was an old man and an old woman. The stranger said to them, "I have brought your grandson."

"We have met many times," said the old man, "but you have never been able to know it. Now I have sent for you for I want to tell you that you are in great danger. Your companion has gone far into the forest and the NYAGWAIHE GOWA is on his trail. At midday to-morrow the enemy will be at your camp. He is full of witchcraft and if you do not act as I tell you he will kill you and kill us. We have many times tried to destroy NYAGWAIHE GOWA, but he is so full of magic that we cannot kill him.

"Go back to your camp, your friend is there now. Cut some basswood sticks and make them into mannikins. When the mannikins are finished put them down in front of your brush house, near the door, and give each one a bow and arrow. When NYAGWAIHE GOWA approaches, you will know it by the roar. Fell trees in the path and be ready with bow and arrows.

"NYAGWAIHE GOWA's life is in his feet. When he raises a foot to cross the trees you have felled you will see a white spot in the sole of the foot; there his heart is. Hit it if you can, for there only will a shot take effect."

The young man went back to camp, cut down basswood trees, and, with the aid of his friend, made two mannikins. He obeyed the old man in everything.

The old man who lived among the rocks was of the GADJIQSA (Husk False Face) people.

The young men sat in their brush house till midday. When they heard NYAGWAIHE GOWA roaring, far off in the ravine, they grew weak. GADJIQSA had told them to keep on the leeward of NYAGWAIHE so he might not scent them.

They were frightened, but said, "We cannot run away, we would not escape. Our only chance is to stay here and kill the enemy. If he kills us he will go to our village and destroy everybody."

As the creature came in sight it was furious. Whenever it came to a tree it sprang at it and tore it to pieces; the smaller trees fell at its touch.

Every time the creature roared, the young men lost their strength and were ready to drop to the ground. When the Bear passed their hiding place and went toward the mannikins and raised his feet in crossing a tree one of the men shot at the white spot and when he was going over a second tree the other man shot him through the other foot. This made NYAGWAIHE rage fearfully. He seized one of the mannikins and bit it through the body, then tore the house to bits, but a little farther on he fell dead.

The young men cut the Bear's hind feet off, for GAD-JIQSA had said that if they failed to do this NYAGWAIHE would come to life. As they cut off the feet the whole body quivered.

The ribs of this Bear were not like those in other animals, they formed one solid bone. They cut the carcass into pieces and burned the pieces to ashes, together with all the bones, for GADJIQSA said, "If even one particle of bone is left, NYAGWAIHE GOWA will come to life, and the hide must be hung over a fire and smoked, otherwise it will retain life and become NYAGWAIHE GOWA himself again."

The young men did exactly as they had been told, then they continued to hunt.

Again a man from the GADJIQSA met one of the friends, and led him to the old man among the rocks, who said, "By killing the Great Bear you saved my people as well as your own. HÁWENIYO (The Great Spirit) has given us power to aid men. It is my wish that you and your people should prosper. There is another enemy to conquer. When you leave your camp, you will go on till you come to a river. There you will camp again, but be on your guard."

The young men set out again. When they came to a river they camped, put up a bark cabin, and while one was building a fire, the other went to look for game.

Soon the man building the fire heard somebody talking loudly, as though making a speech. He went toward the voice and saw the speaker in a valley beyond a low hill. He crept forward cautiously so as not to be seen. On a slight elevation stood a man surrounded by many people. The man said, "To-morrow we start for the village from which the two friends came. At the journey's end we will have a great feast."

The young man, who was listening, knew that these people were GÉNOⁿSKWA (Frost and Cold) and that they were going to his village to eat all the people. He was frightened at their great number; he went back to the bark cabin, scattered the brands and put out the fire. When his friend came and asked why he had no fire, he said, "Don't talk so loudly, there are many GÉNOⁿSKWA under the hill; they are going to destroy our people."

"We must hurry home," said the other, and they started at once.

The next morning they heard the approach of the

GÉNOᵑSKWA. The sound was like heavy thunder. It was evident that they traveled much faster than the two men.

One of the friends said to the other, who was a swift runner, "Run to the village and warn the people!"

He ran to the village, and said, "The GÉNOᵑSKWA are coming. You may die, but do not die without a struggle." Then he hurried back to his comrade.

The comrade said, "I will stay near the enemy and detain him all I can."

That night the GÉNOᵑSKWA chief said, "No one must go far. If he does and is away when the feast begins he will lose his share of it."

The two men listening heard what the chief said. They couldn't think of any way to save themselves or their people. The people of the village were so frightened that they ran from place to place not knowing what to do.

When the GÉNOᵑSKWA were near the village the chief said, "Let us halt and rest."

The two friends sat in a sheltered place near the bank of a river. All at once they saw a man with a smiling face. When he came up he said, "I will save you and your people. I will conquer the GÉNOᵑSKWAS. HÁWENIYO has sent me to aid you. You must stay here and listen, I will go alone and fight the enemy."

With a smiling face and telling the people, who were running for their lives, not to be frightened if they heard a terrible noise, the stranger went into the valley where the GÉNOᵑSKWAS had halted to rest.

Soon a noise as of a desperate battle was heard and the two men, who had been told to listen, saw steam, from the sweat of the GÉNOᵑSKWA people, rising above the hill.

The sound came at intervals, but decreased in volume. At last it ceased altogether and the men saw the stranger coming. When he was near, he said, "I am thankful that I was able to destroy them. The GÉNOᵑSKWAS are dead and your people are safe. HÁWENIYO sends me to aid his people. Wherever there is witchcraft I am sent against it. I am sure to kill whomever I pursue. If a witch crawls into a tree, I shoot the tree; it opens and the witch comes out. I am he whom you call 'Lightning.'"

The stranger disappeared and the two men went to

where the Génoⁿskwas army had been. Only piles of stones were left. The stones of the earth are from this battle and the killing of the Génoⁿskwas.

It was through the two purified young men that our forefathers were saved from death and lived to great old age. They foretold what would be. And to this day we hold to the teachings of those men. They obtained their religion in the upper world.

Lightning is the forerunner of Spring. Warm weather destroyed the Génoⁿskwas (Frost and Cold).

THE TRIALS AND DEATH OF INCHWORM

[Told by Johnny John]

Characters

Dónyakdane, Inchworm, who was also called Dáda-wénye (He who travels everywhere)

Ganyâqde^n, Mud turtle, who was also called Háne^n-yowa'ne (Big Bones)

Wa'yo^n....Rabbit, also called Daqsi'des (Long Foot)

Gáqga', Raven, also called Shagonagâes (Always Chasing)

Gásyondetha, Lightning Lion, or Meteor, also called Hogées (Long Horns)

No^{n}gwatgwa, Fox, also called He^{n}hgéowane (Big Tail)

Nyagwaihe ....The Ancient of Bears

Dzodjógis .... Blackbird

Nondzáqgwe .... Woodcock

Dzainos gowa ....Blue Lizard

Géha ....Wind

INCHWORM lived in a little dirt cabin in the center of a big forest. He had plenty of meat and provisions of all kinds. One morning a messenger came to his cabin and said, "They want you to come to Dry Island, two days from now, to be present at a meeting."

"I will be there," said the old man, but, after the messenger had gone, he began to wonder what the meeting was for, and if he ought to go.

96

Two days later, Inchworm, starting before sunrise and traveling very fast, at midday reached a large lake. He stood near the water and looking around asked in his mind, "Where is Dry Island?" After a while he saw, off in the western part of the lake, a small island. He walked along the shore till he was opposite the island, then went into the water and swam till he came to it. He went ashore, looked around and thought, "Well, where are the people? I can't stay here long; it's too dry. But I have promised to be at the meeting."

Then he saw, at the northern end of the island, a crowd of people. He went to the place and when the chiefs saw him they called out, "All are present. Now we will begin."

The four chiefs: Meteor, Rabbit, Raven and Fox, sat down and began to talk about Inchworm. They were of one mind; they wanted Inchworm to move away from the forest where his home was.

Inchworm didn't want to go away from a place where he had lived a long time, he said, "I am satisfied with my home. I like the country around there. Why should I leave it?"

The chiefs tried to make him consent to move, but he wouldn't, his answer was always, "I am satisfied with my home. Why should I leave it?"

The chiefs were losing patience and getting angry with him when all at once they heard a noise at the southern end of the island; they heard Mud Turtle coming and he was scolding. When he came to where the people were assembled, he said, "I want you to leave my island."

"Be quiet!" said one of the chiefs. "Don't drive my people away, they are peaceable people."

"I won't be quiet," said Turtle. "This is my island, I do as I please here. I don't want you around. Go away!"

"We will go across the lake," said the chief.

Turtle followed the crowd to the edge of the lake. There everybody jumped into the water, and swam away. When they came out on mainland one of the chiefs said, "We will sit down here."

The people sat down, and again the chiefs tried to make

Inchworm say that he would leave his place in the woods, when he refused they talked to him and scolded till they saw a dark object coming toward them, then they stopped talking and watched. At last Rabbit said, "That is an enemy of ours; that is Blue Lizard. I am going. I don't want him to chase me."

He stood up and called to the people to come with him. All went, except Inchworm. He thought, "Lizard doesn't want to kill me; I'll stay here."

When Blue Lizard came up he asked, "Where is the council?"

"The chiefs have gone to the other side of the lake," said Inchworm.

"I thought I would come to the meeting," said Lizard. "I am friendly, I don't want to kill anybody. Why did they go away?"

"They are afraid of you," said Inchworm. "I don't like those chiefs. I can't say anything to them; they won't listen; they want me to leave the forest where I live."

"Why do they want you to leave your home?" asked Lizard. "I think you had better go back to your cabin and stay there. I will stay here till they come again and if they are cross, because I have sent you back to the woods, I will fight them. It won't do to drive a person out of the place where his home is; that's why I want you to go back. Don't be afraid of those people. I will fight them!"

Inchworm went home and Blue Lizard waited for the people to come back.

When Inchworm got home he cooked some meat, ate it, and then went to sleep. While sleeping he dreamed that somebody came to his cabin, and said, "I am here to tell you that trouble is coming and to tell you what to do. If you want to live, pile up meat on your couch and under it, then start off. Go north till you come to a high cliff; climb the cliff and stay there till morning, your life depends upon this." The voice stopped.

Inchworm piled meat on to the couch, and under it, threw his blanket over the couch, and started off, going toward the North. When he came to a cliff he climbed it and lay down where there was nice green grass, and soon he was asleep.

The council sent NYAGWAIHE (the Ancient of Bears) to kill Inchworm. He went into Inchworm's cabin, pulled the skin blanket from the couch and saying in his mind, "Here is the man I'm to kill," he ate all the meat, thinking he was eating Inchworm. Then he went back to the council, and said, "Inchworm is dead; I've killed him."

The next morning Inchworm woke up and started for home. When he got there, he found that the meat he had put on the couch and under it had been eaten, not even a bone was left. He cleaned his house, cooked, and after he had eaten he said in his mind, "I'll go to Dry Island and say a few words to Turtle, but first I'll send a messenger to tell him that I am coming."

He called Yellowbird and sent him to tell Turtle that he would be there in two days, that he wanted to say a few words to him.

Yellowbird did as he was told. Turtle said, "Let him come. This is the way to do; when a person wants to talk with me, he should send a messenger to tell me that he is coming."

After two days Inchworm started. He reached the lake and swam across to the island, then looked around for Turtle's house. Soon he saw an underground house in the middle of the island and going to it knocked on the door. When Turtle got up to open the door he began to scold and he scolded till he came out of the house. Inchworm was frightened and backed away. Turtle laughed, stopped scolding, and said, "Come back, I am ready to talk."

Inchworm said, "I came to talk about the council that was here, and to ask you to be my friend. You are of the same mind that I am: you want to keep your home as long as you live. Those chiefs say that I must leave the forest where I have always been. I don't want to leave, I want you to be my friend so we can hold the places where we live."

Turtle said, "I like what you say, and I will help you. I will tell you what to do. Whenever you want to come here send a messenger to say that you are coming."

"Now I am going," said Inchworm. When he got to

the lake, he ran on the water, he didn't swim as he had
when coming. He traveled quickly and was soon at home.

Some days later Inchworm heard, off in the East, a
loud noise, then he heard it again and nearer his house.
"Well," said he in his mind, "my friend said he would
tell me what to do if an enemy came. I don't think that
noise is made by anyone coming to fight with me." But
he stayed in the cabin and watched. Soon he saw NYAG-
WAIHE so near the cabin that there was no chance to run
away from him. Then Inchworm thought, "It must be
that the end of my life has come."

NYAGWAIHE came in, but Inchworm wasn't afraid. He
laughed, and said, "You are a fine looking man, I will
give you a name that will help you always. I will call you
SHAGÓYA'DOGÉDAS (He drives them away)."

"I don't like that name, I never act in that way."

"I will call you SHAGÓNOGES (He torments them)."

"I don't want that name."

"I will call you DAE^{n}DZONGO (Soaked with Earth)."

"That will do, I'll take that name."

(Inchworm didn't know that each night the chiefs held a
council to devise a way to kill him.)

NYAGWAIHE went off and soon Inchworm heard the
voice that had spoken to him in the night. It was the
voice of GÉHA (Wind) and the voice said, "I am here to
help you. People are coming to kill you. I will tell you
how to overpower them. At the northern end of this forest
you will find a weed called awéondágo^n; gather that weed
and plant it around your house; get four white flint stones
and put one stone at each corner of the house, outside.
Then bring wood and pile it up around the house. On
the tenth day set fire to the wood. That day the chiefs
will come to kill you. This is all."

"Why do the chiefs want to kill me," asked Inchworm.
The voice didn't answer.

Inchworm put on his best clothes, took his bow and
arrows and went for the weed. In the woods he couldn't
walk very fast. Before he got far, night came. He looked
around for a hollow tree, found one, and crept into it.
The next morning he went on, traveled all day asking in
his mind, "When will I get to the end of my journey?"

Another night came. He looked around for a hollow tree, found one and crawled into it. When almost asleep he heard a noise like footsteps. He listened. The steps came nearer and he heard two men talking, one said, "I think this is a hollow tree," the other said, "Let's crawl into it, but first we must know how big the hole is. Pound on the tree and find out."

Inchworm backed into the hole as far as he could, and kept still.

The two men were of the Woodcock people. They crawled into the hole, and soon one of them said, "It seems to me there is somebody in here."

"I don't think there is anyone here, but ourselves," said the other man.

The next morning the two men got out of the tree and went off toward the West. Soon after Inchworm crawled out and looked around. When he saw the two men he whooped; they heard him and one asked the other, "Who is that whooping? Let's go back, maybe it's the man we are hunting for."

They found Inchworm sitting on the ground near the hollow tree.

"Where did you come from?" asked one of the men.

"From Broken Land."

"Do you know the man who lives in the woods?"

"I don't know him."

"Why are you here? Where are you going?"

"I'm traveling through the forest to see how the country looks where the sun goes down."

"We are going to that country," said one of the men. "We will go with you."

"I am not going now. I must stop and hunt for game."

"We will stay with you; maybe we can help you. Where will you camp?"

"I will look around and see where there is a good place. You can look for one too."

Inchworm went in one direction, the two men in another. When Inchworm got out of sight, he started off toward the North.

At midday the two men came back to the hollow tree, but Inchworm wasn't there.

Just at midday Inchworm reached the edge of the forest and began to look for the weed. He found it and in a short time gathered a big bundle of it, then he started for home. Near sunset he came to the hollow tree and found the two men there; they had killed game and were roasting some of the meat. When they saw Inchworm, one asked, "Where have you been all day?"

"Oh, around here, not far away," said Inchworm.

"We have plenty of meat," said the man. "Come and eat with us."

Inchworm put his bundle down, ate, and rested. The next morning when the men began to cook, Inchworm said, "I will go into the woods a little way, I will be back before you are through eating." And, taking his bundle, he started off toward the East. When out of sight, he ran as fast as he could and was at home before midday. He put down his bundle of weeds and went for the white flint, found the stones and took them to the cabin.

The next morning he went into the forest to look for dry boughs and pieces of wood. When he had gathered a large pile he carried it home, a load at a time, and put it down near the cabin. At the end of six days he said in his mind, "I have enough wood, now I will plant the *awéondágo^n*."

He planted the weed; put a white flint stone at each corner of the cabin outside, and piled up the wood around the cabin.

The next morning Inchworm said in his mind, "At midday the chiefs will come." Just before midday he set fire to the wood; it blazed up quickly, made a great fire.

When the chiefs came Rabbit said, "Inchworm's house is burning up."

GÁSYONDETHA (Meteor) said, "Let us find out which one of us has the greatest power," and he sprang into the fire. The burning was not as wide as he thought; he came down between the fire and the cabin and straight on to a sharp flint stone, he was impaled and couldn't move. He saw that the cabin was not burning, that there were beautiful plants growing around it, and they were

covered with bright red blossoms. He began to cry and
he cried louder and louder.

Inchworm said, "Somebody is crying; I'll go and see
who it is."

When he saw Meteor he asked, "What are you doing
there?"

The man was crying so hard that at first he couldn't
answer, but after a while he said, "I came here to visit
you."

"Where are the other chiefs?"

"They are in the fire." They had jumped in to test
their power, and not able to get out had burned to death.

Inchworm said, "You came here to kill me," and he
reproached Meteor till the man gave up his enmity, and
said, "I will be your friend and give you my power."
Then Inchworm stopped his reproaches.

"Let us go into the cabin," said the chief.

Inchworm was angry; he asked, "Do you think this
is your cabin?"

"No."

"Then why did you say, 'Let us go in'?"

"I just said it, that's all. I didn't mean anything
wrong."

"Well, we will be friends," said Inchworm. He went
into the cabin and, looking back, thought, "Where is my
friend?" He went out and found Meteor standing on
the flint stone; he couldn't move. Inchworm took him
by the hand and pulled him from the flint. Then they
went into the cabin and sat down and talked, and became
good friends.

Just at sundown the fire around the cabin went out.
The weeds that Inchworm had planted kept the cabin
from burning.

One morning after Meteor had made Inchworm a long
visit, he said, "I am going home now," and he started off.

Inchworm was alone, but he had plenty to eat and
was happy. One morning he heard footsteps outside; he
sat still, but he said in his mind, "Meteor is coming again."

He listened and when some one knocked on the door, he
called out, "Why don't you come in?"

The door opened slowly; Inchworm watched sharply,

soon a beautiful woman of the Blackbird people came in, and said to him, "I have come to marry you, my old folks sent me here."

Inchworm hung his head, "What shall I do?" thought he, then he looked up, and asked, "Will trouble come of this?"

"No," said the woman, "I want to live in peace."

"I'll marry you," said Inchworm.

Some days later the woman began to scold; she scolded all day.

Toward night Inchworm said, "I am tired. You scold all the time, you must go home."

"I'll stop scolding," said the woman.

"I don't believe you. It won't be quiet with you here, you must go."

He went to where she was sitting, took her by the hair, dragged her to the door and pushed her out. When she was outside he said, "Now go away, and never come back to this cabin."

She went away, crying.

One morning, a few days later, Inchworm sat on the flint stone at one corner of his house, and said to himself, "I feel weak this morning." He looked around in the woods and thought, "I wish my wife were here, I am sorry that I drove her away."

He thought about it all day. Towards night a man came, and said, "I have come with a message from your friend, who lives on Dry Island. He wants to visit you."

Inchworm said, "Tell him to come two days from now."

Two days later, Inchworm, forgetting that Turtle was coming, said in his mind, "I'm going East this morning." He traveled along till at midday he came to the end of the forest and off in the distance saw a village. He went to the village, but every house was empty. At last, at the east end of the village he saw smoke and going toward it found a hut. In the hut was a very old woman. When she heard some one come in she stood up and raised a mallet. Inchworm saw the mallet and hurried out of the hut as fast as he could. Outside he stood around to see what would happen. Just then he remembered about Turtle's visit.

"I must go home," thought he. "My friend is coming to-day, but first I'll burn this old woman's hut. I don't like the way she has acted toward me."

He burned the hut with the old woman in it, then ran home as fast as he could, but when he came to the clearing where his cabin had been there was nothing there but a pile of dead coals.

"My friend has burned my house," said he. "I'll kill my friend. If I can't kill him, I'll punish him in some way," and he hurried off to Dry Island.

When he came to Turtle's house in the middle of the island he jumped into it, but no one was there. He went outside, set fire to the place and waited around till only dead coals were left, then he went to the other side of the lake. As he stood on the bank, listening, he heard some one scolding; Turtle had come back to Dry Island and found his house burned. He was mad and kept saying, "I'll kill my friend! I'll kill my friend!" He crossed the lake and went to where Inchworm was waiting for him. Right away they began to fight. They fought all day and all night, fought five days and five nights, and then their bodies were gone, only their heads were left. The heads fought till the seventh morning, then, worn out, both died at the same time.

GÁQGA'

Characters

RAVEN was traveling but he didn't know whence he came or whither he was going. As he journeyed along he was thinking, "How did I come to be alive? Where did I come from? Where am I going?" After traveling a long time he saw a smoke and going toward it saw four hunters—blackbirds. Afraid to go near them he hid in the forest and watched.

The next morning after the hunters had started away, Raven crept up to their camp, stole their meat, carried it into the woods and made a camp for himself. He was lonely and he said, "I wish there were other people here." Looking around he saw a house west of his camp and going to it found Robin and his wife and five children. Raven ate the youngest child, then ate the other four. The father and mother tried to drive him away, but could not. When at last Raven went off he left old Rabin and his wife crying for their children.

Sometime after this, Raven saw a camp off in the south-

106

east and going there found a family of Sparrows. He was afraid of the old people and he ran off, but they followed him, caught up and hit him on the head till they drove him far away.

"It is a shame to let such little people beat me!" thought Raven. But he was afraid to go back.

Now Raven had gone far from his camp; he hunted everywhere in the forest but couldn't find it. "Well," said he at last, "let it go, I don't care!" and he walked away toward the North. Just before dark, he found a camp and going towards it saw four men and a large quantity of meat. He hid in the forest and the next morning, looking toward the camp, he again saw the hunters.

"I'll. wait till they go away," thought Raven, "then I'll steal their meat." Soon he heard the men moving around, then all was quiet and he knew that they had gone. He crept slowly toward the camp, but when he reached it he didn't find even one bite of meat—they were the hunters from whom he had stolen before. They had finished hunting, had packed their meat and started for home.

Raven was disappointed. He walked on and toward night found another camp. Creeping near it, he again saw the four hunters. He listened to what they were saying.

One said, "I wonder who stole our meat that day?"

Another said, "I think the thief is walking around in the woods, I think his name is Raven."

"Oh," thought Raven, "they are talking about me. They will be on the watch. How can I get their meat?" Then he said, "Let them fall asleep and sleep soundly!"

That minute the four hunters fell asleep. Raven went up boldly, took their meat, carried it off into the woods and hid it, saying, "This is the kind of man I am!"

The next morning the four hunters missed their meat. One said, "Somebody has stolen my meat!"

Another asked, "Who has stolen my meat?"

The third said, "I dreamed that I saw Raven around here and he started off toward the Southwest."

Then the four said, "Let us follow the direction given by the dream."

The hunters started to follow the thief. Soon they came to the place where he was camped. Raven had been out all night and now he was sleeping soundly.

One of the men said, "We must kill him."

"No," said another, "let him live, he didn't kill us while we were asleep."

They took their meat and went away.

When Raven woke up, he was very hungry, but the meat was gone. "Well," thought he, "I must hunt for something to eat." He traveled around in every direction but found no game. About midday he heard the noise of people. He listened a while then went on till he came to a house. A man inside the house was singing and the song said, "Raven is coming! Look out! Be careful! Raven is coming!"

"Why does he sing about me?" thought Raven, "I'll go in and find out."

He went into the house and found Ground-bird and his wife and four children.

"I have come to stay a few days with you," said Raven.

"Very well," said the man.

That night Raven ate the four children, then he lay down and slept.

The next morning the father and mother asked, "Where are our children?"

Raven said, "I dreamed that a man came and carried your children off, and my dream told me which way he went. I will go with you and hunt for them."

When the three had traveled some distance Raven said, "The man who stole your children lives on that high cliff over there. I can't go there with you, for I don't like that man. I will wait here till you come back."

As soon as the father and mother were out of sight, Raven ran off. He traveled till he came to where there were many of his own people. They were dancing and he sat down to watch them.

Soon Muck-worm was seen coming from the East. The people stopped dancing and ran in every direction, but Muck-worm pursued them and catching one after another by the neck he threw them aside dead.

Raven, who was watching, thought, "What sort of a

man is that? I wish he would see me. He can't throw me off dead, in that way."

Muck-worm, after killing many of the Raven people, started toward the West, Raven followed him. Muck-worm kept on for a long time without seeming to know that there was anyone behind him, but at last he stopped, looked back, and asked, "What do you want?"

"I don't want anything," said Raven, "I've come to be company for you."

"I don't want company," said Muck-worm.

Raven was frightened. Both men stood still for a minute then Muck-worm sprang at Raven and caught him. He would have killed him, but Raven screamed so loudly that many of his people heard the cry and came to his aid. They flew at Muck-worm and pecked him to death.

THE THUNDER BOY

Characters

Híno' ....Thunder
Híno'hoháwa^{n}k ....Thunder's Son
Yege^{n}hdji, In one version of this story Yege^{n}hji's mother was He^{n}es (Panther)

A POOR old woman lived in a smoky little cabin in the woods. She was only skin and bones and she cried all the time, both day and night. Her blanket was so old and dirty that nobody could have told of what kind of skin it was made.

This old woman had had seven daughters. Six had been carried off, one after another; the seventh daughter died.

The daughter who died had been buried some time when one night her mother heard crying. She took a torch and going out toward the grave found a naked baby. She wrapped the baby in her blanket and took it home.

The baby, a little boy, grew very fast. One day when the grandmother came home from gathering wood he was not in the house and she couldn't find him.

That night there was a storm with thunder and lightning. In the morning when the child came back the grandmother asked, "Where have you been, my grandson?"

"I have been with my father; he took me home with him."

"Who is your father?"

"Híno' is my father. He took me home first, then we came back and were around here all night."

"Was my daughter your mother?" asked the old woman.

"She was," answered the boy, "and Híno' is my father."

The old woman believed her grandson. As the boy grew he often made a noise like the noise of thunder and whenever Híno' came to the neighborhood the child went out and helped his father; he was Híno'hohÁwa^{n}k, son of Híno'.

After a time the boy asked his grandmother where his six aunts were, and she said, "Far from here there is a mother and son who live by playing dice. Your aunts went there with a company of people; they played, were beaten and their heads were cut off. Many men and women have gone to the same place and have lost their heads."

"I will go and kill that woman and her son," said the boy.

The grandmother tried to keep him at home but he wouldn't stay with her. He was ragged and dirty. He asked her to make him two pairs of moccasins. She made them, and, for a pouch, she gave him the skin of a flying squirrel.

The boy started off toward the West and after a while he came to a large opening where there was a bark house with a pole in front of it, and on the pole hung a skin blanket. He heard a great noise and saw that at one end of the opening old men were betting and boys were playing ball.

When people saw him, one said to another, "Who is that boy? Where did he come from?"

Soon an old man went up to Híno'hohÁwa^{n}k, gave him a club and asked him to play.

He played ball so well that the same man came to him, and said, "We want you to play dice, my people will bet on you."

"I don't know how to play dice," answered the boy.

"We will risk our heads on you," said the man.

Young Híno' followed the old man to the pole that stood by the bark house. The betting woman was sitting there on an elk skin. In front of her was a white stone bowl as smooth as glass. Híno'hoháwaⁿk knelt down beside the bowl.

The woman said, "You must play first."

"No," said he, "you must play first."

The woman took up her dice, which were round and made out of stone. She blew on them, threw them into the bowl, shook the bowl, and called out, "Game! Game!"

The dice flew up in the air, became crows and cawed as they went out of sight. Soon they came down, cawing; as they touched the bowl they were stones again.

The woman had three plays in which to get a count of seventeen. She threw three times, but made no score. Then young Híno' took dice out of his pouch made of the skin of a flying squirrel. The woman insisted on his using her dice, but he refused. He put his dice in the bowl and shook the bowl. The dice became wild ducks and flew into the air.

The ducks went very high, all the people heard them as they rose. When they came down and touched the bowl they were stones and scored ten.

Híno' shook the bowl again, and called "Game! Game!"

The old woman called "No game! No game!"

The ducks flew up and when they came down they scored another ten. He tried a third time and scored ten, then he called to the people to come and see him cut off the head of the betting woman.

"Wait," said the woman, "You must play ball with my son. If he loses, he will lose his head."

Híno' asked the old men what he should do. Seeing how powerful he was, they said, "Play."

He went to the ball ground—he was ragged and looked very poor. Only the two played. Híno'hoháwaⁿk sprang forward and knocked the club out of Yegeⁿhdji's hand. The young man ran for his club, but before he could get it, Híno'hohá sent the ball through the goal. This was repeated seven times, and Híno''s son won the game.

Then he said to the people, "Now you can destroy the old woman and her son."

They did. Then the young boy said, "I am going to bring my grandmother to this place and we will have this long house to live in,"

As he traveled toward home, he sang praises of himself, and his grandmother heard him when he was a long way off. When he came to the cabin he told her what he had done, and said, "We must go there and live in the long house."

She made ready and started, but it took a long time to reach the place, for friends went with them. When all had settled in houses built around the opening Híno' hohÁ called the people to the long house for a dance. The grandmother threw away her old blanket and put on the clothes left by the gambling woman and then she looked like a young girl.

After a time Híno'hohÁ went off with Híno', his father, and stayed with him all Winter.

When Spring came the grandmother was uneasy about the boy, but one day she heard Thunder off in the West and soon her grandson came to the cabin.

"Where have you been?" asked she.

"On a great mountain far off in the West. I have been with my father, helping the nations and protecting men."

The boy stayed with his grandmother that Spring and Summer. Once in a while when it began to storm, he went away, but he always came back when the storm was over. The two lived a long time in this way, but at last the boy said, "You have a brother living in the West. Some wizard stole him from you. I must go and find him."

And he went West to look for his uncle.

Híno'hohÁ traveled till he came to a cabin. In the cabin a woman was sitting by a fire. When he asked where his uncle was she wouldn't answer. Taking his war club from his pouch, he struck her on the head and killed her. Then he went out and walked around the house, mourning and looking for his uncle. At last he heard a man groaning. He looked up in the trees for he couldn't see anyone on the ground, but the man was not in a tree.

He followed the sound and soon came to a large slippery elm tree. A man lay under the tree; he was held down by great roots; his head came out between two roots on one side and his feet between two roots on the other side. The tree stood on the middle of his body. He was calling to his nephew to give him a smoke.

Híno'hohá said, "Oh, my poor uncle, how badly off you are! I will give you a smoke right away."

He kicked the tree over, saying, "Rise up, uncle!"

The man stood up at once, and was well. Híno'hohá took out his pouch and gave the old man a stone pipe and Indian tobacco, and he grew strong. Then he told his nephew how a woman had enticed him to go with her, then she ate him up and put his bones under the elm tree.

The uncle and nephew went to the long house. The old grandmother was surprised and glad and the three lived happily together till one day the nephew went off in a storm and when the storm was over he brought back a wife. Then when he went off with a storm his wife was uneasy. The woman didn't know where she was from. In a terrible storm Híno'hohá had brought her home on his back.

After a time she had a son and when the boy was old enough to run around, the uncle, whose bones had lain under the elm tree, began to teach him, and soon the child was able to make a noise like the roar of thunder.

One day the child followed his mother out of the house; he had a little dog and that followed too. As the boy was running along somebody seized him and rushed off. The dog ran after him, and, jumping to snatch him away, caught hold of his feet and pulled off his moccasins; the dog carried the moccasins home.

When the mother saw the moccasins, she knew that her boy was gone. The father was off in a storm. When he came home the woman asked if he had taken the boy away.

"I have not," said he.

"Oh, he is lost; he is lost!" cried the woman.

"He is safe," said Híno'hohá. "He has many relatives around the world, uncles and cousins."

The boy was gone all Winter, but one day in Spring he came home with his father. Then Híno'hohá said to his family, "We must all go and live with my father."

The old grandmother said, "I can't go; it is far and I am old."

"I will carry you," said the grandson.

Then HINO'HOHÁ began to thunder, and lightning flew around. The long house was torn to pieces and blazed up in flames. All the rocks and houses and trees in the opening were destroyed. HÍNO'HOHÁ and his people rose up in the air. The East wind blew and it bore them to the high mountain in the West and there they found old HÍNO'.

And to this day the Thunder family live on that mountain in caves and among rocks.

GRANDFATHER AND GRANDSON AND AN EAGLE WOMAN

[Told by John Armstrong]

Characters

DAGWANOEⁿYENT ....Cyclone or Whirlwind
GÁSYONDETHA ....Meteor
DŌ'NYONDA ....Bald Eagle

A GRANDFATHER and grandson lived far away from any village. All the people of their nation had been carried off. The grandfather was very careful of his grandson for he was the only comfort he had.

One day the boy ran into the cabin, and said, "Grandfather, I heard something out in the woods crying, '*kidjidi! kidjidi!*'"

"Oh," said the grandfather, "that was a chickadee, that is the first game hunters kill."

The boy went out with his bow and arrows and after many attempts he killed a chickadee. When he took it home the old man danced with joy, singing as he danced, "My grandson will be a great hunter! My grandson will be a great hunter!"

Another day the boy ran in crying, "O Grandfather, I've seen something with four legs, and a tail with four black stripes around it!"

"That was a coon," said the grandfather. "That is the second game hunters kill."

The boy killed a coon, and the old man danced and sang, "Oh, my grandson will be a great hunter! Oh, my grandson will be a great hunter!"

The next day the boy ran in crying, "O, Grandfather, I've seen a strange thing walking on two legs. Red skin hangs from its head, and it makes a great noise."

"That was a turkey," said the grandfather. "That is the third game a hunter kills."

The boy went to the woods and when he saw a flock of turkeys, he ran till he caught one of them. Again the old man danced and sang, "My grandson will be a great hunter."

The boy went out another day and saw a long creature with thin legs and something, like the branches of a tree, on its head. He was frightened; he ran home and told his grandfather what he had seen. The old man said, "That is the fourth and largest game; that was a deer. When a man can kill a deer he is a good hunter."

The next day the boy killed a deer.

The old man didn't dance or sing this time; it was a solemn occasion. He taught the boy how to dress the deer and stretch the skin, then he said, "You are a young man now. You needn't run in to tell me what you have seen, kill anything that comes along. A man that can kill a deer can kill all kinds of game. When hunting you can go in any direction except the North, wicked women live in the North; women who have killed many of our people."

The young man went toward the South, but he kept thinking about the women who had killed his relatives and at last he turned and went North. After a time he came to a tree that was covered with scratches, like the scratches made by a coon's nails. He said in his mind, "It must be that there are a great many coons in this tree."

He threw off his blanket, took a stick and his bow and arrows and climbed up till he came to a hole in the tree; he looked into the hole and, seeing a number of coons, poked his stick down, killed two or three of them, pulled them up and threw them to the ground. As he did this he looked down and he saw, near the foot of the tree, a beautiful young woman.

As soon as he saw her, she called out, "Come down, I want to talk to you."

He paid no attention to the woman, but kept on killing coons. She called again and again. At last he went to the other side of the tree, turned himself into a red-headed woodpecker and went up the tree pecking the bark. When he got to the top he shot an arrow off toward home. The arrow whizzed through the air, making a noise like a woodpecker.

The woman, thinking that the boy was in the arrow, hurried after it.

The young man took his own form, slipped down from the tree, put on his clothes, gathered up the coons and went home. The grandfather was glad to get the coons, but when he knew where his grandson had been he was angry. "You must not go there again," said he. "If you do, great harm will come to us."

The next day the young man started off toward the South, but when out of sight he turned and went North. He went beyond the first tree and came to a second tree covered with scratches. He climbed the tree and killed a number of coons, then he looked down and saw, sitting on a log, near the foot of the tree, the same young woman. As soon as he saw her, she began to urge him to come down. She talked with enticing words. He knew that he ought not to go, but the feeling came into his heart that he wanted to. He went half way and stopped. Again the woman urged. At last he went to the ground and sat down on the end of the log—the woman was sitting in the middle.

"Why do you sit so far away?" asked she, "A young man and a young woman sit near each other when they talk."

He drew a little nearer, then she urged him to come up close to her. At last he sat by her side. She told him stories and talked till he fell asleep then she put him in a skin bag, took the bag on her shoulders and hurried off through the air.

After a long time, the woman came to the ground, took the young man out of the bag, roused him, and asked, "Do you know this place?"

"Yes, my grandfather used to fish here."

"I don't believe it," said the woman, "Point out something you remember."

"There are the poles we put up; and there is the old kettle we cooked in." He willed that she should see those things; he bewitched her eyes.

Again she told him stories till she put him to sleep. A second time she carried him far away. When she came to the ground and opened the bag, the young man found that he was on the shelf of a high cliff. On narrow places near him were other men, some alive, some half eaten up. "Oh," thought he, "my grandfather was right, there are bad women in the North." He called to the man nearest him and asked how he came there.

"A woman brought me here; other women brought these other men to where they are; many men have been eaten up; you and I will be eaten when they come to us."

The young man thought how he might escape. All at once he remembered that, on a time, a great spider had appeared to him in a dream, and had promised to help him when in trouble, and he cried, "O Spider, help me now!"

Right away an enormous spider was there on the top of the cliff and it began weaving threads for a rope. When the rope was long enough the spider let it down and the young man climbed up on it. Then he let the rope down and drew up the men on the cliff one after another. All the men went home except the young man. He set out for the home of the woman who had deceived him.

He found the woman living in an old house with her mother and he said to her, "I have come to marry you."

The woman said, "I have a very bad mother, I'm afraid that she will kill you; she sent me to deceive you and carry you to the cliff."

"I'll try to save myself," said the young man.

The old woman slept at the end of the house. In the night she began to groan and roll around on the ground.

The young woman said, "Strike my mother on the head with the corn pounder."

He struck her, and asked, "What is the matter, Mother-in-law?"

"I dreamed that my son-in-law killed the white beaver in the lake and made a feast for the DAGWANOE^{n}YENTS."

"Go to sleep now," said the son-in-law, "I'll do that to-morrow."

The next morning he went to the lake and killed the beaver with a single arrow, but as soon as he lifted it out of the water the lake rose up and pursued him with fury. The young man knew the water was so poisonous that flesh that it touched instantly dropped from the bones, so he ran for his life. He reached the house and threw the beaver down. That minute the water disappeared.

The old woman was raging, she said, "Oh, my poor son, my poor son! I thought that my son-in-law's bones would be in the lake."

The beaver was dressed and cooked. The man invited the DAGWANOE^{n}YENTS and the GÁSYONDETHAS to come to the feast. They came; the house was full of horrid heads with long hair. When the dinner was eaten to the last morsel, the heads began to smack their lips. "A splendid feast!" said they. "A grand dinner the old woman's son has made us! How sweet his flesh was!"

The old woman was furious; she seized a club and drove the guests away.

The next night the old woman rolled around the house and down to the fire, crying, "*Agi! Agi!*"

"Oh," said the wife. "This time my mother will dream that you and she must go to the sweat house, you first and then she. Now strike her with the corn pounder."

He struck her and she called out, "I dreamed that my son-in-law went to the sweat house and then I went."

"Go to sleep, Mother-in-law, I'll attend to that to-morrow."

In the morning the sweat house was heated. As soon as the young man went in, the old woman danced around outside and sang "Let there be heat to kill him! Let there be heat to kill him!"

When she thought he was dead she went in, but she found him comfortable and happy. Now it was her turn to sweat. The son-in-law closed the sweat house, then he danced and sang "Let it become flint, first at a red and then at a white heat."

Right away the house was flint and red hot.

The old woman was burned up.

"Now," said the young man to his wife, "You brought me most of the journey on your back, you know the way; take me to my home."

She put him on her back, carried him over the fields and the woods, past the fishing grounds where he had said that his grandfather used to fish, past the trees scratched by the coons, and at last brought him to his grandfather's house, and they lived there happily.

The women in this story were eagles.

THE GREAT SPIRIT OVERPOWERS THE COLD AND FROST OF WINTER, STONE COATS

Characters

GÉNOⁿSKWA.........Stone Coats (Frost and Cold)

IN the old time when men got lost while hunting it was supposed the Winter God (Stone Coat) ate them up.

Once three Senecas started off on the war-path, going toward the West. At night they camped in a deep ravine at the head of a stream.

When they had made a fire, a fine looking man came and said to them, "I think it is right to do what I am going to do. I have come to tell you that there are many people, man-eaters, on the war-path. To-night they will make their camp in sight of yours. One of you must go to their fire and say, 'Hallo! I've found your fire. Where are you going?'

"They will answer, 'We are on the war-path.' The man must say, 'I am on the war-path too.' They will say, 'Well, we will fight.' Then the man must leave them and come back to your camp."

The stranger disappeared and soon people came and camped a short distance from the Seneca camp. One of the three Senecas said, "I will go over there." As he approached he called out, "Hallo! I've found your fire! Where are you going?"

"We are on the war-path."

"So am I," answered the Seneca.

"Well, we must fight," said the chief of the Stone Coats.

As the man turned to go away he saw stone clothing leaning against a tree; the owner of the clothes was lying on the ground.

122

The next morning the Stone Coat warriors came up the ravine toward the Seneca camp. They made a terrible noise for they sang, "We are going to eat up the Seneca nation! We are going to eat up the Seneca nation!"

When they were about half way through the ravine, they gave a war whoop and moved forward quickly. But that moment huge rocks began to roll down on them and great trees to fall on them. The Senecas saw a strange man running along on top of the rocks and trees. Whenever he saw a Stone Coat head sticking up, he struck it and killed the man.

Of all the warriors only one was left alive and he was never seen again. All the time the stranger was throwing rocks and trees he sang, and the song said, that the Seneca nation could stand against anything, could stand against the whole world.

When the battle was over, the stranger came to the three men, and said. "I am he whom you call HÁWENIYO (Great Spirit). I have saved you. I did not make the Stone Coats, some one else made them. I want you, the Seneca people to be the most active of all tribes, in war, in games and in hunting."

The stranger disappeared and the three Senecas went home.

One day a Seneca, who was out hunting in the woods, saw that a Stone Coat was following him; he was frightened and began to run. When he saw that the Stone Coat was gaining on him, he climbed a tree that had fallen part way and lodged on another tree.

Stone Coat came to the tree and stopped but he couldn't see the man for he couldn't look up. Taking a finger from his pocket he placed it on the palm of his hand. The finger raised up and pointed at the man. The man was a swift runner. He slipped down from the tree, snatched the finger and ran off with it. Stone Coat shouted after him, begged and promised to be his friend forever if he would give him the finger. The man, afraid of being deceived, wouldn't go near Stone Coat, but he threw the finger back to him. Ever after this, this man and the Stone Coats were good friends.

MAN-EATER AND HIS BROTHER WHIRLWIND

Characters

DAGWANOE^{n}YENT ....Whirlwind or Cyclone

ONGWEIAS ....Man-eater

A MAN and his three nephews lived together, but there was a partition in the house; the old man lived on one side of the partition and the nephews on the other. There was no door between; they talked through the partition.

The old man was a ONGWEIAS (Man-eater). He was brother of the DAGWANOE^{n}YENT who chased the panther and her cubs.—But that is another story.

When the uncle went hunting, he started on a run. The young men could hear the sound of his going. They also hunted. When the old man came home, the nephews heard him throw down a body and cut it up, then they heard him eating and crunching bones. Afterward he spoke to them, asked if they had all come back from hunting and they answered, "We are all here."

One morning, after the old man had gone, the youngest brother started off by himself. A short distance from the house lay a big log; moss had grown over it. When the young man put his foot on the log to cross it, he saw a man fastened to the tree.

The man said, "I am glad you have come. I am tormented here. If you will take me home, I will be a brother to you and stay with you as long as you live."

"I don't think I can take you home," said the young man. "My uncle is a man-eater. But I will talk with

124

my brothers, and to-morrow I will come and tell you what
they say.''

That night when the old man asked if they had all come
back from hunting, the youngest brother said, ''We have
found a man and he wants to be our brother and live
with us. You must not harm him.''

The old man promised not to harm the stranger, and
said, ''I will give him a name. He will be called 'The
Found One.' ''

The brothers brought the man to the house and when he
had grown strong he was a swifter runner than the man-
eater.

One morning the three brothers and The Found One
started off hunting. In the afternoon the old man came
home. At night he asked, ''Are you all there?''

One brother answered, ''No, our eldest brother has not
come.''

The old man was surprised. He told the second brother
that he must start early the next morning and follow his
brother's tracks.

In the morning the young man set out and soon he
found his brother's tracks and followed them. After a
while, he came to an opening. In the middle of the opening sat an old woman; the tracks went toward her. The
young man made up his mind to inquire for his brother,
and going up to the woman, he asked, ''Have you seen my
brother?''

No answer; the woman was deaf. He pushed her, she
struck him and that minute he turned to bones. Now
two brothers were gone.

That night when the man-eater asked if all his nephews
were at home, the youngest said, ''No, two of my brothers
have not come back.''

''You must follow their tracks,'' said the old man, ''and
find out what has happened.''

Early in the morning the young man started. When
he reached the opening and saw the gray-haired woman, it
came to his mind that she had killed his brothers. He
stepped back, got a good start, ran and sprang on to her
back, then he asked, ''Have you seen my brothers?''

The woman didn't answer. He jumped off from her

back, then on again. She tried in every way to hit him. At last she touched him and that minute he became bones— three brothers were gone.

That night when the man-eater asked, "Are you all there?" Found One answered. "I am alone, my brothers have not come home."

The old man said, "To-morrow morning go into the woods and cut some crotched sticks, set them up outside of the house and build a platform on them. Put as many stones on the platform as you can and then start off for your uncle, Whirlwind. You can't help finding him. As soon as you see him, shoot him in the forehead; he will fly in the direction the arrow came from."

The next morning the man made a platform, and, after putting as many large stones on it as possible, he started in the direction the uncle pointed out. About midday he heard a great noise and when he came out in a broad opening he saw Whirlwind on a rock, eating the rock, biting off large pieces of it.

He shot an arrow at the old man's forehead, saying at the same time, "I've come for you, Uncle."

The great Head stopped eating and came toward him. Found One shot a second arrow; the Head followed the arrow. When Found One shot the third arrow, he was back at the house. He called to the old man-eater, "Uncle, I've come!"

There was a terrible wind and the noise of falling trees. Then Whirlwind stood on the platform and began to eat the stones; his crunching could be heard a long way off.

The man-eater said to Whirlwind, "Brother, I sent for you and you have come. My three nephews went hunting and did not come back. I am going for them, if I don't return you will come after me."

The next morning Found One was alone. Whirlwind came, stood on the platform and called out, "Have they come back?"

"They have not," answered Found One.

"Well, I am going after my brother. He oughtn't to eat men if he cannot go anywhere without getting lost!"

Whirlwind went high in the air and saw the old woman. She knew he was looking at her. He came down where he thought she was and bit at her; she wasn't there; he bit gravel. He flew up and looking down couldn't see her. After looking a long time and not seeing her, he hid behind a cloud and watched. At last he saw her in the ground. Then he plunged down, and, biting deep into the earth, killed the old woman, saying meanwhile, "My brother shouldn't eat people if he is such a coward that he cannot kill an old woman."

Found One came and Whirlwind told him to put the bones of his brothers and uncle together, then go to a big hickory tree that stood near, push it and call out, "Rise up, or the tree will fall on you!"

Found One did as told.

The four men sprang up and were running off when Whirlwind called to them and they came back. Then Whirlwind's brother said, "I give up! I will never eat a man again."

The old men, their nephews and Found One went home together and they are said to be in the mountains now. Whirlwind is still living.

OWL AND HIS JEALOUS WIFE

[Told by John Jimison]

Characters

O'ówa .... Owl (horned)
Nosgwais .... Toad
Dzóega .... Raccoon
The Invisible man was the Wind

THERE was a man and wife, O'ówa people (owls), who quarreled every night. When morning came, all was pleasant again.

One night a visitor came and as soon as O'ówa saw him, he went out of the house and off into the woods. The visitor said, "It is strange that O'ówa went just as I came. I will go, and come another time."

After a while O'ówa came back. He was jealous and scolded his wife till they began to fight. He beat her and then started off, saying, "I am going to get another wife; I'll not be bothered this way."

The woman followed him, crying. At last he grew sorry and went back with her. In the morning he said, "I had a dream and it told me I must kill a bear and be back before the dew is off the grass."

He started, but when out of sight he went to a woman's house and stayed there all day. Towards night he thought he would go home, but on the way he met a nice looking woman, "Where are you going?" asked he.

"I am going home."

"I will go with you."

"All right, if you can overtake me," said the woman, and off she ran, O'ówa after her. They ran all night toward the North. (The woman was a partridge.) About noon of the following day they came to a house and the woman went in. O'ówa followed, but he lost sight of her. In the house were two old men. O'ówa asked, "Did you see a woman pass?"

The men sat with their heads down and didn't answer. O'ówa repeated the question. One of the men looked up, and said, "It seems to me that I hear something."

"It seems to me that I hear something," said the other old man.

"Get our canoe," said the first man.

Going to another part of the cabin, the second man came back with a bark canoe and two basswood knives.

"Now," said the first man, "I will catch the game that has come to us."

O'ówa drew back. "Be careful, old man," said he, "I came to ask a question. I'll not harm you." He started to run, the old men followed him. After a time O'ówa turned and running back to the house got a mallet he had seen there. The first man to appear he knocked down with a blow on the head; the second he treated in the same way.

Then one man said to the other, "Get up and do the best you can. It would be strange for us to be beaten by our game."

Again they were knocked down.

O'ówa thought, "These men are NOSGWAIS (Toads). I cannot kill them." And he ran off.

After a while he came upon a woman's tracks and he followed them all day. When night came he thought he would soon overtake her, but the tracks were not the woman's tracks; he had made a circle. At daybreak he was far back and seeing his own tracks he said, "Another man is following the woman. When I overtake him, I will kill him."

Again he came to the house of the two NOSGWAIS men. When he asked for the woman, they caught him and threw him into their canoe, then they began to dispute as to which one should cut up the game. At last they pushed back the canoe and left it. O'ówa could not get up; he was fastened to the canoe.

Towards night he heard somebody say, "You think you are going to die?"

"Yes, I think so," said O'ówa.

"You will not," said the invisible man. "At the end of the canoe is a string and on it hang the hearts of the two old men. Wait till dark then move and you will get loose and can get out of the canoe. I will give you light to see where the hearts are. Squeeze them and you will kill the old men. The canoe has great power, the Nosgwais use it when they travel. I will teach you the song that belongs to it."

O'ówa was so weak he could hardly speak, the teacher sang, "*Gayeihe one^n Owaqdendi ne okho^{n}wa^n* (My canoe has started)."

When he finished singing, O'ówa said, "I have learned the song."

As soon as it was dark, O'ówa began to move and as he moved he gained strength. Looking around he saw a pale light at the end of the canoe. He found the hearts and took them from the string; as he crushed them he heard screams and groans. He put the hearts under the canoe and pounded them, then the cries ceased.

O'ówa lay down and slept. The next morning he said, "Now I have something to travel in and I will soon overtake that woman." And carrying the canoe outside he turned it toward the North, got into it and began to sing.

The canoe started off so swiftly that only the whiz of the air could be heard. As it went on it rose higher and higher. O'ówa began to be afraid that the canoe was carrying him to some bad place. It went higher and faster and he grew more and more afraid. All at once he heard a scrambling behind, as of some one trying to get into the canoe, and looking around he saw a man, who said, "How fast you go! I was bound to get in so I jumped. You are afraid that the canoe is going to carry you away. The reason the canoe goes higher and higher and faster and faster is that you keep repeating the song.

You must change the words, then you can guide it. I forgot to tell you this last night.''

As the man finished speaking, he stepped from the stern of the canoe into the air and disappeared.

O'ówA now sang, "My canoe is going down! My canoe is going down!" In a flash the canoe came to the ground. "This is not what I wanted," said O'ówA, "I wanted to come lower but not to the ground."

Again he sang the first song; the canoe flew up like an arrow and off toward the North faster than before. As it went along O'ówA saw the tracks of the woman ahead. Higher and higher went the canoe, the wind whizzed frightfully.

"I am getting too high," thought O'ówA and he changed his song to, "My canoe must go lower, My canoe must go lower." It came down but its speed was so great that O'ówA was troubled and began to sing, "My canoe must stop! My canoe must stop!" He came to the ground, but he had lost the woman's tracks and he was far from his own country.

Again he sat in the canoe but this time he sang, "Let my canoe travel just above the trees." The canoe obeyed but it soon came to an opening. Then, as there were no trees, it came to the ground.

O'ówA thought, "I will go back to my wife," and he began to sing.

The canoe rose in the air going higher and higher as it went toward the South. It went up till it struck the Blue. The strength of the canoe was in the fore end and as it struck against the Blue it broke and the canoe came down. O'ówA fell in at the smoke-hole of his own house.

"Get up!" screamed his wife, "You have put the fire out."

He couldn't move, she pulled him up, and asked, "Where have you been? You said you would be back before the dew was off the grass."

The woman was jealous. From words they began to quarrel and fight. At last O'ówA said, "I'll not stay here."

The canoe had such power that if broken it soon became whole again. The man sat in it and began to sing. The canoe floated away and soon was over a village. Then O'ówA sang, "Let my canoe come down." It came to the ground, and O'ówA left in and went to the village. To the first man he met, he said, "I have come to get men to go to war."

The man said, "I will call the people together."

When the people had assembled O'ówA said, "An enemy is coming. I want volunteers to go against him."

Ten men agreed to go. (The people of this village were Racoons.)

They traveled for a long time but found no enemy to fight. At last they met a man and captured him.

The man said, "A captive is always permitted to sing his last war-song."

The party talked it over, and said, "That is fair and according to rule."

They released the captive and forming a line on each side let him walk through, singing as he went. He sang, "*Djinónehe, Ágadyéngwâq oyâ'de,*" repeating the same words all the time.

The chief said, "He sings, 'I wish there were a hole!'"

"No," said the captive, "that is only the way the song goes."

As he walked he rubbed the ground with his feet to see if he could find a hole. At last he found one and dropped into it. The men grabbed at him as he was disappearing, but caught only the end of his tail. It broke off and that is why woodchucks have short tails, for the captive was a woodchuck.

When Woodchuck got away O'ówA scolded and abused the Racoon men. They got mad and pounded him till they thought he was dead, then they left him and went home.

O'ówA's wife was angry at his delay, and taking a basswood knife she started off to find him for she thought he was making love to some woman. When she found his canoe, she took a club and broke it to pieces, then went to the village and asked where O'ówA was.

The men who had killed him said, "His body is over there not far away, you will find the pieces."

One of the men said, "I will go with you."

The woman found O'ówʌ's body and left it where she found it.   She went home with the Racoon man and became his wife.   When she found that he already had a wife, she was jealous and began to quarrel with the woman and then to fight with her.   The two fought till both died.

Racoon felt sad and lonesome and soon he began to cry, and he cried till he changed to a dove and still he cried, and Indians called him the crying dove (mourning dove), and that dove cries yet.

OKTEONDO^n AND HIS UNCLE

[Told by Andrew Johnny-John]

Characters

OKTEONDO^n lived in the woods with his uncle, HAI-
ENTHWÛS. In front of the uncle's house was a great
elm tree. The boy lay at the foot of this tree till the roots
grew over and around his body, binding him firmly to the
earth.

HAIENTHWÛS was very fond of his nephew. He always
brought him food: everything that he liked to eat and
drink, venison, squashes, dried berries. Whatever the boy
wanted the old man gave him.

The first work HAIENTHWÛS did each morning was to
put corn in a stone mortar to make meal. He struck one
blow with the pestle and with that blow crushed the corn.
People far and near heard the blow and all said, "OKTE-
ONDO^n's uncle is well-to-do and strong."

The old man cooked the meal, carried a plenty to his
nephew and ate his own share. Some days he went to
the forest for fire-wood. He burned logs into pieces of
such length as he could carry easily. When the fires on
one log were burning well, he would light fires on other
logs and go from one log to another keeping the fires in

order. When the pieces were burned off and ready, the old man carried them home.

As he threw down the blocks they made a deep, pleasant sound on the earth and all the people in the region and to the most distant places heard the noise, and said, "OKTEONDO^n's uncle is well-to-do and strong."

Some days the old man went out to plant beans and squashes or dig wild potatoes. One Spring morning in the planting season, he went to his clearing in the woods with two baskets of seeds strapped to his belt. When starting he left a plenty of food with his nephew, and said, "I am going to plant these seeds."

The old man was in the field, making holes in the ground with a stick forked at one end and sharp at the other, dropping seeds in these holes and closing them, when all at once he heard a song that said: "I am going to rise. I am going to rise."

He knew it was his nephew's song, and dropping the pointed stick he hurried home, forgetting all about the seeds. As he ran the baskets struck the trees on both sides of the narrow trail and scattered the seeds till all were lost.

When HAIENTHWÛS reached the house he saw that his nephew was on one elbow and the tree leaned toward the earth, with the roots starting out of the ground.

"Well, Nephew, what is the matter?" asked the old man.

"I want some water, Uncle."

The old man gave his nephew water, pushed the tree back to its place and then looking into his baskets saw they were empty. He spent the rest of the day on his hands and knees picking up what seeds he could find.

Another day he went out to strip bark from a slippery elm tree, to make strings, but before starting he gave OKTEONDO^n everything he needed. When he had stripped off a good deal of bark and was tying it in bundles, HAIENTHWÛS heard the song again: "I am rising. I am rising!" The minute he heard those words, he threw a bundle of bark on his back and ran toward home. As he hurried along, the bundle struck the trees, first on one side and then on the other side of the trail. One piece of bark slipped out at one place and another at another till there was nothing left on the old man's shoulders but the straps.

"What is the matter, Nephew?" asked the old man when he saw OKTEONDO^n resting on an elbow and the tree leaning to one side.

"Oh, I'm thirsty, Uncle."

HAIENTHWÛS brought him water, then straightened up the tree and went back to the woods. He picked up the pieces of bark on both sides of the trail till he came to the place where he had stripped them from the tree. That minute he again heard the song, "I am rising. I am rising."

"Poor boy, I wonder what he wants now," said the uncle, running home a third time. When about half way he heard the song repeated, then came a tremendous crash which was heard over the whole country.

All the people said: "OKTEONDO^n has come to manhood; he has got up."

When the old man reached home the great elm had fallen and his nephew was gone. He saw footprints far apart, long steps on the ground.

That night the young man came to his uncle's house and they had a talk.

The old man said, "You have grown up. You are now a man. You can go where you please, but I don't want you to go toward the North. If you do something evil will come upon you, you'll have bad luck."

The young man hunted for some time. He was a swift runner. He never killed deer or other game in the woods. He always drove the animals home and killed them at his uncle's door. After he had hunted in the West, South and East, he remembered his uncle's warning and wondering what it could mean, he made up his mind to go North and find out.

So one morning, when out of sight of his uncle's house, he turned to the North and ran swiftly till he came to a large opening in which there was a lake. The air was still; the lake calm and beautiful. Everything was so pleasing to look upon that the young man thought his uncle didn't want him to see the place because it was so agreeable he would want to stay there. Around the lake was a sandy beach, and a forest came to the edge of the sand, leaving a clean space around the water. In the middle of the lake was a wooded island.

OKTEONDO[n] stood looking toward the island when he heard some one call once and then a second time. Soon a dark spot appeared on the water and grew in size. At last a man was seen and he was singing as his canoe moved on.

When quite near, OKTEONDO[n] saw that the canoe was pushed by two rows of geese, one row on each side of the canoe, while the man sang, "Now wild geese's feet row my canoe."

When the canoe touched land, the man jumped out, and said to OKTEONDO[n], "I am glad you have come. I am glad we have met here."

The stranger walked along the sand a while, then turned to OKTEONDO[n], and said, "You are my own brother, we are of the same size."

They stood back to back, measured, and found they were of the same height.

"This shows," said the stranger, "that you are my brother. Your uncle is my uncle too, your bow and arrows are just like mine."

He went to the canoe, got his bow and two arrows and put them by OKTEONDO[n]'s bow and arrows. They were exactly alike.

"These bows and arrows," said the stranger, "were made by the same man, our uncle HAIENTHWÛS. You are a fast runner, so am I, you run with the same swiftness that I do. This proves that we are brothers."

The beach where they stood jutted out into the lake and directly opposite, on the other side of the lake, was a similar point.

The stranger said, "Let us shoot our arrows together, straight across the water to the point over there, then run along the shore and catch them."

OKTEONDO[n] was willing. They shot the arrows at the same instant then ran around the lake till they reached the point where they saw the arrows coming through the air. They caught them before they came to the ground.

"Let us shoot them back," said the stranger.

They stood shoulder to shoulder, let the arrows fly and then running along the shore came to the point from which they had started and caught the arrows before they came to the ground.

"We are brothers," said the stranger. "Your uncle used to tell me not to come here just as he has told you not to, but I came and have remained ever since because the hunting is good. Now you have come. We have another uncle living near here. He gave me this canoe and these geese to row it and take it to whatever place I want to go. He has given me an island in the middle of this lake, a beautiful place full of game. I am in need of nothing; whatever I want I find here. You must go with me to see the island. Get into the canoe."

While the canoe was on the shore the geese were swimming around in the water.

The stranger pushed the canoe to the edge of the water, and sang, "Come here, my geese. Come here, my geese."

The geese ranged themselves on both sides of the canoe and when the two men were seated, the stranger sang: "Row me home, my geese. Row me home, my geese."

The geese pushed the canoe in the direction of the island. The song continued. The geese went so fast that the canoe was almost lifted out of the water.

When the canoe touched shore, the stranger said to the geese, "You may go and feed a while." Then he drew the canoe on to land, took out his bow and arrows and told his brother to come with him and see the island.

Along the water there was a sandy beach, next to that soft grass and farther in thick woods.

The two men walked along till they came to a high bank where the water was deep, then the stranger said: "This is my playground and when anyone comes here with me he and I try to see who has the longest breath."

He took a smooth, round, white stone and threw it into the water, some distance from the shore. The water was so clear that the stone could be seen at the bottom. The stranger dived into the water but did not reach the bottom. Coming up he clambered on shore and said to Okteondo^n, "Now you try!"

The young man took off his clothes and sprang into

the water. While he was trying to get the stone, the stranger took his clothes and his bow and arrows and running to the landing place jumped into the canoe and called the geese, and in a minute he was out on the water going towards the main land at great speed.

When OKTEONDO^n came out of the water and could see no one, he ran to the place where they had landed and from there he saw, far out on the lake, a black speck that soon disappeared.

Left without clothes or weapons he walked along the shore not knowing what to do. After a time he heard a man groan and it seemed to him that the sound came from the ground. He looked around and at last saw a nose sticking up through the sand.

As soon as he saw the nose a man spoke to him, and said, "My Nephew, I am sorry for you. You are poor and naked. Your brother, SHÁGOWENOTHA, left me here too. I will tell you what to do. On the other side of the island you will find a soft maple tree. In that tree, near the ground, is a hole and in the hole is my pouch with a flint and a pipe in it. Bring the pouch here as quickly as you can."

The young man ran across the island, found the pouch, brought it to the old man, and said, "I have brought the pouch, my Uncle."

"Well, Nephew, go to work now and make three bows and three arrows."

OKTEONDO^n whittled out, with his uncle's flint knife, three small bows and three arrows. When these were ready the uncle said: "Find a basswood stick and make three dolls out of it."

When the dolls were ready, the uncle said, "Now run around the woods of this island and when it is midday you will come to a large tree. Climb the tree and fasten one doll and a bow and arrow on a crotch and say to the doll, 'If anyone comes to fight with you, you must kill him.' When you have done this, slip down and run around the island in every direction till the middle of the afternoon when you will come to a second large tree. Climb the tree and fix a doll in a crotch and say to it, 'If anyone comes to fight you, you must kill him.' Come

down and run around a third time in every direction till
it is nearly dark, then put the third doll on the third tree
and tell it to kill any person who attacks it.''

The young man followed the orders given him. He put
three dolls on three trees and at dusk came back to his
uncle, and said, ''My Uncle, I have done as you told me
to do.''

''Very well, Nephew, now bury yourself up to your
nose in the sand. Your brother will come early to-morrow
morning and say, 'I will see if I can find any of my
brother's blood.' He is the servant of a man-eater and
his work is to entice people to this island where they can
be caught and eaten.''

The young man buried himself in the sand, with the
point of his nose sticking out, and waited till the next
morning when SHÁGOWENOTHA came in his canoe, and
said, ''My geese, feed here while I see if I can find any
of my brother's blood.''

He started off on a run. OKTEONDO^n jumped up, ran
to the canoe, pushed it into the water, and sang, ''Now
my geese, row me home. Now my geese, row me home.''

In a minute the canoe was shooting over the lake. When
he was well out OKTEONDO^n heard his brother shout,
''Come back! come back!'' but he paid no heed to the
cries; he went on and the geese never stopped till they
reached the opposite shore.

When OKTEONDO^n landed he said to the geese, ''Feed
here till I call you.'' Then he put the canoe under
water so no man could see it, and went to a house nearby.
In the house he saw his bow and arrows that had been
taken away by his brother, and many arms and much
venison and dried green corn. He ate all he wanted.

That night the uncle on the island listened and heard a
canoe come. In the canoe was the man-eater and his
three dogs.

When they had landed, the man-eater said to the dogs:
''Run around and see what you can find.''

The dogs found the tracks made by the young man in
running over the island to put the three dolls on the
trees, and they followed them.

About midnight they came to the first doll and began to

howl and bark. The man-eater hurried to them, but before
he got there a man on the tree shot an arrow and killed
the foremost dog.

When the man-eater saw that one of his dogs was dead,
he was furious and drawing his bow sent an arrow through
the man on the tree; down the man fell. The two remaining dogs rushed at him and tore his body apart, when that
was done the dead man was gone and the dogs threw
bits of wood out of their mouths. The man had become
a doll again.

The man-eater said to the two dogs, "There is good
game on the island. Run and find it." The dogs ran
around till they came, between midnight and daylight, to
the tree on which the second doll was fixed. As they ran
up, the doll became a man. They barked furiously. The
man let fly an arrow and killed one of the two dogs.

The man-eater killed the man, the man fell to the ground
and was torn to pieces by the remaining dog; the flesh
turned to bits of wood which the dog threw out of his
mouth.

The man-eater raged more than ever and said to the
third dog, "Run now and find good game."

The dog ran till day was coming then he found the third
doll. The doll turned to a man and the man killed the
dog. When the man-eater came and found his last dog
dead he shot the man, the man tumbled from the tree
and when he struck the ground the man-eater saw only a
small stick.

"Very well," said the man-eater. "I will go home now,
but I will come again to-night."

He went home and the following night he came back
to the island with three other dogs. He set the dogs on
the trail. They soon found OKTEONDOⁿ's brother and
began to bark. The man-eater hurried up to kill the
game, the man began to cry out and beg, saying, "I am
your servant. Don't kill me. I am your servant. Don't
kill me."

But the man-eater wouldn't believe him. He drew his
bow and killed him, flung his body into the canoe and went
home.

The next morning OKTEONDOⁿ went to the shore of the lake, called the geese and started for the island, singing, "Row, my geese. Row, my geese."

When he got to the landing place he told the geese to feed nearby, and drawing the canoe to the shore, he went to see his uncle.

"Well, Uncle," said the young man, "I have come back to see you."

"My Nephew, the dogs seized your brother. He begged for his life but the man-eater killed him, flung his body into the canoe and carried it home. Now I have this to tell you. You have a sister who was brought to this island. The man-eater carried her to his own place. You must rescue her. You can go to his house at midday for at that time he is never there."

The young man called the geese, launched the canoe and hurried away.

The geese went so quickly that in a little while Okteondo^n saw the man-eater's house. At the door stood a woman watching for him. She knew her brother was coming and she ran to the landing place carrying two pieces of basswood bark.

"You must not step on the ground," said she. "If you do, the man-eater will find your tracks and kill you."

Before leaving the shore, Okteondo^n sank his canoe out of sight and told the geese to go far away to feed. His sister put one piece of bark near the edge of the water for him to step on and the other before that. When he stood on the second piece she took up the first and put it in front, and so it went on. He stepped from one piece of bark to another till he came to the house, then she hid him under her couch and made ready for the man-eater. She thought if everything were ready for him she wouldn't have to leave her side of the house.

When the man-eater came home, he sat down on his own side of the fire and the dogs lay down near him.

The woman had a large bark bowl full of thigh bones. The bowl was hidden behind the couch on which she sat and under which her brother was lying.

After a while the man-eater asked for water, the woman told him she had put water right there near him; he could help himself. He ate his supper and lay down on his couch. The dogs sniffed something and went toward the couch where the woman sat making moccasins.

The man-eater sat up on his couch, and said: "Some kind of game has come to visit you."

"Your dogs are attacking me," said the woman. "I must defend myself," and reaching behind her she took a large thigh bone out of the bowl and struck the foremost dog with it. He howled, went back and lay down.

The man-eater lay down on his couch again, but soon the dogs started up a second time, came nearer the woman than before and barked furiously. Then the man-eater said, "There must be something near you, my dogs wouldn't lie."

"If you think so, you ought to have killed me long ago," said the woman and she picked up another bone and hit one of the dogs a hard blow on the snout. They went away and lay down in their places.

At daylight the man-eater rose up, called his dogs and went off hunting.

After a while the woman saw one of the dogs coming back. Soon all three of them came in and directly the man-eater appeared. The dogs barked louder than ever and the man-eater said, "There must be game here, my dogs are true."

"They are barking at me all the time," said the woman. "You ought to have killed me long ago, not leave me here to be treated in this way." She took up another bone and gave each dog such a blow that it ran out of the house.

The man-eater said: "Come, my dogs, we'll go hunting." And he went, this time, a long distance.

The woman told OKTEONDO[n] to come out from under the couch. She got pieces of basswood bark and placed them before him, one after another, till he came to the water. He raised the canoe, called the geese, and he and his sister sat in the canoe; he sang and the geese pushed them swiftly through the water. They were far out on the lake when all at once they saw that they were going back to the shore. There was a hook in the canoe, a line was tied to it and the man-eater was pulling in the line as fast as he could.

The woman took a round white stone and broke the hook, freed the canoe, and out it went into the lake again.

The man-eater took another hook, fastened it to a line, threw the line out and caught the canoe. He was pulling it to shore when the woman broke the second hook. The man-eater was in a terrible rage for the second hook was his last and he could not catch the canoe again with a line. But he was determined to destroy Okteondo^n and his sister, so he lay down on the beach and began to drink. He drank so fast that the water ran in a great stream towards him. He was drinking up the lake.

When the canoe was straight in front of the man-eater's open mouth, Okteondo^n shot an arrow and pierced his stomach. The water of the lake rushed out with such force that the canoe was carried to where it had been before. They were moving on quickly and were near the island when all at once the man-eater caused the lake to freeze over. The canoe was fastened in thick ice.

The man-eater came running over the frozen lake and was near the canoe when Okteondo^n said, "It must be done; the ice must thaw!"

The ice thawed quicker than it had frozen and became so weak that when the man-eater was about to seize the canoe, he broke through the ice and sank to the bottom of the lake.

Then Okteondo^n said, "Creatures under the water I give this man-eater to you. Devour him!" They devoured him at once. A little blood that rose to the top was all that was seen of the man-eater.

The brother and sister went to the island. Okteondo^n left the canoe on shore and going to his uncle, who was buried in the sand, said, "Uncle, I have come back and my sister is with me."

The uncle said, "Fill my pipe with dry bark."

The young man did as he was bidden, then put the pipe in his uncle's mouth. The old man drew in smoke and let it come out through his nose, his eyes and his ears. As he smoked he grew strong and soon he said, "Nephew, draw me up," and Okteondo^n drew him out of the sand.

The more the old man smoked the stronger he grew.

The smoke spread out over the lake and was beautiful. Soon he said, "Now we will go to the canoe."

When the three were in the canoe, the young man said to the geese, "Go to the place where you first saw me," and then he sang, "Row me, my geese. Row me, my geese."

The geese swept the canoe over the lake quickly and then OKTEONDO^n said to them, "I will free you now, but you will be seen year after year and people will call you wild geese, and you will always fly in the same form that you had in pushing the canoe—a flock pointed in front and broad behind."

The geese flew away and OKTEONDO^n with his sister and uncle went on till they came to HAIENTHWÛS' home. Then they all lived together again.

TREE WORM AND HIS MOTHER-IN-LAW, BARKWORM

Characters

HÁIENDONIS ...He, woodmaker (A large tree worm)

YENO^{n}GAA ....She, Shingled Hair

YENOGEAU^n ....Ear Enter (Barkworm)

GÁSYONDETHA ....Meteor

HAIENDONIS was walking along with all of his effects in a bundle. He didn't know where he came from or where he was going, though he knew he was going in a northerly direction. Wherever darkness overtook him, there he put his bundle on the ground, went inside of it and spent the night, if he didn't find a hollow tree to sleep in.

He traveled a long time. Then one morning he came to a precipice. It was very far to the bottom and he didn't know how he was to get down with so large a pack on his back.

At last he put the pack on the ground and going to a basswood tree stripped it of bark, split the bark into strings, tied the strings together and made a long rope. Then fastening one end of the rope to a hemlock tree on the edge of the precipice, he let the other end down, took hold of the rope near the tree and lowered himself. Soon he was at the end of the rope, and he clung there. The bundle on his back pulled the upper part of his body over till he was in nearly a horizontal position, face upward. He couldn't see where he was. He almost touched

146

the ground, but he didn't know it. He thought, "What
can I do? I can't hang here long. Maybe I had better
let go and fall. I can't get up and I can't go down."

He decided to let go of the rope and fall. As soon as
he dropped the rope, the pack on his back touched the
ground and his head rested on the pack, but he thought
he was falling all the time. At last he said to himself,
"I am tired of falling. I'll try and turn over a little so
I can see where I am going."

He turned and found that he was on the ground. Saying, "Oh, how I've been delayed by not knowing that the
ground was at the end of the rope!" he got up and went
on.

When night came HÁIENDONIS slept in a hollow tree or
in his bundle. He traveled many days. When he was
tired of traveling he looked around for a good place to
live in. At last he stopped where the trees were only a
short distance apart. He built a cabin, took his pack inside and arranged his blankets, pouches, ladles, and bark
bowls. The next morning he went out to hunt for food.
He saw a deer, pointed at it, and the deer fell dead. Every
kind of game was under his control, when he went home
he didn't carry the game. He stood near the house, and
said, "Let the game I have killed be piled up here at the
door. Let it be dressed and hung up to dry." In the
morning the meat was drying and a pile of skins lay at
the door.

One day, when HÁIENDONIS was hunting, he saw a
GÁSYONDETHA and pointing his finger at him killed him,
for he wanted the skin for a pouch. Going farther he
killed a panther and then a fox. "Now," thought he,
"I'll have three new pouches." The next morning the
three skins were hanging on the side of the cabin. "What
will I do with these pouches?" thought HÁIENDONIS, then,
taking down the skin of GÁSYONDETHA he said to it, "Stand
here, alive!" That instant GÁSYONDETHA stood alive before him.

HÁIENDONIS brought the three skin pouches to life and
had them stand inside the house.

Soon it was known that a man, who was full of witchcraft, had settled down in the neighborhood. That if he

wanted to kill an animal or a man he had only to point a finger at them. People were afraid of him.

Not far from HÁIENDONIS' house lived a woman and her three daughters. The woman was full of witchcraft and had come there to settle down because no one wanted to live near her.

One day this woman said to her daughters, "We will grind corn and make bread."

Each woman had a pounder. Soon the corn was flour and the mother made it into bread. Then she filled a basket and said to the eldest daughter, "I want you to go to HÁIENDONIS and see if he will marry you."

The girl, whose name was DEYÓNDE^{n}NIGO^{n}GENYOS, started with the basket.

HÁIENDONIS saw a girl coming with a basket on her back, and he thought, "There is a woman coming, I think she is coming to see me. I wonder if she wants to marry me?" Then he said to his pouches, "GÁSYONDETHA, go over there and stand by the tree! You, Panther, go and stand a little nearer this way; and you, Fox, stand at the door."

When the girl was near, HÁIENDONIS began to smoke his pipe. She walked along with her head down and did not see GÁSYONDETHA till she was right at his side. Then, looking up, and seeing such a fierce person, she turned and ran. As she ran, the bread fell out of the basket and when she reached home she had lost it all.

"What is the matter?" asked Barkworm, her mother.

The girl was out of breath and couldn't answer.

HÁIENDONIS laughed and watched the girl till she got home.

After a few days the mother said, "We will grind corn and make bread."

The girls pounded corn into flour and Barkworm made the flour into bread. Then she said to her second daughter, "Take the basket and go to HÁIENDONIS, your sister is a coward."

HÁIENDONIS saw the girl coming, with a basket on her back, and said, "Here comes another woman, she will soon be spilling her bread."

He stationed the pouches as before. The girl came with

her head down till she reached GÁSYONDETHA, then, looking up and seeing him, she said, "I'm not afraid of you!"
and went on. She passed the panther and came to the
door of the cabin. In the doorway stood a man switching
something against the door. The girl was frightened; she
screamed, turned around, and began to run. As she ran
she spilled the bread out of her basket.

HÁIENDONIS laughed, and watched the girl till she
reached home.

After a few days Barkworm said to her daughters,
"We will try again." She made bread, filled a basket with
it, and said to her youngest daughter, YENOⁿGAA, "You
must go this time. Don't notice anything or be afraid
of anything. Go straight into the house."

When HÁIENDONIS saw the girl coming, he said, "It is
strange how little those women care for bread. There is
another one coming and when she gets near she will turn
and run, spilling her bread as she goes."

When the girl came to where GÁSYONDETHA stood she
looked at him, then she gave him a blow, and he fell to
the ground, and was nothing but a skin pouch. She
treated Panther in the same way. When she came to the
door, Fox stood there, the wind was switching his tail
against the door, this had frightened the second sister,
but YENOⁿGAA was not afraid. She struck Fox and down
he went, nothing but a skin pouch.

When HÁIENDONIS saw the girl knocking down his
guards, he thought, "She will come in! I will get my
pipe and pretend to be an old man."

As the girl pushed the skin door aside she asked, "Where
is HÁIENDONIS?"

No answer. She asked again, then an old man sitting
there, said, "It seems to me that I hear a woman speaking."

The girl spoke louder.

The the old man looked up and said, "I don't think he
is at home. I don't think he will be here for ten days."

"Very well," said the girl, "I will come in ten days."
And she went home.

At the end of ten days, the girl set out again. When
HÁIENDONIS saw her coming, he said, "Now I will be a
little boy."

This time the girl paid no attention to the pouches. She went straight to the door and stood there.

"Come in!" said a little boy.

She pushed the door aside, and asked, "Where is HÁIEN-DONIS?"

"He went out a little while ago," said the boy. "He has gone to the other side of the world."

"How long will he be gone?"

"He said he would be back in ten days."

"Very well. I will come again in ten days."

At the end of ten days, HÁIENDONIS saw the girl coming and he thought, "I'll be invisible this time."

The girl went into the house and put her basket down. Seeing nobody she said, "I will wait a while," and she sat down on HÁIENDONIS' couch.

HÁIENDONIS laughed. The girl jumped up and ran home, forgetting her basket.

"Where is your basket?" asked Barkworm.

The girl gave no answer, but her mother knew where it was.

HÁIENDONIS had cleaned the intestines of the game he had killed, filled them with blood and meat, cooked them and hung them up over his couch, some of these intestines clung to the girl. Barkworm took them, and said, "Thank you, my daughter. This is good meat. You must go again to-morrow."

The next morning the girl started. When HÁIENDONIS saw her coming, he laughed, and said, "I think this time all the intestines will go."

She found him in his real form. He asked, "What were you doing with the basket you left here yesterday?"

"It was full of marriage bread. My mother sent me to stay with you," said the girl.

HÁIENDONIS did not drive her away. He ate of the marriage bread and that made her his wife.

The next day YENOⁿGAA said, "I want to go to my mother."

"You can go," said her husband.

Old Barkworm and her two elder daughters were evil-minded, poisonous persons. Barkworm now began to give her youngest daughter as much power as possible and to instruct her how to control HÁIENDONIS. "You must make him come and live with us," said she.

When YENOⁿGAA came back, HÁIENDONIS looked at her and right away he knew she was going to try to control him.

Each time she tried, she failed. But she went often to her mother to get more power and witchcraft. HÁIEN-DONIS wondered why she acted this way. At last he said to himself, "I will destroy all of her people." The next time she started for her mother's, he followed, circled around, got ahead of her and reached the old woman's house first.

He sprang into the house, and said to old Barkworm, "I am here to fight with you."

They were fighting when YENOⁿGAA came. She stood at one side powerless to help either her husband or her mother and sisters.

HÁIENDONIS killed Barkworm and two of her daughters, then he said to his wife, "Go off a little way."

She went, and he set fire to the house. It blazed up high, then burned to the ground. When the fire died down, something among the coals popped; a horned owl flew to the trees, and hooted; a second pop and a screech owl called out; at the third pop a common owl flew to the top of a tree.

"Now we will go home," said HÁIENDONIS.

The woman stood still, looking in one direction; she was dazed. He pulled her along by the arm, and said, "Come home," then she started.

The minute the old woman was killed, people, even at the edge of the world, knew it, and a shout of joy was given that sounded all over the world.

HÁIENDONIS put saliva on his hands, rubbed his wife's head and pulled her hair, which till then had been short, and right away it became long and beautiful. Now they lived in HÁIENDONIS' house and were happy.

COLD AND FROST, OR STONE COAT WOMEN

Characters

Hĭno' ....Thunder
Gḗnoⁿskwa ....Stone Coat (Cold and Frost)

ONCE four men started off on a hunting expedition. They went in canoes up a large river. These men were the first men to make a canoe. When the chief of the party said, "We will land at King Fisher's place," the men were glad for they had been out a number of days. After they had drawn their canoes to the bank the chief said, "Each man must do his best, must bring in all the game he can."

The next morning the chief asked the sun, the moon and the stars to help them, and give them success in getting game.

The men were good hunters and soon they had plenty of meat. Then two of the party said, "We are going farther into the forest to hunt for elk."

"You must be careful," said the old man, "and not go too far away from a trail; something might happen."

One of the men was stubborn, he always wanted his own way. He wouldn't follow the old man's advice. But he went farther than he intended.

When night came all the party returned to camp except the subborn man and as they gathered around the fire they talked of him and said he must have gone far into the forest.

The man traveled all day. When night overtook him he built a fire. After a while he heard voices and looking across the river that was near where he had camped, he saw two women and a baby. The baby was crying. One of the women sat down and nursed it. The man was glad that there were people around.

Soon one of the women noticed that there was a man on the opposite side of the river, and she called out, "How did you cross, brother?"

It seemed strange to him that he could hear her words from such a distance, but he told her to come straight toward his fire.

Again the woman asked, "How did you cross, brother?" and he repeated, "Come straight toward my fire." She asked a third time, and a third time he answered, "Come straight toward my fire." He began to be frightened, began to think that maybe they were Stone Coats, though they looked like women.

The younger woman asked, "Can we stay all night by your fire?"

"If you come over, you may stay by my fire," answered the man.

Looking sharply at the women he knew now that they were not human beings. One said to the other, "If we go higher up, we may find a place to cross," and they started. Soon they came to the log where the man had crossed. When he saw them coming, he ran some distance down stream, crossed at a ford and went to a point opposite his fire. When they came to his fire and saw that he was where they had been, one called out, "Why did you run away from us? Nothing will happen to you. Come back. We won't harm you." One of the women picked up his tomahawk and drew her finger along the edge of it. "I wonder if this would take a person's life?" said she.

"Yes," called the man, "it would take any one's life. Put it down!"

She laid it down. They urged him to come to the fire. When he refused they were angry and were determined to get at him. They started for the crossing, saying, "Wait where you are till we come over."

"Very well," answered the man, but when he saw them crossing he ran to the ford and when they reached the place where he had been he was on the opposite side, by the fire.

The women couldn't walk side by side, one followed the other, the younger woman carried the baby.

When they saw the man standing by his fire the elder woman called to him, "A time will come when I will get at you!"

"You kill people," said the man.

"You are not able to kill any one," replied the woman.

"I'll show you what I can do," said the man. He drew his tomahawk and struck a rock; great pieces split off.

"I think he can kill us," said the woman.

Picking up his bow the man aimed at a tree; the arrow went straight to the mark. The woman, seeing his skill, was astonished and thought, "He is a man to be feared."

"That man must be Hĭno' (Thunder)," said the younger woman.

"He is dodging around," said the elder, "but I will kill him!" She was angry because he tried to keep away from them.

When the man saw the women recrossing the river he went into the river and under the water. They couldn't see him. He stayed in the river till daylight, then he started off toward the camp where his companions were. He was a swift runner, but about midday he heard a voice say, "Now I have caught you!"

When he knew that the women were behind him he did his best, but his strength was failing. Finding that he couldn't escape by running, he climbed a tree. He had just reached a place in the thick branches when the elder woman came and stood under the tree. Her daughter, who was carrying the child, ran up; the mother nursed the child and then said, "We must hurry and overtake him!" (Stone Coats, because of their clothing, couldn't look up, so the woman didn't see the man.) When she wanted to know how far away he was, she took a tiny finger out of her bosom and put it on the palm of her hand. The finger stood erect and pointed straight at the man.

That minute the man slipped down, snatched the finger and ran off. The finger was of great service; the man could run faster. It was an adviser also and pointed out the road to be taken. The man consulted the finger to find how far he was from camp and in what direction it was. The finger raised a little and pointed in a certain direction. After he had run some distance he consulted the finger again. It hardly rose from his hand. He knew then that he was near his comrades. When he reached camp, he ate, regained his strength and then told his story, but he didn't tell about the finger. The chief of the party said, "We must gather up our things and go home."

When the men were in their canoes and were pushing away from the bank, they saw a woman coming. She was crying. When near enough she called out, "Give back what you have taken and you will be successful. If you return what belongs to me, you will have good luck."

"What did you take from her?" asked the chief. "Whatever it was it may be true that we will have good luck if you give it back."

The man drew out the finger and showed it to his comrades.

"Let her have it if she will promise not to molest us again," said the chief.

The man put the finger on the palm of his hand and reached it toward the woman as far as he could and she reached to get it. She slipped, fell into the river, and sank. They saw only bubbles.

"Let us be off quickly!" said the man, and they rowed away as fast as they could. They reached home in safety. The man kept the finger. He became very expert in hunting for he always consulted the finger. When he put it on his palm and asked where game was, it rose and pointed in the direction the animal would be found. And as long as the man lived he had a supply of all things good to eat.

THE GANYO GOWA

[A Delaware story told by John Armstrong]

Characters

GANYO GOWA.............Great Game (White deer)

A N old man lived in a forest. All of his relatives had
been carried off. He was alone except for an infant
that had been left without parents. He fed the child and
it grew fast. When the boy was five or six years of age
he asked where his father and mother were. "An enemy
killed them," answered the old man, and he would say
no more.

The second time the boy asked, the old man said, "They
went in the direction of the GANYO GOWA (great game),"
but he wouldn't tell in what direction that was.

One day the little boy started off to look for GANYO
GOWA. He had not gone far when he came to a lake and
on the lake was a beautiful swan. He aimed an arrow
at the swan and killed it. Then he didn't know how to
get the bird for he hadn't a canoe. At last he made a
bark string, fastened a stone to the end of it, threw the
stone beyond the swan, and drew the bird in. He shook
the bird till it was small and putting it on his back, started
for home. When near the house he placed the swan on the
ground, struck it till it was as large as when he killed it,
and going into the house he said to his grandfather, "I've
killed the GANYO GOWA."

"You shouldn't have killed that bird," said his grandfather. "Take it back to the lake and bring it to life.
That is not the GANYO GOWA."

The boy took the swan to the lake, put it on the water, and, giving it a push, said, "Go off and live in the water." The bird came to life and swam away.

When the boy again asked about his parents, the old man said, "A creature that lives in a wizard spring killed them," and he told where the spring was.

The boy started and at midday came to the spring. The water looked cool and refreshing, he wanted to drink, but was afraid to; he put his foot into the water to see what would happen. The instant his foot touched the water, a terrible creature caught it and pulled his leg off.

Now the boy had but one leg. "Well," thought he, "I'll try again, I may as well lose the other leg." The instant his foot touched the water his leg was off.

Then saying, "though I've lost my legs, I'll kill this creature." He pulled hairs out of his head and braided them into a rope, put a wooden hook on the end of the rope and cut off bits of his own flesh for bait.

As soon as he dropped the hook into the spring the creature swallowed it. When the boy jerked the creature out on to the ground it cried pitifully and begged to be thrown into the water.

The boy put the hook into the spring a second time and drew out another creature like the first. When they begged to be thrown back, he said, "I can do nothing for you till I have my legs." They gave him his legs; he spat on them, put them to his body, and was as well as ever. Then he gathered a great quantity of dry wood and branches and setting fire to the pile, burned up the Wizards of the Spring.

Then he traveled on till he came to a small house in an opening in the forest. On the top of the house sat two white, horned owls. As soon as the owls saw the boy, they called out to some one in the house, "Wake up, old man. Somebody is coming."

The boy ran into the house, and found there an old white-haired man, who was sleeping, and in his bosom was a beautiful white deer. Straightway the deer left the old man and going to the boy crept into his bosom.

The boy started for home and as he went all the animals in the world and all the birds in the world followed him.

When he reached the edge of the forest, the white-haired old man woke up and finding himself alone, said, "My brother must have another grandson; he has been here and stolen my white deer." And taking a club he followed the boy.

When he overtook him he asked, "Why did you steal my white deer?"

"What do you want of the deer?" asked the boy, "You are an old man. I am young; the deer will be more useful for me than for you."

The man caught the boy, pounded his head flat, and, leaving him for dead, took the white deer and went home. He sat down in his house and fell asleep with the deer in his bosom.

When the boy came to his senses and found that his head was flattened out he put up both hands and pressed it back into shape. Then he went again to the old man's house. No sooner was he inside the house than the deer was in his bosom, and when he started for home all the birds and beasts in the world followed him. The minute he reached the edge of the forest the old man woke up and pursued him.

The boy beat the old man to death with a club, then went on till he came to his grandfather's house. When he told what he had done his grandfather cried, and said, "You have killed my brother!"

That night, while the boy was sleeping, the old man stuck three arrows in his back, when he woke up his back was stiff and sore and he said to himself, "My grandfather has been trying to kill me."

He pulled the arrows out and said to the old man, "You have tried to kill me. Now I'll go away and leave you here alone."

Early in the morning the boy started off toward the West, taking with him the white deer and all the game that runs and flies. He traveled on till he came to an opening in the forest and saw a house. Then he put the deer in a hollow tree and went toward the house. On the way he met a boy of his own size.

"Where do you come from?" asked the strange boy.

"From the East."

"That is the country of the GANYO GOWA, the deer that commands all the birds and animals that live in the world."

"The GANYO GOWA belongs to me," said the boy.

"Can you call any kind of game you want?"

"I can."

"Will you come with me and kill coons?"

The two boys went on till they came to a large tree covered with coon scratches. They climbed the tree and killed many coons. They carried the coons to the house and each boy made himself a coon skin blanket.

The two boys were so happy that they decided to live together always. So the boy from the East went to the hollow tree and taking the white deer out told it to go wherever it wished. He liberated the GANYO GOWA and from that time animals and birds roam the world at will.

WOLF AND THE OLD WOMAN'S GRANDSON

Characters

DADYOEⁿDZADÁSES, One name for Wolf—He who
  travels around the world
HADJOQDJA .... Skin Man
OTSOON .... Turkey
GÁQGA' .... Raven

AN old woman and her grandson lived together in a
forest. They were poor, for the woman had no one
to help her and her grandson was a little boy. The woman
cried all the time. Each day she went to the forest for
fire-wood and whether going or coming she cried without
ceasing. She felled a tree by burning it, then, when it
was on the ground, she burned the trunk and limbs into
pieces short enough to carry.

One day the boy asked, "Grandmother, why do you
cry?"

She didn't answer.

The next day he asked again, "Grandmother, why do
you cry all the time?"

"Once," said the old woman, "I had many brothers
and relatives, but now they are dead." And taking the
boy by the hand she led him to a door that opened into
a room he had never seen before. In the room were
weapons of every kind; bows and arrows, flint knives, ball
clubs, balls covered with beads, and many turtle-shell
rattles.

160

The boy wondered at what he saw and wanted to touch the weapons. His grandmother said, "You must never touch these things or come into this room."

The next morning the old woman started for wood and as soon as she was out of sight the boy went to the room, took a ball, a club, and a rattle and went out of doors to play. He threw the ball. It went far East and he ran till he found it in a clearing. The clearing was so beautiful that the boy was glad to be there. He stayed a long time but was home before his grandmother came with the wood.

The next day the boy played ball and was home before his grandmother came. He did this a number of days, but one day he made such a noise with the rattle that the old woman heard it. She hurried home, found the boy, scolded him, and asked, "Didn't I tell you not to touch those things?"

"Don't scold, Grandmother," said the boy, "but tell me where my father and mother and my brothers and cousins are."

"You'll never see them," answered the old woman. "There is a man, far away in the East, who carries off people and eats them. He has eaten all our relatives. His name is DADYOE^{n}DZADÁSES (Wolf)."

"Make me four pairs of moccasins," said the boy. "I am going to bring our relatives back."

"You are not going. You are too small," said his grandmother, but nevertheless she began to get him ready for the road.

When ready, the boy started off. He traveled many days and at last came to a broad opening in a forest. In the middle of the opening was a house and in a field close by was a man who looked like an inflated skin. He was on a platform and was swinging back and forth from north to south and watching a big strawberry patch.

The boy stopped just at the edge of the forest and calling a mole, said to it, "I want to borrow your coat for a while."

The boy took off his blanket, hid it behind a tree, made himself small, put on the skin of the mole and went under the leaves and under the ground till he came to the place where the skin man was swinging, then he called out, "Come down, my friend, I want to talk to you."

The skin man (HADJOQDJA) dropped to the ground and the boy promised to free him and give him back his body if he would tell him the secret of the opening.

HADJOQDJA said, "Wolf lives in that house over there. Every day he goes around the world. He catches and kills people, brings them home and eats them. He has three sisters, who live in the house with him. They are great witches. Each day they cook human flesh and pounded green corn, for Wolf will eat nothing else. The sisters spend most of their time driving elk out of this field. Neither Wolf nor his sisters have hearts in their bodies. No one can kill them, for their lives are in another place. In a corner of the house is a couch, under the couch is a lake, on that lake a loon is swimming around, under the right wing of the loon are four hearts. The largest heart is Wolf's, the second largest belongs to the eldest sister, the smallest belongs to the youngest sister. If you pinch one of those hearts its owner will fall to the ground, if you crush it its owner will die."

The boy gave HADJOQDJA a piece of false wampum that he had made of weeds and colored with strawberry juice, and said, "The sisters are calling you. Tell them you were making this wampum, that is why you waited so long. I will make myself like their brother and come to the house spitting blood. When I am in the house I will cause an elk to run across the strawberry patch. You must give the alarm and while the sisters are chasing the elk, I will take the hearts away from the loon."

When HADJOQDJA reached the house the sisters asked, "What have you been doing?"

"I've been making wampum."

The sisters wanted the wampum. HADJOQDJA divided it between them then told them that their brother was sick.

The boy went back to the mole and gave him his coat, then he took Wolf's form and crossed the field, spitting blood. When he went into the house the youngest sister looked at him and said, "This isn't our brother." The sisters tried the boy with different kinds of food but he wouldn't eat anything till they brought him human flesh and pounded green corn, then he ate.

While the boy was eating HADJOQDJA called, "An elk is in the strawberry patch!"

The sisters caught up their clubs and ran out to drive the elk away. The boy went to the couch and raised it up. Underneath was a lake and on the lake a loon was swimming. He called the loon to him and asked for the hearts. The loon, uncertain whether to give the hearts or not, raised its left wing.

"Oh, no," said the boy, "the hearts are under your right wing, raise that."

The loon, satisfied now, gave up the hearts. The boy took them and left the house just as the sisters were coming back from chasing the elk. Taking his own form he called to them, "I've got your hearts! I've got your hearts!"

They started after him with their clubs. As the eldest sister was about to catch him he pinched her heart and she fell to the ground; when the second sister was near he pinched her heart and she fell; the third sister he treated in the same manner. But right away they were on their feet and following him. Again he pinched their hearts and they fell.

When the boy had amused himself long enough he crushed the hearts, one after another, and the three sisters died. He cut a piece of flesh from each sister and made a stew for Wolf.

When the man-eater came and found that his sisters were not in the house, he was angry. HADJOQDJA told him that they were chasing elk that had been in the strawberry patch. He sat down to eat but found the meat so tough that he cried out, "What stuff is this?"

HADJOQDJA was bold, for the boy stood close by holding the man-eater's heart: he answered, "You are eating your sisters' flesh."

"I've killed your sisters!" called out the boy.

The man-eater rushed at him; the boy ran toward a rock and as the man-eater came near he pinched his heart and he fell to the ground. When the boy stopped pinching the man-eater sprang up. Again the boy pinched the heart and again the man-eater fell. No matter how he tried,

Wolf could only go as far as the boy let him. When tired of the sport, the boy struck the heart against the rock; the man-eater fell and died at once.

On every side of the rock were piles of human bones; the boy gathered the bones into one great pile, then placing HADJOQDJA, the skin man, on the ground with his head to the West, his feet to the east, he went to a tall hickory tree that stood close by, and shouted, "Rise up and run, or the tree will fall on you."

A crowd of people sprang up and ran in every direction. HADJOQDJA had his body again. The boy said to him, "In the whole world there is no such strawberry patch as the man-eater's, henceforth it belongs to you and to me."

The boy's father and mother and relatives were among the people he had raised up. Telling them to come with him he went to his grandmother's cabin. The old woman was happy now. She gathered up the clothes and weapons she had kept so long and went, with her grandson and relatives, to the strawberry patch in the opening in the forest. The other men, whom the boy had rescued, brought their families and settled close by; there were many kinds of people among them: the OTSOON and GÁQGA' and others. The boy and his relatives belonged to the OTSOON people, so did HADJOQDJA, the Skin Man.

A RACE BETWEEN BEAR AND TURTLE

Characters

HANÓWA .... Turtle

NOⁿGWATGWA ....Fox

DASIDOWANES ....One name for Bear (Big Feet)

AN old man was going along, slowly and surely, by
himself. After a while he met a man, who asked,
"Where are you going?"

"I am going to the East to see what kind of people live
there."

"You will never reach that place," said the stranger,
"It is far off and you are too old and fat for the road."

Each man went his way.

Soon the old man met another person, a lean man, who
asked, "Where are you going?"

"I'm going to the East to see how people live in that
place."

"You will never get there," said the lean man. "You
are too fat, you can't travel. How do you keep so fat?"

"When I come to a village and find people lying around,
I bore a hole in each one who pleases me, and suck his
fat out. That is my way of keeping fat."

"I'll try it," said the young man. "I am too lean."

Each went his own road. Soon the lean man came to
an opening and at the edge of the woods saw an animal
asleep. He crawled up, carefully, and began making a
hole in its body near the tail. The animal sprang up, hit
the man a heavy blow with its heels and ran off.

"The next time I see that fat, old fellow I'll pay him

for fooling me," said the lean man. He went farther and met the old man a second time. "How do you keep so fat?" asked the lean man.

"I do it by eating fish. I put my tail through a hole in the ice; a fish bites. I pull the fish out and eat it. That is how I keep fat."

"I'll try that," thought the lean man. He traveled on till he came to a river and found a good place to fish. He made a hole in the ice, stuck his tail into the hole, and waited, waited till his tail began to bite and ache, then he tried to pull it out, but it was fast in the ice. He pulled till at last he pulled his tail off; left it in the hole. He went his way, but through losing his tail he was changed, was another kind of person. When summer came he traveled around till he met the fat man.

"Where are you going?" asked the lean man.

"I am going East to see who lives there."

"You will never reach that place," said the lean man. "You are too fat. Come and run a race with me."

"Very well, you may run on land, I'll run in the water. We'll start to-morrow."

The fat man collected a number of his people and posted them in the river from the starting place to the end of the course, and told each man to stick out his head when the runner came almost up to him. The wager was heads.

They started. The lean man ran with all his might, but every little while the fat man stuck his head out of the water, he was always in advance. When the lean man came to the goal the fat man was there before him.

"You've won the race," said the lean man.

"Of course I have!" said the fat man, and seizing the lean man by the neck he dragged him to a rock and cut his head off.

The fat man's friends came out of the river, looked at the dead runner, and said, "Oh, what a fool! Oh, what a fool!"

The lean man was a bear. Before he lost his tail, he was a fox. Since that time all bears have been stub-tailed. The fat man was a turtle. As all turtles look alike he easily deceived the lean man.

THE GRANDMOTHER AND GRANDSON

A GRANDMOTHER and her grandson lived by themselves. After the boy had become quite large his grandmother said, "Here are the bow and arrows that your uncle had. A witch killed him, you may take the bow and arrows and learn to use them."

The next morning she said, "Go out and try to kill birds. Go as far as you like, but don't go North." She gave him a breakfast of parched corn. [1]

The boy went through the woods shooting birds and by the middle of the day, he thought, "I will go home now, my Grandmother will be glad; I've killed so many birds."

The old woman was glad, she dressed the birds, pounded corn, made hominy and cooked the birds with the hominy.

The next morning she gave the boy parched corn to eat, and as he was starting off she cautioned him against going North. By the middle of the day he had a larger string of birds than before.

When he came home his grandmother said, "Thank you, Grandson, we are well off now, we will have plenty to eat."

That night she talked to him, said, "My Grandson, you must always hunt on the South side, never go toward the North. You and I are the only persons left of our people. If you listen to my words, and are obedient, we shall live."

The next morning, after a breakfast of parched corn, the boy started off. He went farther than on the previous days and saw a different kind of game, such game as he had not seen before. While the birds were feeding he got around in front of them, took aim and hit one with an

[1] Hunters always eat parched corn, for they don't get hungry as soon on that as on other foods.

arrow. It ran a little way and fell dead; the rest escaped. He went up to the one he had killed, pulled out the arrow, tied a bark string around the bird, threw it over his shoulder and started for home. When he stood at the door he said to his grandmother, "I have larger game this time."

The old woman was glad. She thanked the boy, and said, "This is what we call turkey."

She dressed the bird and cooked part of it. They ate together and the grandmother was well pleased.

The next day she sent the boy off again. He went a long way before he found game. About midday he killed another turkey, tied bark around its body, swung it on his back and went home thinking how far off game had gone.

The next morning the boy started away as usual. After he had gone a short distance he began to wonder why his grandmother had forbidden him to go North when game was getting so scarce in the South. He decided to go North anyhow and turning he went in that direction. He saw a great many birds but presently some one called out, "I've caught you, Nephew!"

Looking up the boy saw a man sitting on the top of several trees the heads of which he had drawn together and tied in a bundle. There he sat as in a nest.

"Well, Nephew," said he, "What would you do if it should rain fish spears?"

"Oh, I should be thankful. We need some."

The boy ran home as fast as he could, caught hold of his grandmother's hand, and said, "Grandmother, we must run and hide!"

"My Grandson," said the old woman, "You have been in the North where I told you not to go."

He pulled her along by the arm, leaped into a spring and went under the ground till they came to a rock. They sat down under the rock and waited a long time. At last the boy said, "The storm is over, we will go home."

When they reached home their house was level with the ground.

"Oh," said the grandmother, "this comes of your going North."

"Never mind, Grandmother," answered the boy, "I'll

have a house soon.'' He walked around a space as large as he wanted the house to be, then commanded a house to fill that space. Immediately the house was there. He and his grandmother were more comfortable than before.

In the morning the boy ate his parched corn and went toward the South, hunting, took a circuit and went North saying, ''Yesterday I had fun with that man. I'll go and see what he will do to-day.''

The birds were so numerous and the boy was so occupied in shooting them that he forgot about the man till a voice called out, ''I've caught you, Nephew! What would you do if I should send a shower of stones?''

''Oh, I should be pleased. Grandmother often needs stones to pound her corn.''

The boy ran home, took his grandmother by the arm and dragged her to the spring.

''Oh, Grandson,'' said the old woman, ''You have been North again!'' and she began to cry.

They went into the spring and under the ground till they came to the rock. Then they sat under the rock and waited. At last the boy said, ''The storm is over, we will go home.''

They found their house level with the ground. The boy encouraged his grandmother and made a new house. The next morning after he had eaten parched corn, he started off toward the South but soon turned North.

''Now,'' thought he, ''I won't hunt, I'll catch my uncle.''

He went some distance, called a mole, and said to it, ''I want you to take me to that tree over there and go almost up to the man who sits on the nest. I will speak to him and then you must bring me back to this place.''

The boy shook himself till he was as small as a flea, then he hid in the mole's fur. When the mole was near enough the boy called out, ''I've caught you, Uncle!''

The man looked around but saw no one, then the boy called out, ''What would you do, Uncle, if a whirlwind should come?''

''Oh, Nephew, don't be so hard on me as that!''

''I didn't talk that way when you asked me about spears and stones,'' said the boy.

The mole went back to the place where he had found the boy, the boy regained his own size, ran home, caught hold of his grandmother and drew her to the spring. They disappeared in the water, went underground, came to the rock and sat under it till the boy stopped the whirlwind. When they came out of the spring they found trees torn up by the roots and their house level with the ground. But right away the boy built a house by walking around a space and commanding it to be there.

The next morning he started off South, but when out of sight of the house he turned and went North to see what had become of his uncle. All the trees were torn up by the roots and he thought, "My uncle must be dead and buried under the trees. I can hunt in safety now." He shot a great many partridges and went home.

The old woman was glad to have her grandson come quietly bringing game. He said, "Grandmother, I've destroyed my uncle, he is no longer on the trees."

"Well," said the grandmother, "you needn't think he was alone in the world; his brother lives in a house farther on."

The next morning the boy ate his parched corn and started off determined to find his other uncle. He came to the place where the three trees were, found them uprooted and his uncle dead. Then he held on his way till he came to an opening and saw a house with smoke rising through the smoke-hole.

"I'll go there and look in," thought he, "that must be the place where my uncle lives." He went to the house, opened the door, looked in and said to an old man sitting there, "Well, Uncle, I've come to visit you."

"Come in, my Nephew," said the old man. "I have a rule which all follow who come here. Everyone who visits me must run with me across this field and back. We bet our heads on the race."

"If that is your rule, we will run," said the boy.

They went outside. The old man made a mark across the opening, and said, "We will run to that post over there at the end of the opening. If I get back and cross this line first, I'll cut your head off: if you cross first, you'll cut off mine."

They stood side by side. The old man called, "Now!"
Off they started, and ran to the post. When half way
back to the line the boy fell, a sharpened deer horn had
stuck into his foot. He sat down, pulled out the horn and
threw it far ahead; it came to the ground right in front of
the old man. He had gone on a good distance while the
boy was sitting down. Now he ran on to the deer horn. He
fell and while he was pulling the horn out of his foot, the
boy ran ahead, crossed the line and called out, "Uncle, I
have won the race."

The old man disputed. When that was no use he begged
for another smoke, but the nephew refused, took a sharp
flint knife from his pocket, seized his uncle by the hair and
cut off his head. Then he pulled the body into the house
and burned the house. The old man's head burst and out
flew owls.

The boy went home and told his grandmother what he
had done, she said, "You have a third uncle farther on.
He, too, has great witchcraft."

The next morning the boy started off to visit the third
uncle. He passed the uprooted trees and the burned house
and went some distance through a forest. When he came
to the edge of the forest, he saw a large opening and a
house at the other side of it, and he said to himself, "That
must be the house of my third uncle."

He went on till he came to the house. Going in he said
to an old man, who was sitting there, "Uncle, I've come
to visit you."

"Oh, Nephew, I am glad you have come," said the old
man, "I have a game to play. Everyone who comes here
plays with me, we bet heads."

"What is the game?"

"We hide here in this room. I will hide and if you don't
find me every time till midday, you are beaten and I'll
cut off your head. If you find me every time, you win and
will cut off my head."

"Very well," said the nephew.

"Now," said the old man, "You must lie down on the
ground and I'll cover you up with an elk skin. When I
am ready, I'll let you know."

The boy lay down and was covered up with the elk

skin. As soon as the old man covered his nephew, the boy turned into a woodtick and got on to his uncle's neck and when the old man called out, "Ready!" the tick called out, "I've found you, Uncle!"

The old man thought the voice came from behind him, he hid again, and again the tick called out, "I've found you, Uncle." He looked everywhere but couldn't see his nephew. Again he hid, for he had the right to keep on hiding till midday. The old man thought the boy was still under the elk skin and he wondered how he could find him. He continued to hide, but was always found.

Every little while the old man ran out to look at the sun and then hurried back into the house to hide. At last he thought, "I'll hide outside," but the boy called out, "That won't do, my Uncle, you said we must hide in the house."

It was almost midday, the old man was frightened. He ran out, got a long pole and punched the sun off towards the East, then he ran in and hid. The boy called out, "I've found you, Uncle."

Again the sun was almost overhead; the old man ran out, took his long pole and pushed it towards the East, and again hid, but was found. At last the sun was straight overhead and the boy called out, "I've found you, Uncle. The game is mine."

The old man begged for one more smoke, but the nephew wouldn't let him have it. He cut off his head, dragged him into the house and set fire to the house. The head burst and out of it flew owls.

The boy went home and told his grandmother what he had done.

She said, "You have a fourth uncle worse than all the others and I advise you not to go near him, harm will come to you if you do."

The next morning the boy went toward the South, then made a circuit to the North. He passed the places he had destroyed and came to an opening with a house in the center. In the house was a very old man.

The boy said to him, "Uncle, I've come to visit you."

"Very well," said the old man, "come in and sit down. I have a game that I play with all who come to visit me.

I play dice. We each have one throw and we bet our heads on it."

"I'll play with you," said the boy, "but first I'll go to the river."

On the river there was a flock of ducks. The boy called to the ducks. They came to the bank and he said to them, "I have to play a game and I want your help. I want six right eyes. I'll bring them back soon."

They agreed, and he took the right eye from six of the ducks and said to the eyes, "When the old man plays, some of you must drop into the bowl with your sight down, but when I play you must all drop in looking up."

When the boy went back to the house he said to the old man, "We will play with my dice."

They spread a deer skin on the ground and put the bowl on it.

The old man wanted to use his own dice, but the boy wouldn't let him.

When the eyes were in the bowl, he asked his uncle to take the first throw.

The old man didn't want to play first, but after disputing some time he took up the bowl and shook it. The eyes went up slowly to the top of the smoke-hole, as ducks, quacking, and came back into the bowl as dice, some right side up and others wrong.

The boy shook the bowl; the dice flew up as ducks, quacking loudly, went out at the smoke-hole and disappeared in the clouds.

The old man kept saying, "No count, no count!"

The boy said, "Count five, count five."

By and by they heard the ducks coming in the distance, and soon they dropped into the bowl as dice, and all were right side up.

"I've won the game!" cried the boy.

The uncle begged to be allowed one smoke, but the nephew refused, cut off his head with a flint knife, and set fire to the house.

The boy took the six eyes, went back to the river and called the ducks. They came, he moistened the eyes with saliva and put each eye in its own place, then he thanked the ducks and set them free. When he reached home and told his grandmother what he had done, she said, "Now you can hunt wherever you like; there is no one to harm you."

The boy was now a man. He could kill deer, bear and other game, but he had to go so far that he always came home late at night. He didn't like this and one day he said to his grandmother, "I am tired of going so far to hunt. I have power to call game to the house. I will sing and game will come."

He went to a white ash tree and brought home wood to make arrows and by night he had a great many arrows. The next morning he brought a deer skin. The old woman sat down. He covered her with the skin, and said, "You must not look out, if you do, I shall leave here never to come back."

He placed the bundle of arrows on the ground outside and began to sing, "Come to me, deer. Come to me, elks. Come to me, bears. Come to me, coons."

Soon there was a great noise in the forest; animals were coming from every side. When they were near enough the young man began to shoot.

Bears, coons and hedgehogs were climbing over the house. The old grandmother was frightened at the noise. She took the deer skin off from her head and looked up through the smoke-hole to see what the trouble was. That instant a white deer sprang over the others, seized the young man on his horns, and ran off through the woods. All the animals followed. The man was still singing.

The old woman opened the door and saw all the animals that had been killed, but her grandson was nowhere to be seen. Then she remembered his words.

While the white deer was rushing through the woods, a pack of wolves came upon its track, overtook it and killed both the deer and the man. That afternoon the clouds in the West were very red, the grandmother thought, "That is a bad sign, my grandson is in trouble." This was the very time the young man was killed.

The next morning the old woman followed the tracks of the game hoping to find her grandson. The animals had beaten a broad trail through the woods. She followed the trail till evening. About the time she saw the red clouds the day before, she came upon the spot where her grandson and the deer were killed. She found pieces of bloody buckskin, but not a bone or a bit of her grandson's body. Then the old grandmother gave him up and started for home, crying as she went.

BALD EAGLE SENDS MUD-TURTLE TO THE EDGE OF THE WORLD

Characters

DŌ'NYONDA .... Eagle

GANYÂQDE^n HANÓWA .... Mud-turtle

ONCE upon a time, a bald-headed old man lived on the top of a mountain, and his wife and three children lived near a lake about half way to the summit of the same mountain.

Each day the old man went down to fish in the lake. On his way home he stopped and gave some of the fish to his wife, and thus they lived well and happily. After they had passed many years in this manner, the old man became curious to know how large the world is.

Being chief of his people he called a council, and said, "I want to know how large the world is. I wish some man would volunteer to find out."

One young man said, "I will go and find out."

"Very well," said the chief, "How long will you be gone?"

"I can't tell, for I don't know how far I shall have to travel."

"Go," said the chief, "And when you return you will tell us about your journey."

The young man started and after traveling two moons he came to a country where everything was white—the forests, the water, the grass. It hurt his feet to walk on the white ground, so he turned back. When he reached home he notified the chief.

The chief said, "I don't believe that he has been to the end of the world, but I will call a council and we will hear what he has to say."

When the people were assembled, the young man said: "I did not go very far, but I went as far as I was able." And he told all he knew of the White Country.

The chief said, "We must send another man."

They sent a second man. He was gone four moons and returned. The chief called a council, and then asked: "Did you go to the end of the world?"

"No," said the man, "but I went as far as I was able to go. Everything was as it is here till I came to the White Country. I traveled two moons in the White Country and could go no farther. I could not have lived had I continued my journey."

The chief sent a third man. He traveled farther than the second man, then came back and related that there were people who lived in white houses and dressed in fur.

The chief was encouraged and he sent a fourth man. As the man traveled he noticed everything. He crossed white rivers and white lakes and was gone eight moons.

On his return, he said, "I came back quicker than I went, for I came a shorter way and reached the green land sooner than I would if I had come on the trail by which I went."

The chief sent a fifth man. He crossed the White Country and beyond that he found a place where there was nothing but rocks. He climbed very high then went down, and so he went up and down till he wore his moccasins off. He was gone ten moons and came back.

At the council called by the chief the man said, "I passed over the White Country, crossed rocky places, and then came straight home. It cannot be very far across the world."

"How did you know the way home?" asked the old man.

"As I went I noticed the trees. The tops of the hemlocks leaned toward the East and our home is in that direction, so I followed the bend of the hemlocks."

The bald-headed chief was learning something all the time.

Many men were sent, one after another, and each returned with a story a little different from that told by others, but still no one satisfied the chief. At last a man said, "I will start and I will go to the end of the world before I come back."

The chief looked at the man and saw that he was very homely, but very strong, and he said, "I think you will do as you promise. You may go."

The chief called a council of the whole nation and each man agreed to make a journey by himself, and then come home and describe all he had seen. The chief and his men went and were gone forty moons. When they came home a council was held and each told what he had seen.

When the man came who had promised to go to the end of the world, he said, "I have been to the end of the world, I have seen all kinds of people, all kinds of game, all kinds of forests and rivers. I have seen things which no one else has ever seen."

The chief was satisfied, he said, "I am chief of all the people, you will be next to me. You'll be second chief."

This was the pay the man got for his journey. He took his position as second chief.

The old chief was Bald Eagle. The first man sent out was Deer. His feet were tender, he could not endure the ice and snow of the White Country. The homely man who went to the end of the world was Mud-turtle.

THE BOY WHO LEARNED THE SONGS
OF BIRDS

TWO brothers lived by themselves and supposed they were the only persons in the world. The younger was a little fellow but he did the thinking for both. Whatever he said the elder brother did. One day he said,—

"Brother, kill a turkey for me. I want two feathers." The young man killed a turkey and brought it home. When he gave it to the little boy he asked, "What are you going to do with the feathers?"

"I want them for a head-dress," answered the boy, and pulling two feathers from the turkey he gave them to his brother and asked him to fix them in a socket in such a way that they would turn with the wind.

When this was done, the little boy fastened the socket to a band and wore the feathers for a head-dress. At night he hung the dead-dress on the wall over his couch but as soon as daylight came he put it on his head. One morning, when going out, he said to his brother, "I like my feathers and I am going to have a dance for them."

The young man watched till the boy disappeared behind a fallen tree. Soon he heard singing and then he heard dancing. He was frightened and said to himself, "Something is the matter with my brother."

When the boy came back, the young man asked, "What were you doing? Were you dancing behind that tree? Why did you go so far? Why didn't you dance right here with me, not go off alone."

"You don't know the songs I sing."

"I can learn them, then I can help you."

"If you want to help me, you may dance."

"It isn't right for me to dance when I don't know how to sing, and haven't feathers in my hair."

"I will change places with you," said the little boy. "You may hunt small game and I will hunt deer. I have hunted birds, for from them I learn songs. Your game does not sing. But maybe I could not kill big game, I am so small, and maybe you couldn't kill birds, you are so large.''

"Well,'' said the elder brother. "You may sing and dance all you want to, I will hunt.''

The young man continued to hunt large game. Often, when coming toward home, he heard his little brother singing and dancing but as soon as the boy saw him he began to do something else, as though he had not been singing or dancing. This frightened the young man and made him think that something was going to happen. Once he asked his brother,—

"Why have you stopped hunting for birds?''

"I listen to their songs,'' said the boy. "That is why I don't shoot them.''

One day he said to his brother, "My feathers are worn out. I want you to kill another turkey.''

The young man killed the largest turkey he could find and brought it home.

"Skin the turkey,'' said the boy, "and make me a pouch.''

When the pouch was finished, the young man gave it to his brother, and asked, "Do you like it?''

"Yes,'' said the boy. "It is just as I wanted it to be.''

While the skin was drying, the boy often put it around his body and went off into the woods. When he came back to the cabin he took the skin off and hung it up.

"You must not go far from the cabin,'' said his brother.

"No,'' answered the boy. "I will stay near home and take care of things.''

Once he said to his brother, "You must stay at home, not go hunting to-day. I want you to learn to sing my songs. What I do now will be for the people who are to come. I will make a rule that the people to come must wear feathers and dance and sing.''

The elder brother studied over this and wondered how a little boy could have such thoughts.

"Now,'' said the boy, "I am going to sing a song. You must listen and learn it.''

He sang a song.

"What is the name of that song?" asked the elder brother.

From singing the songs of the birds the boy had grown very wise. He said,—

"It is the song the people will sing when they wear feathers on their heads (War-song). You must be careful in singing it; if not, you will fall to the ground senseless. I sing what I have heard the birds sing. I give thanks as I have heard them do when I was hunting. I dance to my songs because I hear the birds sing and see them dance. We must do as they do. It will make us feel glad and happy."

One day when the brothers. were out looking around, they saw a large bird sitting on a tree. When the bird began to sing, the young man knew that his brother had learned its song for he had heard him sing it. "You are very wise," said he to the boy, "I think the Great Spirit tells the birds to teach us songs," and he began singing a song of his own, different from those his brother sang.

"Do you think I could dance to your song?" asked the little boy. "I'll try if you will sing it again."

Instead of singing, the elder brother said, "I will tell you the words of my song, they are, 'I am glad to see the day. I am thankful for the sunbeams.'"

"I know the song," said the boy. "It is different from mine. There isn't as much joy in it. When we are sad we will sing your song and gain courage. Now you must hunt for your kind of game and I will hunt for mine."

As the young man was starting off, the boy jumped into his turkey skin, and said, "Brother, I will go with you."

"Oh no," said his brother, "I go too far. You would get tired."

The boy insisted and at last the young man said, "You may go part of the way, but all of the way would be too far."

When they had gone a long distance, the young man said, "This is far enough for you to go. You must go back now."

The boy went home hopping and running exactly like a turkey.

The young man noticed that his brother was wearing his turkey skin all the time, that he wore it nights. He didn't like this and he asked him to take it off.

"You made it for me," said the boy. "I like to wear it."

The young man was fond of the boy so he didn't say any more. Afterward, when he mentioned the turkey skin, he always received the same answer: "You made it for me, and I like to wear it."

The boy played like a turkey and when he saw wild turkeys he imitated the noise they made. He was learning the habits of a turkey. The young man worried over this.

The boy no longer wore feathers on his head, and his voice began to change; it didn't sound like his voice. At last his brother told him to take the skin off.

The boy said, "I can't take it off. You will have to help me."

The young man pulled but couldn't get the skin off. It had grown to the boy's body.

Turkey said, "I shall stay with you always, but you must be careful; something is going to happen."

He was very wise now; his advice was better than ever; it was beyond the comprehension of his brother.

Once, when the young man came home, he couldn't find Turkey but the next morning he heard him on the roof of the cabin making the noise that a turkey makes at daybreak. He felt strangely, felt that his brother had become a real turkey. Soon he heard him jump down, then he came into the cabin, and said, "Brother, a woman is coming. I think she is coming for you. You must be careful. Something is going to happen to us. If you go with her, I shall follow you."

When the woman came near the cabin she saw a turkey standing in front of it. She looked at the bird but didn't say anything. Going into the cabin she said to the young man, "I have come for you."

"I will tell my brother and find out what he thinks about it," answered the young man. The woman didn't know the turkey she saw outside was the young man's brother.

He went to Turkey, and said, "A woman has come."

"Didn't I tell you one was coming. She is full of witch-craft and she will try to destroy us. You must tell her that you are not ready to go, that you will start to-morrow. Something bad is going to happen to us."

The young man said to the woman, "I will go with you as soon as I can get ready."

Turkey determined to stay in the house that night. He hopped in and perched on a roost his brother made for him. The woman thought the boy was a tame turkey.

The next morning neither of the brothers could eat. The elder said, "I must go with this woman."

"It is wrong to go," said Turkey, "She has great power. It will be hard to outwit her."

When the woman and the young man started, Turkey followed them till he saw them turn and go toward the West, then he went back to the cabin. He was very lonely. The next morning he said to himself: "Poor brother, that woman has taken him away from me. She is going to kill him. I must go and see what is happening to him."

He traveled toward the West till he came to an opening in the woods. In the opening was a cabin.

"That must be the place," thought the boy.

An old woman who was in the cabin said to her daughter, "There is a turkey outside. It is tame. Maybe it has come to stay with us."

Right away the young man knew that his little brother had come. The women took a fancy to the turkey. They didn't think of trying to kill it. Toward night one of the women wanted to shut it up so it couldn't go away but the boy ran out and perched on the roof so as to see and hear everything.

The next morning, when the young man came out of the cabin, his brother followed him, and asked: "Brother, how can you stay here and be abused by the old woman and her daughter? They don't give you anything to eat. They are going to kill you. I have come to tell you this and to tell you that I am going to save you."

Turkey started toward the East. As his brother watched him, he said, "I am glad he can go where he wants to."

Turkey was angry at the women. When he reached

home, he thought, "I must get out of this skin, get my own form. I've been a turkey long enough," and he pulled and worked till at last he freed himself. He hung the skin up and put the feather band around his head, then he began to study over how he could free his brother. After a while he said, "This is what I will do," and going out he called to his medicine, Moose. As soon as he called Moose was there.

The boy said to it, "Go to the West, to where the old woman and her daughter live, when my brother comes out of the cabin, seize him and throw him onto your back, then run with all your strength. Take off your feathers (horns) and I will put mine onto your head; yours are too heavy to run with."

The Moose held its head down; the boy took off its horns and put his feather band in their place, saying, "When you come back, I will give you your feathers."

Moose ran off in the direction of the old woman's cabin and the boy said to himself, "He will soon come back." In a short time he heard a noise and going outside saw his brother clinging to Moose's back; he was so weak that he couldn't get off alone.

"I told you that something bad would happen," said the boy, "Now you have your punishment." To Moose he said, "Stand here a while." He helped his brother into the cabin and when he came back he changed feathers with Moose and sent him away.

"I am glad to have you back," said the boy to his brother. "We are free now from the old woman and her daughter and can live together in peace."

They lived together ever after and continued to learn the songs of birds.

From birds came all the Indian songs and dances.

THE COMING OF SPRING

OR

THE WADYO^{n}YO^{n}DYES GIRLS

Characters

ONEQSAS ....Mushroom-eater (A Bird)

WADYO^{n}YO^{n}DYES ....One of the Wild Duck family

SGANO^{n}HSES GOWA ....One of the Thunder family

DWÂAU^{n}HDANE GE^n ....Two Feathers (A Rabbit)

DOTGEHONDAGWE..Half Red-headed (A Woodpecker)

AN uncle and his two nephews lived in a cabin in the woods. Each day the uncle went to hunt and to dig wild potatoes.

The younger of the two nephews did not know that he had a brother. The uncle kept his elder nephew hidden in an old couch for fear that the daughters of SGANO^{n}HSES GOWA would come and carry him away. Though the uncle brought home a plenty of good potatoes, he gave his younger nephew poor ones.

As the boy grew older, he began to wonder why he and his uncle were always alone. One day, when he asked if there were people living near them, the old man said, "Far off in the West there are bad people. They have carried away our people, one after another, till we are the only ones left."

The boy wondered why his uncle gave him poor potatoes. He saw him put a plenty of large potatoes in the kettle in the evening, but in the morning only small ones were left. One night he made up his mind to keep awake and find out what became of the large potatoes. He tore a hole in the deer skin he slept under and watched his uncle.

Toward the middle of the night the uncle got up, stirred the fire, and going to an old couch in the corner, called out, "Nephew! Nephew! It is time to get up." When there was no answer, he struck the couch with a switch and called, "Nephew! Nephew! Are you ready to eat?" Then the top of the couch came up and a young man appeared.

The two men sat down by the fire. The potatoes, covered with moss, were simmering. The uncle uncovered them, picked out the largest and best and gave them to the young man. After the two had eaten heartily, the old man took a turtle rattle and kept time while the young man danced.

The little boy thought, "That must be my brother. Now I'll have fun."

When the young man hid himself in the couch, the uncle covered up the fire and lay down in his own place.

The next morning, as soon as his uncle had gone out to dig potatoes, the little boy began cooking. When all was ready he went to the couch, raised the cover, and said, "Come out, Brother, come out, we'll eat and then dance."

"No," said the young man, "I cannot come out in the daytime. If I did those WADYO^{n}YO^{n}DYES girls who live off in the West, would hear me."

"Never mind," said the little boy, "They'll not hear you."

"Yes they will, and they will come and carry me off. They don't know that I am here, but if I make a noise in the daytime, they will hear it and come for me."

No matter what the young man said the boy teased and begged till he came out of the couch. They ate and then began to dance. Suddenly they heard a noise like thunder, a noise that made the earth shake.

"What's that?" asked the little boy.

"That's SGANO^{n}HSES GOWA getting her daughters ready to come for me," said his brother. "She is getting ready to push the canoe from the top of the house."

The young man crept into the couch and covered himself. The little boy kept shaking the turtle skin rattle and dancing.

Soon two women appeared sailing in a canoe through the air. They were singing and their song said, "We are coming for Two Feathers, we are coming for Two Feathers."

They looked in at the smoke-hole and asked, "Where is your brother?"

"I have no brother," said the little boy, "I've only an uncle. He is old. He is off digging potatoes."

"There is a young man in the house."

"No, I'm all alone."

"You are not telling the truth. You'll suffer if you lie to us the next time we come."

In the evening when the uncle came, he asked, "What have you been doing to-day? Did you find your brother?"

"Have I a brother?" asked the boy.

"Wasn't there someone here to-day?"

"No."

"What did those women come for? I heard them."

"There wasn't anyone here to-day."

The uncle said no more, but the next morning, when starting off he said, "Go out of doors and play. I don't want you to stay in the house."

The old man was scarcely out of sight when the boy ran to the couch and began to beg his brother to come out. At last the young man came and the two amused themselves till the elder brother heard the women coming.

"Now," said he, "I shall have to go," but he hid in the couch.

Soon a canoe grazed the top of the house and two women came in and one asked, "Where is your brother?"

"I have no brother, I've only an old uncle," said the boy, "I dance to keep from being lonesome."

The women looked around and seeing beautiful red hair hanging out of the couch, they raised the cover and there was the young man. The three got into the canoe and it rose in the air and sailed away toward the West.

When the uncle heard the singing he ran home as fast as he could for he knew what had happened. He went into the house, sat down, and cried bitterly.

"Don't cry, Uncle," said the little boy. "Don't cry, I'll bring my brother back."

He ran out, gathered a bundle of red willows, came home, scraped off the bark and threw it on the fire. Thick smoke rose up and shot off toward the West; the boy sprang into the smoke and was borne away. He overtook the canoe and the young man knew that his little brother was following to rescue him.

One of the sisters were sitting in the prow of the canoe, paddling, the other in the stern, steering. When Two Feathers turned to look at his brother, the woman in the prow struck him a blow on the side of his head, with her paddle, and cried, "Sit still! Don't look around!"

As she struck, the little boy sprang into the canoe and screamed, "Don't you strike my brother!"

Then he said, "Let this canoe turn around and take my brother home!"

Instantly the canoe turned, and, in spite of all the women could do, it sailed back faster than it had come. As it was nearing the uncle's house, the women began to beg the boy to let his brother go with them.

They said, "We will give you whatever you want, only let him go."

In his mind the boy asked, "What can I take and let my brother go?" Then he said, "If each one of you will give me a piece of flesh large enough to make a moccasin, I'll let my brother go with you."

They consented. He took his flint knife and cut out of each woman the piece he wanted. He put the pieces on his feet and they fitted nicely, immediately he was at home and the canoe sailed off toward the West. When his uncle asked where his brother was, he said, "I brought him almost home, but I let him go when the women gave me these beautiful moccasins, with these moccasins on I can do anything I want to, I can kill those women."

After a few days, ONEQSAS, for that was the boy's name, had such power from his moccasins that he knew the women were tormenting his brother. He told his uncle, and said, "I am going after Two Feathers."

He gathered a bundle of willows, scraped off the bark, threw it on the fire and when a thick smoke rose up he sprang into it and shot off toward the West. He came down at the edge of a clearing in a great forest. Near the opposite end of the clearing was a long house[1] and not far away, at the edge of the woods, was a hut where a grandmother lived with her three grandchildren, a boy and two girls.

"I'll go to that hut," thought ONEQSAS. In the hut he found a boy of his own age and size, just like him; half of the boy's hair was black and half was red; the hair on the crown of his head was black, that on the sides was red, his name was DOTGEHONDAGWE (Half Red-headed).

"Who are you?" asked ONEQSAS, "You must be my brother."

The two looked at each other, and seeing that they were of the same size and that one looked exactly like the other, each called the other, "Brother."

"You must stay with us," said the strange boy. "I have two sisters and a grandmother."

When old GAQSHÍNYC came home, her grandson said, "I have a brother here, he is going to live with us."

"How can he live with us?" asked the grandmother. "We are poor."

"He is poor too; he will be satisfied with what we can give him."

At last the old woman said, "Let him stay." Then the grandson asked, "What are they doing at the long house?"

"The chief's daughters have brought a man from the East, from the Wampum people. Each night they hang him up and make him cry, for his tears are wampum beads."

"Can we go to the long house?" asked the boy.

"We can go, and maybe we'll get a chance to pick up some of the wampum."

When night came, the old woman and her grandson and ONEQSAS went to the long house. ONEQSAS said to his friend, "We will gather some dry rushes and if the chief will let us go inside the long house, we will light pipes for the people."

When they had gathered the rushes the old woman asked the chief if she might go in and have a chance to

---

[1] The Indian council house.

pick up wampum, and if her grandsons might carry lighted rushes to the men who wanted to smoke.

The chief said, "Let the old woman in, she is a good woman. Let her have a chance, and let the boys in, too."

Two Feathers was hanging from a post driven into the ground near the fire. When he saw his brother he smiled. Everyone who saw him smile asked in their mind, "How can that poor man smile?"

When the house was full of people, the chief told his daughters to take fire-brands and hold them to the young man's body. They burned him on one side and then on the other. He cried bitterly and as the tears fell they changed into beautiful wampum, falling in a shower. The people scrambled for the beads. The old grandmother got a few. After a while they stopped the burning. The people rested and smoked till the chief said, "Burn him again!" Then ONEQSAS took off one of his moccasins and told his friend to put it on and to stick his foot in the fire as soon as the sisters began to burn the young man.

The instant the moccasin touched the fire, one of the sisters screamed with pain and she didn't stop screaming till the boy took his foot away from the fire. The people asked what the matter was, but the girl wouldn't tell.

The other sister was about to burn Two Feathers when ONEQSAS put his foot in the fire: she dropped the brand and screamed as if in terrible pain.

The grandmother and two boys went outside, then ONEQSAS said, "Let all who are in the house fall asleep and sleep soundly."

As soon as the people were asleep, ONEQSAS freed his brother, carried him outside, and then he fastened the door, and walking around the house he repeated, "Let this house turn to stone and let the stone be red hot! Let this house turn to stone and let the stone be red hot!"

Right away the house was stone and the stone was red hot. All the people inside were burned up.

Then ONEQSAS said to the old woman, "Grandmother, you must come home with me. You will be a good wife for my uncle."

When the two brothers and the grandmother and her grandson reached the old man's house, they found him mourning for his nephews. He had been tormented by foxes that came to the door, knocked and called out, "We are here, Uncle!" Soon after the nephews went into the house a fox came and called out, "I've come, Uncle!"

"Let him in," said ONEQSAS.

The fox ran to the fire to get ashes to throw into the old man's face. ONEQSAS caught him, and said, "Now I'll punish you!" He tied the animal's forelegs together with a bark rope and hung him up in the smoke-hole. Tears rolled out of his eyes and made dark streaks along his cheeks; his face and nose were black with soot; his hair that had been white became tawny from smoke. When he was almost dead, ONEQSAS took him down, threw him outdoors, and said, "Be off, and never come here again!"

Since that time foxes have black noses and their fur is a tawny yellow.

THE CREATION OF MEN (INDIANS)

[Told by "Esq" Johnson]

"Esq" Johnson's account of the origin of Good and Evil as it was told him by old men.

———

SHAGODYOWEG is often translated False Face, but the literal meaning is "The Great One Who Protects Them (Mankind)" from sickness and pestilence, and is considered to be of the Wind People.

ABOVE, in the center of the Blue, people lived before there was any earth down here. In the middle of the village up there stood a tree covered with white blossoms; when the tree was in bloom, its blossoms gave light to the people and when the blossoms fell, there was darkness.

One time a woman in that village dreamed and in her dream an *oñgwe*[1] said to her, "That tree with white blossoms on it must be pulled up by the roots."

When the woman told her dream, the people were silent. Some time passed and the woman dreamed again.

The *oñgwe* in her dream, said, "A circle must be dug around the tree and the tree pulled up by the roots, then something giving more and better light will come."

The woman told her dream a second time, but still the people took no heed of it. She dreamed a third time and again was told that the tree must be pulled up. Then a man said, "I think we should give heed to this dream; we

———

[1] Man (Indian).

may have better light and the people will have cause to rejoice." His advice was listened to, men cut around the roots of the tree; when the roots were loosened the tree sank down, and disappeared.

The chief of the people said, "I did not heed this dream for I knew something would happen to the people if the tree were pulled up." He was angry and ordered that the woman, who had the dream, should be brought and pushed into the hole left by the tree. Men caught her and threw her into the hole. Now that the tree with white blossoms was gone it was dark all the time. .

The woman fell and fell. The hole was deep and long, but at last she came out into bright light, into our sky, and looking down she saw only water.

It is well known that in very ancient days all animals had the gift of speech by which they communicated with one another as freely as human beings do at the present time.

Down under the Blue there was just one enormous body of water on which there were multitudes of various kinds of water fowl and aquatic animals amusing themselves after their own fashion. One of the duck family looked up and saw a dark object coming down from the sky.

The duck cried out to the other birds and animals, "Some strange being is coming down to us."

A council was called at once to decide how they could prepare a resting place for this being, who might not be fitted to live on the water as they did. A duck said, "I'll dive and find if there is any bottom to this water." After a time, the duck came to the surface, shot into the air and fell back, lifeless. Several water birds made the same attempt with a similar result.

All the people that lived in the water were there.

Loon said to fish-hawk, "Go and meet that creature in the air and hold it till we are ready for you to come down."

Fish-hawk went and they saw him meet the woman, for it was a woman.

Turtle said, "I'll take care of her."

Loon said, "You can't, you are too fond of eating."

Horned snake said, "I'll take care of her. She can sit between my horns. I'll carry her wherever I go."

Loon said, "You can't care for her. You are poisonous, you would kill her."

Meanwhile one person after another was trying to bring earth from the bottom of the sea. At last Hell-diver brought up a little. Loon was chief and when Hell-diver came up, he sent all that kind of people after more dirt. Loon said, "Put the dirt on Turtle's back." Turtle was willing, and as fast as the divers brought dirt, Beaver, with his tail, pounded it down on Turtle's back, to make it solid. When Loon thought there was enough dirt, Fish-hawk came down with the woman.

The beaver and duck people kept at work making the earth larger and larger. As it grew, more Beavers and Ducks were ordered to work. Bushes began to grow, little red bushes, like water reeds.

Soon the woman gave birth to a child, a girl. The child quickly grew to be a young woman and to be very active. She walked here and there and watched the birds and animals and once when she was wandering around she met a nice looking young man. They fell in love with each other and by their union came night and day. At daybreak the young woman went to meet her husband, at twilight she came home and the man went away.

One evening, after they had parted, the young woman turned to look at her husband, and saw a big Turtle walking along where the man had just been. She thought, "A Turtle has deceived me!"

She told her mother about the man, and said, "I am going to die, you must put my body in the ground and cover it up well. Two stalks will grow from my breasts and on each stalk an ear will come. When the ears are ripe you must pick them and give one to each of the boys that are born to me."

The younger woman gave birth to twin boys, and died. The mother buried her daughter and soon two stalks came up out of her grave. And this was the origin of corn.

The boys grew quickly; they were strong and healthy, but the younger was an awkward, ugly looking, disagreeable fellow, with a head like a lump of rough flint.

Once when the elder brother was off by himself, he was lonesome and he thought he would try to make something, so he took mud and when he had molded it into the shape he wanted, he put it down, and asked, "Can't you jump?"

It didn't move, then he blew on it till at last it jumped. And he had created the grasshopper. Then he thought he would make something that would fly higher, so of red clay he made the cherry bird. After he had the clay molded, he set it up and told it to fly in the air. The bird flew and lighted on a bough—this was the first bird. One after another he made all of the birds of the air.

Then he thought he would make something that would run on the ground, so he shaped a deer, brought it to life, and said to it, "You must run fast and go everywhere in the world." He blew on it, and pushed it, and it ran off. In the same way he made different kinds of animals. Then he thought, "Maybe I can make something like myself." Out of the mud he made something that looked like himself, but now, in some way, he found that he had a spirit in his body and he wanted the thing he had lying on the ground to have a spirit too. He wanted to give it some of his own but didn't know how. At last he bent down and blew into its mouth. He hadn't blown into the mouth of any other creature he had made. The image began to move; the young man raised it up, made it stand on its feet, and told it to whoop.

The new man whooped; he had a fine voice. Then he walked off a little way and turned and looked at the young man.

The elder brother had a special place to sit when he made all these creatures. About the time he made man, the younger brother found the place and, while watching his brother, he thought, "I will make a man too." He went away alone, made something as nearly like himself as he could and brought it to life. It didn't look like a man. It was a strange creature, and when its maker saw that it wasn't a man, but some ugly, deformed thing, he said to it, "My brother has made a man, he is over there, go and kill him."

The elder brother was watching the younger, for he was afraid he would make some harmful animal. When he heard him tell the creature he had made to go and destroy man, he went back to his own place, caught cherry bird and pulling out the hind leg of grasshopper, gave it to the bird, and said, "Go and scare my brother." As the bird took up the leg the bird became very large and the leg was like the leg of a man, and it was bloody. The bird flew near, perched on a limb and called out, "*Gowa! gowa!*" When the younger brother saw what the bird had in its beak, he left his work, ran home and said to his grandmother, "A bird came and perched just where I was at work. My brother made it frighten me. I was afraid it would pull my leg out, so I ran."

When the elder brother came the grandmother said, "You shouldn't frighten your brother."

The first man made was wandering about alone. The young man saw him once in a while and saw that he was lonesome. Then he said to himself, "I will make something like my grandmother." He made it out of mud, breathed into it and told it to walk; then he found the man, and said, "I give you this one, you must always go together."

When the woman sat down by the man he thought that her arm was in the way and his was also. He said, "We will cut them off." They cut them off and laid them one side. When the elder brother came along and saw what they had done he said to himself, "This won't do. I will give them blood and pain," and from himself he gave them blood and pain, then he put their arms on and healed them (before that they had neither blood nor pain).

To the man and woman, he said, "I have made you, you will have children like yourselves. You must hunt the animals I have made, kill them and eat their flesh; that will be your food. I am going above the Blue. You will not live forever. You will die and your spirit will go above the Blue."

When the younger brother found that the elder brother had gone away, he saw the man and woman and talked with them. He said "I am going to make a man." He got earth and formed it as best he could, blew into its mouth and told it to stand up and whoop. It said, "Ho, ho!" He pushed it from behind and made it leap. It was a frog, as large as a man.

The younger brother was angry, and he said, "I can't

make a man. My brother has made a man and a woman and other animals. What I have made shall turn to man-eaters and animal-eaters and eat up what my brother has made."

When the elder brother looked down from the Blue and saw that the animals his brother had made were trying to eat up the people and animals he had made, he came down, put the man-eaters in the ground, and told them to stay there as long as the earth remained. This work done, he went back above the Blue.

When the younger brother found that his animals were in the ground he was angry, and said, "I will try again to make a man." He got mud and began. Every little while, he went and looked at the man his brother had made. When his man was finished and brought to life, he was an ugly-looking creature. His maker told him to whoop. He could only say, "Ho! ho!" And this was SHAGODYO-WEG GOWA. His maker said, "Go and eat all the creatures my brother has made."

When the elder brother saw what was taking place, he came from the Blue to put SHAGODYOWEG into the ground, but that one spoke first and said, "Do not destroy me. I want to live on the earth. I will be your servant and help you. I will go around in the woods, the ashes of fire will be my medicine for men. If anyone is sick I will take ashes and scatter over them and they will be well."

The elder brother couldn't put SHAGODYOWEG into the ground for he had spoken first, so he let him stay on earth.

The younger brother said to his grandmother, "I have tried to make a man, but I cannot. Now I will cause the people my brother has made to do all manner of evil."

The elder brother went back to the Blue.

THE BUFFALO WOMEN

[Told by Titus]

Characters

DZOGÉON ....Little people (Fairies)
NYAGWAIHE ....The Ancient of Bears
SHAGODYOWEG GOWA.....False Face (Wind People)
DIGIÁ'GOⁿ GOWA ....Buffalo

A BOY and his mother lived near the Allegheny River, at a place called Carydon. One foggy morning, just at daylight, the boy went to the river. He heard rowing and soon saw two little people (*Dzogéon*) coming in a stone canoe. They came to near where he was standing and landed.

One of them said to him, "We have come on purpose to talk with you for you are up early mornings. We are on a buffalo hunt. There are three buffaloes, two old ones and a young one that run under the ground. If they stop in this part of the country they will destroy all the people, for they are full of witchcraft and poison. A great many years ago your grandfather chased these buffaloes, but he could not overtake them. Two days from now come to this place early in the morning and we will tell you about our hunt."

When the time came, the boy went to the river and soon the two little men came to him, and said, "We have killed the two old buffaloes; the young one escaped, ran off toward the West. We let him go, for only a common man can kill him. Now we are going home."

The little men got into their stone canoe, rowed away, and were never seen again.

Some time after this the Senecas collected a war party to go against the Cherokees. One of the party was the best runner of the Senecas.

Before the party reached the Cherokee country, they met the Cherokees and every Seneca was killed except the fast runner. He escaped from the enemy, got out of reach and started home on a different trail from the one the party had taken when coming. The third day, near noon, he came to a deer-lick and sat down to rest. As he sat there, he saw tracks that looked like the tracks of a very large bear; he got up and followed them till they stopped at a tall elm tree, then he saw that they were not the tracks of an ordinary bear but of one of the old kind, the great bear, NYAGWAIHE, and he thought, "No matter if I die, I will see this creature."

The tree was hollow, the man climbed up and looking into the hole saw the bear. It had no hair and its skin was as smooth as a man's.

The Seneca thought, "I mustn't bother this creature, I'll go back to the deer-lick." He hurried down the tree and ran off as fast as he could. As he ran he heard a terrible noise and looking around saw that the animal had come out of the hole and was following him. Going back some distance he ran forward and sprang into the deer-lick, sinking almost to his waist in the mud. He couldn't get out of the lick and could only with great difficulty take a step forward, dragging one foot after the other. When the bear came to the lick it sprang at the man and sank in the mud. It worked its way to the middle of the lick and there sank out of sight.

When the man reached solid ground he ran till he came to a fallen tree, then he sat down and began to think. He didn't know what to do, he had nothing to eat and was too tired to hunt. Soon a stranger came to him, and said, "You think that you are going to die?"

"I do."

"You will not. I have come to save you. Go to where I just came from, off in that direction," said he, pointing to one side, "you will find a fire and over it a kettle of meat. Rest and eat. Men will come and bother you but pay no attention to them. When you sit down to eat, one will say, 'Throw a piece over this way,' another will say, 'Throw a piece over this way.' But pay no heed to them. If you throw even one morsel you are lost; they will kill you.''

The man went as directed and found a kettle of meat and hulled corn. As he ate, it seemed as though a crowd formed in a circle around him. Each man of the crowd began to beg for a piece of meat. They begged all night, but he paid no attention to their begging.

In the morning, after the Seneca had traveled a short distance, he met the stranger who sent him to the kettle. The stranger said, "I am glad that you did as I told you. Go toward the East and when it is near night, sit down by a tree. I will come to you."

The man traveled all day. Near sunset he found a fallen tree and sat down.

Soon the stranger came. He said, "Follow my tracks back till you come to a fire. Over the fire is a kettle full of meat and hulled corn. You will be tormented as you were last night, but pay no heed to the begging. If you escape to-night, you will have no more trouble."

The Seneca went as directed. He found a fire and hanging over the fire a kettle. The kettle was full of meat and hulled corn.

That night men begged for meat as the night before but the Seneca paid no attention to them. The next morning the stranger came to him, and said, "If you keep on your way, you will reach home safe and well."

As he started along, the Seneca turned to look at his friend and saw, instead of a man, a SHAGODYOWEG GOWA. Towards night he got hungry and thought he had better look for game. He saw a deer, killed it with an arrow, and building a fire he roasted pieces of the meat and ate them. He was now strong and well.

The next afternoon he shot a deer, built a fire, roasted pieces of meat and ate them. When night came he lay down by the fire but he couldn't sleep. After a while two women came to his fire and one of them asked, "Are you awake?"

"I am awake."

"I want you to marry my daughter," said the woman.

The man saw that the girl was good looking and he consented to marry her. He didn't know where to go and thought if he married he would have company and after a time might find his way home.

The next morning the mother said, "We will go home."

The three walked on till midday, then they came to a village where, it seemed to the young man, a good number of people were living. They stopped at one of the cabins. The mother-in-law said to him, "This is our home. You will stay with us."

The young man stayed a long time with his wife's parents. One night he heard the beating of a drum and heard his father-in-law say, "Eh! Eh!" The old man seemed frightened by the call.

The call meant that the chief of the village—the young buffalo that escaped from the DzoGÉON and now lived under a hill close by, was to have a dance, and that all the people of the village must come to it.

The next morning everyone went to the place where the drum was beaten, and dancing began. The crowd danced all day and all night. Young Buffalo and his two wives came out and danced. In the morning they went around among the crowd. Buffalo was very jealous. He pushed men away from his wives and wanted to fight. Then he went under the hill and his wives followed him.

The next day the old man said to his son-in-law, "Buffalo's wives will soon come out and go to the river for water. They will pass near you, but you must not speak or smile. Their husband is a bad man. If you speak or smile, he will know it and will harm you."

The young man didn't heed his father-in-law's words. The two women went to the river for water. As they came back, they smiled and looked pleasant and the young man asked them for a drink. They gave it to him and went on.

The old man said, "You didn't do as I told you to. Now the chief will come out and say that he is going to challenge a man to a foot race. He will name you."

Soon young Buffalo came and pointing at the Seneca said, "I challenge this stranger to run a race with me.

If I am a better runner than he is, I will take his life: if he is better than I am, he may take mine. We will begin early to-morrow morning and run around and around the hill. The one who is ahead at sundown will be the winner.''

The old man said to his son-in-law, ''You must have an extra pair of moccasins to put on when yours wear out.''

The next morning young Buffalo came and said, ''Now we will start!'' and off he went.

At midday the young man's friends called to him to do his best for the chief was gaining on him, that he had just gone around the turn ahead. Soon he heard the chief's friends tell him to do his best for the young man was gaining on him.

Buffalo got tired, went crooked and soon the young man overtook him. He didn't know how he was going to kill Buffalo for his side was one immense rib—these buffaloes were not like the buffaloes of to-day. He shot from behind, the arrow went in up to the feathers, only a bit of it stuck out.

The two ran around once more. As they came near the stopping place, the crowd called to the young man to shoot again. He did and killed the buffalo. So the words of the DzoGÉON were true—a common man killed young Buffalo. The people crowded around the Seneca and thanked him for what he had done.

His father-in-law said to the crowd, ''Now, each man is free to go where he wants to.''

The old man and his wife with their daughter and son-in-law went home.

Then the mother-in-law said to the young man, ''Get ready, you must visit your mother.''

Soon after the young man and his wife and her mother started. They were ten days on the road. It was Spring, the time of sugar making. When they were near his mother's house, his mother-in-law said, ''My daughter and I will stop in this swamp. Your mother is making sugar. We will stay here, but we will help her all we can.''

The young man saw his mother and at night went to the house, leaving the two women in the swamp. In the night the wife and mother collected all the sap and gathered a great quantity of wood.

The next morning, when the mother and son went to the woods, they found no sap in the troughs under the trees, but when they came to the boiling place they found the big trough full and a great pile of wood close by. This work went on for some days, then the woman said to her son-in-law, "It is time for me to go back to my husband. You are free now. Have no hard feelings. I shall take my daughter with me; you must stay with your mother. There are many girls who want to marry you but the girl you must marry is the granddaughter of the woman who lives in the house at the edge of the village. They are poor and the girl takes care of her grandmother."

"As you leave us, call out. When some one asks why you call, tell them that you have found buffalo tracks in the swamp. Let them come and shoot us; we will get home sooner."

They parted, the wife and mother-in-law going one way, the young man the other. As he went he called out. When men asked why he called, he said, "I've found buffalo tracks near the end of the swamp."

Hunters went out and soon overtook the buffaloes and shot them. When the buffaloes fell the hunters thought they had killed them, that they were dead, but they were not. When they were shot their loads dropped off and right away they were back at their old home. They left their bodies behind and people ate them, but their spirits went back to the old man and were buffaloes again.

The young man had been gone so long that the Senecas thought him a great man. Women wanted him for their daughters, but he refused every offer and married the granddaughter of the old woman who lived at the edge of the village.

THE GHOST WOMAN

IN a Seneca village there was a young man who was an orphan. He had neither home nor relatives. He lived first with one family and then with another.

One fall, when the men were getting ready to go deer hunting, the young man asked if he could go. The hunters didn't want him and he was left alone.

Then he said, "I'll go by myself," and he started. Towards night he came to an opening in the woods and saw a brush house over by the bushes.

He went to the house and looked in; there was no one there. The young man thought that the other hunters had built the house and spent a night there. He went in, kindled a fire, made a place to sleep on, and lay down.

About midnight he heard someone come in and, opening his eyes, he saw a woman. She looked at him but didn't speak, then she moved toward his couch and stopped again.

At last she said, "I have come to help you. You must not be afraid. I will stay all night in the cabin."

He said, "If you will help me, you may stay."

"I have passed through this world," said the woman, "I know that you are poor; that you have no relatives and are alone; the hunters didn't want you to go with them. This is why I came to help you. To-morrow start early and travel till it is time to camp, then I will be there."

Towards daylight the woman left the cabin.

In the morning the young man started on. Towards dark, when he thought it was time to stop, he looked for a spring, found one and had just finished his camp when night came.

In the night the woman came as before. The next day the man had good luck. He killed every kind of game.

The woman stayed with him till the hunting season was over. No hunter in the woods had killed as much game as he had. When he was ready to go home the woman said, "I will go with you to the first camp you made."

They spent the night at that camping place. The next morning, she said, "I will stay here. When you get home everybody will find out that you have brought all kinds of meat and skins. One and another will come to you and say, 'You must marry my daughter,' an old woman will say, 'You must marry my granddaughter.' Don't listen to them. Come back next year and you will have good luck. When you are getting ready, if a man wants to come with you, don't let him. Come alone. We will meet here."

They parted, and the young man continued his journey, carrying on his back a heavy load of game.

In the village he found some of the hunters. Others came soon after. All boasted of the game they had killed.

The young man said, "I will give each man as much meat as he wants, if he will go to my camp and get it."

Many went and brought back all the meat they could carry; still there was meat left.

Every woman who had a daughter or a granddaughter, asked the young man to come and live with them. At last the chief asked him to marry his daughter. The man was afraid that if he refused harm would come to him, for the chief was a powerful person. He consented and married the chief's daughter.

When the hunting season came, a great many men, and the chief, who thought his son-in-law was the best hunter in the tribe, wanted to go hunting with him, but he said, "I'm not going this year."

The hunters started off one after another. When all had gone, the young man went alone to the camp where he was to meet the woman.

Early in the night she came in, stopped by the door, and said, "I am sorry you didn't do as I told you to. Now I cannot stay with you," and she disappeared.

Day after day the man hunted but he saw no large game. He shot small game, squirrels and birds, for he was hungry. He went back to the village and had to tell the people that he had seen no game.

The woman was a ghost woman.

WÍSHAKON AND HIS FRIEND VISIT THE PLÉTHOAK (THUNDERS)

[A Delaware story told by John Armstrong]

Characters

WÍSHAKON
PLÉTHOAK ....Thunders—Thunder is Plétho

AN old man and a little boy lived together with great affection. They were not relatives; they called each other "Friend."

One day the old man put on new moccasins, fixed new feathers in his head-dress, trimmed his hair and painted his face.

The little boy, watching him, asked, "What are you going to do, my friend?"

"I'm going on a long journey, I want to see what there is in the world."

"May I go with you?"

"If your father and mother are willing."

The boy asked his parents and they gave their consent. His friend gave him a new bow and arrows, trimmed his hair, painted his face and put a new feather in his head-dress. Then they set out together.

When night came, they made a fire in the woods, ate and slept.

They traveled many days. At last they came to a lake so broad that they could not cross it.

"How can we get to the other side?" asked the boy.

"We'll make a canoe," said his friend.

"Will it take long to make a canoe?"

"It will not."

The old man looked around in the woods till he found a hickory tree. He pulled the tree up, stripped the bark off and made a large canoe. The next morning they put their bows and arrows into the canoe and started to cross the lake. Toward night they came to a low island and, without going on shore, they fastened their canoe to the bullrushes.

"How can we sleep here?" asked the boy. "Maybe in the water there are creatures that will come out and kill us."

"We are safe here," said the old man.

"If the wind blows, we will be carried out into the lake," said the boy.

"The wind will not blow."

The boy and his friend lay down and fell asleep. About midnight the boy heard the water roar and it seemed to him that the canoe was moving swiftly. He thought the wind was blowing. He sat up. It was clear overhead, and the wind wasn't blowing.

"The water must be running very fast," thought the boy; and putting his hand out he touched the water and found that it was going with great swiftness. He roused the old man by reaching his feet and shaking them.

"Get up, friend," said he, "something is the trouble. The water is running by very fast. Where is the lake going?"

"Lie down," said the old man, "no harm will come to us."

The boy lay down, but couldn't sleep. Just at daybreak a voice spoke to him, and, opening his eyes, he saw a fine looking man, ornamented with paint and feathers. He saw also that the canoe was on dry land.

The stranger wakened the old man, and said, "Come with me!"

Taking their bows and arrows the old man and the boy followed the stranger, who led them to a long house.[1] There were many persons inside, some asleep, some awake. When the old man of the house met them he said to their guide, "Oh, you have brought them?"

[1] The Indian council house.

Then he turned to the two friends, and said, "I am glad that you have come. You have heard of us. We are the people whom you call Thunder. We bring rain to make corn and beans and squashes grow. We put it in your mind to come on this journey from the East. We want you to help us. You are more powerful than we are. We want you to kill some of our enemies."

Old man Thunder placed food before the friends, corn, beans, and squash, and said, "We have plenty of this food. We take a little from a great many fields. When you see a small or withered squash, or bad kernels of corn on an ear, or dried-up beans in a pod you may know that we have taken our part from them. We have taken the spirit and left the shell. If you see a whole field of withered corn, you may know that we have taken the spirit from it, but we seldom destroy a whole field; we take only a little."

After the friends had eaten, the old chief said, "On a hill is a great hemlock tree. On that tree is a porcupine of enormous size. He hurls his quills and kills everyone who approaches him. We Thunders are afraid to go near the tree. We want you to destroy this porcupine."

As they started for the hill the little boy went ahead. The old man and the Thunders laughed to see him, and the old man said, "I think my little friend might try his luck first." The boy heard this and was greatly pleased.

They stopped some distance from the tree. No one would venture near it. The boy went into the ground and forward till he was directly under the porcupine. Then he put his head and arms out of the ground, took aim and sent an arrow into the porcupine's body. The porcupine moved a little. The boy sent another arrow, and still another. The porcupine, feeling something, raised up his quills and shot them off in every direction, then groaned, rolled from the tree, and fell to the ground dead.

The Thunders came up, cut open the porcupine, took out its entrails, and ate its flesh.

All wondered at the power of the little boy. Old man Thunder said, "We have another enemy, a sunfish that lives in our river here and lets no one come near for water.''

The boy said, ''I can kill him.''

The next day the Thunders and the old man went near enough to show the boy where the sunfish lived. A great tree had fallen into the river, under the trunk of this tree the sunfish had its home. The boy saw the fish. He sent an arrow and the arrow went straight to the heart of the sunfish and the sunfish came to the surface and died. The Thunders sprang into the water, pulled the body out and dragged it off to Old Thunder's house.

The next day Old Thunder said, ''We have one more enemy. Every day there flies past here a creature as big as a cloud. He brings sickness here and many of our people die. If we could kill this creature, few of us would die. He passes here from the West, early in the morning, and goes back in the evening.''

The next morning the old man and the boy went out and hid in the grass. Soon they saw the creature coming from the West. When it was over the place where the two were hidden, the boy sent an arrow into its body. The creature didn't fall, but it turned and went slowly back in the direction from which it came.

Old man Thunder was very thankful. He said to the two friends, ''You may stay here and live with us.''

The old man said, ''I cannot help you, but my little friend, WÍSHAKON, may stay. He is so powerful that he will be of great assistance to you.''

''We will go to your place to-night,'' said old man Thunder. ''We will carry you with us in the clouds.''

When they came to the old man's place, the council house was full of people. As Thunders entered they began to dance. When they shook their heads, lightning flashed around the room.

The chiefs said, ''Our grandfathers are here to-night. They may do us harm.''

For a little while Thunders quieted down. Again they got excited in the dance and shook their heads till lightning flashed everywhere and the people were frightened. When they had danced as long as they wanted to, they went home, leaving the old man, but taking WÍSHAKON with them, and to this day the little boy goes with them everywhere.

After the great Thunders roar we hear the little fellow with his alto voice, and we say, "That is WÍSHAKON," and we burn tobacco saying, "This is all we have to give," and we thank him for rain.

THE ADVENTURES OF HANÍSHÉONON

[Told by John Jimison]

Characters

GENDÁGAHÂDÉ^{n}YATHA ....June-bug
HANISHÉONO^n ....Muck-worm
O'NOWÉHDA ....Angleworm
OTGÓNDAHE^n .... Snake (red-bellied)
O'SHONYÚQDA ....Corn-worm
SEHDO^{n}HGWADE ....Wood-tick

A MAN lived in the ground. His name was HANÍSHÉONO^n. One morning this man thought, "I ought to go around the world and find people." He came out of the ground and went off through the woods. After a while he saw a cabin, and going near it he peeped through a crack and saw a blind woman, Corn-worm. He stood around thinking what to do.

At last he said, "I'll go in there and have sport with her."

When inside HANÍSHÉONO^n picked up live coals and put them on the woman's head.

She began to cry and to say, "Oh, my head aches! My head aches!" She didn't know there were coals on her head. Then she thought she heard some one moving around. Picking up a club, she raised it and ran toward the noise screaming, "I'll kill you! I'll kill you!" She struck out and nearly hit HANÍSHÉONO^n.

He was frightened; he thought, "She will kill me if I

211

stay here. I'll get away." He left the cabin and traveled on. At last he came to another cabin. Looking through a crack he saw an old blind man, and thought, "I'll have sport with him."

As soon as Haníshéono^n was in the house, he took up a bucket, that stood there full of water, and poured the water on to the old man's head.

"What a rain!" said the old man. "My house leaks. I'll go to a corner where it is dry," and getting up he went to the other end of the cabin. Haníshéono^n followed him and poured more water on his head.

"It leaks here, too!" said the old man. "I'll sit where I was before and I'll smoke."

Taking a pipe out of a pouch he put tobacco into it and lighted it. Haníshéono^n poured water into the pipe and put out the fire.

"I thought there was fire in my pipe," said the old man.

He got a second coal. Haníshéono^n poured water into the pipe a second time. A third time the old man put in a coal and that time Haníshéono^n let him smoke, but he took a black flint and struck him on the thigh, saying, "That's the way I do when I want some one to stop."

Then he went out and set the old man's house on fire, saying, "I'll burn him up, I don't want blind men around here."

The old man said, "It's hot here. I think my house is burning. I don't want to be burnt to death," and taking a flint knife he stabbed himself in the breast; blood gushed out and ran across the hut.

When nothing was left of the hut but coals, Haníshéono^n saw that a stream of blood came from under the coals and flowed toward the West. (The door of the hut opened to the West). Right away the blood turned to the old man; he was alive again. Haníshéono^n said to him, "If you want to stay alive you must live under the ground." The old man crawled into the ground.

This is why angleworms are in the ground now.

Haníshéono^n went on till he came to a house where another old man lived and going in, he said, "Uncle, I've come to visit you."

"I'm glad that you've come, Nephew; I get lonesome sometimes."

"Haven't you a game to play?" asked HANÍSHÉONOⁿ.

"I have no game."

"Well, I have one," and taking hold of the old man, HANÍSHÉONOⁿ began to pull him to pieces. He pulled off his arms and legs, and killed him. Then he made up his mind to bring him to life and he began to put the pieces together. As he joined the pieces he pulled them out and when the man came to life he was very long and thin, and HANÍSHÉONOⁿ said, "You are OTGÓNDAHEⁿ (Red Belly, a snake)."

HANÍSHÉONOⁿ went off toward the West and coming to a house he walked in and looked around. A man was sitting by the fire.

HANÍSHÉONOⁿ said, "Uncle, I've come to visit you."

"Very well," said the man, "I'm lonesome."

"Why do you live here?"

"I like to track game."

"Do you catch any?"

"Yes, I've just caught a deer."

"Where is your trap?"

"Down in Open Rocks."

"Come and show it to me."

They went out together and HANÍSHÉONOⁿ found that at a place where large rocks nearly met at one end, the man had suspended a tree in such a way that if it were touched by an animal trying to pass, it would fall and catch it.

"Try it yourself," said the man.

HANÍSHÉONOⁿ didn't think it was much of a trap; he laughed at it, but when he tried to go under the tree he was caught. The man let him out, but HANÍSHÉONOⁿ was angry. He threw the old man down, jumped on him and killed him, then said, "I'll fix him up again, but I don't want to make another snake." He broke each arm into two pieces and each leg into four pieces, pulled out the body, made it longer, and put three legs on each side, and small bits of the arms on the man's face, one each side of his nose. Then he said, "I've finished you!" He had changed the man into an *Ongwe'*.

This time HANÍSHÉONOⁿ went toward the West. After

a while he came to a clean, beautiful forest—there was no underbrush—and seeing a house he went to it and found an old woman sitting by a fire.

"I've come to visit you," said HANÍSHÉONO^n.

"I don't want you to visit me, I don't like you," said the woman.

"Why do you live here?" asked HANÍSHÉONO^n.

"To watch. If I see a man, I kill him."

"That is wrong," said HANÍSHÉONO^n. "I'm going around to fix this world over. If I see people doing wrong I punish them," and catching the old woman by the hair, he pulled her out of the house. She was very angry and HANÍSHÉONO^n was afraid of her. He ran off and she after him. When she overtook him he began to cry and beg. The woman said, "You began this, now I'll kill you."

HANÍSHÉONO^n picked up a large piece of flint and threw it at her head; it bounded back and hit him. He fell over, but soon sprang up and threw a second stone. This time he killed the woman.

"I'll not bring her to life," said he, and he pounded the body till it was a mass of blood and bones. Then he sat down and watched a little stream of blood that came from the mass. When the blood dried, a very small thin insect came from it. "I didn't kill you, after all," said HANÍSHÉONO^n. "Now you can live forever and I'll call you SEHDO^{n}HGWADE" (Wood-tick). She was a mosquito before.

When HANÍSHÉONO^n came to another house, he heard some one singing. He stood at one side of the house and listened. The song said, "HANÍSHÉONO^n is walking around this earth. HANÍSHÉONO^n is walking around this earth."

"Somebody is singing about me," thought HANÍSHÉONO^n.

The singing stopped and he heard a man say, "Last night I dreamed that HANÍSHÉONO^n came here and was standing outside."

"How does he know that I'm standing outside?" thought HANÍSHÉONO^n.

He went in, and said, "Yes, I'm here."

The man laughed, and asked, "Which way did you come?"

"I came out of the ground. Wouldn't you like a new blanket?" asked Haníshéono^n.

"I would like a new blanket, mine is worn out."

Haníshéono^n got some slate stone, dug out two small bowls and gave them to him.

"How can I wear these?" asked the man.

"I'll fix them," said Haníshéono^n, and he put one on each side of the man's back and fastened them on so they couldn't come off. And the man, who had been a wood-worm before, was changed to a June-bug.

"Now I have finished my work," said Haníshéono^n, and he went home to the hole in the ground under the center of the Blue. He was a great power and that was why he was called Haníshéono^n. Whenever he came out of his house under the ground, he chased people and changed them to something worse than they were before.

Haníshéono^n stayed at home a long time. One morning he heard steps and he said to himself, "Somebody is coming to visit me." Soon there was a kick at the door and a woman came in. "You are at home," said she.

"I am."

"You have been doing bad things," said the woman. "I don't want you to harm people. I gave you power and if you don't stop making bad use of it, I will punish you."

"I shan't stop doing as I am doing, for I am doing right."

The woman was angry. She threw flint stones at Haníshéono^n, hit him on the head and stunned him, then she pounded him till his bones were crushed.

"Now," said she, "You'll be this way forever."

She had taken his power away and changed him to a common muckworm.

The narrator says that Haníshéono^n was an evil spirit and that spirits like him are still walking around in the world.

STONE COAT, COLD AND FROST

Character

GÉNOⁿSKWA.........Stone Coat (Cold and Frost)

A LONG time ago some Senecas went out to hunt. A Stone Coat came to their camp and said, "I want to stay in your camp. If you will let me stay, you will have good luck." The hunters let him stay and from that time on they had great luck.

When it was time for them to go home, Stone Coat said, "I will pack up each man's load of meat and skins." They had dried meat, buckskins, and fur.

Stone Coat packed in a bundle what he thought each man could carry, then he shook the bundle till it became small. He told the men when they got home to throw the bundles on the ground and they would be as large as when he packed them.

Then he bade them good-bye, saying, "I hope you will come here next Winter and we can be together again."

The next Winter those hunters went to the same hunting ground. A young Stone Coat came to their camp, and said, "My father has sent me to bring one of your party to his place."

One of the men volunteered to go.

"Maybe," said he, "we will live longer by doing as he wishes." And he went with the young Stone Coat.

When they came to Stone Coat's house the old man said, "My son, I sent for you because I want you to marry my daughter. You need not be afraid, I will make my people understand that they are not to harm you."

The man married Stone Coat's daughter.

The old man got something that looked like a bone and

216

rubbed it over his son-in-law's hands, feet and body, then told him to go hunting. The young man felt himself grow strong and felt that he could carry anything he laid his eyes on.

There was a young Stone Coat who loved the old man's daughter and had wanted to marry her. He was angry at the Seneca and going to him, he said, "You and I must have a foot-race. If I outrun you and win I will cut off your head and take your wife. If you win you may cut off my head."

When the day came for the race, all of the Stone Coat people assembled.

The father-in-law said to the Seneca, "You needn't be afraid, I will help you." And taking a substance out of a stone box he rubbed it over the young man's body.

The opponents locked hands and ran. When they reached a certain small tree they were to let go of hands and run on, but Stone Coat held to the young man's hand till they had bent down the hemlock tree and were nearly at the end of it, then Stone Coat let go. The tree sprang up and sent the Seneca a long distance back beyond the crowd, but he hurried forward, outran Stone Coat and cut off his head.

RAIN OLD MAN AND THE HORNED SNAKE
(LIGHTNING)

ONCE, when the Senecas were at war with the Cherokees, they got very hungry and seeing a bear they
chased it till it came to a den and one of the men followed
it into the den. When some distance in, he no longer
saw the bear but he saw a fire and around it a number of
men. A very old man looked up, and asked, "Why did
you try to shoot one of my men? I sent him out to entice
you to us. I want to send word to the oldest man in your
camp. Tell him from me that his friend is here and in
need of tobacco. To-morrow as many of your people as
care to can come to us."

The young man went back to camp and the next day
five of his companions, each with a pouch of tobacco went
to the den. When they gave the tobacco to the old man,
he was glad, and said, "This will last me a long time."

One of the men in the den said, "I am tired."

"Lie down," said the old man.

He lay down. The old man got up and going to him
rubbed his body from the feet to the top of the head. Then,
putting down a vessel he had been holding in his hand,
he unjointed every joint in the man's body and cut the
body to pieces. He put each piece into a mortar and taking a pestle pounded the flesh and bones to jelly and
poured the mass into a bowl. Then he took the bowl and
the other vessel to another part of the den. After a time
he came back, sat down and began to smoke.

Soon he called, "Come out, Nephew, you have slept long
enough."

When the man came out, he looked as light and fresh
as a young boy.

One of the Senecas asked, "Can you do this for me?"

"I can," said the old man, "if you want me to."

The Seneca lay down and the old man did with him

exactly as he had with the other man. After he had carried the two vessels to another part of the den he came back and began to smoke. Soon he called, "Come out, Nephew, you have slept long enough."

The man rose up and came out fresh and young. He felt no weight in his body.

Another Seneca asked to be treated in the same way, the old man consented, and he too came out light and young.

A third Seneca asked the old man to change him, but he refused, saying, "I have done enough, now I will tell you why I did this. There is a wide opening extending from one end of the world to the other. In this opening there is a great rock and in the rock is a person with enormous horns. He is our enemy and we have tried to kill him, but cannot. I want the men, whom I have made young and strong, to try and crush the rock and destroy this person. But first you two must test your strength."

The two went outside and shot at a rock; it crumbled to pieces. They shot at a large tree; it fell to the ground, only a stump was left.

"Now," said the old man, "you may go to the opening and see what you can do. You will never die for *we* never die. Your companions can stay here. I always help my grandchildren. I cover their trail whenever they need to hide it. It is I who makes rain come."

The two went to the opening and seeing the rock, shot at it. Then they went back to the old man.

He asked, "Did you use all of your strength?"

"We could have struck harder," said one of the men.

"Go back," said the old man, "and use all of your strength."

This time they struck the rock with all their strength. After listening a while they heard someone coming, and soon saw a man and, strapped on his back was the head of an enormous horned snake—they had killed the snake.

The two men said, "Our work is done, Rain Old Man's enemy, the great horned snake, is dead."

And they went back to their camp.

WHIRLWIND AND HER HUSBAND

[Told·by Peter White]

Character

DAGWANOEⁿYENT .... Whirlwind

AN old man and his nephew lived together in a bark house in the woods. The old man made the boy live on fungus and told him always to go South to find it, he must never go toward the North.

Each day the uncle went off hunting, but he never brought home any game. He lived on chestnut pudding and bear's oil.

For a long time the nephew couldn't find out how his uncle made the pudding, but one day he discovered that the old man had a little kettle, that he put a speck of chestnut in the kettle and then said, "Swell kettle! Swell kettle!" And soon he had a good sized kettle and it was full of pudding.

The next day, after his uncle had gone hunting, the young man found the kettle and had a good meal of pudding and each day after that, as soon as his uncle was out of sight, he made pudding.

The young man began to wonder why his uncle always cautioned him not to go North, and after thinking over it a while he made up his mind to find out. He started and traveled till he came to a house. In the house he found a supply of deer and bear meat hanging up around the walls, and many skins full of bear's oil. A woman sat in the middle of the room, with her head bent down. A

220

little boy was crawling around. When the boy saw the young man, he clapped his hands and laughed.

The woman took no notice of what was going on. The young man played a while with the child, then started for home taking along a piece of meat that he had hidden under his blanket.

Things went on in this way for a number of years. The uncle started off to hunt. The young man went to the long house and played with the boy. The woman never moved or spoke.

The boy was perhaps fifteen years old when one day he said to the young man, "You and I are cousins. Your uncle is my father and this woman sitting here is my mother."

The young man asked, "Why does she never speak?"

The boy didn't know. The young man asked the woman different questions but she wouldn't answer. Then he took his bow and shot an arrow at a skin of bear's oil which hung above her head. The arrow cut the skin and the oil ran out and fell on to the woman's head and face. She was very angry, but she didn't speak.

The meat in the house was game that the uncle brought. He came late in the day, after his nephew had gone home. So in all those years they never met at the long house. That evening when the uncle came and found the skin broken and the oil spilt over the woman's head, he suspected that his nephew had been there.

When he reached home, he asked, "Have you been at the long house?"

"I have," said the nephew. "I have been there every day for many years. I have eaten meat there. I haven't eaten fungus for a long time."

"Did you break the skin and let the oil out?"

"I did," said the nephew.

"You have done great harm," said the uncle, "That woman is full of witchcraft. She will destroy us."

The next morning the old man started off as usual. The young man stayed at home, he was angry. He raised the cover of the couch, took out the little kettle, put water into it and a large piece of chestnut. When the water boiled, he began to strike the kettle, and say, "Swell kettle! Swell kettle!" The kettle came up as high as the couch. The young man stood on the couch, when the kettle rose higher he got on to the shelf, when it was as high as the shelf, he went out of the smoke-hole on to the roof.

He enjoyed the increase of the pudding, thinking how angry his uncle would be when he came home.

When the old man came, he asked, "What have you been doing; making chestnut pudding?"

"That is an old habit with me. I have been eating chestnut pudding for years."

"You have destroyed us both," said the uncle, who was very angry. "You have enraged the woman and now she will never stop till she kills us."

The next morning, just at daybreak, they heard a terrible noise off in the direction of the long house. Trees began to moan. The sound grew louder and louder, then came the cracking of limbs and the falling of trees. An awful storm was coming, and the woman was in the middle of the storm. She swept over the house, tore it from the ground, caught up the uncle and carried him away. The nephew had hidden, she didn't find him.

That day the young man went to the long house, as usual. The woman was sitting there silent and motionless, as if nothing had happened. He asked the boy what his mother had done with his father.

"I don't know what she has done with him," said the boy. "She went off with him and came back without him. To-morrow she will come for you."

The young man went home to make ready for the woman's coming. He had a mole for his medicine; he crept into the mole and the mole went deep into the ground under the torn-down house.

In the morning the woman came with terrible fury, uprooting all the trees in her path, but she couldn't find the young man. After she had gone, he came from his hiding place and went to the long house. The woman sat there as silent and motionless as before.

"Where were you this morning?" asked the boy. "My mother couldn't find you."

"I was right there under the house."

When he went home, he prepared for the storm and at

daylight the next morning it came. He was in the mole and the mole was in the ground and the woman didn't find him. At last she made herself into a whirlwind, whirled around and around. Then swooping down, she dug a deep hole in the earth, lifted the ground and went to the sky, carrying the mole along in the dirt. The mole fell and the young man was killed. The woman went home satisfied.

The mole breathed into the young man's mouth and by putting breath in and drawing it out brought him to life, and right away he set out to find his uncle. He went beyond the long house, traveled as fast as he could all day and all night, carrying the mole with him.

The next morning at daybreak the woman came with a terrible storm. The young man went into the mole and under the ground and when the woman couldn't find him she went back to the long house.

The young man traveled a second day and night. The next morning the woman came again with a terrible storm. She found where her nephew was and scooping up the earth she carried him far into the sky. The mole fell to the ground, the young man was killed and the woman went home, satisfied.

The mole brought the young man to life, and, putting the mole in his belt, he ran on as fast as he could. That night he slept deep in the ground between two great rocks on a mountain. At daybreak the woman came, but she couldn't find him. That day the young man traveled till he came to a house in an opening, and near the house, under the roots of a great elm, he found his uncle. The tree was standing on his breast. The old man was only skin and bones, but as soon as he saw his nephew he begged for a smoke.

"Poor uncle," said the young man, "I'll give you a smoke." He pushed the tree over, got the old man out and gave him a pipe and tobacco. As soon as he had smoked, he was well and strong.

The next morning the woman came again. By watching, the nephew had discovered that she came in a narrow path and that it was possible to get away from her. He told his uncle to run toward the West and keep out of the path, then he went into the mole and the mole went under the ground. The woman became a whirlwind, scooped up the ground and carried the mole to the sky. The mole fell and the young man was killed, but, as before, the mole brought him to life. He followed the woman to the long house and found her sitting there silent and motionless. He shot an arrow at her and killed her. Then he gathered a pile of dry bark and wood, poured bear's oil over it, put the body on the pile and burned it up and throwing the charred bones in every direction, he said to the boy, "We will go to my uncle."

They found the old man in the second long house and they stayed there for a time. But the woman came to life, and suspecting they were at the long house she went there in a terrible rage.

The young man sent his uncle and the boy away. He had found out the woman's habits and strength. He knew that, after a certain force was spent, she became weak and couldn't travel fast. While she was a whirlwind, he stayed out of her path. When she hadn't found him and her strength was used up, she turned to go home, but she had to travel slowly. She could no longer go through the air. The young man followed her and killed her with an arrow, then he called his uncle and the boy. The three piled up wood, built a great fire and burned the body to ashes, then picking up the bones they carried them to the long house and pounded them to powder. This powder the young man divided into three parts and put into three skin bags and tied each bag up tight. One bag he gave to his uncle, one he gave to his cousin, and the third he put into his own pouch, saying, "I will keep it here. She shall never come to life again. When we are out in a storm we must always stand apart so that the force in these powders cannot unite."

They went to their first home and soon there was a house and a supply of every kind of dried meat, and the three lived together and were happy.

Peter White said that the Indians used to think that all trees came from the pine tree. That once the pine trees got to disputing, quarreling over which was the tallest and which was the strongest and which had the most power. One tree declared that he had; another said he had. At last one lofty pine got so angry that he struck his nephew on the head and pressed him down with such strength that he crowded his branches together and spread them out. After that the nephew was a hemlock. All hemlocks came from this pine which the wrath of the great pine had maimed and spread out.

THE BIRD MEDICINE

A SENECA named Bloody Hand had great love for the birds of the air that ate flesh and for the animals of the earth that ate flesh. When he killed a deer, he cut the flesh into pieces and called birds to eat it, or he gave it to the wolves. Sometimes he carried home a small piece, but usually he gave all of the pieces to the birds and beasts.

The Senecas went on the war-path and this man went with them. He was killed and scalped. The birds of the air saw him and they held a council. One said, "We can bring him to life if we can get his scalp. The man who killed him has hung up the scalp by the door of his house. We will send for it."

They sent Hawk. Hawk's bill was sharp and strong. He twisted the scalp from the place where it was tied and carried it to the birds.

One of the birds said, "Now we will make medicine and to find out how strong it is, we'll try to bring that tree to life that is lying over there on the ground."

In this bird medicine was a bit of the flesh of each of the birds.[1]

When making the medicine, the birds caused a corn stalk to come up out of the ground. They broke the stalk and in it was blood. They put some of the blood in their medicine, healed the stalk and it disappeared.

They caused a squash vine to come out of the ground and right away there were squashes on the vine, they used some of the seeds for their medicine, and the vine disappeared.

When the medicine was ready, part of the birds sat on one side of the tree and part on the other side and they sang their medicine song and sprinkled medicine on the tree and the ground.

[1] They were birds of the ancient time, not such birds as live now.

Above the clouds is a great bird called SKADA'GÉA, In-the-Mist, he is chief of all birds; they sent the head man of the Ravens to tell him what they were doing—this is why Ravens always sing "Caw! Caw!" when flying—The Eagle is a chief under the great bird above.

When the birds saw that the tree was getting green and coming to life the leader said, "This is enough, we know how our medicine will act. Now we must appoint some one to carry it into our friend's body."

They chose Chickadee. Chickadee drank the medicine then went into the man's mouth and down into his stomach; threw the medicine out and came back.

The other birds rubbed the man's body with medicine, sat around him and sang. They sang two days and two nights then found that the body was growing warm.

All at once the man, who had been dead, felt as though he had been wakened from sleep. He heard singing and he listened. He understood the words of the song. He moved a little; the birds drew back, but kept singing.

The chief of the birds said to the man, "We have brought you to life, now we will give you some of our medicine. If any of your people are wounded by an arrow or bruised by a fall use the medicine and right away they will be well. When you use it, burn tobacco and think of us."

"When you think of us and come together and burn tobacco you will renew and strengthen the medicine. When the tobacco is burning call out, 'Let all the beasts and birds on earth smell this tobacco.'"

Bloody Hand went home, selected a few men and gave to each one of them a little of the bird medicine, taught them how to use it and how to sing the songs. He said, "You must never laugh at these songs. If you laugh at them, bad luck will come to you. No one may sing the songs unless he has the medicine; the songs would be poison (*otgo*[n]) for him."

Solomon O'Bail, an old Indian on the Cattaraugus Reservation, had, in 1883, about a tablespoonful of this bird medicine, in the form of dust. When using it, he put a particle at the east side of a cup, another particle on the west side and another on the side towards the sick man's lips, then poured water into the cup. If all the dust remained on top of the water, the sick man would live; if it sank to the bottom he would die. If it mixed with the water and dissolved, he would recover. If it dissolved, the patient drank the liquid.

The medicine is so powerful that the sick man after drinking it can eat only pure white food, such as white beans and white corn; the odor of meat cooking is bad for him. When a man is sick, the family hang a blanket in front of him so they will have time to find where a caller has been. For if he has stopped on the way to look at a dead person, the sick man will die at once.

The beginning of the bird song is, ''Now this is the medicine to take. Now this is the medicine to take.'' When the medicine is swallowed the song says, ''Now it begins to work. Now it begins to work; to work all over his body.''

The man who gives the medicine sings and dances, saying, ''They (the Spirits) have come and cured the sick man, and I let them go with thanks. I have got to the field, I have got to the mountain, I have got to the falls; I have got beyond the clouds. Now we are together where the tobacco is.''

When a sick man wants to take the bird medicine, he must give a handful of Indian tobacco to the man who has it. That man will put a bit of the tobacco in the fire and say to the medicine as he holds it in his hand, ''Smell of the tobacco for I am going to use you.'' Then taking a cup he goes to running water, gives some of the water to the stream, pronounces the sick man's name, and dipping the cup down stream, takes what water it gets, this water he uses to try the medicine in.

HAGOWANE AND HIS TEN SONS

Characters

HÓNGÂK ....Wild Geese
HAGOWANE
OTHÄGWE^{n}DA ....Flint
O^{n}WE^{n}AUNT ....Blue Snake
DAGWANOE^{n}YENT .... Whirlwind
DJIÄYE^n ....Spider
GASYONDETHA ....Meteor
TSODI′QGWADO^n ....Snake
DEWAQSO^{n}THWÛS ....Flea
HANÓWA ....Turtle
DÕ′NYONDA ....Eagle
HADIA′DES ....Black-snake

A T HETGE^{n}GASTENDE lived a man of great power named
HAGOWANE. He belonged to the Eagle family. One
day this man started off to hunt. Taking his canoe he
sailed across the lake in front of his house and leaving
the canoe traveled for five days toward the West, then he
collected wood and made a camp. The first day he hunted,
he killed five bears and six deer, brought them to camp
and said to himself, "I have had bad luck to-day."

The second day he killed ten bears and twelve deer and
brought them to camp. That night he skinned and roasted
the fifteen bears and eighteen deer and finished the work
before daylight.

The next day he went for more game. He killed twenty-four deer and twenty bears, brought them to camp, skinned and roasted them, finishing exactly at midnight. Then he said to himself, "I have enough now."

Putting the meat into one pile he tied it up with bark strings and shook it, saying, "I want you to be small." It shrank to a little package that he hung to his belt. In the same way, he made the skins into a small package that he hung to his belt. Then he set out for home.

When HAGOWANE came to the lake he looked everywhere for his canoe, but couldn't find it. He saw a man coming toward him.

When they met, the man asked, "What have you lost?"

"I have lost my canoe," answered HAGOWANE.

"The man who lives on that island over there was here yesterday. He took your canoe."

"Who is the man?"

"He is one of the Turtle family."

"How can I get my canoe?"

"Give me what meat you have and I will get it for you."

"What am I to eat if I do that?"

"Well, I will do better. I will bring the canoe if you will take your meat home, keep half and put the other half outside your house for me."

"Very well," answered HAGOWANE.

The man himself had taken the canoe to the island and now he brought it back, "That man on the island," said he, "is an ugly fellow; he nearly killed me."

When HAGOWANE got home, he drew the canoe to a place of safety among the rocks. Then he took the packages of meat from his belt, untied and threw them down. That minute they regained their natural size. He piled the meat up inside of his house and tanned the skins, but he didn't pay HANDZOYAS for bringing back the canoe.

After a time a woman of the Wild Goose family came to HAGOWANE's house bringing a basket of bread. She said, "My mother sent me to ask you to take me for a wife."

The man hung his head a while, thinking. At last he said to himself, "I suppose nothing bad will come of this." Then he looked at the girl, and said, "I am willing."

The girl was glad. She placed the marriage bread before him. He ate some of it, and said, "I am thankful. I have not tasted of bread for many years."

The two lived happily. Each year for ten years a son was born to them.

Then one morning when HAGOWANE was sitting on a rock outside the house, he said to himself, "I am tired of staying here, I am going away."

He sat in his canoe and rowed across the lake. After a time his wife missed him. She looked everywhere, but could get no trace of him.

When the eldest boy was almost a young man, he said to his mother, "I am going to search for my father till I find out where he is."

"You will get lost on the way," said his mother.

"Oh, no, I will not," replied he.

After a time the mother gave her consent and the boy set out traveling always toward the North. While crossing a rocky place, he came upon a trail. "These footprints look like my father's," thought he, and he followed them. Soon he came to a cross trail, "I wonder where this comes from and where it goes," thought he. "When I come back, I will find out."

Not far from the cross trail, the boy saw a house and as the trail he was following entered it, he went in and looking around saw one old man in the south-east corner, another in the south-west, a third in the north-west and a fourth in the north-east corner and each one was smoking.

The first old man raised his head, looked at the boy and asked, "Well, my grandson, what are you doing here? If you want to see your father come to me, I will show him to you."

The boy went to him, the old man seized him by the hair, bent his head over a bark bowl and cut it off.

"I am glad of young game," said he, "It must be worth eating, it is just the right age," and he began to cut up the body.

At home they waited long for tidings from the eldest brother. When none came, the second son said, "I must go and find my brother."

"Oh, my son," said the mother, "do not go, some misfortune has befallen your brother."

"I must go," answered the boy. "I cannot help going. I want to find my father and my brother," and he made ready for the journey. He put on a shirt, leggings and moccasins of meteor skin and took bow and arrows. The mother cried but she couldn't prevent his going.

He went North, as his brother had done, followed the same trail till he came to the cross trail and went into the house where the four old men were sitting.

The old man in the north-west corner called out, "My grandson, do you want to see your father? Come here."

The boy went and looking into a bowl half full of water saw the face of his father and the face of his brother. Then the old man seized him by the hair and cut off his head.

Nine of the brothers went, one after another, and all were killed by the four old men in the house near the cross trail. Then Yellow Flint, the tenth and youngest son, though he was still small and young, said to his mother, "I must follow my brothers."

"Oh, my son," said the mother, "you cannot go. There are four old men living near the trail. They are called HADIA'DES. They have great power."

"But I must go. I want to find my father and my brothers."

"You will never see them again, they are dead."

"Can't I kill those old men?"

"Maybe you can, if I give you my power."

"Give it to me. I must kill them."

"I will go and bring it," said the mother.

She went West to a rough and rocky place and came back with a slate rock mannikin about half the length of her little finger.

"Here," said she, "put this mannikin between your belt and your body and you can do what you like; you can change yourself to whatever form you please."

The boy put the mannikin between his belt and his body, took a bow made of hickory and arrows of red willow pointed with wasp stings, and went toward the North, as his brothers had. He found a fresh trail, and thought, "Maybe this is my father's trail." After a while he came to the cross trail running from east to west. He stood still and thought, "Where does this trail come from and where does it go? I will find out."

He went toward the East till he came to a wide opening and saw a cloud of dust moving toward him. "I must hurry back," said he to himself, "or something may happen to me."

When he turned, the great cloud approached quickly. Soon it touched him and he grew so weak that he fell to the ground. Looking up he saw a long-legged person rushing on. He sprang to his feet, climbed a tree and shot off a wasp sting-pointed arrow. The arrow hit the man in the cloud and killed him. The long-legged stranger was Djiäye^n (Spider).

The boy went East again, another cloud of dust rushed toward him, but he turned aside. After the cloud passed, he ran on till he came to the place where the trails crossed and going northward from there came to the house where the four old men sat smoking. After standing outside a while, he found a crack and looking in saw the brothers.

"I wonder if those are the men that my mother told me about," thought he, "I will kill them if I can, if I can't I will burn down their house."

He took the mannikin from his belt and placed it on his hand. It stood up and he said to it, "I am going to ask you a question. I want to kill those old men, how am I to do it?"

The mannikin said, "You must climb that high rock over there and call out, 'I, Othägwe^{n}da, am on this high rock!' You will find sharp flint stones up there. Take a handful of them and throwing them toward the house say, 'I want it to be hot.'"

The boy put the mannikin in his belt and listened to the conversation of the old men.

One said, "I think Othägwe^{n}da is around here."

"Oh," replied the man in the south-east corner. "You said that all the family were dead."

"I think a little boy is left," said the old man in the south-west corner.

"I think they are all dead except the old woman," said the man in the north-east corner.

"Well," said the old man in the north-west corner,

"It seems to me that one is lurking around here some-where."

"If you think so, hunt for him," said the old man in the south-west.

OTHÄGWE^{n}DA sprang on to the house and sat with his feet in the smoke-hole.

The old man looked all around, but could find no one.

The boy drew his bow and shot through the smoke-hole, shot each one of the brothers. The arrows went deep into their bodies, but the men were not hurt. They didn't know that they had been hit.

The boy sprang from the house and landed far away, then he climbed the rock and called out, "I, OTHÄGWE^{n}DA, am on this high rock!" He heard one of the brothers say, "My back is sore. I feel as though my bones were broken."

The boy picked up a handful of sharp flint stones and threw them at the house, saying, "I want you to be red hot and burn up those old men and their house."

The flints went straight to the house; a few pieces went beyond. Those that struck the house set it on fire; those that fell beyond burned the forest; everything was blazing in and around the place. Then the boy threw a second handful of flints, saying, "I want you to cut off the heads of those old men." The flint struck each man's neck in such a way that his head dropped off.

The boy stood on the rock and watched the fire till only coals remained. All at once there was an explosion and Whirlwind, a great head, flew towards him, knocked him off of the rock and rising high in the air went straight West.

The boy sprang to his feet and looking up saw Whirl-wind going higher and higher. Soon he heard a crash as Whirlwind struck the Blue, then the head came down again. When it reached the ground, OTHÄGWE^{n}DA ran forward quickly and crushed it with a white flint stone.

The boy searched through the coals, with a pointed stick. At the north-west corner of the coals of the house he came upon a trail running towards the north-west, and he fol-lowed it till he came to an opening. A cloud of dust rushed toward him. He ran into the forest and waited.

The cloud stopped at the edge of the forest, and from it came an enormous Spider.

"Oh," said the Spider, "I thought somebody was on the trail. My master is fooling me. I thought he had found another one of the Goose family."

Spider turned back, running as fast as he could. The boy followed till Spider reached a house which was sunken in the ground. The boy listened outside and soon he heard some one crying. He thought, "That sounds like my father's voice; he must be in there."

He took out the mannikin, placed it on his hand. It came to life, stood up, and the boy asked, "How am I to kill the Spider that lives in this house?"

"Go to a tree just west of here," said the mannikin, "Climb to the top of it, and call out, 'I am Othägwe^{n}da, and I am more powerful than anything under the Blue, I can kill any kind of game on earth.' When you have spoken these words, cut a limb from the tree, throw it towards the house and tell it to split open Spider's heart; the heart is in the ground under the house. When Spider is dead, rescue your father and burn the house."

The boy did as the mannikin said. He cut off a limb of the tree, spat on it, and straightway it was alive and he threw it towards the house, saying, "Split Spider's heart in two."

The limb went under the house to where the heart was hidden. That instant Spider stretched out and died. The boy slipped down from the tree and went to the house. Spider lay dead in the middle of the room. Under the couch lay a man who seemed to be almost dead. Othägwe^{n}da raised the couch and found his father. The flesh was gone from his legs and arms and he was barely alive.

"My father," said the boy, "You must go home."

"My son," said Hagowane, "You will die if you stay here."

"There is no danger now," answered the boy.

Then he put the mannikin on his hand and asked, "What shall I do with my father?"

The mannikin answered, "Rub saliva over him and flesh will come on his bones."

The boy did this and his father was as strong and well as ever.

"Now," said he, "I am Hodio^{n}sko^n (the Trickster). I have heard old people say that when he dies he comes to life again. We will go home."

"You can go," said Othägwe^{n}da, "but I must find my brothers."

When Hagowane reached home, his wife looked at him and cried, "Oh, my dear son, I wish you were here. I have seen something strange."

"Why do you talk in that way?" asked Hagowane. "Why do you cry? Are you sorry that I have come?"

"You are not alive."

"Yes, I am."

"No, you are not." And thinking he was a ghost she drove him on to the rocks, and there he had to stay.

After his father had gone, the boy burned Spider's house. When only coals were left, something shot up and flew westward. It alighted on the plain and became a Sandpiper.

"This is the way I do, this is why I say that I can kill anybody," cried the boy, and going around the edge of the opening on the eastern side he found a broad trail and followed it till he came to a cross trail. He stood at the four corners of the two trails, one going North and South, the other East and West, put the mannikin on his hand, and said, "I want you to tell me what I am to do."

"At the foot of that tree over there you will find a bark bowl; beyond the tree is a medicine spring; on the other side of the spring a plant is growing. Put the plant in the bowl and fill the bowl with water from the spring. Here, where the trail crosses, dig a hole and put the bowl into it with the plant standing in the water. Then stay close by and see what will happen."

The boy put the mannikin away and went to the pine tree that grew in the north-west, between the northern and western trails. He found the spring and farther on a plant with bright red blossoms. He did as the mannikin had told him to, then put the bowl in the ground at the crossing of the trails and standing aside watched and listened.

Soon he heard a noise in the forest like a heavy wind coming from the North. Nearer and nearer it came, with a terrible cloud of dust, and nothing could be seen till the cloud stopped at the crossing. Then, in the middle of it, the boy saw the skeleton of Blue Lizard. The skeleton walked up to the plant and ate one of its red blossoms. Though the skeleton had no place to hide the blossom, it vanished. The boy wondered greatly. "It is nothing but bones," thought he, "Where does food go?"

The skeleton grew sick. It jumped around till arms, legs, head and ribs fell apart.

OTHÄGWE^{n}DA laughed, but just then he heard the noise of a heavy wind and saw it coming from the South, with a great cloud of dust. The cloud stopped at the crossing and the boy saw the skeleton of Snake. It went to the bowl and ate a blossom. That minute it began to shake and soon it fell to pieces, became a pile of bones. Then a terrible wind came from the East and stopped at the crossing. In the middle of the cloud of dust was the skeleton of NYAGWAIHE, the Ancient of Bears. It ate a blossom and then began to tremble and to disjoint; soon it was only a pile of bones. From the West came the skeleton of the Ancient of Winged Snakes. When it had turned to bones the boy put the mannikin on his hand, and asked, "Is it finished?"

"It is," said the mannikin. "All the trails are clear. If you go to the end of the southern trail you will find three of your brothers."

When the boy came to the end of the southern trail, he couldn't see anything, but after looking around a while, he found a rock with an opening in it. He went to the opening and down into the ground. It was dark there and he thought, "Maybe there are other skeletons here, but I must go on."

At last he came to a place where there was no fire but a plenty of light, and just beyond he found three of his brothers. The eldest called out, "Oh, my brother, you must hurry away, the skeleton will come soon."

"I will kill it," said the boy.

"My brother, if you stay here, you will not live."

"I have come to take you away," said OTHÄGWE^{n}DA.

"We cannot walk," answered the three. "The skeleton has eaten our flesh."

The boy looked at his brothers and saw that their legs and arms were simply bones. He rubbed the bones with saliva and they were covered with flesh.

"You must go home," said OTHÄGWEⁿDA. "I am going for my other brothers."

The three went home. When their mother saw them, she cried out, and, thinking them ghosts, seized a club and drove them away. They found their father and sat on the rock with him.

The boy went back to the crossing and followed the eastern trail till he came to the end of it. At first he didn't see anything and he wondered where the Ancient of Bears came from. Then he found an opening in the ground and went down into it. "There must be other skeletons here," thought he, "but I must go on."

Soon he came to a place where there was a bright light from rotten wood which was packed up there, and farther on he found three of his brothers. All their flesh had been eaten and they were too weak to move; he brought flesh to their bones and sent them home. The mother drove them away as she had their father and brothers.

OTHÄGWEⁿDA went back to the crossing and followed the northern trail till he came to a small opening. While he was looking around, a whirlwind came upon him and he ran to the shelter of a maple tree that stood near by. Soon he heard a heavy blow on the opposite side of the tree. He looked and saw an Oⁿwɪ (Winged-snake), lying dead at the foot of the tree. Coming in the whirlwind, it had struck the tree and been killed.

The boy went to the edge of the opening but right away he heard a second whirlwind coming. "I shall die this time," thought he, for he saw that a great number of winged-snakes were in the whirlwind. He hid behind the tree and the whirlwind rushed by, then he ran to the other side of the opening.

The boy put the mannikin on his hand; it stood up, alive, and he asked, "What can I do with the snakes that are chasing me?"

"You must make a fire across the trail."

He gathered boughs and sticks, made a large, long pile, set fire to the west end of it, and said to the wind, "My grandfather, blow gently on the west end of this pile."

His grandfather heard him and soon there was a mighty fire. When it was burning fiercely the boy said, "Grandfather, let the breeze die down." Straightway it stopped blowing. When the whirlwind of snakes came again, the snakes were swept into the fire and every one of them perished.

Free of the snakes, the boy hurried along the northern trail till he saw a whirlwind going toward the north-east, then he took out the mannikin and asked, "Which way must I go?"

"North," answered the mannikin.

As the boy traveled along he saw a trail going toward the north-west, but he went straight ahead. When he came to the end of the trail he found an opening in the ground near a birch tree. He went into the opening and soon came to a place where an old man sat smoking. "What can that old man be doing?" thought he.

The old man straightened up, and said, "I am weak this morning. It seems to me that somebody is around here."

He raised his head and looked around and as he looked his eyes seemed to project from his head.

He saw Othägwe͏ⁿda, and said, "My nephew, I am glad that you have come. I will find out what luck you have."

He took a rattle made of a Dagwanoe͏ⁿyent and shook it, saying, "*Sáwa, Sáwa!*"

"Stop," said the boy. "I will try your luck first."

"No, my nephew, I will try first," said the old man whose name was Dewaqso͏ⁿthwûs (Flea). They disputed till they came to blows. The old man threw down his rattle and struck at the boy and his own arm fell off. He struck with the other hand and that arm fell off. Then he kicked at him with one leg and that fell off; with the other and that dropped. The old man was now only head and body. The arms and legs tried to get back to their places on the body, but the boy pushed them away and shot an arrow through the old man. The arrow took root and became a small tree. Flea tried to bite the boy but as he made the attempt his head flew off.

The boy pounded the body, jumped and danced around it, and said, "Oh, my uncle is in pieces now!"

In the old man's house he found the last three of his brothers, weak and wretched as the others had been. He cured them and sent them home. The mother drove them from the house and they sat down on the rock with their father and brothers.

After his brothers had gone OTHÄGWE^{n}DA took out the mannikin and asked, "Is there anything on the north-east trail?"

"You will rescue people if you go there," answered the mannikin.

"Is there anything bad on the north-west trail?"

"There is."

At the end of the north-west trail, the boy found a house without a door. "How can I get into this house," thought he. Looking through a crack he saw an old woman of the Blue Snake people; she was singing and the song said, "OTHÄGWE^{n}DA is coming. OTHÄGWE^{n}DA is coming!"

"She knows that I am here," thought the boy.

Presently she said, "I will go out and play a while."

The boy didn't see how the woman got out of the house, but all at once he saw her going along the trail that ran toward the West; he followed her. She went into a small lake and down deep in the water. Then he saw a tail come to the surface and begin to move around in a circle. On the tail were two little things like fins. They rubbed against each other and made beautiful music. In the water the old woman was a fish. After a while she came partly out of the water but seeing the boy she drew back, and said, "My grandson, don't kill me. I have never harmed any of your people."

"I will spare you if you will give me something that will be useful to me."

"I will give you a fin. Keep it to find your luck with."

"How can I use it?"

"When you lie down, put it under your head. You will have a dream and the dream will tell you what you want to know."

The boy went home with the old woman and looking around saw an opening in the ground and in it many people almost dead. He got them out, rubbed them with saliva, healed them and sent each man to his own home. When all had gone, he asked the old woman why she had captured these people and shut them up.

"I did not shut them up," said the woman. "My husband is a man-eater. He brought them here. He lives on another trail. His name is DEWAQSOⁿTHWÛS (The Weeper—Flea)."

"Was that man your husband? I have killed him."

"I am glad," said the woman. "Your people are safe now, for you have destroyed their greatest enemy."

OTHÄGWEⁿDA traveled on the north-east trail till he came to a house where he heard singing. The song said, "The youngest son of the HÓNGÂK (Goose) woman is going everywhere in the world. We wish he would come to us."

The song stopped and the woman said, "I feel badly. Let us go and throw rocks." They went to a place where there were white flint rocks as large as a house. The woman picked up one of the rocks and threw it into the air. It came down on her head, but didn't hurt her. Then she threw it to the man, who caught it and threw it back.

When tired of playing they went to the house. The man said, "I feel as though some one were here." Looking around he saw the boy, and he asked, "My grandson, what are you doing here?"

"I have come to visit you."

"My grandson," said the woman, "I am glad you have come, we have been waiting for you. You have killed the man-eater and the skeletons. Now we want you to free the men who are in an opening under our house."

The boy found many men in the opening which the man-eater had forced this man and woman to guard. He liberated them, and sent each man to his own home.

"Now," said OTHÄGWEⁿDA, "let all the trails disappear. Trails must not be made across the world to deceive people."

The trails disappeared, then the boy went home. When

he saw his father and nine brother sitting on a large flat rock he asked, "Why don't you go into the house?"

"Your mother wouldn't let us stay in the house; she drove us out," answered HAGOWANE.

The boy went into the house, and asked, "Mother, are you sorry that I found my father and my brothers?"

"Did you find them and send them home?"

"I did."

The woman was glad then. She welcomed her husband and sons. They came in, and all were happy.

COON DECEIVES CRAWFISH

[Told by Mrs. Sim Logan]

Characters

ODJÍE'DA ....Crawfish
DJOE'AGA? ....Coon

ONE day a coon was walking out. As he went slowly along the bank of a stream, he thought of his enemies, the crawfish, and wondered how he could kill them. At last he stood still and thought out a plan: he would go along the stream till he found a half-decayed log; he would take some of the soft, rotten wood, the punk of the log, and rub it over his face and around his eyes till he looked half-decayed himself, then he would wait for his enemies.

He hurried along and soon found a log. He rubbed his face with punk then stretched himself across the log, half of his body hanging down on one side and his head and neck on the other side. Lying in this lifeless way he looked as though he had been a long time dead.

By and by a crawfish, that was walking along and looking around, chanced to see Coon, and he thought, "There is a dead man!" He was surprised, and said in his own mind, "I'll go and see if he is really dead."

He went to the log. Coon did not stir. Flies were crawling over his face and body.

"Why, this is our enemy," said Crawfish, "and he is dead! This is good news to tell. I'll notify all of my people."

He started off immediately. When he thought he was near enough home to make some one hear, he screamed,

243

"*Go-gwa! go-gwa!*" then he ran on, every little while halt-
ing to scream "*Go-gwa! go-gwa!*"

Some one heard the cry and notified the chief that a
runner was coming with important news. The people went
to the edge of the village and waited. When the runner
came in sight, the chief said, "Let half of the people stand
on one side of the path and half on the other, that he
may come to me quickly."

When the runner stood in front of the chief of the
Crawfish nation the chief asked, "What news have you
brought?"

"Great news! As I came along the creek I saw, not very
far from here, a dead man hanging across a log, I went
to the log and found that the dead man was our great
enemy, Coon. He has been dead a long time, flies are
crawling over his face."

The chief said, "This is great news, the best we have
ever heard. Our enemy is dead! We will go and look at
him. The man who found him will lead us to the place."

Before starting they sang and as the song ended they
gave a shout that filled the valley and went up to the top
of the mountains. Some, in a hurry to see their enemy,
pushed ahead, but the chief ordered them to stand back
and move forward in order.

When the runner said they were half way, the chief
told the people to halt and sing. They sang the same song
and again the shout filled the valley and went to the top
of the mountains.

When they came to the place, the chief told the men to
form in a circle around the log, but not to go up to the
man hanging across it till they were sure that he was dead.

After a while each man said to the chief, "He is dead
and has been for a long time."

The chief said, "This is the best thing that has ever
happened, but we must be perfectly sure that Coon is
dead. We will sing and shout and then the bravest man
among us will go up to the body, reach into the mouth and,
if possible, pull out the heart, then we shall know that our
enemy is dead."

At the end of the song and the shout a man went up
and put his hand into Coon's mouth, but he sprang back

with a cry and he looked as though he were frightened and wanted to run away.

When they asked, "What is the matter?" he said, "Coon is alive."

The men called him a liar, and said, "You want to fool us. Coon is half rotten, and you say he is alive."

The chief called on another man whom he said always told the truth. The people sang and shouted, then the man stepped boldly up to the body, but he sprang back. The chief and the people were astonished when the man said, "Coon is alive!" There the body hung, head down, no one had seen it move, and the face was black.

The chief called out a third man, the best man in the Crawfish nation. The people sang and shouted, then the man went up to the body. He had just reached out to touch it when Coon sprang up, and dashing in among his enemies began to fight them. He pulled out their arms, pounded their heads, and killed them. Of all the Crawfish nation only one man escaped. That one found himself alone on a high hill and, not knowing which way to go, was terribly frightened.

"I shall die," thought Crawfish, "for how can I get back to the water. I shall die here alone." He crawled along slowly, for he was weak and thirsty. At last he saw a tree, then he said in his own mind, "I'll go and ask that tree what it is." When he came to the tree he spoke up and asked, "What kind of a tree are you?" The tree answered, "I am a black oak."

Crawfish was discouraged—black oaks grow far from water—and he said to himself, "I shall die here alone," but he crawled along slowly. After a time he saw another tree and when he came near it, he spoke up and asked, "What kind of a tree are you?" The tree answered, "I am a butternut."

Now butternut trees grow nearer the water than oaks do, so Crawfish knew he was going in the right direction, but his courage almost gave out for he was so thirsty and weak that he could scarcely move. Still he crawled on. After a long time he came to another tree, and asked as before, "What kind of tree are you?" The tree answered, "I am a cottonwood."

Crawfish was encouraged and began to think that maybe he would live till he came to some stream, for he knew that one was not far away. He crawled along and soon came to another tree. He asked, ''What kind of a tree are you?'' ''I am a willow,'' answered the tree.

Now Crawfish was so glad that he screamed and laughed and called out, ''I'm near water! I'm near water!'' Soon he came to low bushes, then he stood up, jumped as far as he could and came down in water. He was so thirsty that he didn't go to the bottom of the stream, but floated on the surface till he had taken a long drink. Then he sank to the bottom, and he still lives there.

THE DESERTED BOY

WHEN the Senecas lived at Canandaigua, one of their medicine men notified them that something terrible was coming, something which would cause great loss of life. The people were frightened. They quarreled with one another and became suspicious even of their children.

One night a great uproar was heard outside; the Cherokees were there. Men, women and children sprang up and fled as fast as they could, going in every direction. Among the people of the village was a woman with a baby only two days old. She also ran, holding the child in her arms. After a time she got so tired that she decided to get rid of the bundle. Coming to a tree with a hole in one side, not far from the ground, she dropped the child into the hole and ran on. In the tree a bear lived and as the bundle fell the mother bear caught it.

When the woman overtook her people, they asked what she had done with her child, but she made no answer.

After many persons had been killed, the Cherokees disappeared, but the Senecas did not go back to their village. They made a new home for themselves.

One Spring a hunter, when out looking for game, came to a chestnut grove. He had not been there long when he saw a bear with cubs. Getting a good chance he killed the mother bear. As she fell over, she hit one of the cubs and it cried out like a child. The other cubs ran up a tree. The man, thinking the cry sounded strangely, went to the place quickly and saw a small boy. The boy jumped up and ran away; the man followed and at last caught him.

"Stop crying, Nephew," said he, "Stop crying, nobody will harm you."

"You made me cry," said the child, "You have killed my mother. Over there are my brothers" (pointing to the tree).

"I wouldn't have killed her if I had seen you first," said the man, "but how came the bear to be your mother."

247

"My real mother threw me away. I was only two days old, but I remember everything. I knew my mother's mind. I was a burden to her when she was running away from some one, so she dropped me into that hollow tree over there. The bear caught me as I fell and said I could be her child and live with her cubs; she nursed me and was good to me."

"I know your real mother," said the man; "but now you will be my son."

The boy didn't like this, but at last he stopped crying, and the man strapped him on to his back and carried him to where a party of hunters were camped.

After this, whenever the man went out to hunt, he tied the boy up so he couldn't get away. One day the child said, "Don't tie me up, I'll never leave you."

He was not tied again and as soon as he was old enough the man let him go with him when he went out to hunt. The boy seemed to know where bears lived, but he never told his father where a mother bear was. The man had always been a poor hunter, but as soon as he found the boy he began to have wonderful luck.

After a while the man said, "It is time to go back to my village."

"My mother will see me, and take me away from you," said the boy.

"Pay no attention to her," said the man. "She threw you away."

When they had been two days in the village, the woman heard that a certain hunter had brought home a little boy he found in the woods. She went to the hunter's cabin and watched every move of the child. The boy was afraid of her. He knew her thoughts when she threw him away and he knew them now. When she asked him who he was, he said, "This man is my father." But she decided that the boy was hers and she began to urge him to go home with her. He wouldn't go. One day when the woman knew the hunter was off in the woods, she went to his house and tried to catch the boy. He ran to the woods, crying from fright. She followed, but after a while lost sight of him and turned back.

When the hunter came home and couldn't find the child,

he looked for tracks and soon discovered that the boy was running away and his mother was following him. He was sorry, for he was afraid he would never see the child again. Then he happened to think that maybe the boy had gone to his old home in the chestnut grove. He went there and found the child.

When he asked, "Why did you leave me?" the child said, "My mother tried to catch me, I thought she wanted to kill me. She called me 'Son,' and I didn't like it. I told her that I had no mother. I want to live here all of the time."

The man built a bark cabin and they stayed in the forest.

One day the boy said, "I wish that I had a boy to play with me."

The man went to the village and brought back one of his sister's boys, a child a little younger than the other boy.

Now there were three in the house. When the man went hunting and left the boys at home he told them not to go far from the house, but each day they ventured farther, till one day they came to a place where the leaves and grass and everything seemed to be moving. They looked closely and saw that a wide strip of land was going along as if on a river. They saw a coon going down with this stream of land. Watching it made them forget everything, but at last the elder boy said, "We must go home now. We'll come to-morrow and stay all day."

The next morning, when the hunter started off, he cautioned the boys not to go far from the house, telling them that if they disobeyed him something would happen to them. But the boys were so anxious to get to the place where they had been the day before that the man wasn't out of sight when they started.

They found the moving ground. It was dry land, but was moving like a river. It was not wide; a person could have jumped across it. The boys saw animals on it, and they thought, "What fun! Why not try it?" They sprang on and sat down.

The younger boy said, "Let's go as far as the stream goes."

They laughed and had a good time.

After going some distance the younger boy said, "I'll get off and run back and come down again." It seemed to him exactly like sliding down hill.

As he got on again, his companion was running up, they passed each other. This time when they were both on, one called to the other, "Don't get off again. Go to the end."

Soon they came to a place where the land seemed to pass into an opening like a great door. The elder boy saw the younger go in, and he thought, "This is great fun!"

Then he heard a noise as if some one were killing his play-mate, that minute he too went in at the door. Then he saw that it was a place to snare game, that no one could get away after coming that far. In an instant an old man with a mallet hit the boy on the head and killed him.

Two Stone Coats lived in this house, and they had such power that they could make everything come to them. Each took a boy and sat down on his own side of the fire to roast him. As the flesh began to cook, fat oozed out, fell on the fire, and sputtered. One body called out to the other, "You are burning!"

"*Guah!*" said one of the Stone Coats, "My game has a voice!"

"*Guah!* My game has a voice," said the other Stone Coat. "This is fine, when one begins to burn it tells the other. It's queer game that talks like this."

When the bodies were sufficiently cooked, the Stone Coats began to eat. When they had eaten the last mouthful and not a particle of flesh or a bone was left, they began to be in terrible pain.

One said to the other, "It must be that strange game is making us sick."

They rolled around and groaned till daylight came, then the two boys were there and the two Stone Coats were dead.

One boy said to the other, "This is why our father warned us not to go far from the house. We'll go home and tell him what happened to us."

As they were starting, the younger boy said, "We must burn up this house. Our uncles have done great harm to people. Henceforth men shall eat animals, not human beings."

The younger boy had the most power. He walked around the house throwing red paint, such as they had to paint their faces with. The paint stopped the stream of land that was going through the house, and set the house on fire.

When the boys were near home, they heard singing and the younger said, "Our father is mourning for us. When we get home you must tell him what happened. He will believe you sooner than he will me, for you are older than I am."

The hunter was sitting by the fire and his song was about the loss of his children.

The elder boy called out, "Father, we've come home. We've not been killed. We shall never die. There is nothing that can harm us."

The man greeted the boys and was glad. They told him of their adventure, and said, "Now we are going farther."

The man said, "Beyond the house you burned, there are other houses and in those houses are uncles of yours, man-eaters."

"I don't care," said the younger boy. "I want to see everything there is in the world."

The man knew that the boys were full of power (witchcraft). The younger boy had control of his uncle's mind and it was through his influence that the man let them do as they liked.

The boy said, "You can stay here and hunt. We'll go and see our uncle who lives beyond Stone Coat's house. Maybe he'll tell us stories. We are lonesome."

The man said, "The first house is three looks from here and they are all three looks apart."

When the boys came to the house they had burned, they halted and looked. They could see some object in the distance, and there was the end of the first look. When they came to that object they looked again, went to the object they saw, and looking off again saw an opening, and said, "Our uncle must live there."

When they reached the opening, they saw a house.

Everything was quiet; there was no one in sight. The younger boy crept up carefully, and making a sudden leap sprang into the house and called out, "I've caught you, Uncle!"

"I'm glad you have come, Nephew," said an old man who was there. "I'm sick. You'll give me medicine."

"What do you want?"

"This, Nephew: when anyone comes to see me, I play hide-and-seek. I'll play with you. If you find me, I lose my head. If I find you boys, you'll lose your heads."

The house was empty, but the younger boy saw, hanging on the posts where they met in a point, a very small bag, and he thought, "My uncle will hide in that bag."

As usual in those days there was a large log on the fire.

The old man said, "The finder must go over the top of that hill out there and when the hider is ready, he will call. You must hide first."

The boys agreed and the old man started off. They heard his bones rattle as he ran. The younger boy said, "I'll go into the log on the fire and you can go behind the sun. When you are ready I'll call."

After a time he shouted, "*Onch!*"

"This is what I do to my nephews," said the old man, and catching up his club he ran into the house and began to strike the posts singing out, "Here you are! Come out!"

The boy in the log looked at his uncle and laughed; the boy behind the sun was also watching him. When the old man's time was up, he said, "Come out! I can't find you."

As he said this, the nephew behind the sun showed himself and, laughing at the old man, came down to the house; the other boy crawled from the heart of the log. The old man laughed loudly, and said, "Now go beyond the hill and I'll hide."

When the boys heard the old man call, they ran to the house. The younger boy caught up the club and did as he had seen his uncle do. At last he stopped striking the posts and called out, "Uncle, you are up there in your medicine bag. Come out!"

The old man came out, laughing and said, "My little nephew, you are full of witchcraft. No one ever found me before."

The boy said, "When a man makes a bet, he must live up to it. You have lost your head." Upon this he caught hold of the old man-eater and cut off his head. The elder boy picked the head up, stuck it against a tree and said, "Hereafter trees shall have heads on them (knots), and the heads will be used to make ladles and bowls."[1]

The boys burned the old man's house and then went on. Three looks away they came to the edge of a forest and saw a house close by. The younger boy said to the elder, "Stay here, I'll go to the house and come back."

There were four witches in the house. As soon as the boy went in, the old woman said to her daughters, "Hurry up and get the kettle over the fire." The boy watched them, thinking that maybe they would kill him.

The elder brother waited a long time, then got out of patience and called his medicine, a mole. It came, and he said, "You must take me to that house. I want to find my brother."

When the water in the kettle was boiling, the old woman said to her eldest daughter, "Lay a skin on the ground and put the animal that has come to us on the skin."

The boy knew that they intended to kill him, but he sat down on the skin. The old woman's second daughter took a mallet from the wall and raised it to strike him, but he said, "Let the mallet come down on the old woman." It struck her a terrible blow on the head. As the girl raised the mallet a second time, he said, "Let it strike the eldest sister."

Right away the three sisters began to fight with one another. The boy kept telling the mallet to strike, first one and then another. For a time there was a terrible struggle, then all was quiet; the sisters were dead.

A voice from under the ground asked, "What are you doing, brother?"

"Oh, the old woman and her daughters have been having a little sport."

[1] To this day trees with knots are said to have "Uncle's head" on them.

"All right," said a voice behind him, and there stood the elder boy. "I was out of patience. We might have gone a long way on our journey. We'll burn up the house."

"I don't want my mind to be different from yours," said the younger boy, "but before we go on we must purify ourselves (swim). When we get to the river, you must be careful, I'll go in first and you will stay on the bank till I call you. Unless we purify ourselves, we will meet with misfortune, for the people where we are going are full of witchcraft."

The water of the river was thick and red. When the elder boy saw his brother go in, he thought, "that must be fun!" and without waiting to be called he waded in. Filth gathered on his body and he sank out of sight. His brother rescued him, then said, "If you had waited till I called, you would have been saved this trouble. Now we will go on till we come to a village where they are playing ball."

They soon came to an opening and saw a crowd of people standing near a pole in the center of the opening. The two went forward and the younger said to the chief, "We have come to challenge you. What are your rules?"

"We wager heads."

"There must be two men on a side," said the boy.

The chief said to the people, "These strangers challenge us to a game of ball. There will be two players on a side!"

"You must be one of those players," said the boy to the chief. Then he commanded a spider to weave a strong web across the ball ground.

The game began. The ball flew off in the direction of the web and hitting it was thrown back. The elder boy caught the ball and ran for the first point, got it, had one inning and called out, "The game is mine! We have the inning! The game is finished."

"It is not," said the chief.

"This is the way we play," said the younger boy. "Whoever gets the first inning wins the game."

"Very well," said the chief, "You have won the heads of the men you played with."

"We bet with you," said the boy. "We don't care who played for you," and running up he caught the chief by the hair, and saying "If it hadn't been for you we should have been far on our way," he cut off his head.

The people asked the boys to be their chief, but they said, "No, our work is done. We have killed all the man-eaters, now we are going home."

DAGWANOEⁿYENT (WHIRLWIND)[1]

TWO brothers, one a young man, the other a small boy, were one day out in the woods together. They heard a great noise overhead and looking up saw a DAGWANOEⁿYENT, an enormous head, flying above them.

The elder brother called out *"Gówe! gówe!"*

The DAGWANOEⁿYENT said, "Thank you. Thank you. You should always sing in that way when you are going to fight. If you do, I will be on your side and kill your enemies for you."

Taking three hairs from his head the DAGWANOEⁿYENT gave them to the brothers, saying, "When you want to escape from danger, get water and draw these hairs along in it. When you take them out, drops of water will hang to them and those drops will bring rain." Then the DAGWANOEⁿYENT went on, leaving the two brothers.

By those hairs the brothers often escaped from their enemies.

Whenever they wanted rain, they had only to draw the hairs through water and then shake off the drops; right away heavy rain fell. The hairs were long kept by the Senecas.

The narrator thinks there is one hair yet. It is owned by a man who lives on the Alleghany Reservation.

[1] Always represented as a head without a body.

HÓTHO (COLD)

ONE day a man who was out hunting met HÓTHO and said to him, "You cannot freeze me, no matter how cold you are."

"I can," said HÓTHO.

They had a long discussion and at last agreed that when night came they would have a trial of strength.

The man went home, carried in wood enough to burn till morning, built a huge fire and made a kettleful of hemlock tea. He stood in front of the fire all night, turning first one side then the other toward the heat, often drinking a cup of hot tea. It was terribly cold and grew colder and colder till near morning.

Just at daybreak, HÓTHO, naked, his hatchet in his hip, came into the house and sat down on a pile of bark by the fire.

"You have beaten me," said he, and that minute it began to grow warm and thaw.

This shows that man can conquer HÓTHO.

FLYING-SQUIRREL AND THE SEASONS

[Told by John Jimison]

Characters

DOSENO' DAIĀ ....Flying-squirrel

DJEONYAIK ....Robin

DOWISDOWE ....Tip-up (a bird)

DEⁿDEⁿDÁNE ....Caterpillar

DJIHOⁿSDŪQGWEⁿ ....Ants

GÁSYONDETHA ....Meteor

FLYING-SQUIRREL was a poor man. He could kill no game and he didn't know how to get food for his wife and children. One day he sat from morning till evening with his head bent down, thinking what he could do.

That night, just as he was going to sleep, a man came in, and said, "War is being forced upon the people across the lake. They want all the assistance they can get. They have sent for you. You are to start two moons from now."

"I will go," said Flying-squirrel.

The stranger left and Flying-squirrel fell asleep. While sleeping he dreamed and his dream said, "I have come to help you. You have promised to go to war. Those people will try to kill you. They will do this to find out how much power you have. I will be there and will save you."

The next morning Flying-squirrel was low-spirited. He sat with his head down. His wife asked what troubled him, but she got no answer.

At midday he raised his head, and said, "I am going to war, and I am thinking how I am to conquer the enemy."

After telling his thoughts, Flying-squirrel was no longer sad. When two moons had passed, he took his bow and arrows, and said, "I am going now and I may be away a long time, but I think we will all live."

Flying-squirrel traveled many days without food or rest, then he said to himself, "I am hungry," but he kept on. Just at midday, he heard a noise behind him that sounded as though some animal were following. He turned and saw ten deer in line. He killed them all, built a fire and roasted the meat. He ate the ten deer and wasn't satisfied. He was still hungry, but he started on. That night, for the first time, he stopped, crawled into a hollow tree, and slept. The next morning he was up early. He felt so much stronger that he wondered how he would feel if he slept longer. He lay down again and was just falling asleep when someone kicked the hollow tree, and said, "You had better come out and go on. If you don't start soon, the animal that lives in this tree will come and kill you."

"Let it come," said Flying-squirrel.

Right away he heard a great noise and felt the earth tremble. Then the tree he was in was torn to pieces. Just as enormous jaws were about to close on him, he sprang into the animal's mouth and fell on his back in its stomach. Soon he knew that the creature was running and he thought, "This is pleasant; I am being rocked, and it is nice and warm in here."

The creature traveled for a long time, then lay down. Flying-squirrel went to sleep and when he woke up, he thought it must be morning. By and by he felt a movement and he said to himself, "The person who is taking care of me is waking up." Then he knew that he was being carried along swiftly. "Now I am traveling fast," thought he as he rocked from side to side.

While the creature was running at great speed what seemed like a terrible gust of wind swept through him and Flying-squirrel was blown out. He got up, and, looking around, saw a great black object going on ahead. Flying-squirrel thought, "Oh, what a dreadful animal has been taking care of me!" The sun was in the middle of the sky and he couldn't tell which way to go. After a while he started, as he thought, toward the West, but he went directly North.

Flying-squirrel traveled many days and nights without food or rest, then he thought, "I am hungry." That minute he heard a noise and turning around saw ten bears in a line. He killed the bears, then built a fire and roasted the meat. After he had eaten the last morsel, he said, "I've had a meal that will last me a long time," and he went on.

He traveled many moons, resting nights, then he was stopped by a precipice so deep that he couldn't see the bottom. As he stood wondering how he could go on he saw a man coming from the East. The man's hair was long and bright. Then he saw a man coming from the West. His hair was fiery red. As he looked another man came from the South. He had long light hair. Then he saw one coming from the direction he himself was going in. That man had a very long nose.

The man from the East spoke to Flying-squirrel, asking, "Which one of the four will you choose?"

Then the man from the West said to the man from the East, "I am sorry that you got ahead and spoke first."

Then he asked Flying-squirrel, "Which one of the four will you choose?"

Each one of the four asked the same question, then the first speaker said, "We have all asked. We don't know which one he will choose, but we will put ourselves to trial and the strongest will be the one to have the care of him."

The bright-haired man said to Flying-squirrel, "You who have come here are the cause of our fighting, but I warn you to be careful. Should the man from the North conquer, he would devour you. Should the man from the South conquer, he would enslave you. The man from the West is my friend, but he is not as powerful as I am. There isn't much chance of his winning."

"Let me talk," said the man from the West. "We are proud. Each one thinks that he is the strongest. I have conquered everything I have met. I have been all over the world. I think that I am the most powerful of the four. My friend, whose hair is bright, is not very powerful; all he can do is to give you light. I can do anything. I can aid you in battle. Look at my hair, it is red, covered with the blood of fighting. I shall be sorry if you fail to choose me. I don't know the other two, but I think they are man-eaters.''

"Let me talk," said the man from the South, the flaxen-haired man. "I have great strength in jumping, and I am a swift runner. When in war people run away, I can overtake them. The man who comes from the North is a friend of mine, but he is not as powerful as I am. You should choose me."

"Let me talk," said the Northern man. "I am a man of great power. No matter how steep a place is, I can climb it. I can overpower every creature that lives in the water, and all the animals that roam around in this world. Only five things do I fear: the Ancient of Bears, Blue Lizard, Whirlwind, the Ice King, and Thunder. I shall be sorry if you don't choose me."

Flying-squirrel didn't speak.

"Stand aside," said the bright-haired man. "The trial of strength must begin."

"Let us begin fairly," said the red-haired man. "Let this man make his choice before we begin."

"Let us have the trial first," said the flaxen-haired man.

"Let us have the trial first and the one who is the strongest will have the care of the man," said the long-nosed one.

"Now begin!" said the flaxen-haired man, and he sprang toward the red-haired man.

The other two advanced, but the red-haired man drew aside, and said, "Wait! Let us have peace." But, after a little he said, "Very well, we will decide it by fighting. You all know how strong I am."

The three consented. The four clinched and went down, the red-haired man at the bottom. As they struggled he still insisted that they should have peace, but when they hurt him, he got angry and fought in earnest, then the three were powerless. He pounded them, killed them all, then said to Flying-squirrel, "I told you what my strength was. Now will you have my care?"

"I am on a journey," said Flying-squirrel. "I want

you to help me all you can. I want you to give me power to change myself to any form I wish for."

"I am the most powerful person in the world," said the red-headed man. "I am he whom you call GÁSYONDETHA (Meteor). I am the oldest person in the world. The three fear me for I have often overpowered them. I will give you power and it will be the same as if I went with you. When you use this power you must say, 'Grandfather, you and I have never failed in anything we have undertaken.' I will give you a piece of flesh, from my head and neck and down my back, long enough for a belt."

Flying-squirrel took his flint knife and cut out the piece of flesh. When he was through, the red-headed man appeared to be dead, but as Flying-squirrel looked at the wound he saw the edges come together and heal.

That minute the man said, "You see what power I have, I cannot die. As for the men you saw me kill, I only sent them home; they are not dead. Now go in the direction I came from and do all you can to help yourself. The bright-haired man will soon be here and it would not be well for us to be together when he comes. I am going."

The red-haired man leaped into the air, and, giving a whoop, called out, "I am the strongest person in the world! No one can conquer me." As he traveled there were sparks in the air.

Flying-squirrel felt limber and strong and he ran on swiftly till night came. Then he lay down under a tree. He was almost asleep when he heard footsteps on the dry leaves. Then a voice said, "Flying-squirrel, I am in search of you. I am sent by the red-haired man. During the night men will come and try to get the belt you are wearing, but nothing will happen for I will be here. Help me gather wood, we must have a fire."

The two gathered wood and made a big fire. As it blazed up they heard one voice and then another and another till there were voices everywhere and those voices said, "Throw away what you have around your waist; it isn't good for you; it will poison you." Their cries increased and their number increased.

Flying-squirrel said in his own mind, "If the fire wasn't

here, that great crowd of people would pounce upon me and kill me.'' He didn't see these men for they were in the dark. They didn't come even to the edge of the light thrown out by the fire. They cried louder and louder till just before dawn, then their cries began to recede and at daybreak all was silent.

Flying-squirrel's protector said, ''You are safe now. Go on in the same direction. At midday you will come to a fallen tree. I will meet you there.''

Flying-squirrel went on till he came to the tree and passed it. He didn't remember the man's words till he came to a second tree, then he said to himself, ''I should have stopped at the first tree,'' and he was about to turn back when he thought, ''What good will it do? I am on a journey. I'll not turn back. If he wanted to give me food, I don't care for it. I'm not hungry,'' and he traveled on.

When night came, he lay down by a tree. Soon he heard footsteps.

Someone stopped near him and said, ''I have come to keep you company. There is a person with me. You may sleep. We will build a fire.''

The sun was in the sky when Flying-squirrel woke up. There was no one around. Those who had come in the night had disappeared. A great many nights passed in the same way: as soon as darkness came and Flying-squirrel lay down to sleep two men came to protect him and just at daylight they disappeared.

At last he came to a precipice and could go no farther. Then he remembered that his friend had given him the power to change to any form he wished.

''My friend,'' said he, ''I will be a black eagle and go down into the ravine and look around.''

That minute he was an eagle. He flapped his wings, flew off, and came back, then flew off quite a distance and began to sink down. After a time he saw that there were trees under him, then he sank as fast as he could and soon was in a beautiful country. He saw a great patch of strawberries. He picked and ate as many as he wanted.

Then, taking his own form, he went on till he came to a house. Stealing up to the house he looked through a crack and saw a very old woman with long white hair. She was sitting with head down but she raised it, and said, "Game has come to me, I smell it."

"This woman wants to kill me," thought Flying-squirrel. "If she touches me, I'll cut off her head."

A second time the woman said, "I smell game," then she called, "Grandson, come in, why do you stand out there?"

"It seems this old woman is my grandmother," said Flying-squirrel. "I'll go in."

The woman said, "I heard, a long time ago, that you were coming. You have been invited by my grandchildren who live beyond the lake. I will carry you over there."

This woman was old Caterpillar and she was called the long-haired woman.

"I don't want you to carry me over," said Flying-squirrel. "I can get there myself."

"Well, Grandson, I have a game that I play with those who come here. We take mallets, go to an opening near here, and run. As we overtake each other we strike with the mallet."

"Very well," said Flying-squirrel, "but you must lend me a mallet."

The old woman brought two mallets, and said, "Take your choice."

One was good, the other was old, he took the old one, and they started for the opening. Just as they came to the edge of the field, the old woman struck Flying-squirrel a heavy blow and ran. He ran after her, overtook her and struck her. She fell but was soon up and after him. When she struck at Flying-squirrel a second time, he dodged and the mallet came down on her knee.

They kept this game up till sunset, then the old woman said, "Let us rest a while." Flying-squirrel sat down but Caterpillar struck him and ran. This time she went along the edge of a high cliff.

All at once she turned and gave Flying-squirrel such a push that he went over the cliff. He fell into a river and a great fish swallowed him.

Soon he heard a woman say, "Sister, we have caught a fish in our trap. Help me get it out."

These sisters were of the Tip-up (water-bird) family.

The women got the fish to the bank and cut it open.

"Oh, Sister!" cried one of the women, "there is a child in this fish! Hurry and tell our mother to come."

Flying-squirrel had changed to an infant. When old Tip-up came, she said, "This boy will be my grandson."

The three women took good care of the child. It grew very fast and soon walked and talked.

One day the boy began to cry.

"What is the trouble, Grandson?" asked the old woman.

"My Grandmother," said the boy, "I am lonesome. I want to see my friends."

"Stop crying, Grandson, I will give you something to play with." She gave him a bright red fox-skin of wonderful power. He stopped crying and was happy.

One day the boy said, "I am going into the woods to shoot birds."

The women cautioned him not to go toward the South. He hunted a long time but found no birds, while off in the South, he heard the beautiful songs of many birds. At last he turned and went toward the South. As he advanced, the singing receded. He followed it on and on till he came to an opening and saw a house. He crept up to the house, looked in through a crack, and saw the long-haired woman who had pushed him over the cliff. She raised her head, and said, "Well, Grandson, come in. Why do you stand outside?"

When the boy went in the old grandmother said, "I have been expecting you. I have a game that I play with those who come here."

"Very well," said the boy, for he knew what the game was. "Now," thought he, "I will serve her as she served me."

They went to the opening. After they had struck each other a number of times, the woman ran along the edge of a high cliff intending to turn and push the boy over, but he overtook her quickly, gave her a terrible push and sent her over the cliff.

"There," said he. "I have thrown her as she threw me. Now I will burn her house."

When the house was in ashes, the boy went home. On

the way he killed a turkey. While the sisters were cooking the turkey they noticed that the boy looked frightened.

"What is the trouble, Grandson?" asked the old woman.

"I am afraid you will scold me. I have killed the long-haired woman."

"We are glad," said the sisters. "She has done us great harm. Now you can go in any direction you like. That woman lived in the South and we were afraid she might kill you."

One day the boy said, "I am traveling. I am on my way to war. I cannot stay here any longer."

The women urged and coaxed, but the boy wouldn't listen to them. He started off. After a while, he came to a lake. As he stood looking at the water and wondering how he could get to the other side, he remembered that once he had had the power of flying and he said in his mind, "I will see if I have that power now." Taking his own form, he went back a short distance, then ran forward and as his feet struck the water he gave a spring and went into the air. He came down and as he touched the water, he sprang again, going forward somewhat. In this way he traveled two days and nights, then reached land. He was hungry. As he looked for game, he happened to think of his belt and that the man who gave it to him promised to help him.

Then he said, "I wish my grandfather would send me a deer."

That minute a deer was in sight. Flying-squirrel killed it, then built a fire and roasted some of the meat. He ate and was satisfied, thanked his grandfather and went on through a forest.

One morning he saw a light ahead and soon he came to a large opening. At one side of the opening was a village. Flying-squirrel went to the village and found that the people who lived there were the people who had summoned him to war. The chief said to the warriors, who stood around, "You must test the strength of this man."

The warriors ran at Flying-squirrel, struck him with their clubs and knocked him down, but he sprang up and fought with them, fought till he had conquered them all, though he had only his hands to fight with. These people were Robins.

The chief of the Robins said to Flying-squirrel, "I see that you have great power. In the center of our village is a pole covered with ice. Whoever climbs to the top of that pole may marry my daughter. To-morrow the people will assemble and each man will try to climb the pole."

Flying-squirrel went to a hut at the edge of the village and asked shelter of an old woman who lived there with her granddaughter.

"I have nothing to eat," said the woman.

"I don't want food," said Flying-squirrel.

She gave him a place to sleep. The next morning there was plenty of meat in the hut. Flying-squirrel had wished for it.

He went to the center of the village, where many people were assembled, and just at midday the chief said, "The time has come."

One man after another tried to climb the pole. The first man went only a short distance, the second went a little farther, the third went still farther, and so on till all had tried and had fallen back. Then Flying-squirrel walked up to the pole, spat on his hands and began to climb. He went up easily, got to the top and called out, "Shall I go farther?"

"No. Come down," said the chief.

The chief thanked the young man, and said, "My daughter is your wife."

The people were angry. They caught Flying-squirrel, took him to a hole between high rocks and fastened him in. He made a motion with his hand; the rocks fell away. "Why should I stay here," thought he, "I will claim my wife."

Another man had claimed the chief's daughter. Flying-squirrel caught that man by the hair and cut off his head. The dead man's friends seized Flying-squirrel, tied him and took him back to the hole in the rocks. When they found the rocks were destroyed, they took him to a second hole and fastened him in securely. He moved his hands and the rocks fell apart.

Flying-squirrel went to the chief's house, and said, "The

next time your people seize me, I will destroy everybody in this village.''

Now the people decided to kill Flying-squirrel by burning him. They piled up a great many logs and dead limbs, leaving a hole in the center of the pile. They caught Flying-squirrel, tied him up in a bundle, dropped him into the hole and set fire to the pile.

"These people mean to burn me up," thought Flying-squirrel. "I'll wait till the fire gets to burning, blazing up high." After a while he moved slightly; the cords that bound him loosened and fell off. He moved again; fire and cinders flew in every direction.

Flying-squirrel went to the chief's house and said to his wife, "I warned your father of what I would do if the people seized me again. Now I will destroy you all."

The woman screamed and begged. When the chief came to see what the trouble was, she said, "My husband is going to destroy you and all of our people."

The chief begged him not to do this, called him friend, and said that he did not know what the people were doing, that on the morrow war would begin. At last Flying-squirrel forgot his anger.

The warriors were to start at midday. Flying-squirrel did not wait for them. Early in the morning he set out alone. On the way he came to a large flat stone. He sat down on the stone, then ground it to dust with his basswood club. Taking a handful of the dust he threw it West, in the direction of the enemy's country. The dust became a cloud and then a whirlwind and Flying-squirrel went with it—he was in the center of the whirlwind.

As the whirlwind approached the enemy's village, Flying-squirrel saw a great many warriors sitting near a large mound. These warriors were of the Ant family. When Flying-squirrel reached the mound, he plunged into the ground; the whirlwind following him. He ran North and South, went from one end of the mound to the other. The whirlwind killed every man that it passed, threw the dirt into the air and leveled the mound.

Then Flying-squirrel saw another mound lower than the first but longer; he plunged into it and was half way through when the chief of the Ants and his warriors came and seeing what was taking place began to fight. Flying-squirrel defended himself, used all his strength and swiftness. Just at midday the whirlwind died down and Flying-squirrel was left to struggle alone.

The top of the mound fell off. Then the battle was out in the open. Other warriors came to help their chief, but soon Robin and his men came up and with Flying-squirrel's help, they defeated the enemy, then the chief said to Flying-squirrel, "You are free now, what we called you for is accomplished."

Flying-squirrel went to the chief's daughter, and said, "Get ready, we will go home."

They started but after one day's journey they were overtaken by the woman's people. The woman was killed, but Flying-squirrel got away, changed to an eagle, went to his grandmother's house, and then took his own form. He looked so old that his grandmother didn't know him. She asked, "Who are you and where did you come from?"

When he told her who he was she was glad that he had come. He said, "I am going to my own home. I have a wife and children."

When he started, he changed to a deer and ran with great swiftness, but all at once he was in a hunting camp. The hunters sprang up and followed him, but he was so swift that after a while they gave up and turned back.

Flying-squirrel came to a lake and stopped. He didn't know how to get to the other side. He forgot his belt. He started to walk around the lake. The cliff grew higher and higher. He went along the edge of the cliff till he came to loose earth, then he slipped and fell. As he fell he thought, "If I were a bird, I could save myself."

That minute he was an eagle. He flew high and far. Then looking down he recognized the place he was passing, and coming to the ground he took his own form. Going cautiously toward a house he looked through a crack and saw an old man smoking. As he looked, the old man called out, "Come in, Nephew. Why do you stand outside?"

"I have found my uncle," said Flying-squirrel, laughing. "I will go in and see what he wants."

"You have been gone a long time," said the old man. "Now we will play ball."

"That is the game I amuse myself with," said Flying-squirrel.

The old man's ball was a head, the clubs were sticks split at the end and tied apart with bark strings. They put their clubs against the head. It went toward the old man's inning. Both ran after it. Flying-squirrel got the ball and hitting it a blow with the butt of his club, said, "You don't know how to play ball."

The ball went to Flying-squirrel's inning and he won the game. The old man begged for a few puffs of smoke.

"You'll not get them," said Flying-squirrel. "I would not have asked for them if you had won," and he cut off the old man's head.

Flying-squirrel traveled on till he heard voices. Then, hiding behind a stump, he listened.

A woman said, "My husband must be dead, if he were alive he would come home."

A second woman said, "Don't cry, my son wants you for a wife. I think your husband has another wife."

Flying-squirrel made himself invisible and followed the woman. He heard the younger one promise to marry the elder one's son. Then the two parted. The younger woman was Flying-squirrel's wife.

Flying-squirrel entered the house with his wife. While she and the children were eating, he made a noise. When she turned to see what caused the noise, he caught up a piece of meat and threw it at her. She thought her daughter threw the meat, and catching up a club she began to beat the girl.

Then Flying-squirrel took his own form, and asked, "Why do you beat the children? I threw the meat."

The woman was frightened and she promised never to strike the children again. Right away she sent her daughter to tell the old woman that Flying-squirrel had come home.

Now Flying-squirrel and his wife settled down in peace. Flying-squirrel had the belt given him by the red-haired man so he always had great power, and food was never lacking in his house.

The four men described as coming from the North, South, East and West are said to personify the Seasons.

THE ADVENTURES OF YELLOWBIRD

Characters

A MAN and his wife and children lived in a little house in the woods. They were destitute and had nothing to eat but the scraps and pieces the man earned in the village.

One day the father said to his eldest son, "You are old enough now to work. Go to the village and ask the chief if he has anything for you to do."

The boy had a little dog that he called Yellowbird (the dog was a bird). After he had named the dog his family called him by the dog's name.

The chief of the village was Daddy-long-legs. When the boy asked for work, the chief said, "Stay with me. I will give you work to do."

The chief grew so fond of the young man that after a time he gave him his youngest daughter for a wife.

One day Yellowbird said to his wife, "I am going away

for a while, I want to see who is in the world." And starting toward the South he traveled all day. When night came he lay down under a tree and slept.

Yellowbird traveled eight days. Then he began to feel weak and hungry, but he was in a forest and there were no signs of anyone living near, so he walked on. After a while he saw, off in the distance, a black object. When he came nearer he found it was a bear asleep on the ground. Yellowbird had neither a knife nor a bow, but looking around he saw a heavy stone. He picked it up and creeping near he threw it at the bear's head. The bear straightened out and died.

Then Yellowbird hunted for a piece of flint to skin the bear with. Not finding flint he took a sharp-edged stone. When he had the skin off, he began to wonder how he could start a fire. He didn't want to eat raw meat. He hunted for a rotten log and when he found one he got punk out of it. Then he struck stones together till sparks flew. With the sparks he lighted the punk and soon he had a good fire. Then he roasted pieces of meat and ate heartily.

Now Yellowbird made up his mind to gather a pile of wood and stay there in the woods as long as he had anything to eat. He rested a good many days. Then, when nothing was left of the bear, he started on.

He had traveled a long time and was getting weak and hungry when he saw, in the distance, something that looked as if a tree were on the ground and the roots were sticking up. When nearer, he saw it was a buck. He killed the buck as he had killed the bear, and making a fire, roasted some of the flesh and ate it.

Yellowbird stayed there in the forest till he had eaten the buck, then he started on. After many days, when he was again getting weak and hungry, and was wondering how he was to get something to eat, he saw a smoke off in the woods. "Someone must have a hunting camp there," thought he.

When near the smoke he crept along carefully, then, not seeing anyone, he went boldly to the fire. Over the fire was a kettle and in the kettle bear's meat was cooking. Yellowbird took the kettle off from the fire, cooled the meat and ate all he wanted. Then he hurried on for he was afraid that, when the owner of the meat found it had been stolen, he would track the thief. When night came, Yellowbird lay down under a tree. Soon he heard dry leaves rattle and he thought, "The man whose meat I stole is tracking me."

The sound came nearer till at last someone stopped by the tree. The young man didn't speak. After a while a woman said, "Well, Yellowbird, are you going to stay here all night?"

"I am," answered Yellowbird.

"I have come to keep you from being lonely."

The young man recognized his wife's voice, and he was glad that she had come.

"I told you," said the woman, "that I should follow you. Hereafter I shall be with you. You'll not see me, but when you come to a fire and find food cooking you must not think that it doesn't belong to you. I shall be the cause of it. I shall be with my father in the daytime and with you at night."

Yellowbird was a great many days' journey from the chief's village, but this woman could travel as fast as thought; wherever her thoughts went there she was.

Before daylight, the woman rose and began cooking. When the food was ready, she awakened Yellowbird. They ate together, then all at once the woman was gone.

Yellowbird traveled till midday, then he saw a smoke and going toward it found a fire and cooked food. He ate all he wanted, gave thanks and traveled on.

Just as the sun went down, Yellowbird saw smoke ahead and soon he came to a small house. Going in he found a kettle of meat boiling over the fire. The meat wasn't quite cooked so he sat down and watched it. He thought, "Maybe this meat belongs to someone else," but when it was done he took it out of the kettle and cooled it.

Just as he was ready to eat he heard footsteps. "Now I'm caught," thought he. He sat with meat in one hand and liver in the other, and listened. The footsteps stopped outside the door and a rap came; the man didn't answer; another rap, he didn't answer. He put the liver and meat into the kettle and crept under a bunk that was there.

The skin door was pushed aside and a woman came in. She laughed, and asked, "Why are you afraid of me? I've come to keep you from being lonely."

"I wasn't afraid," said Yellowbird, coming from under the bunk, "I saw a mouse and thought I would catch it."

They ate and then slept. Before daylight food was ready. They ate, and the woman disappeared.

At midday Yellowbird saw smoke ahead and when he came to the fire found food ready, hulled corn and venison. He ate, gave thanks and went on. He didn't know how far or where he was going. At night he again found a house, and food ready. When he was about to eat someone came to the door. Yellowbird forgot the chief's daughter. He was frightened, and thought, "The owner of the house has come, he'll kill me." And taking up a club he went to the door to hit the man as he came in. When the chief's daughter pushed the door open, Yellowbird threw the club down.

The woman said, "I think you were going to kill me?"

"I was not, I was trying to kill a mouse."

They ate and slept. Before daylight food was ready. They ate again, then the woman disappeared and the young man went on. At midday he found food prepared for him. In the evening he came to a hut and went in. He stirred the fire and watched the kettle. When the meat was cooked, he took the kettle off the fire and was about to eat a piece of meat when he heard a noise outside. Again he forgot the chief's daughter and when a woman called, "Are you asleep?" he didn't answer.

"Can I come in?" asked she.

"Who are you? Where did you come from?" asked he.

"I came from the North."

After a long time Yellowbird said, "Come in."

The woman came in, laughing, and said, "It grows harder and harder to get to you. Why is this?"

"When I first came here," said Yellowbird, "people attacked me. I thought they had come back."

The woman laughed. She knew why he didn't remember her. The next morning, while they were eating, she said, "At midday you will come to an opening and a long flat. The flat is guarded by women. Just before midday you will find food ready. After eating, creep up to the edge of the opening and watch. If the women are in groups, run to a large hickory tree on the opposite side of the flat. When in the middle of the flat, call out, '*Gowe! Gowe!* I'm bound to run away.' "

Yellowbird started. Just before midday he came to a fire and found meat cooking. He took the kettle off, cooled the meat and ate as fast as he could, then he hurried along. Exactly at midday he came to the edge of an opening and saw women sitting around here and there in groups. They were eating. He saw the hickory tree and ran toward it. No one noticed him. When he came to the middle of the flat he shouted, "*Gowe! Gowe!* I'm bound to run away."

The women, who were of the White Heron family, sprang up and ran after him. They almost overtook him before he reached the woods on the other side of the opening. The chief's daughter was there to encourage and praise him. She said, "I shall come to you to-night for the last time." He left her and continued his journey. At sunset he saw a cabin, went in, and found food cooking. He poured the meat into a bark bowl and was ready to eat when he heard the rustle of dry leaves. He listened, and thought, "The Heron women are coming to kill me."

This time the chief's daughter didn't rap, she called out, "I've come to visit you."

Yellowbird seized a club, held it up ready to strike, then said, "Well, come in!"

When he saw his wife he sprang back and dropped the club.

She said, "You were going to strike me."

"I was not. I was trying to hit a mouse," said Yellowbird.

The woman laughed. They ate and then lay down but didn't sleep. They talked all night. The woman said, "This is the last time you will see me. Hereafter another person will care for you. You must travel in the same direction. Your happiness is at the end of this trail."

Before daylight the chief's daughter cooked a large quantity of food.—Food was always at hand. We are not told how it came to be there.

While eating she said, "To-morrow at midday you will come to a pond of bright water. On the bank you'll find a tree turned up by the roots. Go around the roots and pick up a bark basket that you'll find there. Fill the basket with water and go on till you come to a village. The chief of that village has a great deal of wampum. Sell him the water for wampum, then say that you'll leave the wampum in his care for a while. Take only one string. Stay a day and a night, then go on. After three days' travel, you will come to a wide opening, at the end of the opening you will find a tree that shines. Pull up that tree, take it with you to the next village and sell it to the chief. My protection ends here. I'll give you food for to-day's journey."

When the food was ready, Yellowbird put the bundle on his back and started. He traveled till hungry, then ate and went on again. At night he slept under a tree. At noon the next day, when looking for a resting place, he saw something so bright that he couldn't look at it. When near he saw that it was water and then he remembered what the chief's daughter had said. He found the basket and filled it. "This is strange water," thought he, but he traveled on, carrying the basket, first in one hand then in the other, till he came to a village. He went to the chief's house, but men standing there wouldn't let him go in.

"I must go straight on," said Yellowbird.

"If you try to we'll cut off your head," said the men. "It's the rule of the place."

They pulled up long flint knives that were sticking in the ground, and were about to cut off his head when the chief called out, "Let the man come in!"

"Where did you come from?" asked the chief.

"From the North."

"How far is your place from here?"

"It takes many days to go there."

"Do you know a man whose name is Daddy-long-legs?"

Yellowbird hung his head in thought, then a voice seemed to say to him, "Raise your head and tell him, the man he asks about is the father of the woman who has protected you so long, your own father-in-law."

Yellowbird raised his head, and said, "I know that chief. I came from his village."

"Do you know a man called Inchworm?"

"I know him. He is my father."

"Do you think you will ever see him again?"

"I do not."

"If you do, carry him this message: 'His mother died here two days ago.'"

When Yellowbird showed the shining water, the chief said, "I have wanted to find this water. I will give you many strings of wampum for it. Where did you get it?"

"From the Pond of Brightness, not far from here."

The chief and Yellowbird went to that pond and when they came back, the chief said, "I am glad that you are Inchworm's son; he and I are old friends."

The next morning Yellowbird said to the chief, "I am going away and I want to leave in your care the wampum you have given me for the bright water. I will take but one string now."

"Very well," said the chief, and he gave him one string.

The young man continued his journey. The first night he slept where darkness overtook him; the second night he slept in a hollow tree; the third night he camped in a hole in the rocks.

The fourth morning he had gone but a short distance, when he came to an opening in the forest and saw just ahead a shining tree. When he came to the tree, he pushed it over, then picked it up, put it across his shoulder and went on till he came to a village. He went to the chief's house and stood outside till the chief called to him to come in.

"Who are you and why have you come?" asked the chief.

"I have come to sell this tree," said Yellowbird.

"I will give you wampum for that tree. I'll give you my daughter and still more wampum if you will go with me to the place where you found the tree."

Yellowbird agreed and the two went to the place, and in the hole where the tree had been they found bright dirt and stones.

The chief said, "There are men who call these 'the eye-breaker stones.'"

Yellowbird married the chief's daughter.

After a while he said to her, "I want to go to my father's village."

"I will go with you," said the woman.

They started. When they came to the flat guarded by the Heron women they stole to the middle of the flat, then called out, "*Gowe! Gowe!* We are bound to run away." And they got to the opposite side of the flat before the Herons overtook them.

When Yellowbird came to his father's home, neither his father nor his mother knew him.

His mother said, "Our house is too poor for you."

"I went out of it to work for the chief," said the young man.

Then the mother recognized her son and was glad to see him.

The young man gave his father a string of wampum, and said, "Buy food with it, and get men to make me a bark house."

When the house was finished Yellowbird opened the door and threw in a string of wampum, then he closed the door and went away. The next morning there were a great many strings of wampum in the house, they had come from his father-in-law's house.

After many moons, a runner came to notify Yellowbird that a woman who lived on an island in a lake wanted him to come to her, and said if he didn't come he would lose his head.

Yellowbird was grieved, he didn't want to leave his wife and children, but that night he started toward the South, running as fast as he could. When he came to the edge of the lake, he said, "Now is the time to show my power to run on water."

He started, and he ran on the water as fast as he had on land. When he was near the middle of the lake, he bent his head down, didn't look forward—the woman on the island made him do this. When she found that he was coming on the water, she threw a pebble telling it to go straight in front of the man and become a rock so high and long that he couldn't pass over it or go around it.

Yellowbird, with head bent down, was running very fast. He struck the rock, fell back in the water and was drowned. High waves rolled up and carried him in the direction from which he came, and toward night his body was thrown on shore.

The Ancient of Bears came, looked at the body, and said, "This man is like the brother of Turtle, the man who always says, 'If my brother is destroyed, I will put an end to this world.' I must bring the man to life."

The Ancient of Bears worked over Yellowbird, used all of his power, and at last brought him to life.

"You are alive," said Bear when Yellowbird opened his eyes. "Now you must go East, to the end of the world. Your brother lives there. You must pacify him. If you don't he will destroy us. Take one of my teeth; it will help you to go quickly. You must hurry, for your brother is angry, he thinks that someone has killed you."

While they stood talking they heard a great roar and far off in the East they saw a column of fire shoot up and spread out over the country.

"Hurry!" said the Ancient of Bears. "If you don't, he will destroy us!"

Yellowbird ran and his speed was so great that he seemed to fly. When he came to the edge of the world where the fire was, he saw a dark figure pushing its head forward.

"My brother," called he, "I want you to stop being angry, I am alive."

"If you are my brother," said Turtle, "you must sing our war song and cross the world four times."

The young man ran to the end of the world and back to his brother. The force of the flame coming up from below the edge of the earth began to diminish. He ran a second time and back: the flame was dying down. When he came back the fourth time, the fire was out.

Turtle said, "Thank you, Brother. Now I want you to tell me where the thing is that I gave you long ago."

"When did you give it to me? What was it?"

"I gave it to you when you were born."

"Maybe my mother is keeping it for me," said Yellowbird. "I'll go and get it."

"Have you anything to help you run faster than you do now?" asked Turtle.

"I have not."

"I'll give you power to go so fast that as soon as you think of a place you will be there. And you shall have the power of turning yourself into anything you like."

He gave him a small piece of something like flesh, and said, "When you want to use this put it in your mouth. Now go as fast as you can."

Yellowbird put the thing in his mouth and started. Right away he was at his father's house, and going in he asked his mother, "Have you anything that my brother gave me long ago?"

"I have," said she, "Here it is, I have never thought of it till now," and she gave him a tiny hand.

Taking the hand, Yellowbird went back to his brother, who, when he saw the hand said, "You are my brother. Now we will go to the woman on the island. You will go ahead, I will follow. If I overtake you, I will cut off your head, for that will increase your speed."

They started and soon the elder brother began to gain on the younger. When he was about to overtake him, Yellowbird changed to a deer and shot ahead. The elder brother changed to a deer and had almost caught up when the younger brother became an elk and ran away from the deer. They held on in this way. Whenever Yellowbird neared his brother, the latter changed into something, and right away the elder brother changed too.

When they came to the edge of the lake, Yellowbird turned into a bass and disappeared in the water, the elder brother became a bass too. At the opposite bank Yellowbird was an eel. The eel touched land and became a man, then an enormous eel sprang to land, became a man, and called, "Stop, Brother, I give up, you have beaten me. The woman who sent for you is chief of a village not far from here. An enormous water monster is destroying her people. She wants you to kill the monster. When you reach her village I will be there."

Yellowbird came to the village and went toward the

chief's house, but two men stood in his way. When they refused to let him pass, he drew out his basswood knife and cut off their heads. He went into the house and said to the chief, "I am angry, for it has cost me much labor to come here. What do you want?"

"I want you to destroy a monster that is killing off my people. He makes rain come, and he can bring water out of the lake to any place where he wants to kill a person. When the person is dead, the water falls back; whomever the water touches it kills. If you destroy this monster, you shall be chief in my place."

Early in the morning Yellowbird and the chief started for the lake. The villages were far apart. When they came to the last village the woman said, "The lake is close by. I will stay here in the village. I don't want Muck-worm to know that we are here; he is a bad man."

While they were talking, rain began to fall. The woman was frightened. "This will kill me," said she.

"It is nothing," said Yellowbird, and he went through the village and into a forest.

Just before coming to an opening he heard a whisper. He looked on all sides but could see no one. Again he heard some one whisper and turning he saw his brother.

"Now," said the brother, "You must use all the power I have given you. The only way to destroy the monster is to go to the lake and cut off its head. Bring its heart, tongue and claws away with you."

Yellowbird went to the lake. The place where the lake had been was covered with sand. There was no water except in the center where there was a hollow. In that hollow lay an enormous Beaver, asleep. Yellowbird cut the monster open, took its heart, tongue and claws and ran for his life. As he reached the forest down came the monster. It leaped toward Yellowbird and barely missed him. Turtle took the heart and pounded it to jelly.

Beaver spoke then to the brothers, and said, "You have great power, you have overcome and destroyed me."

Beaver went back to the hollow in the sand and as he went the forest moved up on both sides and occupied the place where the lake had been.

Turtle said to his brother, "Keep the claws, but give the

tongue to the chief as a proof that you have destroyed the monster."

The woman made Yellowbird chief in her place and became his wife.

Yellowbird changed to an Eagle—his new wife was an Eagle. He went high in the air and when he came to the ground, he was at his old home with his wife and children.

One day he sat very still as though listening. All at once he said, "Off in the West people are crying, I must find out what is troubling them."

The next morning Yellowbird started off, he traveled all day and at night crawled into a hollow tree.

Soon a voice asked, "What would you do if Whirlwind came?"

"I would be pleased."

The speaker went away and soon Yellowbird heard heavy wind and rain coming from the South. Whirlwind leveled the trees to the ground, struck the tree Yellowbird was in, raised it up, carried it away, whirled it over and over, played with it. Yellowbird got impatient; it was almost morning, still he was whirling through the air.

At last the tree fell into the sea and was torn to pieces. Yellowbird lay on one of the boughs. He fastened two or three boughs together and sat on them as on a raft. The water rolled up big waves, "My raft will go to pieces and I'll be drowned," thought he.

Someone laughed, and said, "You are a fool! You don't think of me, even when you are in trouble. You know that I am always behind you, waiting to hear you say, 'I wish my brother were here.' Sit on my back, I'll carry you ashore."

When they reached shore, Turtle asked, "Where is what I gave you?"

"I have lost it," said Yellowbird.

"No you haven't."

When Yellowbird found what he thought he had lost, he traveled on till he came to a place where the earth troubled people. It became soft, heaved up and rolled over their homes.

Then Yellowbird said to himself, "My Brother, I wish you were here."

That minute Turtle was at his side. "I thank you," said he, "for thinking of me. The people here do wrong. They kill and eat one another. If they will cease doing that, they will have no more trouble."

Yellowbird sent a runner to tell the people to assemble and when they had come together, he said, "You kill and eat one another. If you will promise to stop doing this, I will tell the earth to keep still. Yonder is a great forest in which there are wild beasts. Kill those beasts and use their flesh for food."

They promised to do as he told them.

When Yellowbird was about to start for home, his elder brother stood by his side, and said, "On your way home pay no heed to anyone."

Yellowbird traveled four days and then came to his own village. He had not been at home long when a runner came to notify him that a woman chief summoned him to be in her village at midday. He rose up and started. As soon as he was out of sight of the house, he changed to an eagle and flew along just high enough to see what was going on below. When he saw a lake, he dropped down to the edge of the water, turned to a duck and swam to the opposite side. Then he changed to a man and traveled on till he came to the village.

At the edge of the village was a cabin. In the cabin lived an old woman and her granddaughter.

When Yellowbird went into the cabin, the old woman asked, "My Grandson, which way did you come?"

"From beyond the lake."

"Why did you come?"

"The chief of the village sent for me. I came because I couldn't help coming."

"My Grandson, I pity you," said the old woman. "When our chief hears of a man who has power, she sends for him and gives him to a serpent that lives in the lake."

"Well," said Yellowbird, "if I am overpowered, your chief and all of her people will be destroyed, my brother will come and punish your chief."

At midday Yellowbird went to the chief's house. When he saw the chief, he said, "I have come. What do you want? I am angry, for you called me from my work."

"I want you to kill a snake that is destroying my people. If you can kill it, I will make you chief in my place. You can try now, for at midday the snake comes out of the lake."

As Yellowbird went toward the lake, the water began to rise and soon the snake appeared. As it lay on the water it was the height of a man. When it reached the shore and came toward Yellowbird, he turned to run. The snake caught him by the feet and drew him into its throat to the arms, but the man stretched out his arms and saved himself from going down. The snake went into the water. The water moved away, piled up on both sides and left the snake on the bottom of the lake, on dry land.

Then over his head somewhere Yellowbird heard his brother laugh, and say, "My Brother, you are a fool, When you saw the snake coming, you should have thought of me. Exert yourself!"

Yellowbird pulled and easily got loose, then he ran between the walls of water, the snake close to his heels. When he reached the bank the water closed up. The elder brother threw a white flint stone at the snake's head and the snake rolled over dead. The water heaved up till it reached the village, then it receded.

Yellowbird went to the chief, and said, "I have killed the snake."

She thanked him, and said, "Now you are chief in my place," but she was not pleased.

Yellowbird went to the lake, turned to a duck and swam out a good distance, then he changed to an eagle and soon was at home.

Yellowbird remained with his wife and children till a runner came with a message from the chief of the village where he had killed the Beaver. She said, "Be here to-morrow at midday."

Yellowbird did not change his form but he ran in the air till he came to a lake. He was running over the lake, but near the water, when he struck against an invisible object and was thrown back. He rose again and ran on, ran swiftly and before he could stop he was in a tangle of grape vines. He bounded back and fell. He was terribly angry and as he rose up, he said, "Why should she send for me and then try to prevent my coming?"

He reached Eagle's house, rushed in and said to her, "I am here and I will punish you!"

He seized the woman by the hair and cut off her head, then he started for home. When well on the way, he met a beautiful, smiling woman, who asked, "May I go with you?"

"Don't bother me," said Yellowbird. "I am traveling."

"Rest a while," said the woman.

"I will not stop. If you speak to me again, I will cut off your head."

"Oh, stop and talk," begged the woman.

Yellowbird turned, and seizing the woman by the hair, cut off her head. Then he went on till he came to his own village.

One day, after Yellowbird had been at home a long time, he heard a terrible noise and going out saw that the earth was cracking open here and there. It cracked more and more, opened great ditches. All at once a man appeared in the air, and said, "You are frightened. You think you and your people are going to die. You will not. Follow me."

Then Yellowbird rose in the air and the two traveled southward followed by all of Yellowbird's people. As they looked back, they saw the village, where Yellowbird had been, sink out of sight and water rise up there. Then the head of Turtle came from under the water and he called out, "*Gowe! Gowe!* This is the kind of man I am."

The guide, whom Yellowbird and his people were following, said, "Your brother is angry because you killed the Eagle woman. To show his power he has destroyed everything."

They traveled on till the air was fragrant. They saw beautiful ripe berries, and then houses where people lived. One house was larger than the others.

The guide said, "The man of controlling power lives there."

They went on and on till they came to a village that Yellowbird recognized. It was his native village.

The guide said, "Now you are at home, and safe."

The people went into their houses and found everything, as it seemed to them, exactly as they had left it—But this village was above the Blue. Their guide was the man of the Blue.

Yellowbird, though he was called after his dog, was not a bird; he was an inchworm. His first wife was a grasshopper.

THE YOUNG WOMAN AND THUNDER

[Told by George Titus]

Characters

OTHÄGWEⁿDONIS ....Flintmaker
OⁿHDAGWÍJA ....Good Ear
DÉONÊYONT ....Red-hot
HADÄE′ONIS ....Netmaker
HÍNO′ ....Thunder
DJONKDJOⁿKWEⁿ ....Chickadee

ONE day a stranger went into a cabin where a man and his wife and four children lived and asked to marry the youngest daughter of the family. The father and mother consented and the stranger married the girl.

After a time he asked his wife to go home with him; her parents were willing and the two started. They hadn't gone far when they came to a cabin and the young man said, "This is my home."

There was nobody in the cabin when the husband and wife came but toward night the woman heard some one coming on the run. Soon a man came in and sat down by the door. Again she heard running; another man came in and sat down; then a third man came.

The three men began talking with one another, relating how far they had traveled and what they had killed.

One said, "I had good luck, I killed a bear."

Finding that he was the only one who had killed anything, the two said, "Go and bring the bear. We'll cook it."

The young woman sat at the opposite end of the room, watching. She saw the man bring in what he called a bear, saw that it was the trunk and head of a man's body. The men cut it up and put it in a kettle to boil. When cooked they ate it.

The three walked back and forth in the room without looking toward the woman. Her husband was there but he didn't talk or eat with the men. They were his brothers but he never ate their kind of food.

Each morning the three brothers went to hunt for game. In the evening they came back and sitting down near the door talked over their journey. Then, if they had killed any game, they brought it into the cabin, cooked and ate it. If they had no game, they ate what was left from the meal of the previous evening.

One day when the young woman went for water, she found a man standing by the spring. The man said to her, "I have come to tell you that to-morrow your husband is going into the ground. As soon as he goes put some of your spittle exactly in the center of the cabin and tell it to answer for you every time your husband speaks. When you have done that hurry to this place."

The next morning the young man said to his wife, "I am going into the ground and I want you to stay in the cabin all the time I am away." He turned around and right where he stood he disappeared.

After doing as she had been told, the woman went to the spring; the stranger was there. Taking an arrow he put the woman into the head of it, and saying, "When the arrow falls, jump out and hurry along the lake, as fast as you can." He shot the arrow into the air.

The husband called to his wife, "Are you there?"

"I am here," answered the spittle.

After a time he called again, "Are you there?"

"I am here," was the answer.

The man was away a number of days and he often asked, "Are you there?" and always received the same answer. When he came above ground and asked, "Where are you, wife?" and her voice answered, "I am here," he looked around but didn't see her, then he found what had been talking to him.

He was terribly angry and right away began to hunt for the woman's tracks. He found them and followed them to the spring, but there they disappeared. He hunted a long time, then, getting discouraged, he called his dog O^{n}HDAGWÍJA (Good Ear), and said, "You didn't take care of my wife while I was gone. Now you must find her."

The man watched the dog. It ran around and around and came back to the spring, then it stopped hunting on the ground, looked up in the air, sniffed and ran toward the North, looking up all the time as if it saw tracks. The man followed the dog. After a while the two came to where the arrow fell, then there were tracks on the ground.

The dog barked and began to run faster, the man urging it on. When they were about to overtake the woman, the stranger who had been at the spring stood in front of her.

Putting her into an arrow, he said, "You will come down on an island in a lake. Run across the island in every direction. I will be there."

When the man and dog came to where the woman met the stranger they lost her tracks. Again the dog ran around smelling the ground, then looking up in the air he saw a trail and followed it.

When Good Ear and his master came to the lake the man changed to a flea and went into the hair behind the dog's ear.

The dog swam to the island, the flea became a man and the two traveled on till they came to where the arrow fell. There they found the woman's tracks and followed them across and around the island.

When they were overtaking the woman the stranger stood in front of her, and, putting her into an arrow, said, "You will come down on the shore of the lake. Run as fast as you can. I can do nothing more for you, but you will soon come to a village and there you will find some one to help you. Now you may know who I am."

As the stranger turned to go the woman saw that he was DJONKDJO^{n}KWE (Chickadee).

When the dog came to where the tracks disappeared on the ground, he saw the trail in the air and knew that the woman had crossed the lake. Again the man turned to a flea and hid in the dog's hair. The dog swam to the shore; the flea became a man, and the two followed the woman's footprints.

When her husband was so near that the woman could hear the dog bark, she came to a house. A man was sitting inside making arrow-heads. The man was OTHÄGWEⁿ-DONIS (Flintmaker). When the woman asked him to help her, he said, "I will do what I can, but hurry along, the man in the next house will help you."

When the dog came Flintmaker threw a handful of arrow-heads at him. Wherever the arrow-heads struck they tore up the trees and the ground, but the dog dodged them all, ran at Flintmaker, caught him by the throat and shook him till he was dead.

At the second house the woman found a man making nets. This man was HADÄE′ONIS (Netmaker).

The woman said to him, "I am running away from a bad man. I want you to help me."

"I'll do what I can," said HADÄE′ONIS, "but hurry on. You will soon come to a house, the people who live there will help you."

When the dog and the man came, HADÄE′ONIS threw out a net. It caught the two and wound around and around them. For a long time they struggled to free themselves. At last the dog broke through the net, ran at HADÄE′ONIS, caught him by the throat and shook him till he was dead.

In the third house the woman found four brothers. When she asked them for help, they went out and chopping down dry trees piled them on her tracks. When they had a high pile, they set it afire, and standing, two at each side of the pile, they waited.

The dog and the man came to the fire, the dog wanted to go around but the man saw that the tracks led into the fire and he said, "No! You must go through."

The dog sprang into the fire and the man followed. When they came out on the other side both dog and man were almost dead. The eldest of the four brothers said, "We will shoot them."

They shot, but arrows had no effect.

Then the old man said, "We must catch them, kill them, and pull their hearts out."

They caught the man and the dog, killed them, pulled out their hearts and put the hearts in a red hot kettle that the old man had heated over the fire. The hearts flew around and around trying to get out of the kettle but the brothers pushed them down and shot at them till they were dead and burned to ashes.

The old man, whose name was DÉONĒYONT (Red-hot), went to the house and told the woman she was safe. He said to her, "You must rest four days then go home."

When the fourth day came, Red-hot said, "It is time to go. Your home is in the South. As you travel you will know where you are."

The woman started. About midday she met a stranger, who said, "Towards night you will find something to eat."

She traveled till the sun went down, then came to a large stump and found there a pot of hulled corn cooked with bear meat, she thought, "This must be what the man meant." She ate the hulled corn and meat then went on till dark. That night she camped under a tree.

The next morning the woman started again. At midday she met the stranger and he told her that she would soon find something to eat. Towards night she came to a stump and found there a pot of hulled corn and bear meat.

The next morning when the woman woke up, the stranger was standing by her. He said, "You are near your father's home and I shall leave you now. I am the one whom men call HI'NO' (Thunder)."

The stranger disappeared and the woman went on till she came in sight of an old house. Then she saw a spring and right away she knew it was the spring where she used to get water. In the house she found her father and mother. They were glad to see her and said "Yâwe^n."

PARTRIDGE AND TURTLE AND THEIR COUSINS WOLVES

[Told by John Armstrong]

TWO brothers, Partridge and Turtle, lived together. Wolves, their cousins, lived in a house not far away. One day old man Wolf said, "You had better all go out hunting."

They started off, going toward the East in Indian file. After a time they said, "We will separate and each man will go where he likes. If anyone sees game, he can call out."

As Turtle was going along, he came to a log that he couldn't get over so he called out. Partridge heard him and running up to see what game he had found, asked, "What is it?"

Turtle said, "I can't get over this log, it is so high."

"But you shouldn't call out," said Partridge. "The men might think you had found game. Don't call again unless you find game," and catching Turtle by the leg he threw him over the log.

Again Turtle came to a log and couldn't get over, so he cried loudly for help. Partridge ran up and seeing what the trouble was caught Turtle by the leg and threw him over as hard as he could, saying, "The next time you come to a log, you go around it."

"But," said Turtle, "our leader told us to go straight ahead and I did as he said."

"Well, don't be afraid; go around the log next time," answered Partridge.

After that Turtle went around the logs. Soon he came

to a river, and near the river he saw a tree loaded with plums; some of the plums had fallen to the ground. Turtle had on a bark apron. He gathered it up, bag shape, and filled it with plums. While he was eating and looking around, he saw Elk coming.

When near where Turtle stood, Elk asked, "Brother, will you give me some of those plums?"

"No, I'm a great deal smaller than you are, I can't knock them off of the tree as easily as you can."

"How do you knock them off?"

"I'll tell you, I go as far away as I can and see them, then run very fast to the tree and strike my head against it."

"Did you do that?"

"Yes. It hurt some, but not very long. You can do the same way and you'll knock off a great many plums."

Elk went some distance then running as fast as he could struck his head against the tree. The blow threw him back and he couldn't get up. Turtle dropped his plums and jumping on to Elk caught him by the neck and choked him to death. Then he called out loudly.

Partridge came running up, and asked, "What have you done now?"

"I'm a man. I've killed an Elk."

Partridge was glad, and asked, "How can we hide this from our cousins? They are great eaters and would soon finish this meat, but you and I are small people we could live on it a long time. If we could find a hollow tree, we could hide the meat in it. While I am hunting for the tree, you go to our cousins and borrow a knife. If they ask why you want the knife tell them you are going to dig mushrooms."

"No," said Turtle, "You must go, you can fly. If I go they will track me and find out what we are doing."

Partridge flew over to where Wolves were hunting.

They asked, "What luck have you had?"

Partridge tried to answer, but he stuttered so he couldn't get out a single word.

"What makes you stutter?" asked his cousins. "You are frightened. Have you done something bad?"

Again Partridge tried to speak, but couldn't.

"Let him alone," said Old Man Wolf, "he'll tell after a while."

Now Partridge stood up straight, his eyes wide open, and tried to say knife, but stuttered out something that sounded like spear. He had made up his mind to say that he was going to cut his brother's hair.

"Do you want a spear?" asked Old Wolf.

"No, knife!"

"Well, give him a knife," said Old Wolf.

Partridge took the knife and going back to where Turtle was the two cut up the Elk and carried it, piece by piece, to a hollow tree that Turtle had found. Then they camped in the tree.

When cold weather came Old Wolf said, "I wonder where our cousins are? Maybe they have starved to death. We must try to find them."

Several of the Wolves started. After traveling a long distance, they saw a smoke coming out of a hollow tree. They went back and said, "We have found Turtle and Partridge, they are living in a hollow tree far off in the woods."

Old Wolf said, "Go to the tree and find out what they are doing."

When the men came to the tree they saw many bones. Partridge had told Turtle not to throw bones out, if he did Wolves would scent them, but Turtle had disobeyed him.

When Wolves saw the bones, they said, "This is why Partridge was so frightened when he came to borrow a knife. They killed a deer and have eaten it up without giving us any." Before this the cousins had always shared with one another. "Now we'll cut the tree down, kill Turtle and Partridge and eat them."

They set to work and soon the tree began to bend over. Turtle saw what his cousins were doing and he screamed, "Let the tree be large! Let the tree be large!"

The tree grew quickly and caught on to another tree. The Wolves began to chop the second tree.

Again Turtle screamed "Let the tree be large!" and it caught to a third tree.

They began to cut the third tree, thinking that all the trees would fall at the same time.

Now Turtle asked Partridge, "Can you carry me in your skirt?"

"I can try. Maybe I can if you hold on tight when I fly."

Partridge flew off and Turtle held on to his skirt till he was too tired to hold any longer. Then he fell, and Wolves, who had followed, said, "Now, we'll punish him."

"What will we do to him?" asked one, "roast him?"

"You can roast me," said Turtle, "but you'll never have a fire again, I'll put it out forever."

Wolves said, "Maybe he could do that. Let's chop him to pieces."

"You can if you want to," said Turtle, "but you'll never have a sharp knife again. My back is made of bone."

"That's true," said Wolves, "We'll take a mallet and pound him to death."

"Yes, pound me to death, but never again will you have a mallet."

Now Old Wolf spoke up, and said, "I know how to kill him. Drag him to the lake and throw him in!"

Turtle began to cry, and to beg, saying, "I shall die if you throw me into the water."

He cried so hard that they agreed that this was the way to kill him. They dragged him to the lake and threw him in, then they sat down on the bank to see him drown.

Soon Turtle stuck up his head and seeing Wolves called out, "You are fools! Didn't you know that water is my home?"

Wolves were so angry that they sent for an Elk to come and drink up the water. But when Elk had drunk the lake dry, they couldn't find Turtle; he had buried himself in the mud. There was nothing to be done; Elk threw up the water and the Wolves went home.

After a long time Turtle was one day out hunting and he met a Wolf. Wolf began to make fun of Turtle's short legs, told him he oughtn't to go where people could see him, he was so ugly.

Turtle looked at Wolf, and said, "Well, if I have short legs I can beat you running. Notify your people and I'll notify mine, and to-morrow we will run a race."

Wolf was greatly pleased, and he came next day, with all his friends.

Now Turtle had stationed six of his friends, all of the same size, and each with a white feather in his headdress, at certain places along the course.

At the starting Wolf left Turtle far behind and turning he called out, "Why don't you come on?"

But when Wolf was some distance along he heard Turtle call, "Why don't you come on?" and looking saw him ahead.

Wolf passed him, then turned and shouted, "Why don't you run faster?"

The third Turtle came up ahead of Wolf, and called, "You'll be beaten if you don't run faster!"

So on to the sixth Turtle. As soon as Wolf passed, the Turtle would hide in the ground and another Turtle spring up ahead of Wolf.

Now the Turtle people sent up a shout of victory. Turtle had reached the goal and beaten Wolf.

Wolf told Turtle, "Hereafter you and your people can live on the hills and I and my people will live in the woods."

And so it is. At this time Partridges, Wolves, and Turtles from being people became what they are now.

THOUSAND-LEGS AND BRIGHT BODY
HIS SON

Characters

Sadzawíski..............Thousand-legs (A Worm)
Doyádastethe ....Bright Body
Dí'dí ....Blue Jay
Shagoyagéntha ....He Hides Them
Gáqga' .... Raven
Yeqsínye ....Spinner (of the Spider Family)
Dewaqso^{n}thwûs ....Flea

THOUSAND-LEGS (a worm) lived in a house with his wife and seven sons; only the youngest of the seven had a name. He was called Bright Body. Bright Body was so small that his father didn't let him go outside, or play around in the house. He stayed under an old couch and played with his dog, a flea.

Thousand-legs was poor, for though he went hunting before sunrise and came back after dark, he brought home very little game. One morning his wife asked, "Can't you get more game? We are hungry."

"I have bad luck," said Thousand-legs.

"Your back often looks as if you had packed lots of game."

"I bring home all I find, I never have any luck."

The woman didn't believe what her husband said.

That evening Thousand-legs brought no game but his

back was covered with fresh blood. His wife said, "There is blood on your back, you must have killed some animal."

"I got hurt," said the man, "A hemlock tree fell on me."

The next morning Thousand-legs was up and off before sunrise. His wife followed him. Just before midday, with a small stone, he killed a large bear. He took the bear on his back and started off. After a while he came to a house and went in. His wife crept up, and listened.

There was a woman in the house who, after she had greeted the man, said, "The next time you come, you must stay, not go away."

"Very well," answered Thousand-legs, then leaving the bear, he came out and started for home.

His wife ran on ahead, always keeping out of sight. When she reached the house, she said to the boys, "Your father has another wife. I can't stay here any longer," and, putting on her panther-skin blanket, she went away.

When Thousand-legs came he asked, "What is the matter? Where is your mother?"

One of the boys said, "She went out early in the morning and was gone all day, but a little while ago she came and put on her panther-skin blanket, then she said she was going away and wasn't coming back."

Thousand-legs hung his head. At last he asked, "Why did she go?"

"She said that you had another wife."

"Well, my sons, I am going to follow your mother. You must stay here while I am gone. If I live I will be back in ten days."

Thousand-legs found his wife's tracks and followed them; he traveled all night. The next morning he saw that the tracks doubled back, but he kept straight ahead, knowing his wife had done this to deceive him. Soon he was on her trail again, going directly West.

After a while Thousand-legs came to a house where a very old man was living. The old man said, "You are traveling?"

"Yes," said Thousand-legs, "I am following the woman whose tracks come to this house."

The old man's name was SHA-GO-YA-GÉNTHA (He Hides

Them). He was of the Toad family. He said, "I don't know where the woman has gone."

"Her tracks stop at your door."

"You can look for her if you want to."

Thousand-legs looked everywhere, but didn't find his wife.

Then the old man said, in his mind, "I will send him off," and he asked. "Do you want me to send you in the direction your wife went?"

"I do."

The old man brought a small white-flint canoe and told Thousand-legs to sit in it. He did, and then the old man pushed the canoe forward. It rose in the air and went with great swiftness till it struck against a high rock. Thousand-legs was thrown out, fell among rocks and was killed.

The seven boys stayed at home till they were very hungry. Then the eldest went out to see if he could find anything for his brothers to eat and when night came he didn't come home.

The next morning the second brother started off to look for the first. The brothers at home waited all day but neither brother came.

The next morning the third brother went to look for the other two, and he didn't come back.

Each day a brother went out till six had gone and not one had returned. Only Bright Body was left, he was under the couch playing with his dog.

At last the boy said in his mind, "It seems to me there is no one in the house; it is very quiet here."

He crawled from under the couch and looking around didn't see anyone. "What has happened?" thought he, "Why have they all gone away?" He listened, but couldn't hear footsteps or voices. After listening a long time, he said, "I think that I hear my mother crying, far off in the West. I must go to her."

He went outside and listened, his dog standing behind him. Again he heard crying and the sound came from a great distance.

"That is my mother," said he, "I must go to her. She is in trouble."

He and his dog rose in the air and went along above the highest trees, always going toward the West.

Bright Body came down at the edge of a village and going into a cabin found two women there, a grandmother and her granddaughter.

He said to the old woman, "I have come to visit you."

"We are poor," said she, "we haven't anything to eat."

"I don't want food," said Bright Body, "I only want shelter at night."

"You can stay," said the old grandmother, whose name was Spinner. She made rope, by rolling strips of bark on her knees.

Bright Body had not been in the cabin long when someone ran up, kicked the door open, and said, "To-night they will burn the woman's feet; her tears are wampum beads. Maybe you can pick up some of the beads."

The messenger ran off to the next cabin, and the grandmother said, "The people of this village are bad people. That man is the servant of Blue Jay, the chief, the rest of the people are of the Raven family."

When night came, Bright Body went to the long house. A great many people were there. Going inside he saw his mother tied to a post. As soon as he came his mother knew he was there.

The chief rose, and said, "Be ready. Look out for the beads!"

The chief's two daughters lighted the torches, for the old grandmothers were going to burn the woman's feet. When they held the torches to her flesh tears ran from her eyes to the floor and as they touched the floor they became beautiful beads. Everyone rushed to pick them up.

Bright Body was watching. When the people were on their knees scrambling for the beads he untied his mother and led her outside. Then he ran around the house and as he ran he repeated, "I want you to be stone and to be red hot! I want you to be stone and to be red hot!"

The house became stone and the stone was red hot. The people were suffocating. They stopped picking up beads and hurried to get out of the house, but there was no way out. For a time there was shouting and screaming, then all was quiet.

Bright Body said to his mother, "We will leave this place," and calling his dog they started.

When going through the village a blue lizard chased Bright Body, but he tore the lizard to pieces and the dog carried the pieces far off in different directions so they could not come together again, and Bright Body said, "Lizard, you thought you were going to kill me, but I am more powerful than you were. I have destroyed you."

When Bright Body came to Spinner's house, he said to her, "I have killed all the people in the village. Now you can live in peace."

She thanked him, and he and his mother and his dog traveled on till they came to their own home. There Bright Body found his six brothers and they all lived together and were happy.

The story doesn't say how the brothers got home or what happened to them.

A YOUNG MAN RESCUED BY A TOAD

Character

NOSGWAIS ....Toad

TWO brothers lived together. The elder hunted but never brought home any game. The younger noticed that his brother's back was always bloody, as though he had been carrying freshly killed game. He couldn't understand this, so one day he followed his brother, saw him kill a deer, throw it over his shoulder and start for home, but he hadn't gone far when a woman approached from one side, took the deer and carried it off.

The next day the younger brother went in the direction the woman had taken. He soon came to a house and going in found a young woman. She laughed and began to talk to him. After talking a while, he started for home. When he had gone some distance, he found that he was going back to the house he had just left.

As he turned to go in the opposite direction his brother came up behind him, and said, "Don't you know that there is a fishhook in your neck?"

The elder brother took out the fishhook, stuck it in a bush and said, "Your safety depends upon getting away from here as quickly as you can." He made his brother small, put him in his arrow, and saying, "When the arrow comes to the ground, get out of it and run for your life," he shot the arrow into the air.

When the woman pulled on the hook and couldn't move it, she followed the line and found the hook in a bush. She was angry, and said, "You cannot escape from me in this way."

She went to the young man's cabin. He wasn't there. She tracked him to her own house and then back to the bush and looking up she saw the trail of the arrow and she followed it till she came to the place where the arrow fell, then she ran on quickly.

As the woman approached, the young man heard her steps and pulling off his moccasins he told them to run to the end of the world. And there, where he stood, he became a stump.

The woman came to the stump, halted, and looking at it said, "This stump is like a man. But the tracks go on," and she hurried away.

The woman reached the end of the world and there stood the moccasins. She rushed back to where she had seen the stump. It wasn't there, but she found fresh tracks and followed them.

When the young man heard the woman coming he took up a stone, threw it behind him, and said, "Let there be a high rock from one end of the world to the other." That minute the rock was there.

The woman came to the rock and could neither go through it nor over it, nor could she crawl under it.

"I never heard of this rock," said she. "It can't go across the world, I'll go around it."

She ran to the end of the world, went back and ran to the opposite end but she couldn't get around the rock. Then going to the place she started from she tried to break the rock by striking her head against it. The rock didn't break, but she struck her head such a blow that she fell back apparently dead. After a long time she opened her eyes and looked up; the rock had disappeared, only a little stone lay there.

"Oh, he is using his power," said the woman, and again she hurried after him.

When the young man heard her coming, he took a pigeon feather out of his pocket, and said, as he threw it behind him, "Let there be a pigeon roost across the world and so many pigeons on it that their droppings will be so deep and high that nothing can get through or over them."

The woman came to the roost and when she couldn't get through the droppings, she said, "I never heard of a pigeon roost that went across the world. I'll go around it."

She went to one end of the world, then to the other, but couldn't go around the roost. Going back to the place she started from she tried to break through with her head, but fell back apparently dead. After a long time she opened her eyes and saw a small feather on the ground; the roost had disappeared. She was angrier than ever and ran on with greater speed.

The young man came to a lake and saw people in the water playing tag. He halted, and said, "Let one of those men become just like me. Let me become a stump."

The woman came to the stump but hearing the laughter of the people playing tag she looked at them and saw that the man far out in the lake was the man she was following.

The people, seeing the woman, called out, "Come and help us catch this man who outswims us."

She sprang into the water, chased the man and at last caught hold of him. That instant he took his own form. Then she knew that she had been fooled. She hurried back to the shore; the stump had disappeared.

Again the woman followed the young man's tracks. As he heard her coming, a man stood in front of him and asked, "What is the trouble?"

"A woman is chasing me."

"I will help you. Get on to my back," said the stranger, stooping down, "I'll throw you on to the side of a hill. Run along the hill till you are forced to descend."

The stranger was Nosgwais (Toad). The young man sat on his back. Nosgwais stretched till his legs were of enormous length, then he threw the young man off a great distance.

The woman came to where the man met Nosgwais. The ground was soft and springy. As she tried to go forward it rose up and threw her back. Looking around she found that she was on the back of an enormous toad. She got off and, running in circles, hunted for the young man's tracks, and after a long time she reached the hill.

When the young man struck the hill, he jumped up and ran on, ran till he fell and, unable to get up, rolled down the hill, going so fast that he didn't realize anything till he struck a house and a voice inside of it said, "Something is in our trap!"

A young woman came, lifted him out of the trap and led him into the house.

"What is the trouble?" asked an old woman who was there.

"A woman is chasing me," said the young man.

"I will help you." She filled a kettle with bear oil and put it over the fire. When the oil began to boil, she said, "Let this man's face look up from the bottom of the kettle."

There was a noise outside, the door opened and the woman came in. "Where is the man I am following?" asked she.

"He ran into this kettle," said the old woman, "that's the last we saw of him."

The woman looked into the kettle, saw the man, and saying, "I knew that I should overtake you!" she plunged into the kettle to seize him. The boiling oil killed her.

The old woman called to the man, and said, "The person who was chasing you is dead."

Her daughter said, "This man will be my husband."

After a time the young man became the father of twin boys. When the boys began to run around, their father said to them, "You must go for your uncle."

They started and after traveling a long time came to a house; in the house was an old man.

One of the boys said to him, "Uncle, we have come for you."

The man got ready and went with them. When they reached home the younger brother greeted the elder, and said, "Now you will always live with us."

And so it was.

A MAN PURSUED BY HIS UNCLE AND BY HIS WIFE

[Told by Johnny John who learned it from his grandmother, "who lived to be one hundred and thirty years old."]

A N old man and his nephew lived together in a forest. Their house had a partition through the middle and a door at each end. The uncle never entered the part occupied by his nephew, and all communication between the two was held by each hearing through the partition what the other said to himself. Each went in and out of his own part of the house when he liked, but neither ever crossed the threshold of the other part.

After a time the nephew discovered his uncle's true nature—he was a man-eater.

One day a woman came to the young man's part of the house. The next morning the uncle said, "My nephew has two ways of breathing."

The young man, speaking to himself, said, "My uncle is mistaken, I am talking to myself."

"My nephew can't deceive me," said the old man. "There are two persons in his part of the house. I am glad that game has come to him—I am going hunting."

When his uncle had gone, the young man said to his wife, "My uncle knows that you are here, now you must do as I tell you. If you don't he will kill and eat you. Three women have been here. He killed and ate each one of them, for they paid no heed to what I told them. Before I go away to hunt, I will bring wood and water and whatever you want, so you need not go out. If you go out, you are lost. My uncle will kill you. As soon as I leave the house he will come back."

The young man started off, but turned back and a second time warned his wife not to disobey him.

The minute the nephew was out of sight in the forest, the uncle came to the door. The old man had the power of commanding things to be done and the person had to obey though they didn't hear or see him.

He said, "Let the woman come out!"

But the woman had power also. When he saw that she didn't come out, he said, "Let the water she is cooking with boil away!"

The water boiled away, but the woman had a plenty more. The old man was angry, and said, "I will get her out in one way or another."

As the young man was coming home, he saw smoke rising from his part of the house. "All is well," thought he. "My uncle has not been able to kill my wife." When he went into the house he praised the woman for her obedience.

That afternoon, about dusk, they heard the old man come into his part of the house and they knew that he hadn't brought any game. He hunted only for people. He called out, "What luck has my nephew had to-day."

"I have had good luck," answered the young man.

The old man began to mutter to himself, to blame his nephew for hiding his uncle's game. At last he said, "I will wait a while then I will have my own."

He heard two persons breathe and he was angry. Determined to have something to eat he pounded bones into bits, put the bits into a kettle, filled the kettle with water and hanging it over the fire made soup.

The young man and his wife were silent. The man had decided to leave his uncle and his plans were laid. He had walked in circles around the house making each circle larger than the preceding one till he had a ring three days' journey in circuit and now he told his wife what she must do.

That night the uncle said, "I am going away for a while. I can find no game around here."

"Well," answered the nephew, "hunters go where they

can find something to kill and they are often gone a long time. I am going farther myself. Game is getting scarce in our neighborhood.''

The young man had power. He caused a house to appear in a place six days' journey away, then he told his wife about the house, and said, ''I have a brother there and I am going to send you to him. This brother is invisible. No stranger has ever seen him. Hitherto he has accompanied me, but now he will aid you.''

The young man took an arrow from his quiver, shook his wife till she was only a couple of inches long, then, taking off the flint point of the arrow, he put her inside the arrow and replacing the point, said, ''In three days I will follow you.''

Putting his arrow on the bow string he drew it and sent the arrow to the East. That instant the call of a woodpecker was heard. The feathers on the arrow were from that bird, and all the way the arrow sang with the voice of a woodpecker.

The young man could see the trail that the arrow left as it went through the air. He went back to the cabin, and waited. In three days his uncle came, but without game.

Talking to himself he asked, ''What luck has my nephew had?''

''Good luck,'' said the young man. ''I have a plenty to eat.''

''I found nothing,'' said the old man. ''This hunting ground is barren, my eyes see no more game. But if I have no fresh meat I have bones. I'll break them up and make soup.''

Then the nephew heard his uncle breaking bones—there was a terrible noise. At last the young man said, ''My uncle makes too much noise.''

''My nephew wouldn't make less noise if he were in my place. I am trying to get something to eat.'' And paying no attention to what his nephew said, the old man kept at work. The next morning, at daybreak, he said, ''I am going hunting. I shall be gone three days.''

''I am glad,'' thought the young man, and as soon as his uncle was out of sight he took the trail that he had made and followed it three days. Then he went directly toward his new cabin. Glancing up he saw the arrow's trail, which looked like a rainbow in the sky. After a while he made a long leap and as he leaped he ran in the air, went up far above the forest and off on a level which was still in the air.

The trail of the arrow was in the form of a rainbow and it seemed to roll up and dissolve in mist as the young man passed over it. It ended where the arrow had struck. In the cabin at the end of the trail he found his wife.

The invisible brother saw the arrow when it struck the ground and burst. He saw the woman come out of the arrow and take her natural size. When she came into the house, he said to her, "I knew you were coming. By obedience to your husband you have been able to make this journey. No one has ever seen me before except my brother and he only two or three times. I know what will come from my uncle's wrath. He will pursue, and, if possible, kill you."

The old man came home and began to talk to his nephew. When he received no answer he was very angry. He knew that his nephew was not at home, and going out he looked for his trail, struck it and found that the footprints were as old as his own, made three days before. Going back to the house he muttered, "I'll follow him to-morrow. The world is small. He cannot escape me. I'll follow him everywhere."

The invisible brother, though a great distance away, heard his uncle talking to himself, heard his threats, heard him say, "My daughter-in-law will never get out of my reach. I can go to the edge of the world very quickly. My nephew is trying to save her. He'll not succeed. I'll eat her flesh."

The next morning the old man set out. He followed his nephew's footprints till night, then, looking up, saw that his own house was near, that he had been going around and around. He was angry, and said, "To-morrow I will get on the right trail."

As soon as daylight came, the old man started again. As he traveled he found that the trail was growing dim, but he kept on till midday, then he saw that he was near his own house.

"Be it so!" said he. "Though my nephew is possessed with the witchcraft of all the animals, I will have his wife's flesh."

He followed the trail three days longer, then he reached the end of it and cried out, exultantly, "My daughter-in-law's flesh is mine!" Looking up in the air he saw his nephew's trail. The trail of the arrow was gone, but the footprints of the nephew remained on the clouds.

As the old man followed on the ground the trail that he saw in the air, he muttered to himself. The invisible brother heard his threats and the three started for a lake that was not far away. The woman took the lead; the husband stepped in her footprints. When they came to the lake, the young man took a clam shell and threw it toward the opposite bank. Immediately the banks came together and the three stepped over. When they had crossed and the lake had again resumed its natural size they looked back but could scarcely see, at one look,[1] the bank they had left. The young man, thinking that when his uncle came to the lake he would be long in crossing, left his wife and went to hunt for game.

The old man came to the lake and ran back and forth looking for a place to cross. At last he called out, "Daughter-in-law, Daughter-in-law, how did you cross the lake?" And though the woman knew he wanted to kill her, she thought, "Why doesn't he throw a clam shell?"

He heard distinctly what she said in her mind and picking up a clam shell he threw it. The banks came together and when the woman looked to see where the old man was she was terrified to find him right there at her side.

He caught her by the hair, and said, "I knew that I should eat your flesh. My nephew has no right to keep game from me."

With one blow he cut off the woman's head. She had been left alone. The invisible brother was not there to warn her.

The woman had twin boys. The old man hid the chil-

[1] As far as one can see. The distance varies, of course, with the position of the spectator and the nature of the country.

dren in a hollow tree, together with the woman's head, then putting the body on his back, he went to the lake, and picking up a clam shell threw it toward the opposite bank. The banks came together and he stepped over. As he looked back, he saw the lake spread out again.

The young man thought that when near home he would see smoke rising from his cabin, but he did not. "My uncle's words have come true," thought he. "She forgot my warning." He was lonesome and discouraged and he determined never to go back to his uncle's house.

While cooking supper, the young man had to go for water. As he stooped down to dip it up he heard a voice say, "Your uncle has killed me! Your uncle has killed me!"

On looking around he saw that the willows were bespattered with blood, and he knew from the blood out of which the voice came that his wife had been killed. He had two proofs now, his uncle's tracks and the speaking blood.

The young man continued to hunt and as he had good luck he didn't go again to the house across the lake. One day when he came from hunting he saw tracks around his fire, two little trails. Though he saw fresh tracks each evening he paid no attention to them. They looked like the tracks of a child but he thought that a little animal made them. At last he noticed that some of his meat was gone and that each day more and more disappeared. Then he resolved to catch the thief. Pieces of meat hung up to dry had been pulled down, dragged out of the house and then pulled along on the ground.

The young man followed the trail till he came to a big log. The log was hollow and the trail disappeared at the opening. He was sure that some animal lived in the tree. The next day he started off, as usual, but after going a short distance into the forest he stopped to watch his house. Soon he saw two little boys come out of the log and run toward the house. They went in and after a while came out dragging a piece of meat. When they reached the log they disappeared in the opening, pulling the meat in after them. The man thought, "To-morrow I will catch those children."

He knew they could talk, for as they pulled the meat along he heard one of them say, "Hurry, father will come!"

The next morning the young man went a short distance into the forest, hid and waited. The time seemed long, but at last the boys came from the log, ran to the house, went in and closed the door. The man hurried home, went into the house and fastened the door behind him. As soon as the children saw him, they began to cry.

"Why do you cry?" asked he, "I am your father. Don't cry."

When they stopped crying, he asked, "How do you know that I am your father?"

One boy was a little larger than the other, and when the man questioned them he answered, "An old man killed our mother. He cut off her head and hid it in a hollow log and he put us in there too. Our mother's head is in the tree now."

"What do you do with the meat you take from here?"

"We feed it to our mother."

"You must stay with me now," said the father. He was kind to them and the boys were glad to stay. He made them playthings, bow and arrows and a ball and club. Whenever he went hunting, they carried meat to their mother.

One day the larger boy said to his father, "My mother is hungry."

"Feed her," said he. "Feed her all she will eat. We have a plenty of meat. You can take as much as you want."

Soon the man saw that the meat was disappearing very fast, faster than he could bring it in. He was frightened.

One of the boys noticed this, and said, "My mother eats a great deal, we can't carry her enough." And he asked his father to go and see her.

The man went to the log and looking in saw two great eyes in a skull.

"What can we do?" asked one of the boys.

"I am afraid," said the father, "that after she has eaten all the meat she will eat us."

"We must go to some place far away," said the boys,

"so that she will have to travel a long time to overtake us. We can't feed her. She never gets enough, and we are tired."

The man knew that it would soon be impossible to satisfy the Head, so he said, "We will go away from here. You will start in the morning and travel till you come to a large village. My dogs will go with you as far as the village, then they will come back to help me."

The boys started and after they had gone quite a distance and were tired, the larger dog said to the larger boy, "Sit on my back."

Then the smaller dog said to the smaller boy, "Sit on my back."

The boys did as told. The dogs ran on swiftly. After a long time they came to a place where trees had been felled, then they said to the boys, "We are near a village. You must walk now."

The boys were unwilling to walk, but the dogs, shaking themselves as if they had just been in water, threw them off and told them to go to the village. The dogs turned then and went back to their master.

The man knew that by going South he would find uncles who would help him, just such powerful men as his old uncle. When the dogs came back, they told their master that they would stay till the last meat was gone, but he must go, for as soon as the meat was eaten the Head would fly in the direction he took. They would delay it all they could, but he must travel fast for his life was in danger.

The man started toward the South and went with great swiftness, for he was a fast runner. Two days after he left, one of the dogs overtook him, and said, "The meat is gone and the Head is trying to find the boys. It can follow as far as they walked but no farther. Be on your guard for it will find your trail."

The dog could see a great distance, it looked back, and said, "The Head is coming! You have always said that no one could outrun you. The time has come when you must exert all your strength."

When the Head started, the dogs left behind did what they could to delay it. They bit it and when it turned to pursue them, they dodged into the ground. It went on and again they sprang at it and when it turned they again escaped into the ground. The trail of the Head could be seen plainly for the bark was gnawed from the trees where the dogs kept it back, delayed it and made it angry.

All at once, far off in the West, one of the little boys said to the other, "Our father is in trouble, our mother is following him."

Soon a dog came up to the man, and said, "The Head is possessed of such power that we don't know how to keep it back. We are doing what we can, but you must run with all your strength."

The man ran with all speed. Seeing a house he darted into it and called out to an old man sitting there, "Uncle, help me! A terrible Head is following me to take my life!"

"I will help you all I can," said the old man, "but hurry to the next house, your aunts live there; they will help you. If I am killed, a dark cloud will go up to the sky."

The man was about half way between the two houses when he heard a terrible noise and looking back saw that the Flying Head had reached his uncle's house and his uncle was fighting it with all his strength. When he turned a second time he saw a great black cloud rise into the sky and he knew that his uncle was dead.

That minute one of the dogs came to the man, and said, "Your uncle is dead. He was never beaten before."

When the Head had devoured the old man's flesh, it rushed after the husband.

The man ran as fast as he could. When almost exhausted, he saw a house, ran into it and called to the women sitting there, "Help me! help me! Something is following me to take my life!"

"Poor man," said one of his aunts. "Hurry on. We will do what we can to delay the Head. Go to the next house. Your mother lives there. Maybe she can help you."

The man wasn't out of sight of the house when he heard a great noise and heard his aunts call to their children to have courage. The Head flew into the house, and bit at everything it came in contact with. The women beat it with clubs. The man heard the blows fall on the skull. When he was half way to his mother's house, all was still at his aunts' house. Suddenly his invisible brother called out, "Run! Run or we are lost!"

The invisible brother urged the man forward, pushed him and he seemed to run faster. The brother urged and pushed till they reached the house.

Then the man cried, "Mother, help me, help me!"

"Poor Son, you are in great trouble," said the mother. "Go on, we will do what we can."

The man hurried through the house. The Head came in as he went out. The dogs ran around the house and urged their master on.

The mother called to her children, "Kill the Head if you can! Fight with all your strength!"

They took their most poisonous weapons and began to strike the Head. One of the women stumbled and fell; the Head devoured her in an instant.

The old mother cautioned her children, telling them to be careful and make no misstep. The youngest girl, remembering there was bears' oil in the house, thought she would boil it and see if she couldn't kill the Head with boiling oil. While the Head was chasing the women through the house, the oil began to boil, then the girl seized the kettle and threw the oil onto the Head. It burned and killed the Head.

"Your brother is free," said the mother. "We ought to have a game of ball. It is our duty to give thanks. The Head will be the ball."

She picked up the Head, carried it out and called in a loud voice, "Here, warriors, is a ball for you to play with."

Soon a great many people, with netted clubs in their hands, came and began to play ball. (These players were animals that lived in the forest.) The man saw them play with his wife's head. Each one struggled to get the ball and in that way they wore it out.

One of the dogs said to him, "Your wife is dead and you are safe."

When it said, "Your wife is dead," the man's strength left him, his arms dropped down, and he was very sad.

"You are sorry," said the invisible brother, "but I am glad. Why should you be sad? She would have devoured you, if they had not killed her. Now there is no one to harm us. Our uncle will not trouble us again."

"Your children are living off in that direction," said he, pointing to the West. "Go and find them." So saying he turned and when the brother looked after him, he had disappeared.

The man and his dogs traveled toward the West. When the dogs left the children they were near a house at the edge of a village. In that house lived an old woman and her granddaughter. One day when the girl was in the woods stooping down to pick up broken boughs, she heard voices. She listened and, as the wind came toward her, she discovered that they were the voices of children. She went home with her wood, told her grandmother that she had heard children crying, and asked her to come to the forest and listen.

"It is a pleasure to know that there are children alive. They must be for us," said the grandmother. "We will go and find them."

When they came to the place where the girl had heard the voices, she said, "Now listen!"

"True," said the grandmother, "there are children in the woods. We must look everywhere till we find them. Maybe they are sent to us because we are alone."

The girl followed the sound, going in the direction from which the wind came, she could hear distinctly and she knew the sound came from near the ground. At last she came to where the boys were. They were apparently about a year old, one a little larger than the other and both were crying. The girl began to comfort the children, to tell them she would be their mother and be kind to them.

While she was talking, her grandmother came. She pitied the children and said to them, "Stop crying. It is the will of the Great Spirit that you should be our children. I will be your grandmother and my granddaughter will be your mother."

"All we have we will give to you," said the girl. "I will love you as your mother would."

The boys stopped crying and went home with the girl. Each boy had the little bow and arrow and ball club that his father had made for him.

"We will take good care of these children," said the grandmother. "There are many people in our village, but not a child. I have lived here a long time, but I have never seen a little child."

When the boys were old enough to hunt for birds, their grandmother gave them bows and arrows and they brought in a good deal of game.

One day the larger boy called, "Grandmother, come and see what I have killed. It is covered with spots. It is over here in the weeds."

"Where is it? Where is it?" asked the grandmother.

The boys led the way, but she could hardly keep in sight of them, the weeds were so high. On reaching the spot she found a fawn a few hours old. She carried the fawn home, and said to herself, "I am thankful that I have these children. They will be great hunters; their game is getting larger. First they killed birds, now they have killed a fawn."

One day the larger boy said, "Our father is coming."

"I am afraid our father is dead," answered the other boy.

The grandmother overheard this and told the boys to go and hunt for birds, she was hungry for bird meat.

The next day, while the children were out, a man came to the house. The invisible brother had told the man that when he came to the old woman's house he must say, "Grandmother, I am glad to see you," and to the girl, "Sister, I am glad to see you." As the man went in, he saluted the old woman as Grandmother, and to the girl he said, Sister.

One of the boys said to the other, "Our father has come!"

"I don't think so," said his brother, "Our father had dogs; there are no dogs with this man." To find out he raised the skin door a little and looking in he saw his father sitting there with his elbow on his knee and his face on his hand.

"We must find the dogs," said the larger boy.

They followed their father's tracks and they hadn't gone far when they found that the dogs had run off in another direction. They tracked the dogs and toward night found them standing by a fallen tree. The dogs heard the children's voices and ran to meet them. They were as glad to see the boys as the boys were to see them.

"We must go home," said the brothers, but they didn't know the way.

The dogs took the lead. It was late at night and very dark when they got home.

When the boys didn't come, the grandmother and granddaughter were frightened. They were waiting for daylight to come so they could hunt for them. When they came, the grandmother asked, "Why did you stay so long and frighten us?"

The father was happy to be with his children again. The girl was the man's sister and the old woman was his grandmother.

They all lived together now and were happy.

A LAZY MAN

Characters

IN Geneseo there was a young man, an orphan, who went around among the people, staying wherever kind-hearted persons would keep him, sleeping on the ground by a brush fire, and eating whatever was given to him. When he was twenty years old, he was as much of a boy as ever.

A chief, who was rich and proud, lived in Geneseo. He had a daughter and two or three sons. One day the orphan stopped near the chief's house where people were burning brush.

One of the chief's sons came out and said to him, "Don't you feel poor and lonely sitting around so?"

"No," said the young man, "I feel as rich as you do."

"Don't you sometimes think you would like to have a wife?"

"Yes, I sometimes think I would like a wife if I could get one."

"What would you think of my sister for a wife? Many men have tried to marry her, but she refuses everyone."

"Oh," said the orphan, looking up, "I would as soon have her as any woman; she is handsome and rich."

"I will ask her to marry you," said the brother, thinking to have fun with his sister.

He went to the house and said to her, "There is a young man out there by the fire, who would like to marry you. Will you be his wife?"

"I will. I would rather marry him than anyone else."

"Shall I tell him so?"

"You may."

He told the young man, who said, "I shall be glad to have her for my wife."

The brother, in fun, repeated this to his sister, who said, "I will go and ask him myself."

She went to the orphan, and asked, "What did my brother say to you?"

He told her, and she said, "I will go with you. Come to-morrow at this time and I'll marry you."

The next morning the girl got leggings and moccasins for the young man. (He had never worn moccasins in Summer.) In the evening he came to where she was. He washed, put on the leggings and embroidered moccasins and tied up his hair. She told him then that he could go home with her, but he must not talk with any of the men, that one of her brothers was always fooling.

The girl became the orphan's wife and he lived in the chief's house. In the Fall when the chief's sons were ready to go deer hunting, the young woman wanted to go. She had a husband and she thought he might be a good hunter.

The man had never hunted but he said, "I will go and try."

When the party had gone some distance, they camped and began to hunt. The young man found a place where there were wild grape vines. He made a swing, then sat in it and swung all day, didn't try to hunt. At night he went home without game. Each morning he went to the swing and each evening he went home without game.

The brothers killed many deer. One day one brother said to the other, "Our brother-in-law gets no game, maybe he doesn't hunt." They agreed to watch him.

The next morning they followed the young man, found him swinging and saw that the ground was smooth around the swing. Then they said, "We will not live with him and feed him. We will leave him, go a day's journey away and camp."

They left the man and woman with only one leg of deer meat.

The young man never ate much; the woman ate most of the meat. When it was gone, she began to be afraid of starving.

One day, while the man was swinging, a horned owl lighted on a tree nearby. He shot the owl and put it under the swing where he could look at it as he swung. His wife was getting very hungry.

That night when he came home without game, she said, "If I have nothing to eat to-morrow, I will be too weak to get up. You ought to kill something."

"Well, maybe to-morrow I will kill something."

The next morning the man went, as usual, to the swing. While swinging he heard a woman crying. He was frightened and stopped swinging. Soon he saw a female panther coming with three cubs. She was crying. As she approached, he heard a terrible roar in the North, the direction from which the panther had come. Then the man saw Whirlwind coming, tearing down all the trees in his path. He stopped on a tree near the swing.

"You know now what harm you have done," said Whirlwind to Panther.

"Why are you angry with the panther?" asked the young man. "What has she done to you?"

"She has torn up my best feather cap."

"Why do you think so much of your cap? It must have been a nice one."

"It was nice."

"What kind of feathers was it made of?"

"It was the skin and feathers of a horned owl."

"What would you think if I gave you another cap?"

"How can you get one?"

The young man picked up the horned owl that he had killed and threw it at Whirlwind. Whirlwind caught it, said, "Thank you, this is better than the one Panther destroyed," and away he flew.

Panther thanked the man, and said, "I am glad that you had the owl, you have saved my life. Now I will help you. Go to that knoll yonder, behind it you will find two bucks fighting. Shoot them both. The one you shoot first will not run; they will fight till they die."

The young man found the bucks and watched them till

they killed each other. Then, taking a large piece of meat, he went home to his wife, who was almost starved.

"I have brought you meat," said he, "I had good luck to-day."

The woman sprang up, threw the meat on the fire and hardly waited for it to cook till she began to eat.

They dragged the bucks home, skinned them, and had plenty of meat. The young woman dried the meat and tanned the skins.

Panther told the man to always hunt near the swing and he would kill a great deal of game.

When they had a large quantity of meat, the man said to his wife, "Your brothers are good hunters. No doubt they have plenty of meat, but I will find them and see."

He started. On the way he killed a deer, and he carried the carcass along. He found the camp and looking in saw the brothers; they were poor and weak.

He went in, and asked, "How are you?"

"We are almost starved," said one of them. "We can find nothing to kill."

"Your sister and I have a plenty. Come and live with us. I have meat here. Eat and then come to my camp."

He gave them the deer and they ate the meat nearly raw, they were so hungry.

When they started for the young man's camp he went ahead, got home quickly and told his wife he had found her brothers nearer starvation than she had been. During the night the brothers came. They were satisfied and remained with their sister and brother-in-law.

After a while they all went back to the village loaded with skins and venison. Now the young man was rich; and he and his wife lived ever after in Geneseo Valley.

SWAN'S DAUGHTERS MARRY EARTH-QUAKE'S SON

Characters

OWÉE YEGO^{n}HDJI ....Old Woman Swan
DÓE^{n}DZOWES ....Split the Earth (Earthquake)
THAGO^{n}HSÓWES ....He Splits His Face
O'ÓWA .... Owl

O NE day Swan said to her two daughters, "My daughters, I have had a great deal of trouble in rearing you. For a long time I've eaten nothing but mushrooms, I am hungry for meat. You are old enough to marry. Earthquake Old Woman lives near here. Her son, Split Face, is a good young man and a great hunter. You must go and marry him."

The girls pounded corn for the marriage bread. The mother baked twenty cakes in the ashes, wrapped them in corn husks, and put them into a basket. She painted long red stripes on each girl's face and combed her long hair.

Then, giving the basket to the elder, she said, "Don't stop till you come to Earthquake's house. Don't ask the way of anyone, or speak to anyone."

The elder sister took the basket and the two started. About midday they saw a middle-aged man of the Owl people. He ran across the trail and called out, "I have lost my arrow! I shot at a bird and the arrow went so far that I can't find it."

"I will help you hunt for it," said the elder sister, putting her basket down on a log.

The younger girl didn't want to look for the arrow. She said, "Mother told us not to stop, or to speak to anyone," but she followed her sister.

The man ran around the girls, seized the basket and carried it off. When the girls couldn't find the arrow, they went back to the log where they had left the basket. It was gone, and right away they knew that the old man had fooled them. They went home and when their mother asked what had become of the basket the second sister said, "We met a man who had lost his arrow. While we were looking for it, he stole our basket."

The mother scolded the elder sister, and said, "You don't care for me. You know that I am hungry for meat, yet you disobey me. We will make bread to-morrow and your younger sister will carry it to Earthquake's house."

The next day the mother made marriage bread, got her daughters ready for the road and gave them the same command as before.

The girls followed the same trail. Again they met Owl and this time the elder sister asked how far it was to Earthquake's house.

"It isn't far," said Owl. "It is right over there," and he pointed to his own house. They went to the house and going in saw Owl's wife and his little boy. They put the basket of marriage bread down near the woman.

Owl told his wife to go to the other side of the fire and pretend to be his sister. He sat down between the two girls and when the little boy called him "Father," he said, "He is my sister's son. His father died yesterday, he is calling for him," and Owl began to cry for his brother-in-law.

Someone was heard coming toward the cabin. Then there was a kick on the door and a man called out, "O'ówa, they want you at the long house!"

Owl said, "My people always call me by a nickname. They are holding a council and can't get along without me. I must go. I'll come back soon," and he went away.

The younger sister said, "This isn't Earthquake's house. If we can get our basket we will go home."

When Owl's wife fell asleep, the younger girl took the basket and said to her sister, "Now we must go."

They started for home. Soon they came to an opening and in the center of the opening was a long house. They crept up cautiously and looking through a crack saw Earthquake and near her sat her son, a nice looking young man. There were two fireplaces in the house and many men and women were sitting around them. Owl was dancing and as he danced people threw pieces of meat and of mush into his mouth. The girls recognized him and knew that they had been fooled again. They went into the house and putting the basket of bread near Earthquake, they sat down, one on each side of the young man.

The mother was glad; she liked the girls. When Owl saw them, he dropped his blanket and ran out of the house.

Swan's daughters lived with Split Face and were happy. He was a good hunter and they had a plenty to eat. After a while their mother-in-law said, "You must carry your mother some meat, she is hungry."

Earthquake took a large quantity of meat, made a pack of it, made the pack small and giving it to the elder sister, said, "Have your mother come back with you, I will give her a fire to live by."

When Swan had eaten enough and was glad, she went home with her daughters. And she lived with them ever after happy and contented.

HODADEIO^n AND HIS SISTER

[Told by George Titus]

Characters

HODADEIO^n
YEYENTHWÛS
HADJISGWAS ....Mush-Eater
ODZI'NÉOWA ....Wasp
DAGWANOE^{n}YENT ....Whirlwind (Big Head)
OTGOEDAQSAIS ....Otgoe' (Wampum)
SHAGODYOWEQ.........One of the Wind Characters
DAGWAHGWEOSES ....Long Eyebrows

HODADEIO^n and his sister, YEYENTHWÛS, lived in a bark house. When the sister went out to plant, she fastened the door of the house so nothing could harm her little brother. She did not let him go out. She got coon's feet for him to play with and made him bows and arrows. When he played, he threw up the coon's feet and told an arrow to strike them and the arrow always hit them before they touched the ground.

One day while the sister was at home, a voice was heard in the loft of the house, saying, "Mush, Brother! Mush, Brother!"

"Who is that?" asked the boy, "I thought we were alone in the house."

"Poor brother," said the sister, "He is only just alive."

"Well, Sister, make him some mush," said the little boy.

The girl uncovered a place under her couch, took out a very small kettle and a little piece of a chestnut, got water, put the least bit scraped from the chestnut into the kettle and boiled it. As it boiled she stirred it and struck the kettle, and as she struck the kettle it grew till at last it was as large as any kettle and was full of mush. When the mush was cooked, she took it off the fire, poured it into a bark bowl and said to HODADEIO^n, "Go up the ladder and feed your brother."

The little boy climbed the ladder and found a man lying in the loft, and saying to him, "I have brought you mush, my Brother," he put the bowl down near him and went away.

The brother, whose name was Mush-eater, took two or three mouthfuls of the mush and the bowl was empty; all the mush was eaten. Then he blew out two or three puffs of breath, rubbed his arms and legs and began to sing.

The boy heard singing and beating of time overhead, and, a little later he heard his brother call out, "Tobacco! tobacco!" and he said, "My Sister, our brother wants to smoke."

"Our poor brother," said the girl, "he is barely alive, he lives on chestnut pudding and tobacco." She got a big pipe, put in tobacco and a coal of fire, gave it to the little boy, and said, "Take it up to our brother."

HODADEIO^n went to the loft, and said, "My Brother, I have come with a pipe for you."

"Thank you," said Mush-eater, and with one puff he so filled the place with smoke that he nearly smothered the boy before he could get away.

Soon a sound was heard as though Mush-eater had blown through the pipe stem and rapped the ashes out of the pipe. Then he began to sing, and they thought his voice was stronger.

YEYENTHWÛs tied the door, fastened in her little brother and went out to plant.

While his sister was gone, the boy thought he would like to make some chestnut mush for his brother and sing and dance for him. He found the kettle under his sister's couch, took the piece of chestnut and scraped every bit of it into the kettle, filled the kettle with water and when the water boiled he began to strike the kettle. He struck it till it was as large as any kettle and full of mush. When he poured the mush out, he had a great bark bowl full.

He took the bowl to the loft, and said, "My Brother, I have made you another bowl of mush."

"Thank you, Brother," said HADJISGWAS, who took the mush and ate it, rubbed himself and began to sing. He was stronger now and sang a regular song. After the boy put away the kettle, he thought, "My brother must have a smoke."

So he took all the tobacco there was, cut it up, put it in the pipe, carried the pipe to the loft, and said, "My Brother, I have brought your pipe. After you have smoked I want you to sing; I will dance."

Mush-eater drew such a puff that the little boy had to hurry down the ladder to get away from the smoke. He wasn't long down when his sister came.

"Oh, Sister," said he, "I've made our brother a bowlful of mush."

"How did you make it?"

"I cut up the chestnut and boiled it."

"Oh, now he will die."

"After he ate the mush I gave him a smoke," said the boy.

"How did you do that?"

"I shaved up the piece of tobacco, put it in the pipe and gave him the pipe."

"Now we will surely lose our brother. You have done great harm," said YEYENTHWÛS.

"Well, my Sister, where are the chestnuts? I will go and get more of them."

"Those chestnuts grow at the eastern end of the world and this side of them, where the tobacco grows, there are witches. Before one comes to the house of the witches there is a river with trees thrown across to walk on. Just beyond the river are two rattlesnakes, one on each side of the trail, and they attack every person who goes that way. If you pass the rattlesnakes safely, you will come to a mountain so steep that no man can climb it.

"There is put one pass through that mountain. Just beyond the pass stand two SHAGODYOWEQS, each one half as tall as a tree. If you should succeed in passing those men and go farther, there are two men at the edge of an opening. The minute those men see any one they give an alarm and women run up and attack whomsoever they find. If you should get by those men and reach a knoll, you would see a house and in front of it a platform on which a woman is walking back and forth. As soon as that woman sees a stranger, she begins to sing, and witches rush out of the house and kill him.''

The next day when YEYENTHWÛS went out to plant, she fastened the door. While she was gone, the little boy heard some living thing moving around outside and he tried to get out and shoot it, but he couldn't open the door. Then he heard a noise on the top of the house, and glancing up saw something looking down at him. He didn't know what kind of a creature it was, but he said, ''You are Speckled Face, anyhow, and I'll shoot you.''

He drew his bow and said to the arrow, ''I want you to go straight to the game.''

The arrow struck and killed the creature. The boy wanted to bring the game in, and not being able to open the door, he dug a hole through the earth near the door, got out, brought in the game, put it in the corn mortar, covered it and when his sister came, he said, ''My sister, I have killed game.''

''Where is it?'' asked she.

''In the corn mortar,'' answered HODADEIO^n. He ran and brought the game to his sister.

''That is a chickadee,'' said she.

YEYENTHWÛS dressed the bird, cooked it on the coals, then began to eat. The boy stood and watched her.

After a while he asked, ''Is it good?''

''It is good,'' said his sister.

He looked a while longer, then asked, ''Are you going to give me some?''

''No, this is the first game you have killed, you mustn't eat of the first, it wouldn't be right.''

The next morning the boy said to his sister, ''You must tie a belt around me, I am going out.''

She had to do as he said, she couldn't help it. She put

the belt on him, and said, "You must not go North or far away. Stay near the house."

Yᴇʏᴇɴᴛʜᴡûs went to her planting and the boy went out to hunt for game. He saw a bird on a tree, and said, "You must be the bird they call Robin." He killed the bird, carried it to the house and put it in the corn mortar. When his sister came he showed it to her.

"Oh," said she, "this is a robin." She dressed, cooked and ate the robin, didn't give the boy even one bite.

The next morning he got up early so as to go hunting in good time. After he had eaten, he said, "My Sister, put on my belt."

She made him ready for the day then both went out, the girl to her planting, the boy to hunt.

After he had been out a while he saw a bird, and said, "I think you are the bird that is called Pigeon."

He killed the bird, carried it home and put it in the corn mortar.

When his sister came she dressed the bird, divided it into two parts, put one part away and cutting the other into pieces said she would make dumplings. She pounded corn-meal, mixed the meat with it, made two dumplings and both ate of them.

The next day the boy went farther than before. He saw a bird running along, and said, "You must be what they call Striped Tail."

He drew his bow and shot the bird. When it ran, he called, "Stop, don't break my best arrow!"

The bird died. The boy had all he could do to carry it home.

He put it in the corn mortar and when his sister came and saw it, she said, "This is a Partridge."

The next morning Hᴏᴅᴀᴅᴇɪᴏⁿ went farther than the day before. He saw a creature coming toward him. He watched it and said, "I think it is you that people call 'Pine Leaves Hanging Down.'" He drew his bow and shot.

When the wounded bird struggled he called out, "Stop! don't break my best arrow."

It stopped struggling and died. He tried to pick it up but he couldn't lift it.

He went to where his sister was planting, and said, "My Sister, I have killed big game. I can't carry it."

She went with him and when she saw the game, she said, "This is what we call Turkey." She carried the turkey home, dressed it, put half away and cooked the other half.

The next day the boy went farther than before. He found tracks all going in the same direction, and said, "My sister never told me that people live around here and that there was a trail." He put his feet in the tracks and found they were as if made by his own feet. Right before him on the trail he saw game coming. He drew his bow, pierced the animal with his arrow and as it went floundering along he called out, "Don't break the arrow; it's my best one."

The animal fell over and died. The boy ran up and pulled out the arrow, then went for his sister.

When she came she said, "This is Coon."

She caught the coon up by one leg, threw it over her shoulder and went home. She cooked a part of the coon and made bread. While the meat was cooking, she skimmed off the oil, telling her brother that she had wanted oil for a long time. When the oil was cool she rubbed it into her hair.

The next day when Hodadeio[n] saw game, he said, "You must be the one they call Big Feathers."

The animal saw him and turned to run. He shot but the creature ran off out of sight. The boy thought, "I have lost my best arrow, but I'll follow the game." He hadn't gone far when he found the animal lying dead on the trail.

He ran for his sister and when she came she thanked him, and said, "This time you have killed a buck."

She brought a strap, braided out of corn husks, so as to carry the meat home on her back. She skinned the buck and divided it. Hodadeio[n] wanted to carry a part, so his sister cut off the feet, tied them together and gave them to him. She carried half of the animal home and went back for the other half.

The next day Hodadeio[n] killed a bear. They had a good meal that night and the sister had plenty of hair oil.

The next day they went out as usual, Hodadeio[n] to

hunt and YEYENTHWÛS to plant. The boy went to the place where he had killed the bear, but he could find no game. Then he went in a circle and as he looked toward the North it seemed very pleasant. There was an opening in front of him and he thought he would go to it, perhaps he would find game.

He went to the middle of the opening where there was a house, he peeped in through a crack, and saw a crowd of naked men of the Wasp people dancing.

Soon one of the men said, "Some one is looking at us."

Another said, "Let us kill him."

HODADEIO^n turned and ran towards the woods. The men chased him to the edge of the opening and then went back.

The boy went home, took a long stick of wood from a pile his sister had gathered, carried it to the edge of the opening, stuck it into the ground and said to it, "When the men in that house over there run after me with clubs, do you fight them and help me."

He brought a second stick, put it down by the first, and spoke to it as he had to the other stick. He kept on in this way till he had a great many sticks standing in the ground. Then he ran to the house and looked in.

The men saw him, and said, "Let us kill him this time."

They ran out, with their clubs, and pursued the boy till they came to the edge of the opening, then the sticks became people and fought with them. They killed all of the naked men.

HODADEIO^n dragged the men, one after another, into the house and burned up the house. Then he carried the sticks back to his sister's wood pile and went on till he came to the stump of a broken tree. The stump became a man and called out, "I have caught you, Nephew."

The boy walked up to the man. The man said, "I am HODIADATGON, the great wizard. What would you do if it should rain spears on you?"

"Oh," said the boy, "my sister and I would be glad, for we have no spears to fish with."

Then he turned and ran as fast as he could. His sister was in the house, he ran around it, and said, "Let our house be stone!" and straightway it was stone.

Just as he went into the house he heard a terrible roar and a great rain of spears came down. Some broke on the roof, others fell to the ground.

When the shower was over, his sister said, "You have been towards the North."

"I have, but I'll not go again."

But while he was at play he thought, "I will go to my uncle and be the first to say, 'I've caught you,'" and he started off. He went as near his uncle as he could without being seen, then called a mole, entered his body and went under the ground up to the roots of the stump where his uncle was.

Then he called out, "What would you say if a fire were to come and burn up that stump and the woods and all there is around here?"

"Oh, my Nephew, don't do that."

"I didn't say, 'Don't do that,' when you sent a rain of spears on me and my sister."

That minute a thick smoke rose and soon the woods were in a blaze. The fire spread to where the old man was. He fell to the ground, his head burst and an owl came out of it and flew away.

Hodadeio[n] went on, but he hadn't gone far when he came to an opening in which there was a house. He crept up to the house and looking in through a crack saw an old man with both eyes closed. All at once the old man called, "Come in, Nephew! Come in!"

The boy went in and the old man said, "I always play dice with people who come to see me. I will play with you." He brought out six night-owl eyes for dice, and said, "If they all turn up the same, the throw will count five, if not it will count one."

The old man wanted the boy to play first, but he refused to. Then the old man put the six eyes into a dish and shook the dish. The eyes went out through the smoke-hole and when they came back to the dish they counted but one.

"Now," said the nephew, "take your dice out of the dish, I have dice of my own."

Hodadeio[n] put in his dice which were wood-cocks' eyes, shook the dish and threw the eyes up. They went through the smoke-hole and high into the air. The boy kept saying, "Let them all come of one color," but the uncle said, "Let them come of different colors." All came alike; the old man lost.

"Nephew," said he, "let me have one smoke."

"Oh, no," said the boy, "I can't do that."

He cut off the old man's head. Then he went on till he came to a third opening. In the center of the opening was a high rock and on the rock was an enormous Head, with big eyes and long hair, a DAGWANOEⁿYENT, (Whirlwind).

The boy went up to the rock and the Head called out, "My Nephew, I've been wishing that you would come to see me. Now we will play hide-and-seek."

HODADEIOⁿ was to hide first—the Head faced the other way. That minute HODADEIOⁿ became a flea and hid in the long bushy hair of DAGWANOEⁿYENT, then he called out in a far away voice, "You can't find me, Uncle; you can't find me."

DAGWANOEⁿYENT looked all around; up in the air, in the trees, everywhere. At last he saw a weed with a knot on its stem, and he said, "Nephew, you are in that knot."

But he wasn't there.

He looked around a second time and saw a knot on one of the trees. "You are in the knot on that tree, Nephew."

"I am not," answered HODADEIOⁿ.

When DAGWANOEⁿYENT couldn't find the boy he was terribly frightened. "There is danger," said he, and he flew off the rock and went far away, then he rose above the clouds and sat on them.

The boy called out from his uncle's long shaggy hair, "You can't find me, Uncle; you can't find me."

"Oh," said the uncle to himself, "I have come to the place where he is. There is danger here," and he flew off to an island in the sea, and there the boy called out, "You can't find me, Uncle; you can't find me."

He could not and he flew back to the rock in the opening, and there the boy called out, "You can't find me, Uncle."

"I have lost the game," said DAGWANOEⁿYENT, "but I didn't bet my head. You may have control of the three women who are pounding corn outside that house at the edge of the opening."

The women were man-eaters. They were angry when they heard these words. They took their clubs and ran toward the boy to strike him. He willed them dead and they dropped to the ground. He cut off their heads and burned up their house.

The uncle and nephew became friends and the uncle said, "Nephew, if ever you get into trouble, think of me and I will help you."

The boy went home, sat down and began to laugh.

His sister asked, "What are you laughing about?"

"I am laughing because I have put an end to my uncle in the first opening, and my uncle who played dice. I have beaten Dagwanoe^{n}yent and frightened him terribly, I have killed the three women who were man-eaters."

The sister said, "I thank you, my Brother. Many persons have been deceived and killed by our uncles and those women."

That night the boy said to his sister, "Make me parched corn meal and two dumplings with bear fat in them. To-morrow I am going to get the chestnuts."

She did as he asked.

The next morning he set out and kept on his way till he came to a river over which a tree had fallen. He went half way across on the tree. Two snakes began to rattle, he went back, caught two chipmunks then came to the tree and walked on it till he reached the snakes. He gave a chipmunk to each one, and said, "You are free now, but I will kill you if you don't leave this place." The snakes ran away.

Hodadeio^n went on till he came to the opening. At the farther end was a mountain. He found the pass, walked in and as he was coming out on the other side he heard all at once, "*Ho^n, ho^n, ho^n, ho^n!*" and saw the two Shagody-oweqs, half as tall as the highest tree.

"Keep still, keep still," said Hodadeio^n, "I have brought you dumplings" and he gave each of them a dumpling. Then he said, "You are free now, you needn't guard this place any longer."

HODADEIO^n traveled on till he saw two white herons. He went into the woods and dug up wild beans. Then he came back and going as near the herons as he dared, he called out "Stop! stop! here are beans for you." When they had eaten the beans he set them free, saying, "Go from here and do not come back."

He went on till he saw the woman walking back and forth on a platform. He peeled bark from a slippery elm tree, marked it off in small pieces and made it turn to wampum. Then he called a mole, and said, "Carry me to the platform."

The mole took him to the platform and before the woman could call out he gave her the wampum, and said, "Keep quiet."

He left the mole and went to a tree where there were great piles of chestnuts. He took a nut, split it, put one half into his bag and hurried back. He had almost reached the woods when the woman on watch, cried, "I have seen a man!"

One of the three sisters ran out and looked at the woman, who changed her words, and called, "I have lied."

The sisters were angry and wanted to kill the woman, she called again, "I have seen a man!"

The mother said, "Do your best, my daughters, do your best. It must be HODADEIO^n. Kill him and finish his family."

They saw HODADEIO^n off in the distance. The eldest sister ran ahead, when she was near the boy she raised her club to strike, but he disappeared in the ground and she struck her kneepan such a blow that she fell and could go no farther.

The next minute HODADEIO^n was up and walking along again. The second sister overtook him and raised her club to strike. He disappeared. She struck her kneepan and fell. The youngest sister tried with the same result and then the old woman. All four were disabled and HODADEIO^n went home, unharmed.

He gave his sister the half chestnut, and said, "Make plenty of mush for our brother."

One day when HODADEIO^n was playing near the house he cried out suddenly and fell to the ground. His sister ran to him, and asked, "What is the matter? Where are you hurt?"

"I'm not hurt."

"Why do you cry?"

"I heard OTGOEDAQSAIS sing a song and call on my name; he says I am his brother."

"That is true," said YEYENTHWÛS, "He is in the East, at the place where the sun comes up. He is tied to a stake and people burn him with brands of fire and torment him to make him cry. His tears are wampum and when they fall people run and pick them up."

"Where does tobacco grow?" asked HODADEIO^n.

"On the other side of the world where Long Eyebrows lives. He stole our tobacco from us and carried it off. No one can conquer him, for he is a great wizard."

That night the boy told his sister to pound parched corn and make meal for him.

In the morning, when he was ready for the road, he put the bundle of food on his back and started. But the bundle was so heavy that at midday he had only reached the edge of the opening where their house was. He sat down there and ate.

YEYENTHWÛS, who was watching him all the time, said, "Poor brother, I think he will come back."

She looked again; he was gone.

In the evening HODADEIO^n hunted for a hollow tree. He found one, crawled in and was lying there quietly when he heard footsteps and soon a man came to the tree and called out, "HODADEIO^n, are you here?"

"I am," answered the boy.

"Well, what would you do if a SHAGODYOWEQ should come to kill you?"

"I would have sport with him."

The man went away and soon a SHAGODYOWEQ came.

HODADEIO^n took aim and hit him with an arrow, then he drew back into the tree and went to sleep. In the morning he saw a trail with trees broken and torn up and after a while he found a SHAGODYOWEQ dead. He pulled out his arrow and went on.

Soon the boy came to a large lake, on the opposite side of the lake was a village. He searched till he found an oak-puff ball. Placing the ball at the edge of the water, he entered it and caused a wind to blow. The ball swept over the lake. HODADEIOⁿ went through the village till he came to the last house on the other side, in that house lived an old woman with her grandson.

When HODADEIOⁿ asked for shelter, the old woman said, "We have nothing to eat."

"I don't want food," said the boy.

"You may stay," said the grandmother.

The next morning, HODADEIOⁿ said to the old woman's grandson, "Let us go hunting."

When they had gone quite a distance, they came to a hollow tree frequented by a bear.

HODADEIOⁿ struck the tree, and said, "Come out!"

The bear came out; HODADEIOⁿ shot it, and the two boys carried the carcass home.

When they dropped it on the ground in front of the door it made a great noise and the grandmother called out, "What is that?"

When she saw the bear she was glad. They dressed the bear and cooked some of the meat. As they sat down to eat, a young girl came in and the old woman asked her to eat. When they were through eating the girl carried a piece of meat home to her mother, who said, "Go back, carry them bread and get some of their meat in exchange."

The girl did as told, and she got two large pieces of meat for her bread.

HODADEIOⁿ said, "Others will come to exchange bread for meat. Let them have it; bread is what we want."

Towards night a man came, kicked the door, threw it open, and said, "I notify you to come to the long house, there is a man there who sheds wampum instead of tears. If you pick up wampum after it has fallen, it is yours. If you get more than others do, it is your good luck."

The next day HODADEIOⁿ, with the old woman and her grandson went to the long house where OTGOEDAQSAIS was tied and tormented with fire-brands. Before going in, each boy got a bundle of dry reeds to light pipes with. There were many people in the house. When the man who was being tortured saw his brother he smiled.

One of the women saw this, and said, "The bound man

smiled when the boys came in; it must be that one of them
is Hodadeio^n."

One of the men said, "It is well these boys have come,
they can bring fire for our pipes."

In the long house were two women who held fire-brands.
First one of the women burned the young man on one side
of his body, then the other burned him on the other side.
Each time the brand touched his flesh he cried out and
wampum fell in showers. The people gathered all they
could, they struggled and fought for it, and when every one
had enough they were sent away.

The chief said, "To-morrow you will come again."

The boys went home together and Hodadeio^n said, "The
man they torture is my brother, and to-morrow I am
going to destroy those people."

The next day when Hodadeio^n went to the long house,
he heard people say that the brands wouldn't burn; they
were not dry enough.

Then the chief said, "We will rest. After a while the
brands will get dry and burn. Let us lie down."

Hodadeio^n brought deep sleep on all. He released his
brother, took him out to his new brother—the old widow's
grandson—and shut the door securely. Then he ran around
the house, and said, "I want this house to be stone and
I want it to be red hot."

Instantly the long house became stone and red hot. The
man-eaters woke up and ran around inside.

One said, "I will go out through the smoke-hole."

Another said, "I will go through the ground."

But not one escaped. On one side of the village Hodad-
eio^n found piles of bones. He collected them under a
hickory tree, pushed the tree and cried out, "Rise or the
tree will fall on you!" A crowd of men sprang up and
among them were many of Hodadeio^n's relatives.

Hodadeio^n took his brother to the old widow's house.
She was glad, and said, "He is my grandson, I came for
him years ago, I was captured and had to live here with
the man-eaters."

"My brother must stay here and rest," said Hodadeio^n.
"I am going away for a while, I have work to do."

He started and as he hurried along he heard the noise,

"Dum! dum! dum!" of Long Eyebrows, preparing tobacco, pounding it with a mallet. The boy went to the
house and found the old man sitting inside pounding and
singing, and his song said, "He makes tobacco, and I am
he." When the rolls were ready he tied them up with
bark strings.

Two or three times HODADEIOⁿ called, "Hello, Uncle,
I've come," but the old man gave no answer.

The boy took a mallet that was lying near and struck
the old man on the head, saying, "I've come to visit you."

Long Eyebrows paid no attention. The boy hit him
again, and said, "Uncle, I've come to visit you."

"I think mice have thrown the stone bowl down," said
Long Eyebrows, but he kept at work. The boy struck him
again. The old man raised his upper eyelids, which hung
down over his face, tied them back with bark strings, then
taking a shell he scraped his eyes out clean, and said, "I
think some one has come in!"

He looked, saw HODADEIOⁿ, and asked, "What are you
here for?"

"I came for tobacco."

"You will get no tobacco," said the old man, "I will
kill you."

He started up, chased HODADEIOⁿ out of doors and
around the house. The boy was far ahead, but at last
he turned and letting two arrows fly killed Long Eyebrows. Then he took tobacco and threw it toward the
West, saying as he threw it, "Go to my sister, YEYENTH-
wûs."

YEYENTHWûs, far off in the West, picked up the rolls
and said, "Thank you, Brother, thank you."

When he had sent all the tobacco home, he went back
to where he had left his brother and the men he had
brought to life.

He told the men to go to their homes. Those who
remembered where their homes were went, those who
didn't know where to go said to him, "We will go home
with you."

The old woman's grandson was one of the man-eaters.
But he promised never to eat human flesh again and
HODADEIOⁿ left him in the house at the edge of the village.

The next morning HODADEIO[n] and his party started. After a while he stopped, and said, "There are two of my uncles with us, they will show the way, I must go on alone."

He wanted to reach home first. When he met his sister he told her how he had brought many of their relatives to life and saved his brother.

"And now," said he, "We must get ready for them."

He marked out spaces with his feet, each space as large as the house he wanted, then he wished for the house, and it was there with everything in it. When the houses were ready, he went out to meet the people who were coming. He gave each one a house, but there were not men enough for the houses he had made.

Then he said, "They are not all here yet."

After he had been home for a long time, he began to hear the sound, "Dum! dum! dum!" very often. Then he remembered the old woman's grandson, and he said to himself, "I will go and see if he is keeping his promise."

As HODADEIO[n] went on he heard the noise, "Dum! dum! dum!" and went toward it till he came to the center of the man-eater's village. He went into a house; no one there. He went into another; no one there. He entered every house; all were empty. At last he saw smoke at the opposite side of the village, and going to the house the smoke came from he found an old man.

The old man rose up, threw off his blanket, and said, "You have caused me misery and pain, now kill me."

"I have not caused you misery and pain," said HODADEIO[n], "It may be that the old woman's grandson is making you all this trouble."

"It is time for him to come," said the old man, "I and my granddaughter are the only persons left in the village."

A young woman came from her hiding place, and HODADEIO[n] said, "If the old woman's grandson is eating human flesh, he must kill me before he eats any more. You must help me all you can. If we fight, we will begin here and go westward. At the end of ten days we will come back, fighting as we come; there will be nothing left of us but our heads."

"You must have a kettle of boiling oil ready to throw

on my skull. But do not mistake me for him, if you do, I shall die and so will you and your grandfather.''

He heard the old man cry out and going to him found that the old woman's grandson was there cutting flesh from his legs and thighs, and saying, ''I don't know where to take the next piece from.''

''My friend,'' said HODADEIO[n], ''you promised not to eat human flesh.''

''Let us fight,'' said the other.

They began to fight, going westward as they struggled, and soon they disappeared in the woods.

At times for a number of days the young woman heard their cries and groans. She heated the fat, and had it ready. One day they came back into the opening, skeletons terrible to look at. They rushed at each other and fell back exhausted. When they closed again, the skeletons were gone, only naked skulls were left.

One of the skulls rolled up to the young woman, and said, ''Now is the time to do as I told you.''

The other skull rolled up that minute and said the same thing. The girl kept her eyes on the second skull and poured the fat on to it.

''Now you have killed me,'' said the other skull. She paid no heed to the words, but, picking up the skull she had poured the fat on, she carried it to the house and soon HODADEIO[n] was in full flesh and health.

The old man said to him, ''You have saved our lives. Now you must have my granddaughter for a wife.''

''Very well,'' said HODADEIO[n], ''but I'll cure you first.''

He spat on the palms of his hands and rubbed the old man where his flesh had been cut off and right away he was well.

''Now,'' said HODADEIO[n], ''I want you to help me.''

They went with him to the edge of the woods where a great many bones were lying on the ground. They gathered them up, put them near a hickory tree, then HODADEIO[n] pushed the tree and called out, ''Rise up, or the tree will fall on you!''

The bones rose up that minute as living men and went back to their own places. HODADEIO[n] and the old man and his granddaughter started for YEYENTHWÛS' home.

After they had gone some distance HODADEIO^n said, "I must go for chestnuts for my brother, I will overtake you."

He traveled till he came to where he could see the woman walking back and forth on a platform. He got slippery elm bark, and turned it into wampum.

Then he called a mole, and said, "Take me to that woman."

He made himself small, went into the mole's body and the mole went under ground till it came to the platform.

Then HODADEIO^n came out of the mole and said to the woman, "I will give you this wampum, if you will not tell the women that I am here."

Then he called all the moles and sent them into the house to find the hearts of the four women. They found them under a couch; HODADEIO^n seized them and started off. That minute the woman on the platform sang out, "HODADEIO^n has come!"

The mother screamed, "Hurry after him, my children, kill him for he is the youngest of his family."

The eldest sister ran ahead. As she was coming near, HODADEIO^n crushed one of the hearts, and she fell to the ground, dead. The second sister came up; he crushed the second heart and she died. The youngest sister was served in the same way. The mother came; he crushed the fourth heart and she died. He ground up the four hearts and burned them together with the four bodies.

The woman on guard was HODADEIO^n's sister. She was boneless, nothing but a skin pouch. Close by was a pile of bones.

The young man took the skin, put it on the pile, and pushing over a hickory tree that stood there, called out, "Rise up or the tree will fall on you."

That moment many people sprang up. With them was HODADEIO^n's sister, now in full flesh. He went to the chestnut tree and taking one nut he threw it to his sister in the West and told the other nuts to follow it.

All the nuts followed the first one and as they went through the end of the house, YEYENTHWÛS collected and stored them away. Then HODADEIO^n wished for the chestnut trees to be around his sister's house.

Now the young man went home with the sister and friends he had found and when they had taken their places there was one person still lacking.

The people were living in a chestnut grove. Two men came to get chestnuts for a person near death.

"Very well," said HODADEIO^n, "I will give you a chestnut, but you must not lose it. Give me your arrow, I will hide the nut. A man will meet you. He will say, 'Stop, my nephews,' and then come towards you, but that minute say to him, 'Let us see who can shoot farthest.' And before he reaches you do you shoot away your arrow and save the chestnut. If you lose this nut, I will not give you another."

They went their way and soon met a man, who said, "O, Nephews, I have waited a long time for you to come."

"Let us see who can shoot farthest," said the man who had the chestnut.

The stranger sprang forward to snatch the arrow, and barely missed it. He was angry, and said, "You are not my nephews. Go your way."

They hurried along, found their arrow and went home.

The next day HODADEIO^n said, "I still have work to do. I must go West this time."

He hadn't gone far when he came to an opening and saw a lake before him, but no land beyond. Between him and the lake was a house from which smoke was rising. He walked up to the house, pushed open the door, went in and found an old man mending moccasins.

The old man looked up and said, "Well, my Nephew, I have been waiting for you a long time. I am from your village. I am ready to go home. But first we will eat together."

He had a kettle of corn and beans with plenty of bear meat in it. After they had eaten, he said, "Now we will go to my island and look for game."

They went to a canoe and stepped in. Then the old man called ducks to row the canoe. They came, small white birds with black heads, and paddled the canoe to the island, the old man singing all the time.

When they landed, the old man said, "I will go to

the upper end of the island; you go to the lower. We will meet in the middle and see how much game each of us has.''

HODADEIO[n] started but soon he heard the old man's song, and, turning around, saw him rowing toward mainland. He shouted for him to come back, but got no answer.

The old man called to the creatures in the lake. ''If the man on the island tries to swim to me eat him.''

And voices out of the water answered, ''We will.''

While standing and looking across the lake the young man heard a voice say, ''Nephew, come to me.''

He went toward the voice, but saw only a pile of bones covered with moss.

The bones asked, ''Nephew, do you think that you are going to die?''

''I do,'' answered the young man.

''A man-eater is coming to kill you,'' said the bones, ''but do me a service and I will tell you how to save yourself. Go to that hollow tree over there and bring my pouch here. Let me smoke then I will tell you what to do.''

HODADEIO[n] brought the pouch, cut and put tobacco into the pipe and lighted it. Smoke went out through all the fissures of the old man's skull and his eyes and his nose and his ears.

When he had finished smoking, he said, ''Put my pouch away.''

The young man put the pouch in the tree, then went back to the bones, which said, ''You must cut some red willows. Of the larger ones make mannikins, of the smaller ones make bows and arrows. Run to three different places on the island and at each place put a mannikin in the crotch of a tree. Give it a bow and arrow and say to it, 'Shoot the dog when it comes.' When you have placed the last one, come to me and from here go to the end of the island, step off the land and walk in water till you come to an overhanging bank opposite the landing place. There the dogs cannot find you.''

HODADEIO[n] did as his uncle told him to do. That evening the man-eater, with four dogs, came in a canoe and began to hunt for HODADEIO[n]. Starting from the pile of bones the dogs went to the tree where the pouch was and back, then they went on till they came to the first mannikin.

The man-eater followed the dogs, singing as he ran, "There are no dogs like mine, there are no dogs like mine."

Suddenly the man-eater saw a man in the crotch of a tree pointing an arrow at one of his dogs. The man let the arrow fly and a dog dropped dead. The man-eater shot the man; when the dogs sprang forward to catch him, the man-eater called out, "Don't eat the body! Don't eat the body!" but when he came up he saw the dogs biting bits of red willow. He called the dogs off and followed the tracks farther. They came to the second mannikin and a second dog was killed. The man-eater was very angry. The dogs ran on and soon he heard them growling fiercely; they had stopped at a pile of bones.

The man-eater took his club, pounded the bones, and said, "I ate your flesh long ago, and still you try to deceive me."

The dogs started on the trail again and ran for a long time. At last they came to the third mannikin. The mannikin killed one of the dogs. The man-eater then killed him, but when he touched the ground he was only a bit of willow.

Daylight began to come. The man-eater said, "I will go home now, but when it is dark I will come again and then I will be sure of the game." He brought his dead dogs to life, got into his canoe and left the island.

When all was quiet and daylight had come HODADEIO^n left his hiding place and went to his uncle, who said, "My Nephew, bring my pouch and let me have a smoke, then I will tell you what to do."

He brought the pouch, filled and lighted the pipe and put it into his uncle's mouth. The skull smoked with great pleasure, letting the smoke out through every seam, through the eyes, the nose, the ears.

"Thank you, my Nephew. Take the pouch back and we will talk."

HODADEIO^n put the pouch away.

Then his uncle said, "Go to the place where the canoe always comes to shore, dig a hole and bury yourself in the sand, leaving out only the end of your nose."

While the young man was covering himself he heard SHAGODYOWEQ, the man who had brought him to the island coming again, singing to the ducks. Soon the canoe scraped on the sand and a voice said, "Now I'll find the place where my nephew has scattered his blood."

As soon as the man was out of sight, HODADEIO^n jumped up, called the ducks, pushed the canoe into the water and began to sing, "Now we paddle, my ducks. Now we paddle."

The canoe was far out in the water when SHAGODYOWEQ saw it. He ran to the shore and screamed, "Let me in! Let me in!"

HODADEIO^n paid no attention to him, but speaking to all the creatures that lived in the lake, he said, "If he tries to swim after me, eat him up."

Then out of the water came as many voices as there were living things in the lake and they all said, "It will be done. It will be done."

SHAGODYOWEQ ran back and forth on the shore, but he could not get away. When night came he climbed a tree. At dusk the man-eater came, with his dogs, and began to look around for HODADEIO^n, whom he thought was on the island yet. At last the dogs come to the tree where SHAGODYOWEG was.

They barked furiously and when the man-eater came up SHAGODYOWEQ cried, "Don't shoot me, I am your servant."

"You can't fool me," said the man-eater, and he let an arrow fly. The man fell to the ground. The man-eater threw the body into his canoe and left the island.

The next morning HODADEIO^n said, "I will go to the man-eater's house."

He pushed out the canoe and sang for the ducks. They came and swam on till towards dark, then HODADEIO^n saw a house near the water. He brought the canoe to shore, hid it under the water, and said to the ducks, "You may go your way till I come."

A woman came out of the house with two pieces of bark. She put one piece of bark by the edge of the water. HODADEIO^n stepped on it, then she put the second piece of bark before the first. He stepped on the second. Then she put the first before the second. He stepped on the first.

In this way he reached the house without leaving a track on the ground.

HODADEIO^n said to the woman, "I have come for you, I am your brother."

"I will go with you," answered the woman, "but you must stay here till midday to-morrow." And she hid him under her couch.

Soon the barking of dogs was heard and then footsteps. The first dog came in with open mouth. The woman threw a bone at him, then hit him on the head.

The man-eater called out, "Oh, you have killed one of my dogs!"

"Why do they run at me?" asked she, "I have done nothing to them."

He called them off, and said, "I had bad luck to-day, I found nothing but a little cub."

He cooked his game with pounded corn, and when he finished eating he said, "My food was good and tender, now I will take a smoke. But it seems to me you have two breaths."

"That is too much to say," answered the woman, "You might as well kill me."

The next morning the man-eater said, "I'll not go hunting on that island again. I'll go on the other side of the lake," and he went away.

When he had been gone some time, the woman said to her brother, "Now you can come out."

He came from under the couch; the two went to the lake and raising the canoe rowed away as quickly as they could.

When in the middle of the lake they heard the man-eater shout, "You can't get away from me!"

He ran to his house, got a hook and line, and saying, "Catch the canoe!" hurled it into the lake.

Straightway the hook was in the canoe and the man-eater was pulling the canoe to shore. All at once the woman saw that the trees on the shore were coming nearer, then she saw the hook and line and she screamed to HODADEIO^n to break the hook. He broke the hook; freed the canoe and it went out again to the middle of the lake.

The man-eater screamed, "You can't get away from

me!'' and he ran along on the bottom of the lake, raging as he went toward them.

Then HODADEIO^n said, ''Let there be ice over the water so thick that nothing can break through, and let our canoe be on the ice.''

When the man-eater thought he was under the canoe, he sprang up with all his might. He struck the ice with such force that it cracked everywhere. The ice didn't break but the man-eater broke his head and died.

HODADEIO^n caused the ice to melt as quickly as it had formed, and with his sister he rowed to the end of the lake, then traveled on land. When they reached home, they went in at the western door, went around on the south side to the east and HODADEIO^n led his sister to her place, which was at the northwest corner.

All the family were at home now, and all were happy.

A LITTLE BOY AND HIS DOG, BEAUTIFUL
EARS

[Told by Mrs. Logan]

A MAN and his wife went into the woods to hunt. They
built a house of hemlock boughs, and lived happily.
After a while a boy was born to them.

The family always had a plenty of meat, for the man
was a good hunter. While he was away in the woods
looking for game, his wife was busy drying meat; bringing
bark to keep the fire; and taking care of the child. Another child was born to them, a girl.

Everything went on well till the boy was old enough to
do chores and his mother began to send him for water.
The spring was some distance from the cabin and the child
was afraid there. Whenever his mother told him to go, he
complained and tried to beg off. But when she seized him
by the hair, dragged him to the door, pushed him out and
threw the bark water vessel after him, he knew that he
must pick up the vessel and go. As soon as he brought
the water, his mother washed her face, combed her hair
carefully, took her strap and hatchet and, telling him she
was going for bark to burn and he must stay with his
sister, she went off somewhere.

This happened every day for a long time.

The woman began to be cruel to the boy. She didn't
give him enough to eat and neglected him in every way.
She seemed to hate him.

When at last the boy told his father that he didn't have
enough to eat, the man noticed that his wife was cross and
cruel to the child and he began to think that something was
wrong. One night as he and the boy were together on one
side of the fire, and his wife and little girl were sleeping
on the other side, he questioned the child about what was

351

done in the house while he was off hunting. The boy told him that at such a time each day his mother sent him to a spring where he was afraid to go; when he came with the water, she washed and combed and then went to the woods for bark.

The man decided to watch his wife. The next morning he started off to hunt, then crept back till he came to a place where he could see his cabin. By and by he saw the skin door open and out came his boy, head first, the water vessel after him.

The boy, crying bitterly, picked up the vessel and started off. The father was angry, but he waited to see what would happen next.

The boy brought the water and soon afterward the mother came out with her strap and hatchet. She walked away and her husband followed cautiously.

The woman went down a hill and walked on till she came to a black ash tree from which the bark could easily be stripped. There she stopped and looked up into the tree. The man crept as near as was possible and not be seen by his wife. After a while she hit the tree with the back of her hatchet; it made a beautiful sound. She waited a minute, then struck the tree a second time; again the same musical sound. The third time she struck the man saw a bird on the top branches of the tree. When the woman struck a fourth time, the bird flew down, and as it touched the ground it became a handsome man. That minute the husband drew his bow and shot, instantly the man turned to a bird, flew up and disappeared in the air.

The woman, seeing her husband, said, "Is it you?"

"It is," said the man, "and now I know why you abuse our boy."

"I abuse him, and I will abuse you, too," said the woman, and she caught up a club and struck her husband till he was helpless.

Then, leaving him on the ground, she ran home, put her children outside and set fire to the cabin. The hemlock boughs blazed up quickly and soon the cabin was in ashes. Then she said to her children, "You must stay here. Everything will be all right." And taking up a handful of ashes, she threw the ashes into the air and said, "Let there be a snowstorm, and let the snow be as high as these trees."

When snow began to fall, the mother said to the little boy, "Here is your dog, keep him with you and take care of your sister." Then she started off.

Snow fell fast and soon the boy and girl were covered up, but they felt as warm and comfortable as if in a house.

After a time the father dragged himself towards home. When near he saw there was no longer a cabin. He searched for his children and at last found them; then he set about building a house of boughs.

When the cabin was ready he said to the boy, "You must stay here and take care of your little sister, and of your dog, Beautiful Ears. Always give him a plenty to eat, as much and as good as you have yourselves. When you go out, carry your sister on your back, never put her down or leave her for a minute. When the dog seems uneasy, you must turn around and go home. I am going in pursuit of your mother," and he started.

In the morning when the boy woke up, he found food cooked and ready to eat. He gave Beautiful Ears his share, then he and his sister ate. Afterward, whenever it was time to eat, food was ready for them.

One day the boy got lonely and he said to his sister and Beautiful Ears, "We will go out and amuse ourselves."

The boy had a bow and arrows; but he couldn't shoot, for he carried his sister on his back. Beautiful Ears ran ahead, then ran back, and was full of life.

The three looked around and enjoyed themselves till the dog began to whine and tease, wanted his master to go home.

Then the boy said to his sister, "Beautiful Ears wants to go back."

A few days later they went out again, went a little farther than the first day. When they got home, food was ready for them. The boy always gave Beautiful Ears his share first.

The third time they went out, the dog ran after a wild turkey. The boy followed the dog. The dog chased the turkey into a clump of bushes. The boy couldn't get into the bushes to shoot the turkey, for his sister was strapped to his back. He thought, "I will unstrap her just for a minute, then we will have a nice fat turkey to eat."

He took the little girl from his back and put her down. Before he reached the bushes she screamed and turning around the brother saw a bear take the child up and run off.

Beautiful Ears and the boy followed the bear. For three or four days the boy heard the dog bark as it ran on ahead, but at last it was out of hearing and he lost trace of it, couldn't follow it any longer.

Now the boy was alone. He had nothing to live for and wished to die.

One day, as he walked along without purpose, he came to the bank of a lake; he climbed a high rock, leaped into the water and lost consciousness. On coming to his senses he thought he was in a beautiful country and he felt happy. But in reality a great fish had swallowed him.

After a few days the fish swam into a small stream. On the bank of that stream lived seven sisters. They had built a cabin and made a fish dam. One morning they went to the dam and found a very large fish.

They pulled it up on to the bank and the eldest sister said, "We will cut it open."

"Wait," said the second sister, "till we boil water to cook it in. We will cut it open carefully; such a large fish must have a lot of spawn."

When everything was ready, the sisters opened the fish. But in place of spawn they found a beautiful boy. They forgot the fish. They washed the boy, cared for him, and rejoiced that such a gift had come to their door.

They said, "We will take good care of this boy. Maybe he will become a great hunter and get meat for us when we are old."

The sisters and their "son," as they called the boy, lived happily together. He soon surprised them by killing large game and by becoming a good hunter, but when they found that while hunting he wandered a long distance from home they were frightened and told him to keep near the house and never go toward the West.

One day the boy said to himself, "I wonder what there is off there where the sun goes down. I'll go and see."

He hadn't gone far when he came to a clearing and saw a cabin. Everything was quiet. He crept up cautiously and peeping in saw an old man sitting with his head bent down to his breast.

That minute the old man called out, "Well, Nephew, you have come."

The boy knew that he was discovered and he answered, "Yes, I have come. I thought I would see what you were doing."

"Well, come in and wait till I get my head up."

The old man picked up a big wooden pin that lay at his side, and taking a mallet drove the pin down his spinal column. Up came his head, and he said, "I have a rule that when a nephew comes I will play a game with him and bet—"

"What do you bet?"

"I bet my head against his."

"Very well," said the boy.

The old man swept the ashes from the fireplace and made it smooth. Then he shook a bowl that had stones in it, and said, "The one who turns the stones all of a color will be the winner. You must throw first."

"No," said the boy, "if you want to play the game you must play first."

At last the old man consented. He shook the bowl; six stones flew out of the smoke-hole, turned to birds and flew off out of hearing.

After a while the boy heard the birds again and soon six stones fell through the smoke-hole into the bowl. The old man bent over and stirred the stones, repeating, "Let them be white! Let them be white!" but he couldn't get them all of one color.

The boy shook the bowl and, as before, six stones went out of the smoke-hole, turned to birds and flew off. The old man began to shake the dish and say, "I wish this, I wish that." When the stones came back to the bowl the boy stirred them and they all turned of one color.

When the old man saw that he had lost the game he wanted to play again.

"Oh, no," said the boy, "that isn't your rule."

"Let me smoke once more."

The boy cut off the old man's head, set fire to the cabin and went home.

After a few days the boy thought he would go again toward the West. He passed the old man's place, came to another opening and saw another cabin. Around the cabin the ground was as smooth as a playground. The boy walked up quietly and peeping into the cabin saw an old man sitting there.

That minute the old man called out, "Is that you, Nephew? Come in. I have been waiting for you."

The boy went in.

"I have a way of passing time," said the old man. "I play a game."

"What is your game?"

"Ball."

"I like that," said the boy.

"I bet my head against my nephew's head."

"Very well," said the boy.

They went to the middle of the opening, at one end of which there were two stakes. They threw the balls; the uncle was the best thrower, but the nephew was the best runner. When he was far ahead, the old man threw a horn after him and the horn stuck in the sole of his foot. He had to sit down and pull it out. While he was sitting there the old man passed him.

The boy spat on his hand, rubbed the spittle into his foot and it was healed. He threw the horn. It hit the old man's foot and he had to sit down and pull it out. The ball rolled on and went between the stakes. At the next throw the result was the same. The old man lost the game.

He wanted to play again, but the boy said, "No, it isn't the rule."

He cut off the old man's head, burned the cabin and went home.

A third time the boy went toward the West, and farther than before. He passed the first and second clearing and coming to a third one saw a great pond covered with thick ice, and near the pond a cabin. He crept up to the cabin and peeping in saw an old man. The old man called out, "Well, Nephew, I am glad to see you. Come in."

The boy went in and said, "I thought I would look in and see you. Now I will go."

"Oh, no; I have a rule. When a nephew comes to see me, I play a game with him. We run a race on the ice and the one who gets to the goal last loses his head. No matter how you get there, only get there first."

When the boy was ready to start he took an oak ball from a nearby tree and said, "Let a high wind come!" He got into the oak ball, a high wind rose, and in a flash he was over the ice. The old man was scarcely half way.

The boy took a white flint stone out of his pouch, threw it toward the middle of the pond and said, "Let this stone melt the ice and boil the water."

In an instant the old man was sinking in boiling water. He cried for mercy, but the boy didn't listen.

The water disappeared; dry land was left where the pond had been. The old man, now a great stone, was in the middle of the space where the pond had been. The boy burned the cabin and went home.

One day a runner came to the home of the seven sisters and said, "The chief has sent me to notify you of the marriage of a certain girl. He wants everyone to come to the gathering."

The sisters knew that the boy had magic power and they were careful of him. When he said, "I want to go to the gathering," they said that bad people would be there and all sorts of games would be played.

He said, "You were afraid to have me go toward the West. I have been there and I have destroyed the dice man, the ball man, and the ice-pond man. Now I am going to this gathering. My mother, father, sister, and my dog, Beautiful Ears, are there."

At last the sisters told him he could go and told him where to find a grandmother who would tell him what to do.

The boy started and after going some distance came to a wide trail and began to meet many people. When night came they all camped together. The next day they went on.

The sisters had said to the boy, "There will be one

woman in the crowd, who will seem to have power over all the others. Don't notice her.''

He soon saw her, but remembering their words, looked at her and went on.

At last he came to the place where his grandmother lived. He said, ''Grandmother, I have come.''

''Poor Grandson,'' said she, ''I have little to give you. I am alone and poor.''

''Don't mind that,'' said the boy; ''we will soon have a plenty to eat.''

He brought in game till the old woman cried, she was so glad. And she hurried around, like a girl, to prepare the food.

She said, ''There is a great gathering at the long house; the chief's daughter is to marry a second time, but first she will destroy her husband, her daughter, and a dog they call Beautiful Ears. She had a son, but no one knows where he is. Her husband is tied up at one end of the long house and every person who goes in must strike him with a burning brand. His tears are wampum beads.

''Her daughter is hanging over the fire and slowly roasting. The dog is at one end of the fire, and every person who passes him gives him a kick. His hair is singed off and he is dying.''

The boy was very angry. When night came he said to his grandmother, ''I am going to the gathering. The seven sisters said that you would tell me what to do. The man they are torturing is my father; the little girl is my sister.''

''I know everything,'' said the old woman, ''and I will help you. I have a pair of moccasins that you must put on when you get to the long house. Stand by the fire and when your mother calls out, 'Burn him!' stick one foot in the fire. The moccasins are made of a woman's flesh and I have power over them.''

When the boy came to where the people were, he made himself very small, played around with the children, and went into the long house with them. His mother was sitting on a high seat in the middle of the room where she could be seen by everyone.

As she gave the order, ''Burn him!'' the boy stuck his foot into the fire. That instant the woman screamed with pain. She felt that a firebrand was burning her flesh. The boy ran out, but when it was about time for the woman to give the order again he was near the fire, and as she was beginning to say, "Burn him!" he put his foot in the fire. That instant she screamed with pain. He tormented her in this way till she died from fright and pain.

The boy led his father and sister out of the house and the dog followed. Then he said, "Let this house become red hot flint!"

Right away the long house was in flames. Some of the people in the house had magic power; their heads burst and their spirits flew through the smoke-hole and off in the air in the form of owls and other birds.

The boy spat on his hands, rubbed his father, sister and dog and they were as well as ever. Then he said, "Now we will go home."

He thanked his grandmother for her help, and they started for the sister's cabin. When they came near, the seven sisters ran to meet them. And they all lived happily together ever after.

QUAIL KILLS COLD WEATHER AND THE THUNDER FAMILY

Characters

POPKPÉKNOS .... Quail

GENO^{n}SKWA ..... Stone Coat (Ice and Cold Weather)

A MAN and his wife lived in an ugly-looking cabin in the forest. They had one child, a little boy. When the boy was four or five years old, another child was born, a boy no longer than a hand. The mother died and the man burned the body. Then, wrapping the baby up in a blanket, he put it in a hollow tree, for he thought it was dead.

Each day the man went to hunt and left the elder boy to play around the cabin. After a time the boy heard something crying in a hollow tree and going to the tree he found a baby. The child was lonely and almost starved. The boy fed it with soup he made of deer intestines.

The child drank the soup with great relish, drank again and again and soon became strong. The boy gave his little brother plenty to eat and at last he came out of the tree.

The two boys played together. The elder boy made the little one a coat of fawn-skin and put it on him. Then, as he ran around, he looked exactly like a chipmunk.

One day the father noticed a decrease of provisions and asked the boy what he had done with the deer intestines.

The boy said, "I eat a good many."

The father looked around the fire and seeing very small tracks, said, "Here are the tracks of a little child."

Then the boy told how he had found his brother, had fed him and made a coat for him, and how they played together.

"Bring him in," said the father.

"He won't come; he is afraid."

"We will catch him. Tell him to come with you and hunt for mice."

The man caught a great many mice, put them in his bosom and his clothes and, going beyond the hollow tree, turned himself into an old stump.

The boy went to the hollow tree, and called, "Come out, Brother, we will play catching mice."

The little fellow came out of the tree and he and his brother ran to the stump, ran around it and caught a number of mice. The child laughed and shouted with joy. Suddenly the stump became a man. The man caught the little boy and ran home. The child screamed and struggled. No use; he couldn't get away; but he wouldn't be pacified. At last his father put a little club in his hand, and said, "Strike that tree!"—A great hickory that stood near the house.

The child struck the tree, the tree fell to the ground. Everything that he hit with his club was killed. He was delighted, he didn't cry any more.

The little fellow stayed now with his brother and the two played while their father was off hunting.

"You must not go towards the North," said their father; "bad people live there."

"Let's go North," said the little one, as soon as his father was out of sight, "I want to find out what is there."

The boys started and went on till they came to wooded and swampy ground, then the little one heard people call, "My father, my father, my father," and he said to himself, "Those people want to hurt my father, I'll kill them."

He piled up stones, made them red hot, and hurled them into the swamp till he had killed all the people there— they were frogs and they sang, "Ho'qwa! Ho'qwa!"

When the boys got home their father was angry, and said, "You must not go to the swamp again, and you must not go West. It is dangerous there too."

The next day when his father had gone hunting, the little boy said to his brother, "I want to know what is in the West, let us go there."

The two traveled West till they came to a tall pine tree. On the top of the tree was a nest made of skins.

"Oh," said the little boy, "that is a queer place for a nest. I would like to see what is in it. I'll climb up there."

Up he went and on the top of the tree he found two naked children, a boy and a girl. They were terribly frightened when they saw him. He pinched the boy till he cried out, "Father! Father! Some strange child has come and is frightening me."

Suddenly a terrible voice was heard in the far West. The voice came nearer and nearer, and a great dark object hurried along in the air till it reached the nest on the top of the tree—It was Old Man Thunder.

The boy raised his club and struck him on the head, crushed him and he fell to the ground, dead.

Then the boy pinched the little girl till she called out, "Mother! Mother! Some strange boy has come and is teasing me."

That minute the voice of Mother Thunder was heard in the West and soon she was at the nest.

The boy raised his club and struck her on the head and she too fell to the ground, dead.

"This Thunder baby will make a splendid tobacco pouch for my father," thought the boy, "I'll take him home."

He struck the boy with his club and threw him to the ground. He threw the little girl also, then he went down himself, and said to his brother, "Now we will go home."

When the boys got home the little one said, "Oh, Father, I have brought you a splendid pouch."

"What have you done now?" asked the father when he saw the Thunder baby. "Old Man Thunder and his wife have never done us any harm. They bring rain and do good, but they will destroy us in revenge for what you have done."

"They'll not harm us," said the boy, "I've killed the whole family."

Another day the father said to the boys, "You mustn't go North, that is the country of the Stone Coats (Ice and Great Cold)."

The elder brother wouldn't go, so the little one started off alone. About midday he heard the loud barking of a Stone Coat's dog and knowing that its master must be near he crawled into the heart of a chestnut tree.

Soon Stone Coat came, looked at the tree, and said, "There is nothing here."

But his dog, as tall as a deer, barked and looked up, so Stone Coat struck the tree with his mallet. The tree split open and the boy fell out.

"What a strange little fellow you are," said Stone Coat, looking at the boy, "You are not big enough to fill a hole in a tooth."

"I'm not here to fill holes in your teeth," said the boy, "I came to go home with you and see how you live."

"All right! come with me."

Stone Coat was enormously tall, he carried two bears in his belt as a common man would carry two squirrels. Once in a while he looked down at the little fellow running by his side, and said, "Oh, you are a curious little creature!"

Stone Coat's house was very large and long. The boy had never seen anything like it.

Stone Coat skinned the two bears, took one himself and put one before his visitor, saying, "Eat this bear or I'll eat you and the bear together."

"If you don't eat your bear before I eat mine, may I kill you?" asked the boy.

"You may kill me," said Stone Coat.

The boy cut off pieces of meat as fast as he could and put them in his mouth, but he kept running in and out, hiding the meat. He was so small that Stone Coat didn't see what he was doing. In a short time all of the flesh of the bear had disappeared, then he said to Stone Coat, "You haven't finished eating your bear. I am going to kill you."

Stone Coat said, "Wait till I show you how to slide down hill."

He took the boy to a long icy hill that ended in a cave,

put him in a bark bowl and sent the bowl down at great speed. Presently the boy ran up to where he had started from.

"Where is my bowl?" asked Stone Coat.

"I don't know; it has gone down somewhere," said the boy.

"Let's see who can kick this log highest," said Stone Coat.

The log was large around, long and very heavy. Stone Coat put his foot under the log and lifted it into the air twice his own length.

The boy put his foot under the log and sent it whistling through the air. It was gone a long time, then came down on Stone Coat's head and crushed him.

"Come home with me," said the boy to Stone Coat's dog.

"Now my father will have a splendid dog," thought he.

When the man saw the dog he cried out, "What have you done? Stone Coat will kill us."

"I've killed Stone Coat. He'll not trouble us," said the boy.

"My boys," said the man, "You must never go Southwest. That is where the people live who are always gambling."

The next day the little boy started off alone; about midday he came to an opening in the woods. At the farther end of the opening was a roof on posts, under the roof was a man whose head was larger than the head of a buffalo. He was shaking dice for the heads of men who came along. Crowds of men were betting in threes. When the game was lost, the big-headed man had the three men stand on one side while he played with three other men. When they lost, they stood with the first three and so on till the number of losers was large enough, then he cut off each man's head.

As the boy came, a large number of men had lost and were waiting to be killed. Hope came to them for they knew that the boy had great power.

The game began again; the boy playing. When the big-headed man threw the dice, the boy caused some to remain in the dish and others to go high and when they came back to be of different colors. He threw; the dice became woodcocks, flew high and came down dice, all of one color.

The two played till the boy won back the men who were waiting to have their heads cut off, and the big-headed man lost his own head.

The crowd shouted, and said, "Now you must be our chief!"

"How could such a little fellow as I am be chief? Maybe my father would like to be your chief, I will ask him."

The boy went home and told his father, but his father would not go to the land of the gamblers, he said, "You have come back from the Southwest, but you must not go to the East, bad men play ball there."

The next day the boy went toward the East till he came to a beautiful plain, a large level space where Wolves and Bears were playing ball with Eagles, Turtles and Beavers.

The boy took the side of the Wolves and Bears and they said, "If you win the game for us, we will make you chief of this country."

The boy won.

He went home and said to his father, "I have won all the beautiful country of the East. You must go there and be chief." The father and his two sons went to that country and there they lived.—This is the story.

The little boy is called Popkpéknos, Quail, and is said to personify Summer or Warm Weather. He kills Stone Coat, a character known to be Ice and Cold Weather, and he also kills the Thunder Family.

GÁQGA' AND SKAGÉDI

[Told by George Titus]

Characters

GÁQGA' .... Raven
SKAGÉDI .... One-half of Anything

A BROTHER and sister lived together. The brother never let his sister go out of the house. When he went hunting, he told his dog to stay at home and get whatever the girl wanted.

One day when the brother was away the girl wanted water, and, not seeing the dog, thought, "What harm can it do? I'll go to the spring and get back quickly."

She ran to the spring, stooped down and filled the bucket, but as she straightened up and rested, putting the bucket at the edge of the spring, someone grasped her from behind, lifted her into the air and carried her off.

The dog followed, barking loudly. He made a spring into the air to catch the girl, but he couldn't reach her.

The brother, hearing the dog bark, hurried home and finding his sister gone, said to the dog, "You have caused great trouble."

The dog felt so badly that he bent his head down, curled it under and became stone.

GÁQGA', the man who stole the girl, took her to an island in the middle of a lake.

Every day GÁQGA' went away and came back with dry fish that he found on the shore of the lake. Sometimes he

366

brought pieces of human flesh which he ate himself, sending the girl to get water for him to drink.

One day when the girl went to the edge of the island to get water, a man stood before her, and said, "I have come here to tell you that GÁQGA' is very hungry and he has made up his mind to kill you to-morrow. He will tell you to bring water and fill the kettle. As soon as this is done he will take up his club to kill you. You must run behind the post that the kettle hangs on. He will strike the post and break his arm, then come to this place as quickly as you can."

The next day GÁQGA' did as the stranger said he would. When he struck at the girl she dodged, his arm hit the post and broke. She ran to the lake; the stranger was there and had a canoe. They sat in the canoe and the man pushed out on to the lake. This man was SKAGÉDI (One-half of anything). When he stepped into the canoe he divided and one-half sat at each end. They crossed the lake and as they touched land the half of SKAGÉDI at the rear end of the canoe was raised up and thrown across the canoe. It struck the front half and joining it became a whole man. The girl was sitting on the bottom of the canoe.

SKAGÉDI's mother was at the landing. She went to the girl and saying, "My daughter come with me," led her to a house.

The girl was now SKAGÉDI's wife. Every time he went out in his canoe he divided himself and one-half sat at each end of the canoe. As soon as he touched land he became one again.

SKAGÉDI had all his life been traveling around on the lake, liberating persons captured by bad men and wizards.

After a time SKAGÉDI's wife gave birth to twin boys. As soon as they were born, the grandmother threw them into the lake. As they touched the water they began to paddle and quickly came to shore.

She threw them in a second time; in a minute they were back; she threw them a third time, and far out. When they swam to shore, she said, "That will do." They began to run around and play.

The boys grew quickly and after a while said to their

father, "You ought to stay at home and let us go out in the canoe and do your work."

"Very well," said SKAGÉDI.

The boys started and after rowing some distance one said to the other, "See, there is something off there on land that looks as if it were breathing. Let us go ashore and find out what it is."

They landed, and going to the spot, found an old house lying flat on the ground, but inside something was breathing and soon they saw that it was a very old man. They got him out from under the house and one of the boys said, "This is our uncle. We must take him home."

The man was willing to go. As they were leaving the place he pointed to a large stone, and said, "That is my dog," and striking it with a switch he called out, "Get up!" The dog rose, shook, stretched himself and followed the man.

When they reached home, the boys said, "Mother, we have found our uncle." She looked at the man and sure enough he was her brother.

The boys said to their grandmother, "You must marry our uncle."

"Very well," said the woman.

After that they all lived together happily.

THE MAN-EATER AND HIS YOUNGER BROTHER

Characters

ONGWEIAS ....Man-Eater

SHAGODYOWEQ GOWA,

       Frost and Great Cold ("People")

TWO brothers went on a hunting expedition. After they had been quite a while in the woods and had good luck in finding game, they built a bark house.

At first they had everything in common, but one day the elder said to the younger, "We must live apart for the future. We will make a partition in the middle of the house and have a door at each end. You will always go out of the door in your part of the house and I will go out of the one in my part."

The younger brother agreed, and they made the partition, then the elder brother said, "Now each one will live by himself. I will not go to your part of the house and you will not come to mine. When we want to say anything we will talk through the partition. You can hunt birds and animals, but I will hunt men and kill them. Neither of us will marry or bring a woman to the house. If I marry, you will kill me if you can. If you marry, I will try to kill you."

Both agreed to this arrangement, and for a long time lived according to it, but one day, when the brothers were out hunting, a woman came to the younger brother's part of the house. The elder brother tracked her, caught her

369

at the door, dragged her into his part of the house, killed and ate her. When the younger brother came home the elder said, "I had good luck to-day, near home."

The younger knew what his brother had done, but all he said was, "It is well to have good luck."

A second time the elder brother tracked a woman to his brother's part of the house. This time he knocked at the door and called out, "Give me a couple of arrows; there is an elk out here."

The woman carried him the arrows and the minute she opened the door he killed her. He dragged the body into his part of the house and ate it up.

When the younger brother came, he talked through the partition as before, but said nothing about the woman.

The next woman who came to him he warned against opening the door, told her not to open it for anyone, even for him; he would come in himself.

The elder brother ran to the door, knocked and called out, "Give me a couple of arrows; there is a bear out here."

The woman sat by the fire, didn't move.

Again he called, "Give me the arrows; the bear will get away."

She didn't stir, and after a while he went into his own part of the house.

When the younger brother came the woman told him what had happened.

While they were whispering, the elder brother called out, "Brother, you are whispering to someone. Who is it? Haven't you a woman in there?"

"I am counting my game," answered the young man.

There was silence for a time, then the young man began whispering cautiously to the woman.

He said, "In the morning my brother and I will have a life and death struggle. You must help me, but it will be difficult for he will make himself like me in form and voice, but strike him if you can."

The woman took a small squash shell and tied it in the young man's hair so she might distinguish him.

The brother again called out, "You have a woman in there. You are whispering to her," but he got no answer.

In the morning the brothers met and began to fight with clubs and flint knives. When their weapons broke, they clinched. Soon both were on the ground. Sometimes one was under, sometimes the other. The elder brother was exactly like the younger and repeated his words. Whenever the younger called to the woman, "Strike him!" the elder cried out, "Strike him!"

The woman couldn't tell which one to strike. At last she caught sight of the squash shell. Then she struck a heavy blow and killed the elder brother. They put the body on a pile of wood and burned it up, then scattered the ashes.

But the young man knew his brother would come to life. He put the woman in a cattail, put the cattail on the point of his arrow and shot it far away to the West. Then he ran through the heart of the post of the house, sprang after the arrow and coming to the ground ran with great speed till he found where the arrow had struck and the cattail burst open. Then he soon overtook the woman and they traveled on together.

He said, "We must travel fast, for my brother will come to life and follow us."

The next morning they heard somebody whoop. The young man said, "That is my brother; he will destroy us if he can."

He changed the woman into a half-decayed stump; hid himself a short distance away, and, taking off his moccasins, told them to run on ahead; to go quickly through swamps and thickets and over hills and mountains and come back to him by a round-about way.

When the elder brother reached the rotten stump, he looked at it and was suspicious but he followed the moccasins and went on swiftly all day and all night, then he turned back. When he came to the place where he had seen the stump, and it wasn't there, he was awfully angry, for he knew he had been fooled. He found his brother's tracks and followed them.

When they heard him whoop, the young man took out of his pouch the jaw of a beaver, stuck the teeth in the ground, and said, "Let beavers come and build a dam across the world so water may rise to my brother's neck, and let the beavers bite him when he tries to cross the dam.''

When the elder brother came up, the dam was built, and the water was neck high; his brother's tracks disappeared at the edge of the water, and he said, "If they have gone through, I can.''

When the water reached his breast, beavers began to bite him. He was forced to turn back and look for another crossing. He ran all day, but could find no end to the dam. Then he cried out, "I have never heard that there was a beaver dam across the world," and turning he ran back to the place he had started from. The dam was gone, all that remained was a beaver's jaw with two teeth in it.

The man-eater hurried along as fast as he could and again the man and woman heard his whoop. The man took a pigeon-feather from his pouch, placed it on the ground, and said, "Let all the pigeons in the world come and leave droppings here.''

All the pigeons in the world came and soon there was a ridge six feet high, made of droppings.

When the elder brother came to the ridge, he said, "Their tracks are here; if they have gone through, I can.''

He tried, and when he couldn't get through he turned back and ran eastward to look for an opening, ran all day. The ridge was everywhere. He went back to the place that he had started from and slept till morning. When he wakened, the ridge was gone; all he found was a pigeon feather sticking in the ground.

After dropping the feather, the younger brother and the woman ran till they came to where an old man sat mending a fish net.

The old man said, "I will delay the man-eater as long as I can. You have an aunt living west of here, beyond her house the trail passes between two rocks that move backward and forward so quickly that whoever tries to go between them is crushed, but beg of your aunt and she will stop them.''

The two hurried on, came to the woman and begged her to help them. She stopped the rocks long enough for them to spring through, then she said, "You will soon reach a river. On the other side of the river you will see a man with a canoe, beckon to him and he will come and take you across. Beyond the river are the Frost people (SHAGO-DYOWEQ GOWA) but they will not harm you. A little animal will come to meet you. Follow it and it will lead you to an opening. In the opening you will find your mother's house."

When the elder brother came to the old man, who was mending a fish net, he pushed him, and called out, "Did anyone pass here?"

The old man didn't answer.

He struck him a blow on the head and asked again, "Did anyone pass here?"

The fisherman threw his net over the man, entangled him and he fell, but after struggling a time he freed himself and hurried on. When he came to the woman who guarded the rocks he begged her to stop them and let him pass. She refused and he watched for a chance to spring through. At last, when he thought the rocks were moving slowly, he jumped. He was caught and half his body was crushed; but he rubbed it with saliva and cured it. Then he hurried on. When he came to the river and saw the man on the opposite bank he shouted to him to come with his canoe and take him across, but the man didn't look up. He shouted again and got no answer, then he swam across.

On that side of the river was a forest where all of the trees had been stripped of bark and killed by the hammering of mudturtle rattles. The hammering had been done by the Frost people in keeping time while they danced. These people turned upon the man-eater, killed him, hammered all the flesh off of his body, then hammered his bones till there wasn't a bit of them left.

When the mother saw her son and his wife she was happy, and said, "I am glad that you have come. I was afraid that your brother, who stole you away from me, would kill you. Now you will stay with me always."

They lived happily ever after.

THE RABBIT BROTHERS

[Told by John Armstrong]

Characters

TONDAYENT ....White Rabbit
DAGWANOE^{n}YENT .... Whirlwind

SIX brothers and a sister lived in a long house in a clearing in the woods. The house stood East and West with a door at each end and a fire in the middle. Three brothers occupied one half of the house and three the other half. Each man was obliged to stay on his own side of the fire, never crossing to the other side, and always to go in and out at his own door, never using the door of the other three.

Whenever the brothers were away hunting, the sister was alone in the house. She had the right to go everywhere and in and out both doors.

The TONDAYENTS lived a long time in this way, then one day the eldest brother asked, "How would it be if I were to marry and bring my wife into the house?"

"Oh," answered the brothers, "it would be well if she didn't abuse us."

He went to an old woman, who lived in the West and had six daughters, and asked, "How would you like to have me marry one of your daughters?"

"Very well," said the mother, "if you would be kind to her and not abuse her."

He promised to be kind, and went home.

The girl made a basketful of marriage bread and the

374

next day came to his house bringing the bread. The brothers were glad. They ate the bread and the woman stayed. Her brother told her that three brothers had one half of the house and three the other half and each three had their own door. The sister was the only person who could go in and out at either door.

For a time the woman was satisfied and the TONDAYENTS were happy, but one day she said to herself, "I'm not going to obey such a silly rule, I'll go out of whichever door I choose."

She crossed the house and went out of the forbidden door. The minute she did this her husband, who was hunting in the woods, in crossing a fallen tree, got the strings of his moccasins tangled on a knot of the tree, fell and hung there, head down, helpless.

Five of the brothers came home from hunting. They missed their brother and waited a long time for him. At last they took torches and started off to look for him. After a long search they found him hanging to the tree stiff and half dead. They carried him home, rubbed him and brought him to life.

The next morning when the man was himself again, he began to scold his wife, who by her disobedience had almost killed him. He said, "You will kill us all. I don't want you any longer. Go home! You can't stay here."

They were both very angry. He started to drive her out, but as he went toward her she held up a skin blanket which she wore over her shoulders and instantly the man's eyes were on the blanket.

The second brother, seeing what the woman had done, screamed, "You have killed my brother! You have taken out his eyes. I will kill you!" and he ran after her. But before he reached her she turned, threw up the blanket, and immediately his eyes were on the blanket.

In the same manner the other brothers followed her and each in turn lost his eyes. All groped their way back to the house and sat down in despair.

Now the young sister was left to keep her brothers alive. Each day she went to the woods to collect roots and oak nuts to feed the blind men. One day, when she went to the river for water, she heard loud laughter and looking up saw a canoe coming and in it were two children, who were having great sport. They drew near, and said to the girl, "You must come and ride with us, it is great fun."

"I cannot," said the girl. "I have to take care of my blind brothers."

"Oh, come a little way," urged the children, "You don't know how nice it is."

"No," said the girl, "I cannot."

"But only a little way, we will let you right out again."

At last, after much urging, the girl got into the canoe; the children turned it and went a short distance. Then she said, "I must get out."

"Oh, go a little farther, just to the next turn."

When they got to the turn she again begged to get out. They said, "Just a bit farther."

Soon they came to a lake. As the girl looked toward the stern to beg the child to let her out, she saw a fat, ugly old man sitting there. Looking to the other end of the canoe she saw the little child was gone; she was alone with the terrible old man.

They went on swiftly and soon came to an island on which there was a bark house. The old man said, "Get out and go into the house."

It was a strange looking house and in it sat a fat old woman. The man said to her, "I have brought nice game for you."

"Thank you! thank you!" answered the old woman, and turning to the girl she said, "Take that bed on the shelf."

The man said, "Let her be well-fed."

They gave her plenty to eat and after a time the girl knew that she was growing fat; her body felt heavy. There was another girl, about her own size, in the house. Waking up one morning she saw a great many hands and feet hanging on the beams and she asked the other girl why they were there.

She said, "Those are the hands and feet of people who have been eaten up. When these men-eaters are hungry, if they haven't fresh meat, they boil dried hands and feet and eat them. When they kill us, to-day or to-morrow, they will eat our bodies and hang up our feet and hands to make soup of when they get hungry.''

As the girl lay thinking of her fate she saw some one looking down through the smoke-hole and she asked, ''Who are you? What are you looking for?''

''I am the son of DAGWANOE^{n}YENT (Whirlwind). I can save you if you do as I tell you. The old woman wants to kill you to-day. She will send you to get the water that you are to boil in. Go to the lake, pick up three round stones, put them side by side at the edge of the water. Some distance from the stones stick a wooden mannikin in the ground. When you have carried two pailfuls of water to the house, I will meet you with a canoe. After the old woman has waited a while she will come to the lake to look for you. She will find the mannikin and think you have turned yourself into it. She will take her club and beat the mannikin and we will gain time.''

Whirlwind's son went away. Soon the old woman called out, ''Here, it's time to get up! Go and bring me some water.''

The old woman got her kettle ready to put over the fire and the girl went to the lake for water. She found three round stones and placed them side by side at the water's edge, stuck a mannikin in the sand and went back to the house. When she went for the third pailful, Whirlwind's son was standing there with one end of his canoe in the sand. The girl put the stones into the canoe and jumped in herself. The young man pushed off the canoe and away they went.

They rowed as fast as they could and were a long way out before the old woman missed the girl. She hurried to the lake and seeing nothing of her walked up and down till she saw the mannikin. Thinking it was the girl she pounded the mannikin with her club till, chancing to look across the lake she saw, in the distance, a canoe and in it Whirlwind's son and the girl.

''Oh, you good-for-nothing creature,'' called she, ''why did you carry off my game?'' And taking out a hook and line she hurled it after the canoe. The hook caught into the canoe and she pulled it rapidly toward the shore.

When the young man saw they were nearing the shore he called to the girl, "Turn the canoe on one side!"

She did so and broke the hook with one of the stones. Then they righted the canoe and hurried on again.

The old woman threw another hook, saying, "I'll kill you both!" They turned the canoe over a second time and broke the hook with the second stone. A third time she threw a hook and a third time they broke it. Then she stooped down and began to drink up the lake, saying, "I'll get you at last; you'll not escape me."

Soon they saw that the canoe was going in a swift current straight to the shore and into the old woman's mouth. Whirlwind's son waited till they were near, then running to the bow of the canoe he ripped up the old woman's body with a sharp flint knife. Out shot the water and carried the canoe to the other shore.

The young man drew the canoe onto the sand and the two went toward his mother's house. Then he asked the girl if she would be his wife. She consented and when they were near the cliffs he said, "I will put you in a hollow stump till I go and see my mother. She lives in the cliff at the head of the creek. She is a cross woman and might harm you."

He left the girl in a stump and went on. When he came to his mother's house two wolves sprang at him and barked furiously.

"Get away, you miserable wolves! Why do your wolves bark at me?" asked he of his mother.

"Because you smell of people."

"That is no reason. I go everywhere. Of course I smell of people." And he struck and scolded the wolves till they slunk away.

After a while he said, "Well, Mother, what would you think if I took a human being for a wife? Would you be like your wolves?"

"I wouldn't be angry, but would you like a human being?"

"Yes, I have a body. You have only a head, but I am like a human being. I have a nice wife out there in a stump, will you go and bring her in?"

The old woman went to the stump. When the girl saw

the Head she was frightened, but the Head said, "Don't be afraid, I will keep my wolves away."

The girl went home with the Head and the three lived happily together. After a while twins were born—two handsome boys. The old grandmother nursed the boys and took great care of them. First she gave them bows and arrows, then she gave them ball clubs. After that they wanted fish spears. She told them they mustn't go away from the house, if they did an old uncle who lived nearby might catch them; but the boys went wherever they liked.

One day they saw a great pine tree and a nest.

One said, "If we go there that old man might see us."

"Oh," said the other, "We'll go and if he shows himself we will kill him."

They went under the tree and made a noise.

Their uncle looked down from his nest and called out, "I saw you first!"

The boys looked up, and said, "Very well."

The old man asked, "What would you do if a storm of fish spears were to come down on you?"

"Oh, we would like it. We'd take some of the spears to fish with. Make them come quickly."

Old man Whirlwind called for a storm of spears to come from the clouds. The boys crept under a big stone. They heard a great noise as of a storm coming toward their hiding place. It passed and when they couldn't hear it any longer they came out. There were a great many spears on the ground. They picked up the best spears they could find, took them home and said to their grandmother, "We have had good luck, our uncle sent a storm of spears."

"Don't go there again," said the old woman, "he will kill you."

The boys laughed. The next morning they went toward the pine tree. When they were near they hired a mole to carry them under the ground till they were at the tree.

When there they called out, "We see you, Uncle."

Then one of the boys asked, "What would you do if a storm of fire should come down on you?"

"I should die," said the old man.

"Let it come!" said the boy.

That minute fire fell from the clouds. The boys hid under a great rock. When the storm was over they found their uncle lying dead on the ground; his head had burst.

When they told their grandmother what they had done, she cried and said, "He was my brother, all the brother I had."

One day when the boys were playing around they found a great hole in the ground and in the hole were six blind men.

"What made you blind?" asked the boys.

"A woman took our eyes from us and stole our sister."

"Maybe our mother is your sister, our father stole us from a man-eater. You must be our uncles. We will find your eyes."

The men told the boys where their home was and the two started off. When they were near the house, one brother said to the other, "You will be a white deer and I will be a wolf and chase you, when you run toward the house the woman will come out and chase me. While she is gone you must steal the eye blanket."

The woman heard a wolf and running out saw it was following a white deer. She picked up a club and chased the wolf. The deer became a boy, found the eye blanket and ran off with it.

When the boys came back to where their uncles were, they separated the eyes, gave a pair to each man. Then they could see their nephews.

After that the six brothers lived with their sister and nephews in old woman Whirlwind's house.

MINK AND HIS UNCLE

Characters

DWÂAUⁿHDANEGEⁿ ....Two Feathers
HATHÓNDES (Giodaga) ....Mink
TÉQDOOⁿHUISHĔ. Woodchuck Leggings—the Deceiver

A MAN and his nephew lived together in a cabin in the woods. The uncle's name was Two Feathers, the nephew's was Mink [1] (HATHÓNDES the listener.).

The uncle and nephew were very poor, their food was the fungus of trees and a kind of wood mushroom.

When they had lived in the woods a long time and the boy was almost a man, his uncle said one day, "To-morrow go to the ravine and listen. As soon as you hear something, come back and tell me what it is. At the bottom of the ravine you will find a log, sit on the log, and listen."

The nephew did as his uncle told him to. He went to the ravine and listened. When he heard the call of a bird he was so frightened that he started up and ran home. Tumbling head first into the cabin, he cried, "Oh, Uncle, I have heard something!"

"Wait, Nephew," said the uncle, "till I light my pipe and let the smoke go up."

When the smoke was rising from the pipe, the boy told what he had heard, imitating the call of the bird.

"Oh, Nephew," said the uncle, "that is nothing, go again to-morrow."

[1] In one version of the story it was Scorched Belly, a name given the boy because his body was red from lying in the hot ashes at the end of the fire.

The next day the boy went to the ravine, sat on the log and listened. Soon he heard the cry of an owl. He ran home and tumbling head first into the cabin, cried, "Oh, Uncle, I have heard something!"

"Wait, Nephew," said the uncle, "till I light my pipe and let the smoke go up."

When the boy told what he had heard, imitating the cry, the uncle said, "That is nothing. Go again to-morrow."

Each day the boy heard the call of a different bird and told his uncle, imitating the call. After several trips to the ravine he heard women singing and their song said, "I am going after the nephew of the Two-Feathered Man."

The boy thought, "I will listen and learn that song." Soon he heard it again, then he went home and when smoke was rising from his uncle's pipe, he told what he had heard and sang the song.

His uncle said, "That is what I wanted you to hear. Two women are coming after me. We must get ready for them."

He put nice skins on his own couch, but threw his nephew's blanket on the ash heap in the corner and told him to lie there while the women were in the house; to keep quiet and not show his face.

The old man put on his best clothes and tried to be as nimble and bright as a young man, and kept sending the boy out to see how near the women were. At last, when they were quite near, the boy ran in crying, "Oh, Uncle, they are here!"

"Lie down on your blanket and don't stir," said Two Feathers.

The women came in bringing a basket of marriage bread. The old man hurried around to make everything pleasant for them, but they were continually looking toward the ash-heap where Mink was.

When night came, Two Feathers spread down a blanket for the women to lie on, and said, "Here is a nice place for you to sleep." But they went over to the ash-heap and lay down near Mink.

The boy was asleep but they smoothed his hair and spoke pleasant words to him.

Early in the morning the women went into the forest and each gathered a back-load of wood. When they put the wood down near the house and pulled out their straps, the wood increased till it was a great pile, then they started for home.

When Mink woke up he was a young man, strong and fine looking.

The uncle said, "You are a man now, you must follow those women. I will get you ready and teach you how to hunt. You will have power. Those women are the daughters of a great chief."

Two Feathers brought an outfit for his nephews: a panther coat, wild-cat leggings, owl-skin moccasins and an otter-skin head-dress with a white heron on it. He smoothed the bird, blew on it, and it came to life. He brought a tobacco pouch made of a fawn while it was spotted. He smoothed the pouch and the fawn came to life. On the pipe-stem sat two pigeons.

The uncle said, "These birds will bring you coals to light your pipe, and whenever you spit while smoking you will spit wampum beads."

He gave him a bow and arrows, and said, "These arrows will never miss."

The young man put on the clothes. They fitted him and were beautiful to look at. He took them off. The cap became a live otter, the coat a live panther, the leggings a pair of wild-cats and the moccasins two owls.

"Now," said Two Feathers. "I will teach you to hunt."

They went a short distance from the cabin.

The uncle said, "You must think what kind of game you want, then call it."

"I will call a deer."

Two Feathers made the call that a young fawn makes, and soon a deer came in sight, and then a second deer and a third came. The young man shot all his arrows away and each arrow killed a deer.

They pulled the arrows out and Two Feathers said, "Always wipe the arrows clean and smooth with your hand. Now that I have as much meat as I need you may start. I will put something on your feet to make you a swift runner, and I will hang up a wampum belt so that I will know if misfortune comes to you."

Two Feathers hung up the belt, and said to his nephew, "When you are well, the wampum will be high; if you are sick, it will lower till it nearly reaches the ground; if you die, it will drag on the ground.

"When you think that I have eaten all of the meat you must come and get me more. Go straight East. About midday you will find a trail; follow it. You will meet Woodchuck Leggings, an old man, but pay no attention to him; hurry along."

The young man started early in the morning and traveled till sunset without meeting anyone. Just at sunset he heard a cry of distress. He thought, "I must be careful, maybe that is the man my uncle told me about." Soon he saw an old man running around a tree, making a great fuss, and acting as though there were coons or something up in the tree. When he saw Mink he called out, "Oh, my dear nephew, come and help me kill these white martins."

The young man, remembering his uncle's words, went along. The old man ran after him, begging him not to leave him, to stop and help kill the martins.

When the young man was far beyond the tree, Woodchuck Leggings cried, "You needn't stop, only point an arrow and shoot, you will kill a martin. Your arrows never miss."

Mink thought, "It will do no harm to shoot an arrow." He shot and killed one of the martins. Then Woodchuck Leggings begged him to kill another; he shot again and hurried along.

The old man picked up the martins and ran after Mink, calling to him to stop and take his arrows. Mink waited for him to come up, then Woodchuck Leggings said, "I know where you are going, I am going there too, but we can't get there to-night. I have a place where we will rest till daylight."

The old man walked fast and kept talking all the time. When it was getting dark, he said, "We must wait till morning. It wouldn't do to get there in the night."

Mink thought this might be true, for his uncle had told him that he would reach the place at sundown.

They gathered a pile of wood and built a fire. Among the pieces of wood was a hickory stick. The old man said, "I can whittle an arrow for myself out of this while you are sleeping. I will sit one side of the fire and you can lie down on the other side. You can go to sleep as soon as you like, old men sleep less than young men."

They skinned the martins and cooked them. After eating, Mink took off his clothes and lay down by the fire, and right away was asleep.

Woodchuck Leggings began whittling. He thought, "There is no hurry, I have him now."

When he had the hickory stick well sharpened he crept up to steal the young man's clothes, but the coat, now a panther, wouldn't let him come near. He fed pieces of meat to the beast till it was pacified. When he reached for the leggings two wild-cats were there and wouldn't let him touch them. He pacified the cats as he had the panther. At last he had the whole outfit, except the bow and arrows, those he forgot. Then he went to Mink and thrust the sharpened hickory stick through his backbone. Mink woke up but he couldn't speak he was in such agony. He saw Woodchuck Leggings throw his dirty clothing down by the fire and hurry off.

Two Feathers knew when his nephew shot the first arrow, for he was watching the wampum and he saw it lower. He felt badly; he knew that Woodchuck Leggings had deceived the young man.

When Woodchuck Leggings thrust the hickory stick into Mink's back, the wampum belt came nearly to the ground. Two Feathers groaned, threw ashes over his head, and said, "I shall mourn for you ten summers."

He watched the wampum, repeating continually, "I shall mourn for you ten summers."

Woodchuck Leggings knew the power of the clothes he had stolen and as he hurried along he smoothed the white heron on the cap, and said, "You must call out when we are near the chief's house." The bird was silent.

When Woodchuck Leggings was near the house, the chief's elder daughter ran out to meet him. Everyone wondered how she could go to such an old man. She called to her younger sister, and asked, "Why don't you speak to our husband? We have been at his uncle's cabin, and now he has come for us."

"That is not the man we went to," said the girl, "I will not go into the house while he is there," and taking her blanket she went to a hut in the corn-field.

Woodchuck Leggings wanted to show his power. He said to his wife, "Ask your mother for a deerskin. I am going to smoke and I shall spit wampum beads."

The mother was pleased and she gave the largest and best deerskin she had.

Woodchuck Leggings drew out his pouch, spotted like a young fawn, and told it to stand up, but it fell down and do what he could it wouldn't stand.

"Oh," said he, "it is timid, there are so many people looking at it."

He took out his pipe and told the birds to get coals; they didn't move, and everyone wondered why he talked to dead things. He smoked and spat, but spittle it remained. After a time he told his wife to roll the skin up and put it away, and when it was unrolled they would find wampum.

The next morning he went out to show his skill as a hunter. He called deer but not one came. At last he killed a small fox. While he was skinning it the heron on his cap kept drooping over. He pushed it back till its white feathers were black. When he got home, he told his wife to cook the fox.

"It smells badly," said she, but she cooked it and as soon as she took the kettle from the fire he began eating the hot meat. Her brothers wouldn't touch it, each one said, "It smells badly."

When Woodchuck Leggings left Mink he was in agony, but about midday he crawled to where the old man's clothes were and, with great effort, put them on, then on his hands and knees he went towards the chief's house. He saw a cornfield and thought, "I will go there first, for I am hungry."

He went to the middle of the field where stalks were put together for a hut. In the hut was a bed made of husks. After eating an ear of corn Mink lay down on the husks and went to sleep.

The younger sister had gone for food and was starting back when her father said, "Your sister is married but you are living out in the cornfield. Stay here!"

She stayed that night, but in the morning she stole off to the hut. She found a man sleeping on the husks. His clothes were in rags and he seemed to be in great pain, but she recognized him and when he woke up, she said, "You are the young man my sister and I went for, but an old man came here for us and my sister is his wife."

Mink told the girl everything just as it had happened and showed her the hickory stick in his back. She made him a soft bed, covered him with a skin blanket, and fed and cared for him. He made her promise not to tell that he was there, for he wanted to punish Woodchuck Leggings.

The next day he said to the girl, "Tell your father that a man has had a dream and that he, as chief, must see it fulfilled. The man's dream said that the chief's son-in-law was to meet him at a sweat-house and that all the people must be there to witness the meeting."

She told her father the dream and he had a sweat-house built and heated. In the house was a great kettle of water and many red hot stones were ready to throw into it.

The chief's ten sons and his son-in-law and all the people of the village came to the sweat-house. Soon they saw an old man coming, led along by the chief's younger daughter. The girl's brothers were ashamed of her and everybody wondered how a beautiful girl could care for such a wretched looking, dirty old man.

Woodchuck Leggings said to the ragged man, "Go into the sweat-house first."

"No," said the ragged man, "We will take our clothes off out here." They stripped and went into the sweat-house.

The hot flint stones were thrown into the kettle and the door was closed. Right away the two men began to sweat. Every minute Mink reached to his back to see if the hickory stick was loosening, and after a time he pulled it out. As Woodchuck Leggings sat bent over Mink suddenly thrust the hickory stick into his back, saying, "I have done just what I wanted to."

Then he went out of the sweat-house, picked up his own clothes and smoothed them. The panther and wild-cats and owls came to life. He smoothed his cap; the heron screamed with joy, then everyone knew that he was the real owner of the clothes.

All this time Two Feathers was crying and singing, "Ten summers I will mourn for him," but once in a while he rubbed off the ashes and looked at the wampum. One day when he looked he saw that the wampum had gone up. Then he was happy for he knew that his nephew was well again. He washed the ashes from his face, brushed his cabin, made a fire and began to cook meat.

The young man dressed and went to the chief's house. The crowd followed. They left the old man in the sweat-house. After eating, Mink sat down to smoke. He shook his pouch; it became a beautiful little fawn, walked around and looked at everyone, then was a pouch again. He filled his pipe. The birds flew and brought coals. He began smoking and spitting, and he spat wampum beads which rolled around everywhere, and the crowd rushed to pick them up.

Early the next morning the young man went to hunt. He called deer. They came and he killed one after another till all of his arrows were used. He pulled out the arrows, cleaned them, and went back to the chief's house and told his wife to send her ten brothers to bring home the deer.

The chief was astonished that so many deer could be killed near the long house. He sent out a runner to tell people to come with their head straps and carry home all the meat they wanted.

Each time the young man smoked he spat wampum and soon the whole village had plenty of meat and plenty of wampum.

One day when Mink was out in the forest, he saw a large birch tree which he thought would make good ladles. He was cutting off a bough when he heard somebody say, "Look here!"

He looked up and saw two beautiful women, one called,

"Come here! Why are you cutting off the limbs of that tree? That is an old man's work."

When he paid no attention to her she said to her sister, "He is a proud fellow, I shall have to go to him. Come along," said she.

Taking hold of Mink she pulled him on to a log. She sat down on one side of him and her sister on the other side and they began to comb his hair. Soon Mink was sound asleep, then one of the women took a canoe out of her pocket and stretched it till it was large enough for three persons to sit in. When the three were in the canoe the younger woman sang, "Fly, my canoe, fly."

The canoe rose in the air and went toward the West. After it had gone a long distance the women brought it to the ground, shook the young man, wakened him, and asked, "Do you know this place?"

"This is the place where my uncle and I used to hunt."

"We must go farther," said the woman, "As far as our ledge of rocks." And putting the young man to sleep they sailed off again toward the West.

When they reached the rocks they took the young man out of the canoe and put him where if he wakened and moved he would fall off or if he didn't move he would starve to death.

Then they sailed away.

Two Feathers knew that his nephew was in great danger for the wampum came down as before. He threw ashes over his head and face and began to mourn.

When the young man woke up he stretched his arms and found that he couldn't reach anything. He looked and couldn't see anything. He heard a noise and thought that some animal was coming to devour him, but, after listening a while he knew that there were men near him, for he heard a groan.

Then he thought, "Those women bring men here for some terrible creature to eat." After a while he heard a noise that sounded like crunching and he knew someone had been killed. At last the creature came to him. It was an enormous Head. It took a bite from one of his legs and flew away over the ledge of rocks.

Mink spat on his hand, rubbed his leg with the saliva and it was well again.

Just at daylight Mink heard a man's voice in the distance. It came nearer and nearer and soon he heard the words, "This is what we, who dwell among the rocks, eat." Looking up he saw a man on the cliff above him. The man held up a roasted squash and began to blow the ashes off from it. He took a bite and smacked his lips to torment Mink, who was hungry, then he swept down between the rocks and showed the squash to men who were starving.

Mink lay on the rocks all day, thinking what to do. He got his bow ready and when he heard a great noise and saw the terrible Head coming he let an arrow fly. It went straight through the Head and the Head fell between the rocks.

When the Squash man came again and looking down said, "This is what we, who dwell among the rocks, eat," Mink sent another arrow and the Squash man fell down between the rocks.

Mink thought, "I have killed the Head and the Squash man, now I must get off from this rock." He leaned over the cliff, ran his fingers down his throat, and, trying very hard, vomited a little. Then he began to sing, "Let a great hemlock tree grow from that, Let a great hemlock tree grow from that."

As he sang a tree began to grow and it grew till its boughs were far above the cliff. Then Mink called, "My friends, I have found a way down. Creep along carefully. If you find a skeleton, push it off."

Several men crawled along. Mink made them go, one at a time, down the tree; last of all he went himself. As he went down, the tree decreased. When he reached the ground it disappeared.

He said to the men, "Those of you who know which way you came can go home; those who do not know may go home with me."

All this time Two Feathers had been mourning. When Mink was near the cabin a voice at the door said, "I have come home, Uncle."

Two Feathers looked at the wampum belt; it had gone up. He was happy, he called, "Wait a minute, my nephew, till I wash off the ashes." When he opened the door there stood a Rabbit. It made great leaps and in an instant was out of reach.

The old man was disappointed; he scolded the Rabbit and shut the door. Soon he heard steps again and a voice called out, "I have come, Uncle."

"That must be my nephew," thought Two Feathers, and he opened the door. It was a Fox.

"Wretched animals!" said the old man, "I will kill you if you torment me when I have mourned so long for my nephew."

He got a strap and a corn pounder, then made a hole in the door just large enough for a man's hand. When an animal came again he was going to kill it.

Mink came and when he called out, the old man said, "Now I will catch you."

It was so quiet inside that the young man wondered what his uncle was doing, and he called a second time, "I have come, Uncle."

"If you have, put your hand through the hole in the door."

Mink put his hand through. Two Feathers caught hold of it and strapped it to the door, then opened the door. When he saw his nephew he was overjoyed.

Mink told the old man everything that had happened, and said, "I will get meat and wood for you, then I will go for my wife."

The men who had come with Mink gathered the wood and took care of the game he killed. When his uncle was well supplied, Mink went for his wife and brought her home.

THE FOX AND RABBIT

[Told by George White]

Characters

TONDAYENT ....White Rabbit

NOⁿGWATGWA .... Fox

ONE day a hunter was going along over a light, freshly
fallen snow. His footsteps made no noise.

All at once he saw a man coming toward him and that
man shouted, "I am a man-eater!"

The hunter ran for his life. He circled around and
around to escape, but the man followed and was gaining
on him. When the hunter saw that he was losing ground,
he took off his moccasins and said to them, "Run ahead as
fast as you can." Then he lay down and became a dead
rabbit, dirty and black.

When the man-eater came up and saw the black, dirty
old body and the fresh tracks going on, he followed the
tracks. When he came to the end of the trail and saw
only moccasins, he was angry, and thought, "That fellow
fooled me, the next time I will eat anything I see."

The man-eater turned back and sure enough the dead
rabbit was gone. He followed the tracks and soon came
upon a man who sat rolling pieces of bark, making rope.

He asked, "Have you seen a hunter pass?"

No answer. He asked again and pushed the rope-maker
till he fell over, then the rope-maker said, "Some one
passed just now."

The man-eater hurried away. The rope-maker sprang

up, ran forward, made a circle and was ahead of the man-eater, then he turned himself into an old tree with dry limbs.

When the man-eater came to the tree, he said, "Maybe he has turned himself into a tree."

He punched the tree and broke off a twig that looked like a nose, but it was dead wood.

"I don't think it is he," said the man-eater, and again he followed the moccasin tracks.

When he overtook the moccasins he said, "That tree was the man and he has fooled me again."

He hurried back and when he came to where the tree had been, it was gone, and where he had thrown down the twig there was blood, then he knew the tree was the man, and he followed the tracks that he found there.

Just as the hunter saw that his enemy was near he chanced to come upon a dead man; he pushed the body on to the trail and when the man-eater came up, he said, "I will eat him this time! He won't fool me again, I'll finish him." And he ate the putrid carcass. The hunter escaped.

The man with the moccasins was a rabbit; the man-eater was a fox.

A WARRIOR CARED FOR BY WOLVES

Characters

ODJÚ
GANOGWIOEO^{n}

AMONG the Senecas there was a war chief named GANOGWIOEO^{n}. Once, with ten men, he went on the warpath to the Cherokee country. They found the Cherokees on the watch and could do nothing.

Then the chief said to his men, "I'll go alone to their village." And after dark, leaving his men in the woods, he went to the Cherokee village.

In the first cabin he came to, he found an old woman and her granddaughter. They didn't see him. He crept into a little place where they kept wood.

After dark the old woman said to her granddaughter, "Maybe GANOGWIOEO^{n} is around here. I'll shut the door," and she spoke a word of warning to ODJÚ, her granddaughter. The chief heard this.

After a while the girl said, "It is time to sleep."

The chief heard this also and heard the girl going up the ladder to sleep above, meanwhile talking with her grandmother, who was below.

The old woman fastened the door of the little wood house, with bark strings and fastened the chief in, leaving the door to the cabin unfastened.

After waiting till the old woman was asleep, the chief went into the cabin. The fire had burned down to coals but he could see the ladder that the girl had climbed. He went up. The girl was not asleep and was about to scream when he said, "If you scream I'll cut off your head. The chief of this village has a daughter. If you will get her to come into the woods with you I will spare your life."

Odjú said, "In the morning, as soon as the grass is dry, I will go to the chief's house and ask his daughter to come with me to gather wood."

Threatening to come back and kill the girl if she failed to do as planned the chief left the cabin.

Early the next morning, Odjú went to the chief's house and said to his daughter, "Come with me and gather wood." (This was the custom in those days.)

The chief's daughter was willing to go and they started. As soon as they came to the forest the Seneca sprang out of his hiding place and ran toward them. Odjú stood still, but the chief's daughter screamed and ran toward home. Ganogwioeo^n caught her, scalped her, and then, giving a war whoop, ran away. Men rushed out of their cabins and pursued him.

The Seneca saw that among the men following him there was one good runner. He hid in a ravine and when the runner came to the entrance of the ravine he shot him with an arrow and pulling off the man's scalp held it up before the people who were following.

When the Seneca came to a second ravine another runner was ahead of the rest. He aimed at the man, but his bow-string broke. The pursuer saw this and rushed into the ravine. The Seneca ran swiftly, but the Cherokee overtook and closed with him. A second and a third man came, then others; they bound Ganogwioeo^n, led him to the village and summoned the people to assemble.

Among the Cherokees there were two women who were looked upon as the head women of the tribe. Each woman had two snakes tattooed on her lips—the upper jaws of the snakes were on the woman's upper lip, and opposite each other, the lower jaws on the lower lip in the same way. When the woman opened her mouth, the snakes seemed to open theirs.

These women said, "This is the way to torment him; tie him near a fire and burn the soles of his feet till they are blistered, then let the water out of the blisters, put kernels of corn inside the skin, and chase him with clubs till he dies."

When Ganogwioeo^n's feet were blistered, the women stripped him and tied a bark rope around his waist.

One old man said, "I want to hold the rope."

The people stood in two lines and at the end of each line were many people. The Seneca had to run between the lines. He ran so fast that he pulled the rope out of the old man's hand, then plunging to one side, he broke through the line and ran with all his strength toward the place where he had left his men.

When running he thought he was going to die, for he was naked and unarmed, far from home, and his feet were raw, but he evaded his enemies and, when night came, crept into a hollow log. In the night he heard steps on the dry leaves, and thought the Cherokees had discovered his hiding place.

Whoever it was came up to the tree and said to someone who was with him, "This man is our friend."

Then he called to Ganogwioeo^n, "You think that you are going to die, but you will not. We will take care of you. Stick out your feet."

The chief put out his feet and right away he felt someone licking them.

After a while one of the strangers said, "We have licked his feet enough. Now we must get him warm, we will go into the tree and one of us lie down on each side of him."

It was very dark in the hollow log, but the man felt someone lie down on either side of him, and soon he was so warm and comfortable that he fell asleep.

Just before daylight the strangers crept out of the log and told the man to stick out his feet. They licked them again, and then said, "We have done all we can now. You will go on till you come to a place where you put a piece of bark. Raise the bark up, you will find something under it."

When the man came out of the log, he found that his feet were better, he could walk comfortably. At midday he came to four posts holding up a bark roof. On the ground, under the roof, was a large piece of bark. He raised the bark and found a piece of flint, a knife and an awl, then he remembered that his men had put those things there a couple of years before, when on the war-path. He took them and went on.

When it began to grow dark he looked for a hollow tree, found one and crawled into it. In the night he heard steps on the dry leaves and a voice said, "Our friend is here."

Then someone said, "Put your feet out."

He did so and again they were licked.

Then the stranger said, "That is enough, we will lie near our friend and keep him warm."

They went into the tree and lay down, but before daylight they crept out, and, after licking the man's feet again, said, "About midday you will find food."

The man went on till he found a bear that apparently had been killed only a few minutes before; it was still warm. When he had skinned the bear and cut out some of the meat, he saw, not far away, a smouldering fire, he blew it and it blazed up. He cut meat into small pieces and roasted it on sticks. When night came he lay down, and soon he heard steps on the leaves as he had the preceding nights, then a voice said, "Our friend is lying down; he isn't going to die; he has plenty to eat. We'll lick his feet."

When they finished, they said to him, "Nothing will happen to you now, you will reach home in safety." And they went away.

The next morning the man, taking some of the meat, went on toward home. That night his friends came again.

They said, "Your feet are well, but you will be cold," and they lay down one on each side of him. Before daylight, when going away, they said, "At midday you will find something to eat and to wear."

The man traveled on till toward midday, then found two young bears, just killed. He skinned the bears, cooked some of the meat, tanned the skins and lay down, very tired.

The next morning he made leggings of the skins, took what meat he wanted and went on.

That night the friends came to him, and said, "To-morrow you will find something to wear on your feet."

About midday the man came upon two fawns, just killed.

He tanned the skins and made moccasins. When night came, he made a fire, cooked meat, ate, and then lay down.

Soon he heard a voice say, "Our friend, you will reach home to-morrow. Now we will tell you why we healed your feet and cared for you. Always when you have been off in the woods hunting and have killed game, you have given the best part of the animal to us, and kept the smallest part for yourself; we are thankful. In the morning you will see us and know who we are."

When daylight came the chief saw two men, as he thought. As soon as he stood up the men took leave of him and started off. Wanting to see his friends as long as he could he turned to look at them and in the twinkle of an eye he saw that one of them was a white and the other a black wolf.

The chief reached home as his friends, the wolves, said he would.

DOGS SAVE THEIR MASTER

THERE was a Seneca, who was very fond of hunting. He had two dogs that were so strong that they could kill a bear.

One winter this man started off to hunt. After traveling two days he camped and began to look for game. He hunted many days and killed a great many animals. One night, just as he was going to sleep, the dogs began to bark furiously. Not far from the camp was a large elm tree with the top broken off. The man had thought the tree was hollow, but he had never examined it. One of the dogs now ran in the direction of this tree, the other followed and by the sound of the barking the man knew that some creature was in the tree.

After a time one of the dogs came back, and said, "My brother, maybe we are going to die to-night. On the tree there is such a creature as we have never seen before. I will watch it, but mark me with a coal, from the end of my mouth to my ear, on each side."

The man did as the dog asked, then the dog said, "Now I will go to the tree and my brother can come and be marked."

He ran off and soon the other dog came and was marked, then the hunter took a torch and went to the tree.

On the broken top was a terrible creature. He could see its head and a part of its body. It had long teeth, enormous eyes, and huge claws. The man had never seen any animal so dreadful. As he went back to camp one of the dogs followed him, and said, "We shall be killed, but we will do what we can to save you. You must hurry to the village. Don't take a torch or a bow with you; they'll be in your way. Put on a new pair of moccasins and take a second pair. I'll lick the soles of your feet so you can run fast."

The dog licked his master's feet, then the man put on

new moccasins and started for home. He had been running a good while when one of the dogs overtook him, and said, "Run faster, the creature has started. It doesn't travel on the ground, but leaps from tree to tree. The only thing I can do is to get between the trees and spring at it as it leaps. When you come to water, stir it up, make it as muddy as you can, then drink of the water. We drink of such water; it is better for us."

The man soon got thirsty. When he came to a spring, he stirred the water up, then drank what he wanted and went on.

He hadn't gone far when the dog came up, and said, "There is a hole in your moccasin."

The man looked and sure enough there was a hole.

"Put on new ones," said the dog.

The dog licked his master's feet and the man put on new moccasins, then the dog went back and the man hurried on.

Soon the other dog ran up, and said, "The creature is coming very fast, we are afraid it will kill you. My brother will come to you once more, but when he gets back he will be killed."

The dog disappeared. The man listened; both dogs were barking, then one bark ceased and he knew the dog was coming to him.

"I have come," said the dog, "to speak to you once more. When I go back I shall attack the creature and do all I can to overpower it, but it will kill me."

The dog went back and the man heard both dogs bark and howl. He knew by the sound that they were fighting. Then only one dog howled; the other was dead.

The man tried to increase his speed, but it was a dark night and he ran against trees and brush. The barking ceased and soon the dog was at his side.

"My brother is dead," said he. "I am alone. The village isn't far away. You must scream. Someone may hear you."

The man began to scream as he ran.

That night there was a dance in the long house and people were sitting around outside. A young man heard the cry of someone in distress and he gave the alarm.

The dog came once more to encourage his master. "Do your best," said he, "You are near the village. I will come once more, then I will pull the creature down and fight it."

The man heard the dog when it got back and knew by the sound that the creature was getting near.

The dog came again and said, "This is the last time you will see me, I shall attack the creature and it will kill me. If the people hear your cries, they will come and rescue you, if not you will be killed."

The dog went back; he had only a short distance to go. The man saw torches; his cries had been heard.

The dog howled in distress, then all was still, and the man knew his friend was dead.

When the man saw the torches, he struggled harder and harder to get to them. As the people met him he fell.

Holding up their torches the men looked ahead and saw a terrible animal; its forelegs were longer than its hind ones. They shot at it, but it disappeared.

In one night the man had made a journey that required two days. They carried him to the village and as soon as he could talk he told what had happened. The people decided to go to the camp in the woods and bring home the meat.

Near the village they found the last dog; it was torn to pieces. Farther on they found the other dog, also torn to pieces. When they reached the camp, they saw that most of the meat had been eaten, what was left they carried home. The animal was never seen again.

THE DESERTED VILLAGE

A GRANDFATHER and grandson lived together. They were the only persons left of a large nation. All their relatives and friends had been killed.

When the boy was old enough, his grandfather made him a bow and arrows and taught him to hunt. He killed small animals at first, but after a while he killed a deer. Each time he brought home game his grandfather danced and rejoiced, and mentioned the name of the game.

The two lived happily together till the grandson was a young man, then one day his grandfather said to him, "You are old enough to marry. I would like to have a woman here to cook. You must go South and find a wife. For an ordinary man it is a long journey but you will go quickly," and giving his grandson a pair of moccasins, he sent him off.

About midday the young man came to an opening in the woods. In the opening was a large village. He went from one house to another; all were empty. Then he went to the long house and looking in saw, on a bench, the body of a young woman. The corpse was ornamented with beautiful beads.

The young man thought, "I'll take some of those beads, they will be nice for my wife, when I find one."

He took what beads he wanted and when outside, said to himself, "I'll go home now and look for a wife some other time."

He started northward, as he thought, and ran along swiftly.

After a while he came to a clearing and to his surprise found it was the same one he had left. Looking at the village and the long house, he thought, "I must have made a mistake."

He took bearings again and hurried toward home. Again he came out in the village.

"It must be that woman brings me here because I have taken her beads. I'll give them back to her."

He went to the long house, put the beads on to the body, and again started for home. On the way he killed a bear and skinned it. Taking some of the meat he rolled it up in the skin, made a pack and carried it along, running as fast as he could, hoping to reach home before night.

At night he came out in the same opening.

"This is strange," thought he, "I'll have to spend the night in the long house."

He kindled a fire, cooked his meat, spread out the bear skin and sat down to eat. As he ate he threw the bones behind him; soon he heard crunching and gnawing.

"Maybe a hungry ghost does that," thought he, "I'll give it some meat."

He threw pieces of meat behind him and heard them eaten.

After he had eaten enough, he crawled under the bear skin to sleep. Soon something began to pull the bear skin from his feet. He sprang up, stirred the fire and put on more wood. All was quiet, and he lay down again. After a while, when the fire had grown dim, something crawled over his body, came up to his breast. He threw his arms around the thing, wrapped it in the bearskin and sprang to his feet. A terrible struggle began. The two wrestled from near the fire to the end of the long house and then down along the other side. When near the place they had started from, the gray of daylight came. That minute what seemed to be a body, dropped to the floor and lay still. The young man lashed the bearskin around it closely, left it on the floor and cooked and ate his breakfast.

He was curious to know what was in the skin, for he thought it must be something connected with the woman. Opening the skin carefully he found only a piece of clotted blood about the size of his fist.

He heated water, dissolved the blood, and, with a wooden ladle he whittled out with his flint knife, he poured some of the blood into the woman's mouth. It went down her throat. Again and again he poured. At last the woman's breast began to move. When he had given her half the blood she breathed.

When she had taken it all, she said, "I am hungry."

The young man pounded corn, made thin gruel and fed her. Soon she was able to sit up and in a little while she was well.

She said, "People lived in this village till a short time ago. Many men from the North have wanted to marry me, when I was unwilling and refused each one of them, they changed me and drove my father and all his people away. I was left here for dead."

"Come," said the young man, "We will go and find your father."

They set out together, and after a while came to a village. Crow, with his large family, lived in the house at the edge of the village. When the young man told Crow the story of the long house and the chief's daughter, Crow said, "My chief is this girl's father. I'll tell him that his daughter is alive."

Crow hurried to the chief's house and said to the chief, "Your daughter is alive."

The mother screamed, "You lie! no one ever came to life after being dead more than ten days." And taking up a club she started to drive Crow out of the house.

"Don't strike him," said the chief, "Maybe our daughter has come to life."

"She has," said Crow, "She is in my house now."

"Tell her to come here," said the chief.

When the chief and his wife saw their daughter they were happy, and, as they were willing, the young man became their son-in-law.

After a few days the man said to his wife, "Borrow your father's bow and arrows, all the young men in the village are to hunt to-morrow; I must go with them."

Each man went alone, starting early. Crow met the young man, and said, "I'll fly high and look around, see where the deer are."

Crow saw ten deer some distance away. He came down and said, "I'll fly behind those deer and drive them toward you, you can kill them."

The young man waited till the deer passed, then when all were in line, he killed the ten with one arrow.

Crow said, "The hunters never give me anything but intestines."

"You may have a whole deer to-day," said the young man. Crow flew home with the news, and asked, "What are our young men good for? The chief's son-in-law has killed ten deer before sunrise."

The other hunters had bad luck.

At night there was a feast and a dance in the long house.

The hunters planned to kill the young man. When in the dance he came to the middle of the long house, by their magic they made him sink deep into the ground, disappear. But Crow knew where he was, and when all were gone he called upon his friend Turkey to dig up the young man.

Turkey came and scratched till at last he had the dirt away, then Crow made a rope and together they drew the young man out of the ground.

The chief decided to leave the enemies of his son-in-law and go with the good people, the friends of his son-in-law, to live in the village where the young man's grandfather lived.

They went there, settled down, and lived happily.

WAR BETWEEN SENECAS AND CHEROKEES

Characters

HATCINONDO^n

HÁWENIYO ....Great Spirit

ENDEKHĀ GEQGWA, Sun (Orb of Day)—The usual word is Geqgwa

NOHNOHSOT .... Heron

HATCINONDO^n was a great warrior, the greatest of all the Senecas. Once, when out with a party of warriors, he came to a high cliff and knowing that the Cherokees were on the lookout he told his men to stay where they were and he would go ahead and see what could be done. He hadn't gone far when a party of Cherokees saw him and started in pursuit.

HATCINONDO^n ran into tall reeds that grew in two great patches with a narrow space between them. He escaped from the first patch and hid in the second one. His pursuers thought he was in the first patch; they watched the narrow space and set fire to the reeds. When the reeds were destroyed they expected to find him dead, burned up.

HATCINONDO^n fell asleep in his hiding place. In the night two men came, wakened him, and said, "Follow us, we have come for you."

He went with the men and after a time one of them pointed at a house, and said, "NOHNOHSOT, the man who lives there, sent for you."

He went to the house, but could find no door. After a while a voice called, "Come in!"

A door opened and he went in and saw a man, who said, "I sent for you and you have come. Are you hungry?"

HATCINONDO^n smiled and said in his mind, "That's a strange question. That's not the way I do; I give food."

NOHNOHSOT laughed, he knew the man's thoughts. He brought out half a loaf of acorn bread, half of a wild apple, and half of a pigeon.

HATCINONDO^n said, "How little will fill me."

"If you eat all of this I will give you more," said NOHNOHSOT.

As the Seneca ate he noticed that each thing became whole again, that he was unable to finish either the loaf, the apple or the pigeon.

When he had eaten all he could, NOHNOHSOT said to him, "Now I will talk with you."

Just then the door was thrown open and Sun came in so quickly and with such brightness that HATCINONDO^n had to hold down his head.

Sun spoke to NOHNOHSOT and right away hurried off towards the East.

Then NOHNOHSOT said, "That is the man you call EN-DEKHĀ GEQGWA' (the orb of day). It is night down below and he is hurrying to the East. He told me of a great battle."

NOHNOHSOT was HÁWENIYO (Great Spirit), and he said, "That is what I expected when I made people, I thought they would fight. Hereafter when you meet an enemy don't run away, go up to him; he can't harm you; no arrow can kill you. I am the cause of the Senecas not fighting with the Cherokees. You will find your warriors where you left them. Now the HADIO^{n}YAGEONO^n (Spirits) are ready to go with you."

HATCINONDO^n went out, passed through an opening, as he thought, and found himself in the reeds. He got back to his party and told the men what he had seen, and they all went home.

Soon after this the Senecas held a council and the warriors decided to go again to the Cherokee country.

When the Senecas and Cherokees met, HATCINONDO^n, remembering what NOHNOHSOT had told him, went straight up to a Cherokee warrior, killed and scalped him, then called out, "I have killed and scalped a man! My name is HATCINONDO^n."

After that there was a battle and many men were killed. But the Senecas won and went home carrying a large number of scalps.

Another party started off to fight the Cherokees. This time HATCINONDO^n was captured; he was tied and led to the Cherokee village.

It was a Cherokee custom when a man was captured to leave it to two women to say how he should be tortured.

The two women decided that HATCINONDO^n was to be bound to a tree and burned to death.

They tied him to a tree and piled dry brush and wood around him. He thought, "Now I am going to die." But, just as the women were setting fire to the brush a terrible rain storm came and every one ran for shelter, leaving the Seneca bound to the tree.

While he was there alone, an old woman came to him, and said, "My Grandson, you think that you are going to die, but you are not. Try to move."

He moved, the thongs fell off and he was free.

The woman said, "I have returned your kindness. Once when your people were making a circle of fire, you saw a toad inside the circle, you took it up and put it in your bosom and when you came to water put it down. I was that toad. Now when I saw you in trouble I brought rain to save you. Go to the river and run with the current."

When the rain was over the Cherokee women came back to the tree and found that their prisoner was gone. They raised an alarm, men ran together, found tracks, and followed them.

When they came to the river, they lost the trail, and after a time they abandoned pursuit and went home.

Two men came and sat down near HATCINONDO^n's hiding place, and one said to the other, "It is strange where that man went."

The Seneca was afraid they would discover where he

was, but at last they went away, then he went down the stream some distance and struck off toward the South.

Toward night he came to an opening and saw three men building a fire. He watched and listened till dark, then crept up to a place opposite the fire and found that the men were asleep; he stole their weapons and provisions.

The next morning he traveled in a circle till he found the trail by which he and his party had come. Soon he saw men sitting around a fire, he crept near and heard Seneca words, then he called *"Goweh! Goweh!"* three times. The men shouted with joy and ran to meet him.

This is their story.

TURTLE ON THE WAR-PATH

A TURTLE lived near a river. One day he thought, "I am lonesome, I'll go on the war-path," and getting into a canoe he rowed up the river, singing "I am on the war-path! I am on the war-path!"

When he had gone a short distance, a man came to the bank, and called, "Friend, stop a minute, I will go too, we will go on the war-path together."

Turtle landed. On the bank stood Deer.

Deer said, "I want to go with you."

Turtle answered, "First, let me see you run. We may get beaten and have to run for our lives, and unless we can run very fast we'll get scalped and killed. Run to that mountain over there, and back."

Deer ran to the mountain and was back in no time.

Turtle said, "You can't go, you don't run fast enough, only fast runners can go with me."

And Turtle started off in his canoe, singing, "I am on the war-path! I am on the war-path!"

Soon another man came to the bank, and called, "Stop! Come to the bank, I want to go on the war-path with you."

Turtle landed and said to the man, "You must let me see you run, I'll not take you unless you can run very fast. Run to the second mountain."

The man was Skunk. He showed his strength and started, but Turtle called, "Come back, that is enough, you can go."

They got into the canoe and started, Turtle singing, "I am on the war-path! I am on the war-path! You, Brother, smell rather strong."

Soon a man called to them, "Stop! you must land, I want to go on the war-path with you."

This man was Bear. Turtle landed and told Bear to run to the mountain. He started off and soon came back.

Turtle said, "You won't do, you don't run fast enough

to suit me," and he pushed off again, singing, "I am on the war-path! I am on the war-path! You, Brother, smell rather strong."

Another man called to them from the bank; they landed and went up. The man was Hedge-hog and he wanted to go on the war-path.

Turtle said, "If you are a good runner I will take you. Run to that mountain over there."

Hedge-hog turned and started to run; his feet crossed each other, he stumbled and nearly rolled over. He had taken but a few steps when Turtle said, "Stop! You'll do, come down to the canoe."

The three started, Turtle singing, "We are on the war-path! We are on the war-path! You, Brother, smell rather strong; You, Brother, have many arrows (his quills)."

Now Elk called from the bank, "Stop! Come to land, I want to go on the war-path."

Turtle landed and told Elk to run to the second mountain and back as quickly as he could.

Elk started, and in a very short time he was back, smashing and breaking limbs and boughs as he came.

Turtle said, "You can't go," and getting into the canoe he started off, singing as before.

Soon a man appeared on the bank, and called, "Bring up the canoe. I'll go with you."

"I'll come and see you run," said Turtle, "I only take fast runners, for something may happen while we are gone, we may have to run for our lives. Go to the second mountain."

Rattlesnake rose up to go.

"Oh, you'll do," said Turtle, "You may come with us."

The four started, Turtle singing, "We are on the war-path! We are on the war-path! You, Brother, smell rather strong; You, Brother, have many arrows; You, Brother, have a black face."

Turtle was going to make war on the Seven Sisters, and their home wasn't far away. The warriors reached the place and pulled the canoe out of the water, then Turtle said, "Each man must choose the place he wants to be in when war begins."

Skunk said, "I will be near the fireplace and will attack the first person I see."

Hedge-hog said, "I'll hide near the house, in that pile of wood, and I will attack the first person who comes for wood."

Rattlesnake said he would get into the skin bucket where they kept dried corn and he would attack the first one who came for corn.

Turtle said, "I'll station myself by the spring and if any one comes for water, there will be a fight."

Early in the morning the mother of the Seven Sisters began to build a fire. Skunk attacked her, and she fell back almost dead. She couldn't open her eyes.

When the Seven Sisters heard their mother scream, they ran to her. They saw the man and began to fight with him. All seven were attacked, but, getting clubs, they pounded Skunk till they killed him. They threw him out of doors then made a fire and one of the sisters went for wood. When she stooped down to pick up sticks she felt a blow on the arm, and looking found that her arm was full of hedge-hog quills.

While the girl was fighting Hedge-hog and screaming, her sisters came and seeing Hedge-hog they picked up pieces of wood and struck him on the head and back till they killed him.

One of the sisters wanted dried corn for breakfast. She went to the bucket and put her hand into it to get the corn, that minute she felt a sharp blow; she saw Rattlesnake and called to her sisters. They came, armed themselves with sticks, and struck Rattlesnake till they killed him. But the sister he had bitten was dead.

After a time the old woman sent one of her daughters to get water. The girl went to the spring and as she stooped over to dip up the water, Turtle caught her by the toe and held on. She tried and tried, but couldn't get him off; then she walked backwards to the house dragging him along.

The old woman was so angry she screamed, "Throw him on the fire and burn him up!"

Turtle laughed, and said, "You couldn't please me

more, I came from Fire and I like to be in it better than anywhere else."

The woman changed her mind, and said, "I'll carry him to the river and drown him."

Turtle cried, "Don't do that! Don't do that! I'll die."

He begged hard, but no use, they took him to the river and threw him in. He sank to the bottom, but right away he rose in the middle of the stream, held out his hand, as if showing scalps, and shouted, "I'm a brave man, and here is where I live." Then he sank out of sight.

THE GREAT SNAKE BATTLE

IN olden times the Indians had a great battle with snakes, and this is how it happened: One day when a man was hunting he saw a rattlesnake and tormented it. He caught the snake, made a hole through its body and putting a bark string through the hole fastened the snake to the ground. Then he built a fire and saying, "Now fight me," he burned the snake alive. Afterwards he tormented many snakes in this way, always challenging them to fight.

One day a man, who was in the woods, heard a great noise and going toward it saw a large number of snakes traveling in one direction. He listened and heard them say, "We will have a battle, DJISSAA (Fire) has challenged us. The battle will be four days from now."

The man hurried back to the village and told the people what he had seen and heard. The chief sent a number of men to the place, and, as far as they could see, there were snakes, all going in one direction. They were going to a council.

The men went back and told the chief. He said, "We can't help it; they will force us to fight, we must get ready."

They drove two rows of stakes the whole length of the village, then, some distance beyond, piled up a great quantity of wood in long lines. On the fourth day they set fire to the wood.

When the snakes came, they sprang through the fire; many of them were burned, but so many rushed into the fire that they put it out. Live snakes climbed over the dead and in spite of the men, who were trying to kill them, they reached the second row of stakes and again they were killed till the living climbed over the dead, got above the second stakes, and were in the village. Then the battle for life began.

The first man killed was DJISSAA, the man who had challenged the snakes. The people fought till the chief, seeing how many were being killed, screamed that he surrendered.

Then a snake, with an enormous body and head, came out of the ground, and said, "I am chief of all the snakes, we will go away from your village if you will promise that as long as the world lasts your people will not injure or torment my people."

The chief promised and the snakes went away.

THE HUNTER WHO BECAME A FISH

TWO brothers started off to hunt. After they had camped they heard a peculiar noise and one of them said, "I am going to find out what that is," and he followed the sound. It seemed to come from inside a hollow tree. Thinking there might be a bear in the tree the young man ran back to camp and said to his brother, "There must be a bear in that tree over there, but it makes a noise like a whirlwind."

They went to the tree and one of them climbed up and looked into the hole. At first he couldn't see anything. Then, at the bottom of the hole, he saw a spotted trout jumping around.

He got the trout out and threw it down to his brother, who said, "This is a curious fish. Let's take it to camp."

"Don't touch it," said the other, "It might be something that will harm us."

But the young man didn't listen; he took the trout to camp, cleaned and ate it.

Right away, he said, "Bring some water, I am thirsty."

Water was brought and he drank and kept drinking, "Couldn't drink enough."

"I think the fish is making you sick," said his brother.

"Get more water," was the answer. "Take my moccasins and fill them."

When the young man was tired of bringing water he said to his brother, "You must go to the spring where you can drink all the water you want."

He went to the spring, drank till he was tired, then rested and drank again. When the other brother went to the spring he was frightened; his brother's mouth was like the mouth of a fish.

"Doesn't your mouth feel strange?" asked he.

The man put up his hand and then knew that his mouth had grown large, but he kept on drinking.

The next time the young man went to the spring his brother was half fish; fish to the waist, and he was still drinking.

Later he went to the spring and found that his brother had become a fish and gone into the water.

The next morning when the young man went to the spring, he saw a great fish far under the water, and the spring had become a pond.

He sat down on the bank and soon the Fish rose to the surface, and said, "My poor brother, go home and tell our father what has happened to me. When you want fish come here and get all you need; this pond will always be full of fish."

The young man went home and told what had taken place. The people came to the pond; the Fish rose to the surface, and said, "I shall not be a fish long, I am going to be a NYAGWAIHE."

Soon the Fish changed to a NYAGWAIHE (a great bear). The Bear stayed around the pond and of each party that came to fish, it killed and ate one man. Nobody saw this, but each party always lost one of its number, and people began to think that if the Bear lived long it would kill a great many men.

A council was called to decide what to do, and three young men promised to kill the Bear. They went to the pond, but never came back.

The Bear's brother said, "I will go to the pond, maybe I can drive him away."

And taking parched corn flour to eat, new moccasins to wear, and a good bow and twelve arrows he went to the pond and camped on the bank.

That night he dreamed that his brother, in the form of a man, came to him, and asked, "Why are you here? I can kill you."

And he answered, "I came to drive you away, for you are doing a great deal of harm."

The man said, "I will start at daylight and run. Follow, and see if you can overtake me."

The next morning the young man went in the direction

the man had indicated, running as fast as he could. Just
at midday he saw bear tracks, and he called out, "Now I'll
overtake you!"

He ran faster than before, ran till dark, then camped
and built a fire. When he opened his bundle of corn flour
it had turned to ants; he had nothing to eat. The Bear
had done this to deprive his brother of food.

While the young man sat by the fire thinking, he heard
some one approaching; he knew it was the Bear and he
had drawn his bow, ready to aim, when the Bear called
out, "Wait, brother, till I talk with you. If you will let
me go I will start early to-morrow morning, and leave
this part of the country forever."

The brother said, "I will let you go."

They parted and the next morning the young man went
back to his village and told the people what had happened
and said, "You can fish in the lake as much as you like;
no one will trouble you."

And so it proved.

TWO SENECA WOMEN ESCAPE FROM
CHEROKEE CAPTIVITY

TWO sisters were gathering wood not far from home. The elder sister had a baby with her, a little boy. A party of Cherokees captured them. When the husband and friends found that the women had been carried away, they called a council, and it was decided not to pursue the Cherokees lest they might kill the women.

When the sisters found that they were near the Cherokee country, the elder sister, who had a flint knife hidden under her blanket, planned an escape. In the night, when the men were asleep, she found that the ends of the ropes binding herself and her sister were on the ground under one of the men, and she knew that if she could cut the ropes she could free herself and sister. She cut them very cautiously.

They were going to leave the baby, but it was about to cry and the mother said, "Let us die together," and she took it.

They were not far away when some one called out, "The women are gone!"

Then they saw firebrands. Each man had taken one and started in pursuit.

The sisters went South, the men went North, for they thought the women would try to get home.

The sisters ran toward the South, as they thought, till they came near a fire and saw a man shaking a squash rattle and singing, then they knew that they were back at the place they had started from.

The elder sister said, "We must try again. When we come to the tree ahead we will go to the next one ahead, and so on."

They traveled in this way till morning, then took the direction toward home. When night came, they rested.

The next day the sisters traveled till dark, then made a

bed on the ground. In the night the younger sister heard a voice say, "Is this where you are resting?"

"It is," she answered.

Then the voice said, "Keep on and you'll come back to the place where you were captured. No danger will meet you. To-morrow you'll find something to eat."

The woman wakened her sister and told her what the voice had said.

The next day, when the sun was in the middle of the sky, the women came upon a deer apparently just killed. They saw a smoke near a log and found a smouldering fire. They kindled the fire and cooked meat, ate a good meal and started on, carrying as much meat as they were able to.

They traveled a number of days and when the meat was about gone they saved what was left for the child.

One night a voice came again to the younger sister, and said, "You are on the right road and will come to your village before many days; you'll find plenty of food."

She told her sister what she had heard. They walked till nearly midday, then she said, "There is something white ahead, what is it?"

It was a patch of wild potatoes. While digging the potatoes the woman saw a smoke and found a few live coals. They gathered sticks and made a fire. After roasting potatoes and eating a plenty, they started on, each taking in a bundle as many potatoes as they were able to carry.

They traveled a number of days longer; the potatoes were almost gone.

Then one night the younger sister heard a voice say, "You'll reach home to-morrow at midday. The people will come together and you will tell them what has happened and sing the song YONTO^{n}WISAS (this song belongs to women). You must sing, 'We have come home. We are here!' When you enter the long house go once around it, and say, 'We have come home.' I want you to know that we are the HADIO^{n}YAGEONO^n, and that we have watched over you."

When the woman wakened she told her sister what the voice had said.

The next day, about noon, they heard chopping and soon they saw their uncle, who was out cutting blocks to make ladles.

They called to him, "Uncle, we've come home!"

He looked at them, and asked, "Are you living women?"

"We are," they answered, and then he cried out he was so glad.

They told the old man what the voice had said, and he called the people together. When all were assembled in the long house, the sisters began to sing as the voice had told them to do. This song is still sung by Seneca women.

The narrator of this story said the HADIO^{n}YAGEONO^n were spirits.

A DEAD MAN SPEAKS THROUGH FIRE

[Told by Henry Jacob]

Characters

NYAGWAIHE ....The Ancient of Bears
DZOGÉO^n ....The Little People

A WOMAN and her son lived in one house, a brother
and sister in another. The old woman's son and the
brother looked alike, were the same height and could
scarcely be told apart; they were great friends.

The old woman's son often visited the brother and
sister, but when the brother found that his friend thought
of marrying the sister when she was old enough (she was
very young), he was displeased and the next time the
young man came to the house he killed him, dug a hole
under the fireplace, put the body into it, filled the hole with
earth, and built a fire.

The mother waited for her son and when he didn't
come she went to the other house, and asked, "Where is
my son?"

"He just started for home, maybe he is in the woods;
he was going to cut twigs for arrows," answered the
young man.

When the woman started for home he ran out, cut wood
quickly, hurried to her house, sat down and began to
whittle out arrows.

When she came in he asked, "Where have you been,
mother?"

422

"I've been at your friend's house."

"Well," said he, "I am going over there a little while."

He put away the arrows, ran home, and said, "My sister, I am afraid that we are going to die. Hurry to the spring, leave your pail there; run in every direction, then come back to the house."

The girl went to the spring, covered the ground with tracks and came back.

Then the brother said, "I'll put you in the head of my arrow and send you off."

He shook the girl till she became very small, then put her in the head of his arrow, and said, "I will shoot toward the East; when the arrow strikes the ground, jump out and run. I'll overtake you."

He shot the arrow up through the smoke-hole. It came down on a stone far off in the East. The arrow burst and the girl came out and began to run as fast as she could.

The young man ran around in circles; made many tracks, then stood on the top of the house. There was a long line across the sky, the trail the arrow had made. He ran off under this trail, came to the spot where the arrow struck the stone, then followed his sister's tracks.

The woman got tired of waiting for her son and went over to see what he was doing. The house was empty. She sat down by the fire, then a voice spoke out of the fire, and said, "My friend killed me! My friend killed me!"

The woman dug down and found her son's body. She went home, became a NYAGWAIHE and followed the girl's tracks to the spring; followed them till she was at the house again. Then she looked through the smoke-hole, saw on the sky the trail of the arrow, and hurrying out ran toward the East.

The young man overtook his sister before she was far from the stone, then they ran on together. After a time they heard a bear roar. The girl trembled and grew weak, but her brother encouraged her. At night they lay down by a tree and slept a little.

The young man dreamed that a woman came to him, and said, "Here is a stone to defend yourself with. To-morrow about midday throw this stone behind you and

say, 'Let there be a ridge of rocks across the world so
high that nothing can climb over or pass it.' ''

In the morning the young man saw at his side the very
stone he had seen in his dream. He took the stone with
him.

Before midday they heard a bear roar. The young
man threw the stone behind him and that minute a ridge
of rocks stretched across the world. The ridge was so
high that no living creature could climb it.

The bear came to the ridge and saw that the tracks
she was following went farther. She clambered up and
fell back.

Howling terribly, she said, "I'll overtake and eat them
both!"

She ran toward the North; could find no end or opening,
then she went back and ran toward the South, and finding
no opening went back and lay down near the tracks.

The next morning she found only a small stone in her
way. She ground it to powder and went on.

The brother and sister had gone far but at midday
they heard the bear roar and knew she was coming. They
reached a great forest; the trees were dried up and leafless.
They saw a house and going in found an old man sitting
by the fire.

They told him their trouble and he said, "I will help
you, but you have another uncle not far from here, he will
help you more than I can."

The old man was chipping flint, when he had a handful
of chips he flung it at the trees and in this way he had
killed all the trees in the forest; he had great witchcraft.

The brother and sister went on.

The old man had a heap of flint chips piled up near
him. When he heard the bear coming he threw handful
after handful of the chips at her, but she didn't turn
away.

She came to the door, and asked, "Have you seen a
young man and a girl?"

"I have not," said he, "I pay no heed to persons who
pass."

The bear seized the old man by the head, crushed him
and killed him. Then she saw tracks and knowing that

the brother and sister had gone ahead, she roared and rushed on.

When they came to the second uncle, he said, "I will help you all I can, but hurry on till you come to the house of another uncle."

He made a trap on the trail, near that a second trap, and then a third one.

When the bear came, she rushed into the first trap; after a long struggle she broke through, then got into the second trap, and only got out of that to fall into the third one.

When she got out of the third trap she went to the old man, and asked, "Have you seen a young man and a girl pass?"

"I have not."

The bear seized the old man and tore him to pieces with her teeth.

When the brother and sister came to the third uncle, he was making a net. His eyes were closed and his eyelids hung on his cheeks. When they called to him he didn't hear them; they called again; he kept at work.

When his nephew got a pounder and hit him on the head he raised his eyebrows and said, "I hear a voice."

"A great bear is following us," said the young man.

"I will help you all I can," said the uncle, "but your grandfather lives in the next house, run to him; he can help you more than I can."

When the bear was near, the old man put a long net on the trail. She was caught in the net, but she struggled and bit till at last she freed herself.

Then going to the old man she asked, "Have you seen a young man and a girl pass this way?"

"I have not," said he.

When the brother and sister came to their grandfather's house they found SHAGODYOWEQ (Wind people) there. These people wore heavy shells. When they saw the brother and sister they told them to go on till they came to the next house, that the people there were very strong, possessed great witchcraft and could help them.

The bear came and after a hard fight killed the Wind people.

When the brother and sister reached the next house an old Dzogέo[1] woman sat in front of it. She told them to go in, she would kill the bear. She had a great deal of bear fat. She told her three sons to make two fires on the tracks of the brother and sister, put a kettle over each fire and fill the kettles with fat. When the fat was boiling, the brothers gathered red willows and made arrows.

The woman stood near the first kettle. The bear came rushing along and asked, "Are the two here whose tracks these are?"

"They are here," said she, "They are in the house."

The bear started to go around the kettles, but the woman said, "You mustn't go that way; those who came before you went through the fire, you must do as they did."

The bear started; overturned the first kettle, got her paws burned and fell back growling. She made for the second kettle, overturned that and was burned still worse. Then the boys killed her with their red willow arrows, and burned her bones to powder so she couldn't come to life.

The Dzogέo woman told the brother and sister to stay with her till they were rested, then her sons would go home with them.

They started, and the Dzogέo boys traveled with them two days, then telling them how to get home they turned back.

Peter White said the Bear woman's son had a tuft of yellow hair hanging down his back from the crown of his head, that when he was killed by his friend, the friend cut off that tuft of hair and fastened it to the top of his own head.

When the Bear woman's son was hunting he could send his arrows home. They would go into the house and to the place where they belonged. After the friend had the tuft of hair his arrows would go home in the same way. The strength was in the tuft of hair.

[1] Very small people who usually live among rocks.

THE FEAST OF THE WHIRLWINDS

Characters

Dzogéo^n ....The Little People
Nyagwaihe ....The Ancient of Bears
Dagwanoe^{n}yent, Whirlwind or Cyclone, always represented as Flying Heads (Heads without bodies)

Dzogéo^n and his uncle lived together in the woods. When the boy was old enough, his uncle taught him how to shoot and took him out hunting.

One day, while the young man was following an elk, a woman called to him, "Come here and rest; you are tired."

At first he paid no heed to the woman's words, but, when she called the third time, he sat down at her side. She talked to him and soon had his head on her lap. She began to search in his hair and right away he was asleep.

When the woman was satisfied that the young man slept soundly, she put him in a basket, put the basket on her back and started off with great swiftness.

She traveled till sunset, then she stopped, put down the basket, roused the young man, and asked, "Do you know this place?"

"I know it," said he, "My uncle and I used to hunt here."

They spent the night there. The next morning the woman searched in Dzogéo^n's hair till he fell asleep, then she put him in the basket and hurried on.

Late in the afternoon she stopped near a lake, put the

427

basket down, shook the young man and asked, "Do you know this lake?"

"I know it, I have been here with my uncle."

The woman took out of her basket a canoe no larger than a walnut, struck it till it became large, then both sat in it and the woman paddled across the lake.

"We will go home now," said she, "I have a mother and I have three sisters married and living in my mother's cabin."

The two traveled on till they came to the cabin. When they stood at the door and the mother saw a stranger with her daughter she called out, "Welcome, Son-in-law, I am glad you have come."

Dzogéo^n became the young woman's husband and they lived on happily till one night the old woman had a dream. She rolled on to the floor and to the edge of the fire.

Her son-in-law jumped up and asked, "What is the matter, Mother-in-law? Are you dreaming?"

She didn't answer, but rolled around muttering to herself, then he said, "I'll make her talk," and taking a corn pounder he hit her a blow on the head.

She stood up then, and said, "Oh, I've had a bad dream, I dreamed that my son-in-law killed NYAGWAIHE."

"I'll do that in the morning," said the young man, "but go to sleep now."

The next morning Dzogéo^n killed the bear, without much trouble, and carried it home.

That night the old woman dreamed that her son-in-law must make a feast for the DAGWANOE^{n}YENTS (Whirlwinds), invite them to it, and provide so much food that they couldn't eat it all.

The next day Dzogéo^n killed a great many elks, deer and bears. There was an abundance of meat; the house was full of it, and still there was more. Then the young man went out and called to the Whirlwinds to come to a feast prepared for them.

They answered quickly and all promised to come. They came in such numbers that there wasn't room for them on the shelves, the floor, or the seats. They began to eat, and they ate with a terrible appetite.

The mother-in-law went around urging them, saying, "Eat, eat your fill, I want every one to have plenty."

They ate and ate and the old woman still urged, hoping the supply would give out and her son-in-law would be killed.

The young man with his wife and her three sisters and their husbands went for more food in case of need. The Whirlwinds ate till their jaws couldn't move.

"We have enough, Mother, enough," said they.

When Dzogέoⁿ heard these words he motioned to the walls and roof of the cabin, and said, "I want your roof and walls to become stone."

The old woman and the Flying Heads, [1] finding that they were in a stone house and couldn't get out, flew around in every direction. The mother-in-law begged for mercy.

"You had no mercy on me," said her son-in-law.

Then he said, "I want this house to be red hot."

As the house grew hot the heads flew about with terrible speed, knocking against the walls and making such a noise as had never been heard in the world before. But at last all was still.

Then Dzogέoⁿ with his wife, her three sisters and their husbands set out for his uncle's cabin. When they reached the lake, it was covered with ice, so thin that it would barely hold up a small bird.

The young man took eight puff balls from an oak tree, made himself and his friends small, and each one entered a puff ball. When the eight balls stood side by side on the ice at the edge of the lake, the young man said, "Let the West wind blow!"

The West wind came and swept the balls over the lake. Dzogέoⁿ and his friends sprang out of the balls, became of natural size and went on their way till they came to the uncle's cabin.

[1] Whirlwind is always represented as a Flying Head.

THUNDER DESTROYS HORNED SNAKE

Characters

DONO^{n}GÁES ....Snake (Long horns)
HÍNO' ....Thunder

A MOTHER and daughter lived in a bark house on the edge of a village. Many men wanted the girl for a wife, for she was nice-looking, but to each man she said, "You are not such a man as I want."

One day the girl and her mother went to the forest to pick up wood. When it began to grow dark they were far from home.

The mother said, "We'll make a fire and stay here all night."

They made a fire and got ready for the night. All at once a man stood near the girl, when she looked up she was amazed, he was so handsome. He had a wampum belt around his body and long feathers in his head-dress.

He said to her, "I have come to marry you."

Her mother was around picking up wood.

The girl said, "I will tell my mother."

The young man stood by the fire and waited for the girl's answer.

When she told her mother that a stranger had come and wanted to marry her, the mother said, "You have refused many good men, now do as you like."

The girl gave the man her mother's answer, and said, "I will be your wife."

"You must go home with me," said the man, and taking off his wampum belt he gave it to the mother, and said, "This will be a proof that we are married."

The woman hung the belt on a tree. She was greatly pleased with her new son-in-law.

The two started off together. They soon reached a large clearing at one end of which was a house.

The man said, "That is our home."

When they went into the house the persons sitting around seemed to be pleased with the young woman.

She was contented and happy till one day her husband said, "I am going to hunt."

He went out and as he closed the door she heard a strange noise, then all was still.

Towards dark she heard the same noise. The door opened and a great snake came in. It put its head on the woman's lap and told her to look for vermin. She found bloodsuckers and angleworms as well as insects. After a while the Snake backed out of the door; the next minute the husband came in as handsome as ever.

"Were you afraid of me?" asked he.

"I wasn't afraid," said the young woman.

The next day the man went to hunt. When he closed the door the woman heard the same kind of noise she had heard the day before. And when she went out to gather wood she saw a great snake sunning itself on the rocks. Then she saw another and another and she began to be very homesick.

About dark her husband came as he had the evening before.

The next day, after he had gone, she began to think about getting away from such a terrible man. She went for wood and while standing in one place, thinking, she heard a voice and turning toward it saw an old man.

He said, "My grandchild, you are unfortunate. The man you are living with is a bad man. We have often tried to kill him, but he is cautious, we can't catch him. There are seven brothers, your husband is the youngest, their hearts are tied together in a bunch and the bunch is hidden under his couch. You must get it; I and my friends will help you all we can."

The young woman found the hearts, hid them under her blanket and hurrying out of the house began to run.

Soon she heard a voice calling, "Stop! Come back!" but she ran the faster.

The voice said, "You can't get away, no matter how you try."

Then strength seemed to leave her, but that minute the stranger, who had called her "grandchild," was at her side.

"I will help you," said he, and taking hold of her blanket he pulled her out of the water. She saw then that she had been in a lake. A great black cloud was above them and Thunder began to shoot his arrows. Soon the woman saw that the stranger had killed the terrible Snake; other men like him were on the shore and they thanked her and said that she had helped them.

The men drew the Snake out of the lake, cut it into pieces, and stuck the head on a pole. Seeing that the eyes looked at the woman in a sharp, ugly way, the grandfather said, "You must come home with us."

They packed pieces of the Snake in separate bundles, then each man took a bundle, and they started. After a while they came to what seemed to the woman to be a house. Inside the house was a very old man. The leader said to him, "This young woman has helped us kill the great Snake."

The old man looked up, and said, "My granddaughter, I thank you."

All the men, except the very old man, hunted, but each day they brought the woman corn and squash, for she couldn't eat their kind of food. They told the names of the persons from whom they stole the corn and squash, and she knew those persons.

One day the old man said to the others, "Maybe you had better take the woman with you; she has power."

They said, "Very well," and then they told her that one of their number was missing, and said, "On a rock in deep water is a terrible bloodsucker. The man shot at him, but he wasn't quick enough and the bloodsucker caught him. Our friend lies there on the rock and we can't rescue him or kill the bloodsucker."

She went with them to the lake. When they came to where the rock was she looked down and saw the bloodsucker. The men tried to kill the bloodsucker by going up to the clouds and shooting arrows down into the water. When each man had tried and failed they asked the woman to shoot. She shot once; the bloodsucker moved. She shot a second time; there was a terrible struggle in the water, then all was quiet.

Soon they saw that the bloodsucker was dead and their friend was free. The man came out of the water and they all went home.

After the woman had been with these men about a year, Old Man Thunder said, "It is time for this woman to go to her mother," and he said to her, "For ten days you mustn't do any work, any pounding or chopping."

The Thunders went with her till she was near home. She thought they walked along as ordinary persons. When they left her she saw that she was standing in water; a heavy shower had just passed over. Her mother's house was close by.

For eight days she refused to work, the ninth day her mother and friends urged her to help them pound corn. She said that she couldn't, but they urged so hard that she took the pounder and struck one blow; the mortar split apart and the corn fell on the ground, such was her terrible strength.

THE FRIENDSHIP OF AN OTTER

ONCE, in the fall of the year, a chief and six or eight families went on a hunting expedition. For many days they found no game. At last the chief, who had as a charm a fawn skin pouch, called the party to his brush house and told each person to take hold of the pouch and say what animal he would kill the next day.

The first man said he would kill a bear. The chief's wife said she would kill a wild goose. As the pouch was passed from one to another, the chief's daughter told her husband not to touch it and when it came near she grasped his hand to keep him from doing so, but he pulled it away and taking hold of the pouch said, "To-morrow, before daylight, I will kill two otters."

At midnight he got up and went to where the river doubled nearly around and there he watched for otters. Soon he saw two and he killed both of them. He was hungry and, as it wasn't daylight, he cut open each otter and took out the heart. He roasted and ate the hearts then went home. Unwittingly he had destroyed the power of the charm.

That day each person came home without game. The chief's wife had said she would get a wild goose, but when she clapped her hands and called, "Let them fall. Let them fall," they all flew over, for the charm was broken.

The chief examined the two otters and when he saw that the hearts had been taken out, he was very angry.

The young man's wife was frightened. She hid a piece of meat and a knife, telling her husband where he would find them in case of need.

The chief said, "My son-in-law has broken the charm, we had better kill him."

The daughter said, "If you kill him, kill me too."

The chief, who didn't want to kill his daughter, said, "We will strip him naked, leave him, and go far away."

434

They stripped the young man, and went off, taking his wife with them.

At midnight when all alone, the young man heard somebody coming on snowshoes—it was Winter. A man pushed the door open, and said, "You think that you are going to die, but you are not, I have come to save you. To-morrow morning follow my tracks to a hollow tree. There is a bear in the tree, kill it and you will have plenty of meat, and the bear's skin will keep you warm, make you a blanket and moccasins."

The next morning the young man could see no tracks except rabbit tracks. He followed them to a hollow tree and found a bear. He killed the bear, skinned it and carried the carcass to the house. Of the skin he made a blanket and moccasins.

At midnight he again heard someone coming on snowshoes.

Then a voice said, "Last night I sent you help, to-night I have come to tell you that your wife will be here to-morrow at midday. She thinks you are dead and she has left her father's camp to come and find you. In the morning send her for her father and the people who are with him, let her say, 'My husband has plenty of meat for you all.' They will be glad for they have no meat."

At midday the young woman came, and the next morning her husband sent her to tell her father and friends to come to his camp.

That night the stranger came to the brush house, and said, "Your father will be glad that you have meat. He will show his charms and give you your choice of them. Take the one he says is of no account, it is wrapped in a piece of bear skin and is my finger that I lost when he caught me in a trap. He will tell you to take one of the other charms, but take that and no other."

The next morning the father-in-law and his people came back. The old chief unwrapped his charms and told his son-in-law to take his choice.

The young man took the one wrapped in bear-skin.

"Oh, that is of no account," said the chief, "Here is a better one."

But the young man said, "I'll keep this one." And

he went out to look for the person to whom the finger belonged. He hadn't gone far when he saw a house in the middle of an opening and in the house he found the stranger, who had befriended him and he gave him the finger.

The old man thanked him, and said, "I will always be your friend and you will succeed in everything you undertake."

As the young man was going home he turned to look at the house. It had disappeared and what he had thought was a field he now saw was a lake.

Ever after this the young man had good luck. He became a great hunter and when his people made war on a neighboring tribe he took many scalps. Whatever he wished for he had. And all this came from the friendship of the Otter whose finger he returned.

HOW CHIPMUNKS GOT THEIR STRIPES

Characters

DZOHÓ'GWAIS ....Chipmunk
DASIDOWANES ....Big Feet (one name for bear)

A GRANDMOTHER and granddaughter were living together. They had a skin blanket, but it was old and a good deal of the hair was worn off.

The two women went to the forest to camp and cut wood and they carried the blanket to cover themselves with at night. They had been in the forest only a few days when they found that their skin blanket was alive and was angry. They threw the blanket down and ran toward home as fast as they could go. Soon they heard the skin following them.

When it seemed very near the grandmother began to sing and her song said, "My granddaughter and I are running for our lives, My granddaughter and I are running for our lives."

When the song ended, the women could scarcely hear the skin following them, but not long afterward they heard it again. When they reached home the skin, now a bear, was so near that as they pushed open the door it clawed at them and scratched their backs, but they got in.

The old woman and her granddaughter were chipmunks. Since that time Chipmunks have stripes on their backs, the result of the scratches given by the bear.

CHILD FED AND CARED FOR BY A PORCUPINE AND A BEAR

A WIDOWER, who had a little son, married a second time, and soon after he took his wife and child and went to the forest to camp and hunt.

The three lived happily till the woman began to think that her husband loved the child better than he did her. This worried her and made her uneasy. She could think of nothing else, and she began to study how to get rid of the boy.

One day, while her husband was hunting, she led the child to a cave in the woods, told him there was a bear in the cave and that he must crawl in and scare it, make it run out at the other end of the opening.

The child crept in. The woman rolled a stone up, closed the opening, and went home.

When the man came from hunting, he missed his boy and asked where he was. The woman said that when she went to gather bark the child was at play near the house, but when she came back she couldn't find him, that she had hunted everywhere. She was afraid he had been carried off by some wild beast.

The father was nearly crazy. He hunted many days for the child, but could only find tracks made by his little moccasins, tracks that the step-mother had made far into the woods, to mislead and deceive the father.

When the child found that it couldn't get out of the cave it began to scream.

All at once a voice said, "Poor child, stop crying, I am your grandmother. I will give you something to eat," and a hand wiped away his tears. Then somebody brought him food that he thought was very nice, though it was only hemlock burrs.

438

The woman in the cave was a porcupine and she gave the boy some of the food she had saved for herself. When he had eaten enough she said, "You are tired, my little grandson, come and lie down."

In this way the woman cared for the child a long time. One day she said, "My burrs are gone. It is Spring now, you'll not be cold out-of-doors. Your step-mother fastened us in here, but I can call my neighbors and they will let us out. When we are out, I must leave you in their care and go to hunt for food."

She went to the opening and called for help. Soon the boy heard a noise and voices outside the cave, and after a while he heard a man ask, "Who can push away this stone?"

The Bird people came and pecked at the stone; they could do nothing. Small animals scratched at the stone, but it didn't move. One after another tried and all failed. At last Wolf said, "I can pull that stone away! I'm the man to do it."

He pushed his long claws under the stone and pulled and pulled till at last his hold gave way and he fell over on his back.

Deer, with his long horns, tried to raise the stone. All tried, each one in his own way, from the smallest to the largest, except a bear that sat off a short distance with three cubs playing near her.

When all had failed, Bear said, "I will try."

She walked slowly to the stone, examined it and made up her mind how to act, then she quickly moved the stone. Looking into the cave she saw Porcupine and a little boy and was so frightened that she ran away from the opening. Others looked in, were frightened and ran till they were far enough away to make sure of escape, then they waited to see what would happen.

Porcupine came out and called to them not to be afraid, and said, "We are very poor, my grandson and I," and she told them how the boy came to be there and that her burrs were gone.

She said, "You are able to care for my grandson and I want to leave him with you."

Even the Bird people said they would care for the child.

"I must know what you can give him to eat," said Porcupine, "and when I find out which one of you can supply food that my grandson can eat I will give him to that one."

Each one brought a little of the food they could furnish and put it down before Porcupine.

Wolf brought what he had to eat, Porcupine looked at it and then asked, "What would you and the boy do in case of danger?"

"We would run."

"No," said Porcupine, "My grandson can't go with you; he couldn't run fast enough."

Deer came with food, but when Porcupine asked, "What would you do in case of danger?" he ran off so swiftly that his horns could be heard knocking against the trees.

Last of all Bear came forward, and said, "Others have failed and though I have a large family of my own, I will take care of the boy and feed him as I feed my cubs; on blackberries, chestnuts and fruit."

When asked what she would do in danger she went back to her cubs, and gave the sign of danger. The cubs crouched down by a log and the mother Bear lay down near them and watched.

"This is what I do," said she. "We lie still till the danger is past. I know where berries grow, I will take the boy there. I know where my Winter quarters will be. My cubs and your grandson will get nourishment by sucking my fat paws."

"You are the one to care for the child," said Porcupine, "I am going for food."

The boy never saw Porcupine again.

When Bear led him to the berries, he thought she took him by the hand, as a human being would.

The cubs became fond of the boy and when their mother was lying asleep in the sun, they pulled his finger-nails to make them long like their own, and tried to teach him to climb trees as they did. At last the boy could almost equal the cubs in climbing for his nails were long and sharp.

One day the mother Bear woke up and couldn't see the boy. Then, a long way off, she saw him high up in a tree. She scolded the cubs, was angry with them, and put the boy's nails back as they were before.

Summer passed and Winter came. Then the mother Bear said, "It is time to go to our den." And she led her cubs and the boy to a hollow tree. The boy thought there was plenty of room in the tree; he and the cubs played together and were happy. The mother Bear slept most of the time, but when there was a noise she wakened in an instant, and said, "Keep still! There is a hunter around." There was a crack in the tree and they could look out. Soon after a warning they would see a man coming. Then the boy thought the mother Bear put her hand in her pocket and drew out something that had two prongs, put it through the crack and moved it to and fro till the hunter was out of sight, then she drew it in.

All went well till one day towards Spring when they heard a hunter coming. Though they all kept very still the mother Bear said to the boy, "I think that our time has come, you can stay here, but we must go. We are bears, but you are a human being. The hunter will take you home and you will be cared for."

The mother Bear put out her two-pronged bough, but she could do nothing; all her magic power was gone.

When the hunter came near he saw claw marks in the bark of the tree.

The mother Bear knew then that the end had come, and she said to her eldest cub, "You must go first, the others will follow."

The eldest crawled out of the tree and that instant the boy heard the whiz of an arrow. As he watched the little bear it semed to throw off a pack. The pack fell to the ground but the little bear itself went straight on, never stopping.

The other little bears followed and each shared the fate of the first. Each time the boy heard the whiz of an arrow and saw the pack fall, but as he saw his friends still running he wasn't frightened.

When her children had gone, the mother Bear said to the boy, "I have to go, you must be obedient and all will be well."

The boy heard a whiz and saw a burden drop to the

ground, but the mother Bear ran on as her children had done.

Now the boy screamed, for he was alone.

The hunter heard the scream and was frightened, but remembering that a child had been lost, he set to work and soon had the boy out of the tree.

The child was naked and unable to talk. The hunter skinned the bears and made him clothing. The boy was terribly grieved but he couldn't speak to let the hunter know how dear the bears were to him.

The hunter took the boy to his father, who was over-joyed to find his child, and ever after took him with him wherever he went.

A BROTHER AND SISTER PURSUED BY A MAN-EATER

[Told by Henry Jacobs]

A MAN-EATER stole a little girl and carried her to his house in the woods. There was a partition in the house. The man-eater stayed on one side of the partition and the girl the other side. He brought deer meat for the girl, but he ate human flesh.

The girl had a brother and he determined to get her away from the man-eater. When he was ready to start, his father gave him a bow and an arrow, the arrow was hollow. He gave him a piece of flint, a pigeon's feather, and the tooth of a beaver, and said, "If you are in great danger throw the flint, the feather, or the tooth behind you."

One day, when the man-eater was off hunting, the brother, who had been watching around, went to the house, saw his sister and told her she must come with him, but they couldn't go home, for if they did the man-eater would find and kill them. The young man shook his sister till she was small.

Then he put her in his arrow, and said, "The arrow will strike a stone at the end of the world; it will burst and you will come out. Then run toward the South as fast as you can. I'll overtake you."

He shot the arrow, then ran in increasing circles around the man-eater's house till he came to a tall hickory tree. He climbed the tree, made a long leap toward the South, came to the ground and followed the trail the arrow had left in the sky.

When the man-eater came home and found the girl gone, he was angry, and said, "I'll find her, no matter where she is."

He changed himself into a bear, found the young man's tracks and followed them around and around the house till he came to where they ended. He searched a long time and at last found the place where the young man had come down when he sprang from the tree.

"Now, I'll get you!" said the man-eater, and he was glad.

In the form of a bear he followed the young man's tracks till he came to the stone where the arrow struck. Then he followed farther till he came to where the brother and sister met.

One day when the two stopped to rest, they heard a bear roar, and the roar said, "You can't get away from me! I'll find you, no matter where you go."

The girl was so frightened that she fell. The young man didn't know what to do, then he remembered that he had a wonderful pair of moccasins that belonged to his mother. He took the moccasins out of his pocket, put them on the ground, and said, "Go West as fast as you can." He put his sister in the arrow and shot it off toward the South, and climbing a tall tree he sprang from it, landed far away, and followed the arrow.

When the man-eater saw the moccasin tracks, he thought they were the girl's tracks and he said, "Now I'll overtake you!"

He ran west all day, ran through swamps and across rough places. Just at dark he came to a rotten log and there he found two moccasins. He tore up the moccasins and roaring, "You'll not get away from me!" he turned and ran back, ran all night and the next day, came to the old track, then ran in circles till he found where the young man struck the ground.

After a long time he came to the stone where the arrow burst, then to the place where the brother and sister met. He had almost overtaken them when the young man thought of the piece of flint his father had given him. He threw the flint behind him, and said, "Be a rock across the world!"

When the man-eater came to the rock, he said, "I never heard of a rock across the world. I'll soon get around this."

He ran a long time, then, thinking that he was going in the wrong direction, turned and went back to the starting place and off in the other direction. After running all day and finding no end to the rock, he went back, a second time, to the starting place. A little piece of flint lay where the rock had been. The man-eater was terribly angry; he broke up the flint and ran on faster than before.

Again the man-eater, in the form of a bear, was getting near. The girl was tired and cried, the young man encouraged her, told her they had friends on the road and would soon have help.

When the bear roared, "I'll have you now!" the young man threw the pigeon feather behind him with the wish that pigeon droppings would block the way.

The man-eater came to the deposit and couldn't get through. He ran all day to get around it, then, thinking that he had gone in the wrong direction, he went back to the starting place and ran in the opposite direction, but finding no end, came back to the starting place and lay down. When he woke up, a pigeon feather was on the trail; the deposit had disappeared. He was mad with rage. He went on swiftly and again was near the brother and sister.

The young man threw the beaver tooth, and said, "Let there be a beaver swamp deep and wide."

The man-eater came to the swamp and tried to cross, but couldn't, saying, "I never heard of a beaver swamp so long that I couldn't go around it." He started toward the West, traveled all day, then went back and off toward the East, but finding no end to the swamp he returned to the starting place and lay down. When he woke up the swamp was gone and on the trail was a beaver's tooth.

The young man thought, "I've nothing more to delay the man-eater. Maybe we will die now." But he encouraged his sister and they ran on and soon came to an opening. In the opening was a house and in the house was an old man. They called him "Uncle" and begged for help.

"I'll do what I can," said he, "but farther on you have another uncle, who will help you more than I can."

The old man was a net-maker. He gathered up his nets

and spread them on the trail. When the man-eater came he got tangled up in the nets and was a long time freeing himself. He wanted to kill the old man, but not seeing him called out, "You have made me lose time, I'll come back and kill you."

The brother and sister came to a village, and when the chief heard the young man's story, he rubbed them with his hands, changed their looks, gave them different clothes and told them to stay with his people.

When the man-eater was near the village, he took his own form and going to the chief said, "A young man has stolen my daughter. I am following him, but I am tired and want to stay here and rest"—he knew that the brother and sister were in the village.

After a while the man-eater said, "I was brought up to have fun."

"We have no time for fun," said the chief, "We are going into the woods to hunt."

The young man knew that the man-eater was looking for tracks, so he went to the edge of the clearing where there was a stump, put down a pair of moccasins, and said to them, "Run all day but come back at night."

The man-eater saw the tracks and followed them. Towards night the moccasins came to the stump, dropped down and were nothing but moccasins. When the man-eater came and saw them he was so mad that he tore them to pieces and tore up the stump.

The chief knew that the man-eater would stay around till he found the brother and sister, so he said to the young man, "I will help you all I can."

He spat on four pieces of bear skin, then gave them to the brother and sister to fasten on to their feet.

"Now," said the chief, "your tracks will be like bear tracks. When the man-eater is getting near, put your sister in an arrow and shoot it toward the West, then spring from a high tree and follow her. You will come to a house where there is an old man. He will tell you what to do."

The man-eater came upon the bear tracks but didn't mind them. After traveling a long distance and finding no other tracks he rubbed his hand over a track and smelt of it, then he knew they were the young man's tracks and he followed them till he came to where the arrow was shot off, and after hunting a while he found where the young man came down when he sprang from the tree.

The brother and sister came to an opening and saw ten boys playing ball. In the middle of the opening was a house and in the house was an old man, who, when he heard the young man's story, said, "I will help you all I can and my boys will help you. I know that man, I am older than he is, but he hasn't as much power as I have. He will come in the form of a bear."

When they heard the bear coming, the boys threw up their clubs, gave a war-whoop, and ran forward. One hit the bear a blow; the bear chased him. Then another gave it a blow, and it turned and chased that one till another boy hit it a blow. This went on till the bear stumbled and fell, then the boys cut off its head. They buried the body but made a ball of the head.

The brother and sister wanted to start for home, but the old man said, "Many people are coming to play games. You must stay and see the sport."

Early the next morning a crowd of people came. Their leader said, "We have come to play games."

"That is what I like," said the old man. "I have ten sons who will play ball with you, but if you want a foot race, I'll run with you myself. I am old, but I can run. Do you know what we bet?"

"We do. You bet heads."

"How many men have you?"

"Fifty."

"Well, we will play ball. If you beat us, you may cut off my head and the head of each one of my ten sons. If we beat you, I'll have your head and the head of each one of your fifty men."

The old man always carried his ball West. The head man of the fifty wanted to carry his ball West.

"No," said the old man, "it is my rule to carry West. You must go East."

They disputed a long time, then the old man brought out a board, black on one side and red on the other, and said, "Choose your color. I'll throw the board up. If it comes down your color, you may carry the ball West; if it comes my color, I'll carry West.''

The head man chose black.

The board went up out of sight. The old man kept saying in his mind, "Red; red; red!" It came down the red side up.

The old man had a ball and the head man had one. They quarreled over the balls but at last agreed to play twice, once with each ball.

They put the old man's ball down; his boys snatched it and ran West. Fifty men followed the ten, but couldn't catch them. They came back, took the head man's ball and ran East. The ten followed and the swiftest runner of the ten snatched the ball and ran West with it. The old man won, and the fifty with their head man lost their lives.

When the brother and sister were ready to start, the old man said, "I'll make a trail for you. Look at the sky and you'll not get lost.''

He took a stick and made a mark on the ground, then he motioned and a line came on the sky.

He said, "If you lose the trail on the ground, you'll see it in the sky. Follow it and you will get home.''

The girl was in a hurry. She said, "We can travel in the night as well as in the day time for we can see the trail along the sky.''

They traveled fast and were not many days in getting home.

A RACOON STORY

AN uncle and nephew lived together. One day when the nephew was in the woods, hunting, a handsome young woman came to the cabin. She had a basketful of bread on her shoulders.

Unstrapping the basket and putting it down in front of the old man, she said, "Here is marriage bread, my father and mother have sent me here to marry your nephew."

"Very well," said the uncle.

When the young man came home, his uncle said, "You are married now."

"I am glad," said the nephew.

After this the young woman cooked and the men hunted. Each day the nephew returned with a heavy load of game. One day while hunting he came to a tree in which there was a large hole and in the hole was a litter of coons. He climbed the tree and threw one coon after another on to the ground.

All at once he heard a woman say, "Come down. Come down, you are tired," then she ran off through the forest.

When the young man went home, he told what had happened. His wife laughed, but said nothing. Not long after, when packing up his game ready to start for home, a woman came up behind him, took him by the arm and led him to a log. They sat down, she pulled his head on to her lap and began to look in his hair.

The man was soon asleep. The woman put him in a basket, put the basket on her back and went to an island in the middle of a lake. Then she took the man out of the basket and asked, "Do you know this place?"

"I know it. This is where my uncle and I used to fish," and giving a spring into the water the man became a bass and escaped.

When he went home, he told his wife what had happened. She laughed, but said nothing.

The man was so frightened that he stayed at home for several days. Then the feeling wore away and he started off to hunt.

As he was packing up his game to go home a woman said, right there at his side, "Stop, wait a while, you must be tired."

They sat down on a log. She drew his head to her lap and began looking in his hair. He was soon asleep. Putting him into a basket the woman carried him to a great ledge of rocks where there was only a foothold, then, taking him out of the basket, she asked, "Do you know this place?"

"I will tell you soon," said the man, looking around.

That minute the woman disappeared.

Soon he heard someone say, "I will fish a while."

A line dropped into the water below and a man began singing and pulling up fish.

At last he said, "I have enough, I'll rest and have something to eat. This is what we people eat when we are among the rocks," and he took a baked squash out of his basket.

The young man said to the rocks, "Stand back a little so that I can string my bow."

The rocks stood back; he strung his bow, and, saying, "Now boast again!" he shot the fisherman.

He heard a loud noise and looking in the direction it came from saw an enormous bat coming toward him. The bat passed a little to one side. The young man took a hemlock leaf from his pocket and dropping it over the rocks, sang, "A tree must grow from this hemlock leaf. A tree must grow from this hemlock leaf."

Soon a tree came in sight. Then the man talked to the tree, said, "Come near, and have many limbs."

As the tree came to a level with the place on the rocks where the young man was sitting, it stopped growing.

He had seen that along the narrow shelf of rocks there were many men. He called to the nearest one to tell all to come and they could escape.

The men crept up, one after another, then went down

on the tree. When all had reached the ground, the young man took a strawberry leaf from his pocket and dropping it said, "Grow and give berries." Then he sang, "Ripen berries. Ripen berries." The vines grew, were covered with blossoms. The blossoms became berries and the berries ripened.

When the men had eaten as many berries as they wanted, the young man picked a leaf from the vines, put it in his pocket and the vines and berries disappeared. Then he said to the men, "Let us go to our wife"—meaning the woman who had captured them.

When they had traveled some distance, the young man killed an elk. Taking the hide he cut it into strings and made a baby board, but one large enough for a grown person. After a while they saw a house and in front of it a woman pounding something.

When she saw them, she began to scold and, holding up the pounder was going to strike them.

The young man said, "Let the pounder stop right there!"

The pounder stopped in the air, half raised.

They seized the woman, strapped her to the board, and, saying, "You must be cold," they set the board up in front of the fire. Just then the young man's wife came and, finding that they were about to roast the woman, she was angry.

She freed her, and said, "You are free now, and I will go home."

She went to the lake and called on Bloodsuckers to stretch across the water. They came and she walked over on them.

Each man went his own way. When the young man got home his wife was there.

The nephew and uncle were racoons.

THE MOOSE WOMAN

A YOUNG MAN, who lived alone with his mother, decided that he would go to the forest and hunt; that he would stay away a year, collect and dry meat, and at the end of the year come home.

He started and after going a long distance, came to a region where he thought there would be plenty of game. He built a bark house and began housekeeping. Each morning he made a fire, cooked his breakfast and ate it, then went out to hunt. He stayed away all day and when he came home at night, he was often so tired that he lay down without eating. He soon had a large quantity of meat but many times he was hungry.

One day, when coming back from a long tramp, he saw smoke rising from the smoke-hole of his cabin. He was frightened, for he was sure the cabin was on fire. He ran as fast as he could, thinking he might save some of the meat he had dried.

On going into the cabin he was surprised to see a fire in the fireplace and his kettle hanging on the crook in such a way as to keep its contents hot. He wondered who had come to cook for him. In all the time he had lived in the forest he had not found a cabin or seen a human being. He saw that the deer he had brought home the evening before was dressed and hung up to dry; that wood had been brought in and piled up near the fire; that everything had been put in order and acorn bread made.

On the way home he had thought that he would lie down as soon as he got to the cabin, but now he was glad to find a warm meal awaiting him. He sat down and ate, thinking, "The person who got this ready will come soon," but no one came.

The next morning he went into the forest to hunt. When on the way home he looked to see if smoke was coming out of his cabin; it was, and again food was ready. Near the fire he found a partly finished braid. Then he knew that his unknown friend was a woman. She had put a number of deer skins to soak to make buckskin. He

thought, "How kind she is," and he made up his mind to
see her, even if he had to stop hunting.

In the morning he started off, as usual, but only went
to a place in the woods where he could watch the cabin.
Soon he saw smoke rising from the cabin, and, creeping
back cautiously, he waited around till a woman came out
for wood. When she went in he followed quickly.

He saw that the woman was young and good-looking
and he said to her, "You have been kind to me, I am
thankful."

She said, "I knew that you were often hungry and I
came to see if you would let me be your wife."

The young man was glad that the woman was willing to
stay. After that she tanned deer skins, dried meat, cooked
for him, and worked hard every day. She was good
natured and kind and her husband loved her.

Before the end of the year a boy was born and then
they were perfectly happy.

When the time came that the man had set to go back
to his mother, his wife said, "I know your promise to your
mother. The time has come for you to go. I have everything ready, I have made moccasins for you and for your
mother, and there is plenty of meat."

"How can I carry the meat?" asked the man, "She
lives a long way off."

"You have only to select the meat you want; I know
how you can carry it."

She knew how he came to the forest, and that he could
reach his village much quicker by going in a canoe down
the river.

Early the next morning she asked him to go to the river
with her—it was not far from the cabin. When they came
to the bank, she took a tiny canoe from her bosom. Her
husband wondered what she was going to do with such a
little plaything.

"Take hold of one end of this," said the woman, "and
pull away from me."

He did and the little canoe stretched and stretched till
it was very long and wide. They placed it at the edge
of the water, then brought basketful after basketful of
meat from the cabin and packed it away in the canoe.

When the canoe was well loaded the woman gave her husband a package, and said, "I want you to put on a new pair of moccasins each morning and throw away the old ones."

Then she cautioned him not to forget her, said, "When people see what a good hunter you are, many women will want to marry you, but you must be true to me, if you are not you will never see me again."

The man promised to come back in the Fall, and they parted.

When he reached home, news spread that such a woman's son had returned from a year's hunting and had brought a great deal of meat. People came to see him and to look at the meat. He told no one, not even his mother, that he was married, so many young girls asked for him. His mother had a nice looking girl whom she liked and she urged her son to marry her, but he refused.

After a while he said to his mother, "I am going to the woods again. I have a cabin there. Some time you will know why I don't marry the girl you have chosen for me."

When he reached the river, he shook the little canoe, as his wife had told him to do. It stretched out, but was not as large as before, for he had no meat to carry. He sat in the canoe and started up the river. When near his cabin, he saw his wife waiting for him and his little boy running around at play.

The husband and wife were very happy again. Another year went by and a second boy was born to them.

Again the woman got her husband ready to carry meat to his mother, she seemed to know that this time he wouldn't come back.

In parting she said to him, "If you marry another woman, you will never see me again, but if you love me and the children you will be true to us and come back. If you are not true, your new wife will soon be sucking her moccasins from hunger, for you will lose your power of killing game."

As before, the man's fame as a hunter brought many good looking girls to ask for him. Again his mother urged him to marry, but he refused and was ready to start for his cabin in the forest when a beautiful girl appeared in the village and came to his mother's house. His mother urged him to marry the girl and he yielded.

The wife in the forest knew what had happened, and she said to her children, "My children, we must go away from here. Your father doesn't love us."

The children were full of play and fun but they were troubled by their mother's tears, for the poor woman was always crying.

After the man had taken a second wife, the meat in his mother's house began to fall away strangely. He could almost see it disappear. Though there was a good supply when the woman came, in a few days but little was left. He went hunting, but couldn't kill anything, not even a rabbit. He went day after day; always the same luck— his power was gone.

One day when the man came home, he found his wife sucking her moccasins, she was so hungry. He cried and sobbed. "This is my punishment," thought he. "She warned me that this would happen if I were untrue to her." Right away he decided to go to his first wife and her children and never leave them again; and he started, without saying a word to his young wife or his mother.

When he reached his cabin in the forest, he found it covered with snow, not a single footprint was to be seen. He went in. The cabin was empty, but the children's moccasins were there and the sight of them made the father very sad. As he was hungry he looked around for food. Near the fireplace he saw three little mounds of ashes, the second smaller than the first, the third smaller than the second. He sat down and wondered what the mounds could mean, for he knew they had been made by his wife as a sign for him should he ever come to the cabin.

At last he made up his mind that he had three children, and he determined to find them.

"My boys," thought he, "are playful and as they followed their mother they must have hacked the trees."

When the mother and her children were starting away, the elder boy said, "We will mark the trail so if our father ever thinks of us and comes back he can follow us."

The woman said, "You musn't do that, your father will

not come back. He has another wife and will never think of his children in the forest.''

But, as they traveled along and played by the way, the boys hacked trees and shot arrows, and now their father was able to track them.

He found that after a day's journey his wife had camped. He saw the ashes of a fire and on a tree nearby four pairs of moccasins. He made a bundle of the moccasins and the next morning when he started off he carried the bundle on his arm.

Again he walked all day and again he found the ashes of a fire and found four pairs of moccasins. He was without food and was tired, but the next morning he traveled on. Toward night, as before, he found the ashes of a fire, and found four pairs of moccasins. He always put the moccasins in his bundle.

About noon the next day he saw, in the distance, a smoke, as from a cabin. He hurried on and as he came near the cabin he saw two boys playing, running around and shooting. They saw him and went into the cabin to tell their mother that a man was coming. She looked out, recognized her husband, and told the boys to stay inside and keep away from the man.

The man didn't know that the children were his own. He supposed they belonged to some one who lived in the cabin. As he was hungry he decided to go in and ask for food. As he entered the woman turned her back but the elder boy knew his father and running to him put his hand on his knee. The father didn't recognize the child so he gently pushed his hand away. The woman turned and saw the act.

''There,'' said she, ''I told you to keep away from him, that he didn't love you.''

Now the man recognized his wife and he begged her to forgive him. He was so earnest and begged so hard that the woman forgave him and brought to him his little daughter whom he had never seen.

Ever afterward the man was true to his wife, who, though she looked exactly like a woman, was of the Moose family. He never again left his home in the forest, and he and his family were happy.

THE ADVENTURES OF GÁNYAGE GOWA

Characters

GÁNYAGE GOWA ....Diver (A Duck)
HÓNGÂK ....Canada Goose
DZAINOS GOWA ....Blue Lizard
DÍ'SDIS ....Woodpecker
DAGWANOE^{n}YENT ..Cyclone or Whirlwind (Big Head)
DZÓTHÁWENDO^n ....Humming Bird
GASYONDETHA ....Meteor
DJEONYAIK .... Robin
DÁDAHWÂT ....White Beaver
HÁNI SHEONO^n .... Muck-worm
ONÓQGO^{n}T GOWA ....Bumble Bee
GANE^{n}ITHA ....Corn Beetle
GENO^{n}SKWA ....Stone Coats (Cold and Frost)
GWI'YEE ....The Phebe Bird
SKADA'GÉA ....In-the-Mist (A Bird)
GÉHA ....Wind
NYAGWAIHE ....The Ancient of Bears
SIGWEONT ....Rattlesnake

G ÁNYAGE GOWA (Diver, a duck) lived by a lake.
One morning he went out in his bark canoe to fish,
but finding no fish he went home and put away his canoe.
Soon afterward he said, "Well, I must go somewhere.
I am tired of staying here," and he walked along the shore

457

till he came near the end of the lake and saw a house. He went to the house and finding no one there and plenty of meat, he ate what meat he wanted and was starting off when he saw a man coming from the lake, with a big load on his back. This old man was I'onwᴇ (Wild Duck).

The two met and greeted each other.

"I came to visit you," said Diver, "I have been in your house."

"Well, come back with me," said Duck.

"No, I must go on."

"Come again, then," said Duck.

Diver swam across the lake and keeping along the bank soon saw another house. Going near he looked in through a crack and saw a large family; a man and woman and their children. He stood around a while then went in.

The man, who was of the Hóɴɢâᴋ people (Canada Goose), greeted him and asked, "Where did you come from?"

"From the other side of the lake," said Diver.

"What did you come for?"

"To see the place. It is pleasant here."

"How far are you going?"

"Around the lake."

The two men became friends and after a while, Goose said, "I will go with you."

"Very well," answered Diver, and they walked along the shore. At midday they came to the mouth of a river and Diver asked, "How can we cross this wide river?"

"We can swim, if you know how," said Duck.

"I do," answered Diver.

They swam across, then walked on till they saw a rock, then many rocks. The path grew narrower and narrower, Goose was ahead, Diver picked up a stone, and, tying a bark string around it, hung the stone on his friend's back without the man's knowing it. He couldn't walk now, kept slipping back.

Diver said, "Come on! I'm in a hurry, I want to get home before dark."

"Then let go of me, don't pull me back."

"I am not pulling you back, I'll go ahead if you want me to. Wait, I will pass you."

When Diver was ahead he said, "Now, come on!"

Goose couldn't walk fast and Diver left him. The trail grew narrow till at last there was none. The name of the place was HEUSDEO'ON (Rocks go to the water).

"I must turn back," thought Diver. "I can't get by these rocks."

There was not room to turn around, so he tried to walk backwards. After a few steps he slipped into the water and began to swim. When past the rocks he came out and walked again. It was nearly sundown and he asked in his mind, "When will I get home?"

Soon it was so dark that he couldn't travel, so, finding a hollow tree, he crawled into it. Not long afterward he heard footsteps on the dry leaves. The sound stopped near the tree. Diver kept very still.

A voice asked, "Are you sleeping in this tree?"

"I am," answered Diver.

"I want you to come out and talk with me."

Diver crawled out and there stood Goose, who asked, "Do you know how angry I am?"

"Why are you angry?" asked Diver. "I urged you to come along, but you wouldn't."

"You did something to stop me. Look at my back."

The flesh was off where the stone had hung.

Goose caught hold of Diver and began to strike him. Diver didn't want to fight. He pulled away and ran, but Goose overtook him and again began to strike. Diver was angry now.

The two fought till dark the next day, then Diver said, "Let us rest a while."

"Very well," said Goose, "You can stay here, I will be back to-morrow."

As soon as Goose was out of sight, Diver ran off. He came to a river and thought, "I will swim across," but the water ran too swiftly. He was carried down stream and into rough water where he couldn't help himself. In the river there was a large rock. Diver was driven against it, and he thought, "Now I am going to die," but after struggling a while, he drew himself out of the water on to the rock.

In the morning Goose went back to the hollow tree and

not finding Diver tracked him to the river, and saying, "I'll catch him!" he sprang into the water and tried to swim, but the water was too swift. It swept him to the rock where Diver was.

"I am going to die now," said Goose.

Diver heard someone talking and when he saw who it was he was frightened. He jumped into the water, and, after struggling a long time, reached land.

Goose was drowned. His body floated to the bank. Diver saw it and said in his mind, "Oh, there is my friend! Did he think he could kill me? Didn't he know that I had more power than he had?"

Diver traveled on and soon reached home. That night he dreamed that he was on a trail going toward the West when, in a large opening in the forest, he saw a NYAG-WAIHE coming from the southwest, and he thought, "I am going to die; that creature will kill me." He kept his face toward his enemy and walked backward to get away. Soon, from the northwest came Blue Lizard. Diver went backward and backward as fast as he could; Bear and Lizard met and began to fight. Diver watched them, wondering which one would conquer. As they fought they came near him. Again he went backward, went till he fell into a hole in the ground. Bear and Lizard fell on to him. Screaming, "Hurry up! Help me! I am going to die," Diver woke up and found himself alone. His blanket was wrapped tight around his body and he was rolling on the floor.

"What a bad dream I've had," said he to himself.

He fell asleep again and again he dreamed of Bear and Lizard, but this time they were in the forest and belonged to him. He made them stand near each other, put a stick across them, sat on it and told them to go toward the West. They reached the end of the earth very quickly. Diver sprang down, and saying, "Stay here!" he went South till he came to a house. In the house was a nice looking old man.

"I have come to see you," said Diver, "I am traveling around the world."

"Where did you come from?" asked the old man.

"I came from Great Lake."

"Why do you travel?"

"Oh, to see the world and find out what kind of people are living in it."

"What is your name?"

"Diver. What is yours?"

"My name is DzÓthÁwendo^{n} (Humming Bird). My master lives near here, you must see him before you visit me."

Going in the direction pointed out, Diver came to a house standing on a high rock. He stood by the rock, and thought, "How can I get up there?" Then he saw a narrow ledge running around and around and following it he came to the house. In the house an old man was sitting by a fire.

Diver greeted him and he asked, "Why did you come here?"

"To see the world."

"Where did you come from?"

"From Great Lake."

"What is your name?"

"Diver. What is yours?"

"I am Dagwanoe^{n}yent" (Whirlwind).

"Will you let me visit you?" asked Diver.

"You can stay here as long as you like."

One morning Whirlwind asked, "Don't you want to go and see my servant?"

"I would like to," answered Diver.

They were soon at Humming Bird's house. They went in, but he was not there.

Whirlwind said, "My servant is not here. He must have gone to the southern end of the world. A very cross people live there. He is trying to subdue them, make them peaceful. You must go home now. Something will come and chase you if you are here at midday."

Diver started, but he hadn't gone far when he saw White Beaver coming. He tried to hide, but could find no place. He tried so hard that he woke up.

He felt sad and worried over his dreams. He was hungry, and he said to himself, "I will get my canoe and try to catch a few fish."

He went far out looking for fish. Seeing a large trout

he jumped after it, but it disappeared; he saw another, jumped again, no fish. Then he looked around carefully and found there was a fish on the right side of the canoe and its shadow was down in the water.

He caught the fish, ate it, and started for home, but he was far out on the lake and didn't know which way to go. He rowed very fast, in the right direction, as he supposed. He reached the shore but saw no house. Leaving his canoe he walked toward home, as he thought.

He walked till night, then came to a hut in the woods. Going near he stopped and listened.

There was a man in the hut and he was saying, "I know how to get power, I can teach anyone who comes here, I know the whole world. I can give power to anyone who wants it. I wish Diver would come. I would show him how strong I am. He thinks he is the strongest man under the Blue."

Diver thought, "Why does he say that? Doesn't he know how strong I am?"

He listened again, GASYONDETHA (Meteor) was the old man and he said, "I am the swiftest runner and the swiftest flyer. I can make light go through the world, I have greater strength than any man. The Geese people tried to chase me; I killed them all, I am the man, who, many years ago, was made chief of all the people under the Blue." He alluded to a council held by Humming Bird and other chiefs.

"I would kill that man if he chased me," thought Diver. "He must be crazy. He talks to himself all the time."

Diver went into the house and said, "You are talking about me."

"No, I am not."

"I will go, then, I thought you were saying things about me."

Diver went outside, picked up two large stones and striking them together, said, "I'll do this way by that man if he follows me."

Meteor came out and asked, "What did you say?"

"I said that you are the best friend I have in the world."

"What did you say about the stones?"

"I said that when my friend traveled he had to carry

these stones and if he went into the water he had to throw them."

Meteor half believed the man and he went into the house. Diver laughed, and thought, "Oh, he is a fool. He believes what I say." He went into the house again.

"Why do you come here?" asked Meteor. "Why don't you go home?"

"I want to stay till to-morrow morning."

"I don't want such a man as you are around."

"I'll not bother you."

"Go away, I don't like you. You are mean."

"I am not mean. I will be quiet."

"Well, stay, but you mustn't talk to me."

When night came, Meteor took his pipe and sitting down by the fire, put coals into it and began to puff.

"Does it taste good?" asked Diver.

Meteor didn't answer.

Soon Diver said, "How the smoke rolls around!"

Meteor was angry and screamed, "Get out of this hut! I don't want you here."

"You said that I could stay till morning."

"Didn't I tell you not to talk?"

"I'll be quiet. Don't put me out."

Meteor was silent.

Diver laughed. After a while he said, "I want to ask a question, 'What is this world made of?'"

Meteor turned around, he was cross, but he didn't speak.

Then Diver asked, "Do you believe the old folks who say that Whirlwind is still alive?"

Meteor didn't speak, he only turned and looked at Diver, then turned back and smoked.

"Do you believe that Wind goes everywhere?" asked Diver.

"I'll throw you out!" screamed Meteor. "I told you not to talk to me."

"Don't throw me out," begged Diver. "I am going to be quiet now."

Meteor sat down.

After a while Diver asked, "Do you believe old folks who say that Híno' makes rain?"

No answer.

"Do you believe persons who say that trouble comes to those who pay no heed to what is told them?"

Meteor looked at Diver, but didn't answer.

"Do you believe old folks who say that water runs day and night?"

Meteor caught up a club and began to strike Diver, who begged hard and promised to be quiet.

"No, get out! I won't have you here!" cried Meteor.

Diver begged still harder. Meteor stopped striking and was calm again. Diver laughed and said to himself, "Whenever I say anything, people lose their anger."

In the middle of the night Diver spoke again. Meteor sprang up. He was very angry.

"Don't be angry," said Diver, "I only want to know things."

"Go to sleep!" said Meteor, "I don't want to talk."

Diver was silent for a little while, then he spoke again. Meteor sprang up.

"Now go!" cried he, "I don't like you."

Diver began to beg, but Meteor seized him by the hair and threw him out of the house.

"Oh, let me in," begged Diver. "I'll stop talking."

"Go away, or I will kill you," said Meteor.

"That is a bad man. I wish that I had power enough to make Wind blow down his house," thought Diver, but he started off. Soon he heard someone coming, looking back and seeing Meteor he crawled into a hollow tree. Meteor knew where Diver was but to fool him he went back a little and hid.

"That is the kind of man I am," said Diver. "He didn't see me," and coming out of the tree he started on. Meteor followed again and overtaking Diver said, "Now I have you and I am going to kill you."

"No, no," cried Diver, "I don't want to bother you."

"Yes, you do."

They began to dispute.

"I want to ask you a question," said Meteor, "How can you make Wind blow down my house?"

"I don't know."

"Why did you ask, what will you do if Wind blows down your house?"

"I didn't ask that, I said there was wind around the lake."

"Do you believe that I can kill you?" asked Meteor.

"Yes, yes," cried Diver, and he kept backing off.

"I am going to kill you now."

"What have I done?"

"You have told lies," said Meteor—but he turned to go away.

"This is the kind of man I am," boasted Diver, laughing.

Meteor heard what he said and coming back, quickly seized and shook him till he cried, "Oh, my friend, don't kill me, I am always on your side."

"I won't stop till I kill you," said Meteor, then he thought, "Why do I kill this man?" and he let Diver get up from the ground where he had thrown him.

"This is the kind of man I am," boasted Diver, laughing.

Now Meteor was terribly angry. He caught Diver and said as he threw him, "Go far West and never come back!"

Diver, as he went through the air, rolled over and over. At last he came down just where the sun sets.

As he fell he said, "I wonder where Meteor is."

Meteor, though far away, heard him and flying through the air came where he was and asked, "What were you saying?"

"I was saying what a nice place this is."

Meteor made no answer.

Diver traveled North till he saw a high rock and on the rock a house. Then he thought, "This is the place I dreamed about." He went into a nearby cabin and found an old man there.

The man greeted him, and asked, "Where did you come from?"

"From Great Lake."

"Why did you come here?"

"I was lonely at home."

"What is your name?"

"Diver. What is yours?"

"Humming Bird."

"Can I stay here?"

"No, you must go first to my master."

"Where does he live?"

"His house is on a great rock near here."

Diver climbed up to the house on the rock and looking in saw an old man sitting by the fire. "That is the same man who threw me West," thought he.

The man turned, looked at Diver, and asked, "Who are you?"

"I am Diver. Who are you?"

"I am Whirlwind."

"Will you let me stay with you a few days?"

"You can stay as long as you like, I am glad to have someone in the house, I am lonely."

One morning Whirlwind asked, "Will you go and see my servant?"

"I will go," said Diver.

They went to Humming Bird's house. Whirlwind looked around and said, "He isn't here, he must have gone to the end of the world. Cross people live there. He is going to try and make them good. If they don't obey him, I shall go and eat them up."

"How far is it from here?"

"You couldn't get there in fifty Winters."

"Then there will be a hundred Winters before your servant comes back."

"Oh, no," said Whirlwind, "my servant travels very fast. He is in a place as soon as he thinks of it."

"I don't believe that," said Diver.

"Get away from here!" screamed Whirlwind. "People are coming to kill you."

Diver started off, but he hadn't gone far when White Beaver overtook him and began to strike him.

"Don't kill me," begged Diver, "I'm not strong enough to fight with you. Don't kill me."

But Beaver didn't listen to his begging. He killed him, and went on. Soon he met a man, greeted him and asked, "Where are you going?"

"To see a man who is dead."

"What is your name?"

"Robin."

"What will you do when you get there?"

"I don't know."

When Robin came to where Diver lay, he dug roots of

different kinds and, making a powder of them, rubbed the powder over the body, and soon Diver was alive again. Robin was a great doctor.

"This is the kind of man I am," said Diver. "Where is White Beaver?"

"Don't speak of him," said Robin, "he must be near."

Diver wouldn't stop boasting and threatening, so Robin went off and left him.

"I'll go back to Whirlwind's house," said Diver.

When Whirlwind saw him he laughed and said, "A man came here to tell me you were dead."

"I shall not die," said Diver. "Haven't you heard old folks say that if $SHODIO^nSKO^n$ died he would soon come to life?"

"Yes. Is that why you came to life?"

"It is."

"Well, I want you to go where the cross people live. Old men have told me that $SHODIO^nSKO^n$ can make cross people quiet."

"I will go," said Diver. When he came down from the rock where Whirlwind's house was, he took hold of the rock and tried to turn it over.

"That must be my friend," thought Whirlwind when he felt the house move.

Diver kept at work and at last over went the rock.

The old man was hurt but he sprang up, and cried, "Oh, my dear friend, I must kill you now."

He tried to catch Diver but his head was dizzy and he fell.

Diver, seeing the old man on the ground with blood coming out of his head, laughed and said, "What did he think? Didn't he know that I was stronger than he was?" He rolled the rock on to the old man and went along.

When he came to the place where the cross people lived he stood near their great earth house and thought, "I'll roll this house over." And, taking hold of one end of it, he lifted it up. People came running out and when they saw a man holding up one end of their house they began to fight him. Diver ran away as fast as he could; the crowd ran after him, but he escaped.

"That's the kind of man I am," boasted he.

He walked till almost dark, then came to a cliff in which there was a large opening. "Someone lives in there," thought he, "I'll go in and see who it is." At first he saw only one man, then he saw another, and another till he counted seven.

"What are you doing in this cliff?" asked he.

"Why do you ask?"

"I go around to make people quiet and happy," said Diver.

"We don't want you here"—these men were the seven Rattlesnake brothers.

"I am going," said Diver.

While leaving the cliff, he saw a house and heard a thumping inside. Looking through a crack he saw an old man, who was pounding something into a thin piece of wood. Soon he put the wooden thing over his face.

"I have never seen such a man as this one," thought Diver. "He is making a mask. I'll take the roof off of his house and then make rain come." Getting on to the hut he threw off the roof.

Old man Woodpecker didn't know the roof was off. Diver went to a spring nearby and shook his wings so furiously that water flew high and came down over where the man sat.

"My house is getting old," thought Woodpecker. "Rain comes in. I'll sit where it is dry."

He stood up and looked around but he couldn't see a dry place. "I'll get someone to cover my house," said he, and leaving his work he started. He heard a noise at the spring and saw a man standing in the water.

"What are you doing there?" asked he.

"I am trying to fish," answered Diver. "When I get the water all out it will be easy."

"That is my spring," said the old man. "If you don't get out of it, I will kill you."

"I am not afraid of you. You are old and weak."

"I can kill you quickly," said Woodpecker.

"You can't, you are too old."

But Diver was afraid. He left the spring. He traveled a long time. One morning he came to a house and looking in saw an old man sitting by a fire. This man was Corn Beetle.

Soon the old man said, "Come in, my nephew, why do you stay outside? If you are here to visit me, come in."

"I have found my uncle," thought Diver, "I'll go in, he wants me."

He went in and asked, "Uncle, what do you want?"

"I have a nice game," said the old man, "that I play when anyone comes to visit me. We wager heads. I have canoes to race with."

"Very well," said Diver, "that is a game I used to play."

The old man brought out two white flint canoes and said, "Take your choice."

Diver looked the canoes over and chose the old one.

"That is the worst one," said the old man. "That canoe can't help you. It will tip over."

It was the canoe that had the greatest power and the old man wanted it himself.

They went to the lake, put their canoes down at the edge of the water and each man sat in his own canoe.

"*Ha one*!" said the old man and the two canoes started.

Diver was soon far ahead, when he reached the end of the lake he asked in his mind, "Where is my uncle?"

After a long time he saw the old man coming. When he pulled his canoe onto the sand, he said, "Let us rest till to-morrow."

Diver pretended to be asleep.

"He is asleep," said the old man to himself.

He pushed the old canoe into the water, sat in it, and said, "Carry me to where the sun goes down." The canoe rushed through the air.

Diver got up and looked at his uncle's canoe, then he sat in it, and said, "I want you to go where my uncle has gone."

He struck the canoe with a white flint stone; it became alive and went very fast, faster than the canoe the uncle had taken. While going through the air Diver sang and his song said, "We are following my uncle's trail. We are following my uncle's trail."

Soon he saw a small, dark speck ahead. It grew larger

and larger, but Diver did not overtake the old man. He got to where the sun goes down, but the old man was there first.

"You cheated me," said Diver. "Now I am going to cut off your head."

"I haven't cheated you, I tried to waken you."

"Why did you come so far?" asked Diver.

"I came to see where the sun goes."

"I think that you tried to run away from me. Now we will go back to the end of the lake."

They were soon back. Then Diver said, "We will sleep a while," but he didn't sleep; he watched the old man till morning.

Then they got into the canoes and started for the old man's home. Diver was there first. When the old man came, Diver took a basswood knife and cut off his head.

Diver walked along till he came to a hemlock forest. While standing among the trees he heard a man say *"Hiyi! Hiyi!"* and looking up saw a man sitting on the limb of a tree.

"I will give you a name," said Diver, "I'll call you *Hiyi*." The man laughed, he was glad to have a name.

After a time Diver came to a river with rocky banks, and, going down to the edge of the water, he saw an ugly looking man. The man greeted him and said, "I am glad you have come. I am hungry. I will eat you."

"Don't kill me," begged Diver, "I'm not good to eat. Do you believe HÁNI SHEONO^n is alive?"

"Yes," said the old man.

"He is dead," said Diver. "He was killed last night."

The old man began to cry aloud, cried till many of his people heard him and came to see why he cried.

"I have heard that HÁNI SHEONO^n (Muck-worm) is dead," said the old man.

Then all began to cry.

"Why do you cry?" asked Diver. "You are free now. You should be glad. I will give you a name, I will call you GENO^{n}SKWA (Cold and Frost). You can't overtake me."

They were angry and followed him. He began to fly. He went up and up till he reached the clouds. He saw people there, and thought, "Who can be living here, I never heard that there were people up in the clouds." Soon he met a man wearing beautiful downy clothes.

The man greeted Diver and asked, "Where are you from?"

"From down below."

"How did you get here?"

"Through the air. I want to give you a name, I will call you SKADAGÉA (In-the-Mist). This is a strange place up here."

"We can see all over the world," said the stranger. "Look straight down."

Diver looked. It didn't seem far, but he could see all over the world.

"Do you know the man who lives by that lake down there?" asked Diver. "He is a mean man."

"You mustn't bother that man," said In-the-Mist, "he is a great power. He is Meteor. We are afraid of him. You must go now, GÉHA (Wind) is coming. He will kill you if you stay here."

Diver came to the earth and looking around, saw a man coming out of the ground.

"Do you live in the ground?" asked Diver.

"I've always lived there," answered the man. "Don't bother me."

"Do you know where Muck-worm's home is?"

"I know. It is in the ground, that is why I live in the ground."

"Do you think you have as much power as he has?" asked Diver.

"I have not," said the man.

"Have you a name?"

"I don't want one."

"I will call you Bumble-bee."

The man hung his head, then raised it and asked, "Can you call me by another name?"

"No, it's the name that suits you best. You are bad looking."

The man cried. He was Winged Ant and he didn't want to be changed.

Diver traveled on till he came to Meteor's house. Meteor

was asleep but he woke up and began to sing, "Where is my friend Diver? Where is my friend Diver? I want to see him."

"Why does he sing about me?" thought Diver, and taking up a mallet he began hitting the old man on the head.

"I think gnats are biting me," said Meteor. He turned over, saw Diver and asked, "What are you doing? Why do you hit me?"

"I haven't hit you. I called you 'Grandfather.' Let us talk and be friends."

"Very well, sit down at the other end of the fire."

The two men talked a long time, disputed as they did before.

At last Diver asked, "What can kill you?"

"A flag stalk that grows in a swamp. If a man were to strike with one of those stalks, it would kill me."

Diver went to a swamp and came back with a flag stalk. He struck Meteor and ran off, thinking he had killed him. Soon he came to a house built on the side of a high rock and he wondered how he could throw it over. As he stood thinking a man greeted him.

"Do you live in that house up there?" asked Diver.

"I live there," said the man. "When I talk, everyone hears me."

"Let me hear you," said Diver.

The man called out "*Wia'a'*" (the call of the Phebe bird).

"That is enough," said Diver. "I am traveling and giving names. Hereafter whoever speaks of you will call you *Gwi'yee* (the Phebe bird). You will be quiet and will not chase people." (This is why the Phebe bird never chases other birds, or people.)

The next morning, Diver thought he would go and see if Meteor was dead.

When near the house he heard singing and the song said, "I will kill Diver as soon as I see him."

The old man stopped singing and began to talk, to say, "My grandson means to kill me."

"I will kill him and burn his house," thought Diver, and piling up brush he set it on fire.

"I think my house is burning," said Meteor. "My grandson is doing this."

He was very angry. He sprang through the fire, and the first thing Diver knew the old man stood near him.

"You have set my house on fire," cried Meteor.

"No I haven't. I saw it burning and came to put out the fire."

The old man didn't believe him. He seized him and pounded him to death. Then Meteor whooped and called out, "This is the kind of man I am. I am the most powerful man under the Blue!"

People all over the world heard him and said, "Diver is dead. Meteor has killed him."

TURKEY'S BROTHER GOES IN SEARCH OF OF A WIFE

Characters

GASYONDETHA ....Meteor
OTSOON ....Turkey
TÉQDOOⁿHUISHĔ, Woodchuck Leggings (the Deceiver)

A N old man had two nephews: one, perhaps, fifteen or sixteen, the other two or three years old. The three lived together in a bark house in the woods.

When the uncle went hunting, the elder brother stayed at home. When the young man was hunting, the uncle was at home, for the younger boy was too small to be left alone.

One day the elder brother said, "Uncle, if you will kill a turkey, I will make a coat for my little brother to wear."

"How can you do that?" asked the uncle.

"Oh, I will skin the turkey and make a feather coat."

The next day the uncle brought home a large, white turkey-gobbler. The young man took the skin off from head, legs and body, in one piece. Then he rubbed the skin and made it soft and when it was ready he put it on the little boy. It fitted him nicely, for he was the same size as the turkey. He put his feet into the skin of the legs and his arms into the wings, and then went around hunting for beechnuts. He could fly onto trees and he looked exactly like a turkey so they called him OTSOON (Turkey).

The uncle and nephews lived together till the elder

474

nephew was old enough to marry. Then the uncle said to him, "I am tired of cooking, I want to eat food cooked by a woman. You are old enough to marry. The chief of a village far from here has three daughters. You can get one of them for the asking."

"Very well, I will go and ask for her," said the young man and he began to get ready.

Turkey wanted to go too, but his brother said, "You must stay at home with our uncle. How can we leave him alone?"

"I don't want to stay here," said Turkey, "I want to go with you."

No matter how the brother and uncle coaxed or scolded Turkey insisted, and at last they told him he could go.

"Now, Nephew," said the uncle, "You must have an outfit. They must see that you are a great man, I will give you what I have."

He brought a coat of wild-cat skin and put it on the young man, then, standing back and looking at him, he said, "That is not good enough."

He brought a lynx-skin; that didn't please him.

"Oh," said he, "I have another coat; that's the one for you."

He brought a *gasyondetha* skin coat with the head for a cap, whenever the wearer was angry the head would roar. In the cap he put two loon feathers that sang all the time.

"This will do!" said the old man. "Now they will see you as you are."

He gave the young man beautiful moccasins, with leggings to match, and a pouch of fisher-skin, whenever an enemy came near the fisher would snap at him and bite him. In the pouch was a pipe. The bowl of the pipe was a bull frog, the stem a water snake. When the young man began to smoke the bull frog croaked and the snake wriggled and tried to swallow the frog.

The uncle said, "Now, my Nephew, go straight toward the West. It is a long journey. We are the only ones left of our nation. All of our people have been captured and carried off, that is why you must go so far for a wife. When half way to the chief's village, you will see a spring on one side of the trail. Don't stop there or touch the water. Farther on, about half way between the spring and the chief's house, you will meet an old man. He is a great thief. Don't stop with him or listen to him."

The brothers set out at sunrise and at midday they came to the spring, though it was a year's journey for an ordinary person. As soon as the elder brother saw the spring he was thirsty and wanted to drink, but Turkey said, "Our uncle told us not to touch that water."

They were passing the spring when the elder brother looked again at the water and this time he was so thirsty that Turkey couldn't keep him from drinking. Lying down he had just touched the water with his lips when something caught him by the hair and pulled him into the spring, but he grasped the creature and, struggling hard, got out of the water bringing the creature with him. It was not a man, though it looked something like one.

It gasped and begged, "Oh, Grandson, throw me back! Oh, Grandson, throw me back!"

"No, you can stay where you are," said the young man. He lay down again to drink and a second creature caught him; he pulled that one out.

"Oh, Grandson," it gasped, "throw me back! Throw me back!"

A third time he lay down to drink and this time he was undisturbed. The water was sweet and cool. When he had finished drinking, he killed the two creatures. With Turkey's help he gathered all the dry sticks to be found, put the creatures on the pile and burned them to ashes, then the two traveled on. In the middle of the afternoon they came to a place where there were many tall trees and around one of them an old man was running as fast as he could go.

When he saw the young man he called to him, "Oh, my Grandson, shoot! Look, such a nice fat coon! Shoot him for me!"

He begged so hard that the young man shot at the coon. The arrow stuck in its body and the coon ran into a hole in the tree, as the young man thought.

"Oh, we must find the coon," said the old man, "You mustn't lose your arrow. Go into the hole and pull him

out, but take off your clothes so as not to spoil them.
You needn't be afraid, I won't touch them. I am going
in too."

The young man took off his coat, leggings and moccasins
and put them on the ground, then climbed the tree, the
old man following him. When they came to the hole, the
young man looked into it and right at hand, as he thought,
saw the coon. He reached in to pull the arrow out, but that
instant the old man pushed him and down he went through
the hollow tree to the very bottom. There was no coon
in the tree.

The old man slipped to the ground, put on the young
man's coat, leggings and moccasins, and taking his pouch
and bow and arrows started off westward, toward the
chief's village.

Turkey cried a long time for his brother, then he flew
on to a tree and sat there moaning.

The elder brother thought, "Now I am in trouble. My
uncle told me not to listen to that old man."

There was no way of getting out of the hole, for the
sides were as smooth as ice. On the ground, at the bottom,
were the bones of people, who had been thrown in by the
old man.

Toward morning the young man remembered that in
his boyhood a great spider had appeared to him in a dream,
and said, "If ever you get into trouble I will help you."

"Oh, Spider!" cried he, "Come and help me now."

That minute a great spider came to the opening and
began to make a web. When the web reached the bottom
of the hole the spider called out, "Now climb!"

The young man started but wasn't half way up when
the web broke.

"Oh, Spider," moaned he, "You are not strong enough
to help me." Then he remembered that in his boyhood
a black snake had appeared to him in a dream and had
promised to help him if ever he were in trouble.

"Oh, Black Snake," cried he, "help me now."

Straightway a black snake looked into the hole, then it
slipped its body down till the end of it reached the ground.
The young man took hold of it. The snake coiled itself
up, brought him to the top, then disappeared.

When Turkey saw his brother he was glad. He flew to the ground, and said, "Now, we must go home."

"No," said the young man, "We must go to the chief's village. I will put on the old man's clothes."

As soon as he had on the stiff leggings, the torn moccasins and the dirty blanket, his voice grew weak and he began to cough, and right away he looked and felt like an old man.

The thief meanwhile felt young and strong and could travel fast. In front of the chief's village was a broad river. When the thief came to it he shouted for some one to ferry him across.

The chief's eldest daughter rowed over in a canoe and seeing a fine looking man, she asked, "Where did you come from, and where are you going?"

"I came from the East. I am going to the chief's house, I am looking for a wife, and I have heard that he has three daughters."

"I am his eldest daughter," said the girl, "I think you would suit me."

"Very well," answered the thief.

"Then you are my husband," said the girl.

She led him to her father's house and showing him a couch covered with beautiful skins, said, "That is your place."

The next evening Turkey and his brother came to the river. The old man shouted for somebody to come and row them over, but his voice was so weak and thin that for a long time he wasn't heard.

At last some one on the opposite bank said, "An old man and a turkey want to cross the river."

The chief's youngest daughter got her canoe and went over. She asked the old man who he was and where he came from.

"I came from the East," said he, "I am looking for a wife."

"Looking for a wife? Why you are too old," said the girl.

"I am young, but maybe I look old. Here is my brother. He is a little boy."

"Did you come from beyond the wizard spring?" asked the girl.

"I did, and I cleared the spring of two strange creatures."

"Did you meet an old man?"

"I did, and that is why I look old; he stole my clothes."

"This is the man we are waiting for," thought the girl, "I'll marry him."

She rowed him across the river, led him to the chief's house and pointing out a couch covered with beautiful skins, said, "That is your place." Above the couch was a smaller one, the girl said, "Your brother can have that place up there."

When the girl's family saw the husband she had chosen they were dissatisfied and tried to persuade the chief to drive him out, but he said, "Let the girl alone, she knows what she is doing."

The husband and wife lived quietly for a number of days, then the husband said, "I am sick, go to your father and ask him for his best bowl."

She brought the bowl and the man filled it with beautiful black wampum.

"Take this wampum to your father," said he, "and say that I give it to him."

"Oh," said the chief when he saw the wampum, "I knew he was a great man. He is the greatest man I have ever heard of. This is beautiful wampum."

When the husband of the eldest sister heard what had happened, he said to his wife, "Ask your father for his best bowl, I am sick."

She brought the bowl, but in place of filling it with wampum he filled it with lizards and foul things.

The chief was angry and said to his daughter, "Go to the river, wash the bowl and scrape it clean."

A few days later the husband of the youngest sister said, "Go and ask your father for his bowl."

She brought the bowl and he filled it with beautiful white wampum.

The chief was delighted, and said, "My son-in-law is a great man; he comes from the Wampum people."

When the thief heard about the white wampum he sent

for the chief's bowl, but again he filled it with lizards and foul things, and again his wife spent a whole day at the river cleaning and scouring the bowl.

Now Wildcat and Fox came to see the youngest sister's husband, for they were his friends. After a while Fox spied Turkey sitting on his shelf over his brother's couch and he said to Wildcat, "That's a nice gobbler up there, can't you get him for us?"

That night Wildcat crawled down the smoke-hole till he could reach Turkey. Turkey was sitting with his eyes wide open. He saw Wildcat and waited till he was near, then he raised his club and struck him such a heavy blow that he fell into the fire, and before he could get out his coat was so singed and burned, that to this day Wildcats have yellow, smoky coats.

Wildcat screamed, "Oh, I've had a fit. I fell into the fire and am burned!"

"You can't have fits here!" said the eldest sister, and jumping up she pushed Wildcat out of the house.

Fox was waiting outside.

"That's not a turkey," said Wildcat, "that's a wizard. He will kill us."

The two hurried off without saying good-bye to their friend.

"Ask your father for his bow and arrows," said the young man to his wife.

She brought them and the next day he killed more deer than had ever been killed in that place. The game was carried to the chief's house and all the people had enough to eat, no man was left without meat, and everybody wondered at the great number of deer killed.

The chief notified the people that there would be a council at daybreak the next morning.

Every one was awake early, except the chief's eldest daughter and her husband; they were sound asleep. While they slept the young man took his coat, leggings, moccasins and pouch from the thief and put them on, then he went to the council.

"Get up," said the mother, shaking her daughter, "your husband must go to the council." Then, glancing at the man, she started back in fright, and cried, "What a looking husband you have!"

As soon as the clothes were gone, the man was old and shrunken, with a face like an owl's.

The young woman woke up and looking at her husband was frightened to see what an ugly old creature he was. She pulled him up, pushed him out of the house, and said, "I won't have you for a husband!"

The thief disappeared and was never seen again.

When the young man went into the council house, he was fine looking and strong. He opened his pouch, took out his pipe, lighted it and began to smoke. The bull frog croaked, the snake wriggled and tried to swallow the frog.

Then all the people said, "We have never seen such a powerful man!"

The young man said to his father-in-law, "Now that I have my clothes, I must go back to my uncle who lives in the East."

"We will go with you," said the chief.

And the people shouted, "We will go too!"

"My brother and I will go ahead," said the young man, and, turning to Turkey he said, "Now, brother, take off your turkey skin and dress as other boys do."

Turkey took off the skin and he looked fine in his new blanket and leggings.

The brothers went home in one day; the chief and his people were a long time on the road. The uncle was glad to see his nephews and to welcome the chief. "This is my story."

THE TWELVE BROTHERS AND THEIR UNCLE, DAGWANOE^{n}YENT

Character

DAGWANOE^{n}YENT ....Whirlwind or Cyclone

ONCE twelve brothers lived together. Everyone knew that these brothers had great power and could do whatever they undertook.

Each morning the twelve started off in different directions to hunt and each evening they came back to the cabin. The eldest of the twelve knew that there were women going around in the world to destroy men and he avoided them.

One day while he was hunting, he saw a red-headed woodpecker tapping on a tree and making a great noise. As he watched the bird, it went around the tree, then went to another tree and around that, then it flew to the ground, became a young woman, and called to him, "Are you not ashamed to point your arrow at a woman? Come and talk to me."

The young man went to her and that was the last he remembered.

The woman carried him to a high rock where there was another woman, who said, "Let his bones drop to the ground!"

The young man's body fell apart, became a heap of bones. Great piles of bones lay around the rock for many men had been brought to the place by the first woman and destroyed by the second.

When night came and their brother did not come home, the eleven said, "Some evil has befallen our brother. He will never come back," and they mourned for him.

After a time the second brother was missing, and he never came back.

While walking along in the forest the young man met two women. They put him to sleep.

Then one said to the other, "We will bury him in the ground. He will stay there till mold covers his face and body, and still he will be alive. We'll leave him there till his brother finds where he is and rescues him."

The ten brothers were greatly frightened. They told their youngest brother, whom they loved much, that he must stay at home, not go roaming around in the forest, for he was young and didn't know the world as well as they did.

A time passed and then one night the third brother was missing. The nine said that he must be dead or he would come home and they mourned for him.

Now three places were empty and the brothers were lonesome and sad.

Time went on till, one after another, ten of the brothers had disappeared, only two were left: the youngest and the one next older.

Then the elder said to his brother, "You must not go into the forest, you must always stay at home where no harm can come to you, for you are the only one I have to depend on when I am old."

"But," said the younger, "Maybe our brothers are captives, maybe they are being tormented by some one, I want to go in search of them."

"You cannot go," said his brother, "You are too young. We have an uncle, who knows everything. Maybe he could bring our brothers back, but he is such a terrible creature that no one can get near him. He wouldn't know that we are his nephews and he would kill us. He lives on a high rock. His long hair has swept the ground around the rock till the ground is as smooth as ice. He has no body, but he has a great head and enormous eyes."

"I must go to this uncle," said the younger man, "and find out where our brothers are."

"If he doesn't tell you, you may travel the whole world and not find them," said his brother.

"What does our uncle live on?"

"He gnaws the bark of hickory trees."

"That is good food. I'll get him plenty of it," said the young man.

He felled the tallest trees he could find and cut out large blocks of bark for his uncle to eat, then he lifted six trees out of the ground by the roots, and said to the trees, "I want you to be small." The trees were small and of each tree he made an arrow. The blunt end of the arrow was the part near the roots.

The elder brother didn't know that the arrows were trees. He was afraid to have his brother go in search of their uncle. He didn't think he could find him and if he did, he thought the old man would kill him.

While the young man was making his arrows, he practised running. One day he thought he heard a groan under his feet. It sounded as though he stepped on a man and hurt him badly. Going back and forth he found the spot the groan seemed to come from. He dug down and came to a living man. The man's face was covered with thick mold and there was no flesh on his body.

The young man carried the skeleton home, and said to his brother, "We have plenty of bear's oil, you must oil this man till he gets his natural size." The man could neither see nor hear.

The next morning the young man started off telling his brother to stay in the house while he was gone, for he should bring his uncle home with him. He ran toward the North till he came to the place his brother had described and saw a terrible Head sitting on a rock. His brother had said, "You must speak first. If the Head speaks first, you will surely die."

The young man's medicine was a mole. He called it, and said, "You must carry me under the ground so the leaves will not rustle. When we are near my uncle, let me out."

He went into the mole and it ran on till near the Head.

When the young man saw his uncle, he was frightened, but he sprang from the mole and with his bow string drawn, cried out, "Uncle, I've come for you!"

He let the arrow fly and as it whizzed through the air it grew to the size of a tree. The tree hit the Head above the eyes. With a loud laugh the Head rolled from the rock and swept along in the air leaving behind it a wide track of fallen trees. It went through the forest as a terrible whirlwind.

The young man was just ahead, running very fast. When his uncle was near he turned and shot another arrow. The arrow became a tree, hit the Head and drove it back a long distance; again the young man was ahead. He shot an arrow whenever he was in danger of being overtaken. Each time the Head was driven back a shorter distance; DAGWANOE^{n}YENT gained on his nephew continually.

While the Head was still a long way off, the elder brother heard a terrible roar and knew that a great whirlwind was coming; he said to himself, "My brother has found our uncle and he will be here soon." He opened the skin-doors,—there was a door at each end of the house, and put a stone pounder against each door. Then he built a big fire.

The younger brother ran into the house, took up a pounder and when his uncle came down at the threshold and rolled in, both brothers began pounding him and they pounded till he rolled to one end of the house and was silent.

Then the younger brother said to him, "I have brought you here, Uncle. Now you must stay with us and tell us where our brothers are."

"I can't stay here," said the Head, "but I will help you and your brothers will come back."

The elder brother had rubbed the mold from the head and face of the dug-up man and had found that he was their brother. DAGWANOE^{n}YENT blew on his nephew and he was sound and well again. Now there were three brothers at home.

At night the Head stayed outside and gnawed the chunks of hickory bark that his nephew had prepared.

After a few days, DAGWANOE^{n}YENT said to his youngest nephew, "I must go home, but first I will take you to the place where your brothers' bones are."

The two started together. The Head, springing high from the ground, made long leaps and didn't stop till it brought the young man to the women on the rock.

As they came to the women, the uncle said, "We must kill these women."

They wanted to make him laugh, but he called out, "Fall and be bones!"

The women were enraged by the words and tried to spit at the old uncle, but he repeated the words and the third time he said them both women rolled off the rock and as they fell their bones made a noise like the pouring out of many shells.

"Scatter their bones!" said the Head.

The young man gathered the bones and threw them in every direction, saying, "Become, such and such, birds."

They became the birds he mentioned, horned owls, hawks, crows and woodpeckers, and disappeared in the air.

"Now," said the Head, "Gather up the bones that are here in piles and make as many bodies as you can, giving each body its own bones. While you are doing this, I'll go off a long distance and come back straight over the forest. When you hear the roar of wind and see trees falling, cry out to the skeletons, 'Rise up or the trees will fall on you!' They will obey you, I will pass over them and go to my own home. If you want me again, you can come for me."

The young man worked as fast as he could. When all the bones were used, he heard the roar of wind and knew that his uncle was coming. Then he called out, "Rise up or the trees will fall on you!"

DAGWANOEⁿYENT, with a terrible roar, swept over the skeletons and they sprang up, men.

In two of the skeletons bones had been interchanged. One man, who, from the shape of his feet, had been called "Sharp-pointed Moccasins" had but one of his own feet. A second man had the other. Both were cripples. One of these cripples, a man-eater, had been enticed from a long distance. Right away he wanted to begin eating his companions. The young man killed him with one blow. In the crowd were nine of the twelve brothers.

Each man found whatever he had brought with him and all separated. Those who did not know where their homes were went with the brothers, and soon the twelve brothers were together again in their own home.

UNCLE AND NEPHEW

[Told by Henry Jacob]

A N uncle and nephew lived off in a forest. There had been a large family, but all were dead except the two. The uncle and nephew were the last of their race.

One day the uncle said, "My nephew, you have grown to be a large boy. Now you must learn to hunt. You may use the bow and arrows that I used when I was young."

The old man took his bow from the wall and cleaned it, for it was smoky. Then he said, "We will make a trial of shooting."

They went out together and the uncle tried first, shot at a tree a long way off. The nephew made a good shot and the uncle said, "That was well done. You can begin hunting. You must hunt between sunrise and sunset and always keep on the sunny side, never go North."

The boy hadn't been out long when he killed a deer.

When he took it home his uncle thanked him, and said, "We can live now; we have plenty of meat."

He cut up the meat, tied bark strings around the pieces and hung them up to dry.

For a while the boy brought game each day, then it became scarce and he had to go far South before coming upon any animals.

One time when the boy was sitting around in the house, his uncle said, "When I was young I had something to amuse myself with. I will get it for you."

He brought a flute and when he blew on it the flute talked, said, "To-morrow you will kill such and such game."

The boy was greatly pleased, and soon learned to play on the flute. The next morning he started off hunting

487

and sure enough he killed exactly what the flute said he would.

That night, after the boy had rested from hunting, he took his flute, and again it said, "You will kill such and such game to-morrow." Again the boy killed exactly what the flute said.

He began to wonder why he must always go South. At last he made up his mind to go North, and, making a circuit, he was soon north of his uncle's cabin. He found elk tracks, followed them and came to a broad opening and in the opening he saw an elk; he ran after it, ran in a circle, and came out in the opening.

All at once he heard a woman call, "Stop! Stop!" but he ran on full speed, after the elk, and again he came out in the opening.

A second time the woman called, "Stop! Stop! Wait and rest."

Looking around, the boy saw that the woman was sitting on a fallen tree. She called, "Come and sit down. I know you are tired. When you have rested you can chase the elk."

He sat down near her and soon his head was on her knees. The boy had very long hair, so long that he kept it tied up, for when he let it down it swept the ground. Now he tied one of his hairs to a root in the ground. After a while he fell asleep. The woman put him in a basket, swung the basket on to her back and started off on a run, then she rose in the air and ran very fast.

The hair stretched till it could stretch no longer, then it pulled them back to the place they started from.

The woman said to herself, "There is witchcraft about this boy, I will try again."

The boy wakened, again she searched in his hair till he closed his eyes, then she asked, "Are you asleep?"

"I am not asleep," said the boy.

After a while she asked again, "Are you asleep?"

He didn't answer; he was asleep.

The woman put him in the basket, swung it on to her back, ran a while, then rose in the air. When she had gone a long distance she came down by the bank of a river, roused the boy, and asked, "Do you know this place?"

"I know it, my uncle and I used to come here to fish."—
He had never been there; he wanted to deceive the woman.

Again she put him to sleep and again she rose in the
air. When she had gone a long distance she came down
on an island, shook the boy, roused him and asked, "Do
you know this place?"

"I know it, my uncle and I used to come here."

Again she put him to sleep, and again she rose in the
air; this time she carried him to the edge of a ravine that
was so deep that the tops of the tallest trees that grew in it
could not be seen.

She put the basket down on the very edge of the cliff,
turned it over, and the boy went headlong into the ravine.
He fell slowly, for he had power. He came to the ground
unhurt, but he could find no way of escape. The sides
of the ravine were like a wall.

The uncle waited and waited. At last he said to himself, "It is late. Something has happened. My nephew
is not coming home. I must find out what the trouble is."

He took the flute down and saw that the mouth-piece
was bloody. Then he said, "They have beaten my poor
nephew, trouble has come to him." As there wasn't much
blood he thought, "Maybe he will free himself and come
back."

The nephew lay down among the rocks in the deep, blind
ravine and tried to sleep, but could not. All at once he
heard a great bird coming. As it swept past him, it caught
a mouthful of flesh out of his arm. He spat on his arm,
rubbed and cured it. When the bird had been gone a
while, he heard it coming again, and as it flew past, it took
a second bite out of his arm. He spat on the arm, rubbed
and cured it.

When daylight came the boy stood up and looking
around saw bones and skeletons on every side, and one man
just alive. He said to himself, "I suppose I shall die here
just as these men have died."

That morning the uncle looked at the flute and seeing
that there was more blood on it than before, he gave up
his nephew as lost. In despair he sat down and cried,
meanwhile scattering ashes over his head and shoulders.

The second night the bird flew past twice, each time

taking a piece of flesh out of the boy's arm. When the bird had gone, the boy fell asleep and dreamed.

In his dream he heard an old woman's voice say, "Grandson, I have come to help you, you think you are going to die, but you are not. Just at sunrise you will vomit. If you vomit up something that looks like a hemlock leaf you may know that you are going to escape from here. Pick up the leaf, stick it in the ground and sing. As you sing the leaf will become a tree. Sit on one of the limbs and keep on singing. The tree will grow till it reaches the top of the cliff, then jump off and run."

Just at sunrise the next morning the boy vomited as the woman of the dream had said he would, and he found a little hemlock leaf. He stuck the leaf in the ground near the wall of the ravine and began to sing. The leaf became a tree, and as the boy sang the tree grew higher and higher. He didn't sit on a limb of the tree, but stayed below and sang till the tree was higher than the top of the cliff, then he gathered all the skeletons and bones into a pile and going to a great hickory tree which stood near he pushed it, and called out, "Rise up and run or the tree will fall on you!"

The bones became living men and the men sprang up and ran away from the tree. Two of them had unequal legs, each had a leg that belonged to the other.

The boy said to the crowd, "Now you must follow me up this tree to the bank above. You must not look back, if you do you will fall."

The limbs of the tree were near together, like a ladder, and the men climbed easily.

The two men with one leg short and one leg long were behind. After climbing quite a distance one of them looked back to see how high up he was. Right away he turned to bones and the bones, rattling through the limbs of the tree, fell to the ground.

Now there was but one man with uneven legs. He went on till near the top of the cliff, then he looked back. Right away he turned to bones and the bones, rattling through the branches of the tree, fell to the ground.

When the boy was some distance away from the cliff, he said to the men who were with him, "Stay here while

I go and bring the woman, who has done all this mischief. She has a mother, who is a wizard. We will punish them both."

He started off and hadn't gone far when he came to the house of the woman who had deceived him. He sat down by her, and said, "I have come!"

Soon her mother came in, and said, "I am glad that my son-in-law has come."

That night the young man heard the old woman groaning. She crawled out of bed on her hands and knees and rolled around on the ground. He took a corn-pounder, struck her, and said, "Mother-in-law, wake up and tell us your dream."

She stood up, and said, "I dreamed that my son-in-law must kill the two white otters that are in the lake."

"Go to sleep," said the young man, "I will do that to-morrow."

The woman went back to her blankets. In the morning she said, "You must kill the two white otters in the lake and bring them home before the door stops shaking after you have slammed it in going out. If you don't, something bad will happen."

The young man tied one of his long hairs to the door, and, unknown to his mother-in-law, kept pulling it to make the door tremble.

He reached the bank of the lake and called to the otters. They came in sight. He threw a round stone, which he had in his pocket, at one of the otters and killed it. Great waves rose up and rushed towards him. The second otter came near, on the top of a wave. He threw the second stone and killed the second otter, then the waves went back.

When the young man came to the house, he called out, "Here, Mother-in-law, are your two otters!"

"Where?" asked she, "Where?"

The two otters were her brothers.

The young man's uncle thought he was dead and often he sat in front of the fire and, with a handful of ashes in each hand, held his hands above his head and let the ashes fall over his hair and face.

At night he often heard some one coming. Then a

voice called out, "Uncle, I have come!" The old man jumped up, brushed off the ashes, went to the door and opened it only to find a fox or an owl. At last he made up his mind not to be deceived again.

The night after the otters were killed, the old woman groaned and rolled around on the ground. The young man hit her with the corn-pounder. She woke up, and said, "I dreamed that my son-in-law must kill the bird on the top of the tall tree."

"Go to sleep, Mother-in-law. I will do that in the morning."

In the morning she said, "If you get back after the door, that you slam in going out, stops swinging, something bad will happen."

The young man fixed the door as before, and going to the tall tree saw, on the very top, a black eagle. He drew his bow. The first arrow that he sent went almost to the top of the tree, but was driven back by the power of the eagle.

He sent a second arrow. It struck the eagle in the heart and brought it to the ground.

The young man picked up the bird and ran to the house. When he came he called out, "Mother-in-law, here is your eagle!"

"*Whu! Whu!*" said she. The eagle was her third brother and had always fed on men killed by his sister and nieces.

"Come outside," said the young man to his wife.

When she was outside, he fastened up the house, walked around it, and said, "I want this house to turn to stone," and immediately it was stone. The old woman and three of her daughters were inside.

They cried out, "Have pity on us! Have pity on us!"

"You had no pity on me," said the young man, and he left them to smother.

Then with his wife he went to the men near the ravine and said to them, "I have brought back this woman. She is the one who threw us over the precipice to die in the ravine."

They stripped a wide piece of bark from a tree, tied the woman on it, with bark straps, and placed it against a tree.

Then the men gathered wood, piled it around her and burned her up.

The young man had two brothers among the. men he had rescued. He told the other men to go to their own homes. Then, with his brothers he went to his uncle's house. When near they heard the old man crying. They listened; he stopped crying and began to sing, "Ten Summers I will mourn for him."

The door was fastened. The young man called out, "Uncle, I have come, let me in!"

"Be off!" answered the old man. "You have deceived me times enough."

The nephew begged to be let in, said he had his brothers with him.

"Be off!" cried the uncle. Then he relented, made a hole in the skin-door, and said, "Put your arm in, I will see if you are my nephew."

The young man put his arm through the hole. The old man tied it to the door with a bark string, then he opened the door cautiously.

When he saw his nephew, he cried out, "Wait, till I clean up a little."

He brushed off the ashes, then he welcomed his nephews, and they lived happily together.

A MAN CHASED BY THE ANCIENT OF LIZARDS

Characters

DAGWANOE^{n}YENT . . . . .Big Head (Whirlwind)
OGE^{n}HWAN . . . . .Gnat
SWE^{n}GEDAIGEA . . . . .Hawk (Hen-hawk)
GASYONDETHA . . . . .Meteor
NYAGWAIHE . . . . .The Ancient of Bears
OSHADA . . . . .Mist or Dusty Vapor
DZAINOS GOWA. .Blue Lizard, the Ancient of Lizards

O NCE there was a large village where people lived
happily and had plenty of meat. At the end of the
village lived a man whom few persons noticed.

One night that man had a dream. His dream said,
"Something is going to happen to the people of this village. You must tell them to move away within ten days."

The next morning the man went to the center of the
village, gathered the people and told his dream. Some
believed in the, dream others did not. Five days later
those who had believed joined those who had not, and
paid no heed to the dream.

The fifth night the man dreamed again and his dream
said, "We know that the people do not heed your warning.
But save yourself. Three days from now take all your
arrows and climb the hill on the east side of the village
till you come to a large rock. The rock is hollow. Go
inside of it and you will find a hole in the ground. Look

through the hole and you will see all that is going on in the village.

"The people will be destroyed by Big Head. Five days from now, at midday, there will be a terrible outcry. When the cry dies away, you must begin to shoot through the hole, for as soon as the people are destroyed the monster will track you. You will save your life if you shoot all your arrows at it before it reaches the hole.

"When the monster is dead, take from the back of its head a piece of skin together with the hair, which is very long. The skin will be of use to you, for it has great power. Wind the hair around your body next to your skin and declare that there is nothing that you cannot do.

"At night, when it is dark enough not to be seen, go North a short distance and you will find a tree turned up by the roots. You must not be frightened. I shall give you something which will be of great use to you."

After this dream the man was gloomy and unhappy. When the time came, he took his bundle of arrows and left the village. He didn't take his wife or children for they did not believe in the dream. Just at sunset he came to a large rock on the side of the hill. He found the opening and going into it crept along till he thought he was under the center of the rock. There he found a space high enough for him to stand in. He lay down and slept.

The next morning a deer was standing near the opening. He killed it, roasted some of the meat and ate it.

The fifth day, as the man sat on the rock, he heard a great noise coming from the South. As the sound approached the village he saw something that looked like smoke, saw that trees were falling, and falling toward the village.

When the noise reached the village, the man took his position opposite the opening in the ground. It seemed to him that the village was right at hand. He heard the screaming of the people and saw the cabins torn to pieces and hurled into the air.

Big Head missed one man, and when all the others were destroyed he laughed, and said, "This world is not large enough for him to hide in."

When the man saw that trees were falling toward the

East, he knew that Big Head had found his trail, and he
strung his bow and began to shoot through the hole as
rapidly as possible. When only two arrows were left, he
saw a great black Head not far away. He shot his last
arrow; the roar ceased, the Head fell and he heard it say,
"You have killed me!"

The man went to where the Head lay and found in it
every arrow he had shot. "I must do as my dream said,"
thought he, so he took a part of the scalp, tied it around his
body and said, "You must always help me. You must not
let me be overpowered by anyone."

He climbed to the top of the hill quickly, for now he
could go very fast. He found a good place and built a
brush hut. "I must have plenty of meat," thought he,
and going out he saw deer, bears and all kinds of game.
He killed what he wanted. To skin the deer and bears he
had merely to take hold of the skin of the head and pull;
with no effort the skin came from the whole carcass. He
made a brush shed and hung the meat up to dry.

When it began to grow dark, the man started toward
the North, as his dream had told him to do. He had not
gone far when he came to a fallen tree, the roots turned
out of the ground. When half way around the tree, he
saw Meteor with his great mouth open.

When Meteor saw that the man wasn't frightened he
laughed and said, "Take one of my teeth, it will be of
great use to you. It will enable you to change yourself
into any form you like."

The man took a double tooth, the one farthest back in
Meteor's jaw.

Then Meteor said, "You will live always and you will
have great power, but you and I must always counsel with
each other. Now we will part."

Meteor flew off through the air and the man went back
to his hut. He made up his mind that the hut would be
his home. He stayed there a long time then getting lonesome, he said to himself, "I will go and see if I can find
people anywhere."

He turned into a hawk and flew toward the southwest.
As he rose high in the air he looked down on the ground.
After a while he saw, in the West, something that made

him think people were living there. Then he began to come down. He came lower and lower and when near the ground saw a village. He said to himself, "I will eat up the people who live in that village."

He turned into a great bear and, beginning at the first house, ate up every person he could find. When he thought he had eaten everybody, he saw, off at the edge of the village, a little hut with smoke rising from it. In the hut he found a man and woman and several children. He ate them all.

"I have finished," said he, and changed himself to a man.

He stood around a while, then, seeing a trail he followed it, but had not gone far when he met a woman who was very handsome.

"Where do you live?" asked he.

"Over there in the cabin at the edge of the village."

"You had better go home with me for there is no one living in that cabin. All the people are dead."

"I must see first," said the woman.

They went back to the village and to the hut where he had found the man, woman, and children. She was the eldest child of the family. Seeing blood on the ground she began to cry. The man put his hand on the top of her head. That minute she was senseless. He shook her and as he shook she became a gnat. He changed himself to a hawk and putting the gnat under his wing flew up and off in the direction of his hut. He got there quickly, then he changed to a man and shook the gnat back to her natural form and size.

"This is your home," said he, "You must take care of the meat and the house."

One night while the two were sitting in the hut, the man heard a noise outside as though someone were coming on a run. The door was pushed open and a man came in, and said, "I have come to warn you. You have made yourself into two. NYAGWAIHE (the Ancient of Bears)—is jealous of you and has said, 'There is a man over there who is very powerful, but I will overpower him and eat him.'"

"To-morrow the Bear will come. You must go East till you reach a high stony hill. When the Bear tries to attack you, jump from one rock to another. It will spring after you. When it falls, you may feel safe. This is what I had to tell you. Now I will go."

The next morning the woman saw that her husband was gloomy and sad.

"What is the matter?" asked she.

"I am thinking of what will happen to me at midday."

The woman had neither seen nor heard the man who spoke to her husband though she was right there in the hut. He and the man who came to him were so powerful in spirit that they alone heard and saw each other.

When it was nearly midday, the man started for the rocks, leaving his wife. He seated himself on the highest rock and waited. Just at midday he heard a great noise, then another nearer; the third was right at the rock.

There was a whoop and a voice said, "I am the strongest of the strong. Nothing can overpower me."

It was NYAGWAIHE (the Ancient of Bears). The Bear leaped on to the rock where the man stood. The man sprang to the next rock, the Bear close behind him. In this way they sprang from one rock to another till the man was tired. As he looked ahead, the next rock looked farther off than the others had been. He made a great effort and just reached it. The Bear was right behind him. It sprang, but falling short, hit its jaws on the edge of the rock and went down.

The man jumped to the ground. As he struck the ground he looked back and saw the rock he had just left turn over on to the Bear.

"That is what I said," thought the man. "There is nothing that can overpower me."

He went back to his hut. He was very happy.

One day when the man and woman were sitting by the fire, they heard somebody approaching the hut. The man opened the door and saw the friend who had twice warned him of danger. The woman saw him too.

The man said, "Your life is in danger but I will try and save you. Rub your wife's head with your hands, she will turn to *oshada* (*oshada* is like the dusty vapor flying on a road in dry weather). Tell her to follow you wherever you go, but she must leave the hut before you do, you will stay here as long as you can, then run directly South. I am going now, but I will come to you again.''

In the morning the man rubbed the woman's head and said, "Let my wife become a dusty vapor.''

While he rubbed, she became a vapor on his hand. With his other hand he brushed the vapor off in the direction it was to go. Then he piled up his meat and said in a loud voice, "I give this meat to you flesh-eating animals that live in the woods.''

He went southward from the hut to an elm tree that was smooth up to where it branched off. He climbed the tree and sat in the crotch. Soon he began to feel weak, and he thought, "There must be something near.'' He looked everywhere but saw no one.

Taking out the Meteor tooth he dampened it with saliva, rubbed his finger over it, then rubbed his eyes, and said, "Now I can see everything that is going on, even down in the ground.''

He looked into the earth and saw, deep down, a tree and on the tree was a monster Lizard. He watched it as it climbed slowly up the tree. When it was near the top the man grew very faint.

The Lizard was the largest of the ancient blue Lizards (DZAINOS GOWA). It came out of the ground in the heart of the tree that the man was sitting on. The man leaped to another tree.

That instant the Lizard was where the man had been sitting and it called out, "You are smart but I shall overpower you.''

It sprang toward the man; the man leaped to another tree and then from tree to tree, the Lizard following.

At the edge of a hill was a great rock. The man ran to the rock and from the rock leaped into the air and came down on a mountain far away. He ran directly south along the ridge of the mountain, then went down on the opposite side to a wide valley. He ran across the valley and had begun to climb a second mountain when he heard the Lizard coming down the mountain he had just descended on the other side of the valley. It was dark now but the man continued to run, ran all night.

In the morning he saw an opening on the other side of

which was a low hill, and smoke of some kind. He reached the foot of the hill and turning saw the Lizard had just come to the opening. It raised its paw and struck the man's footprint on the trail. That instant the man fell to the ground. As he fell his friend was there and said, "Get up! You will die if you fall in this way."

He lifted him and pushed him into a run, urging him to hurry. The man felt stronger and again ran fast from valley to valley, the Lizard always about the same distance behind.

All at once the man fell again. Right away his friend was there. He lifted him to his feet saying, "Keep up courage," and pushed him into a run. Again he felt stronger and ran faster.

It was a very dark night; he ran against a great maple tree. As he hit the tree he went straight through. This happened many times in the night. Whenever the man hit a tree he went through it.

For eight days and nights the Lizard chased the man. When it found out that he went through trees it threw its power ahead and made the trees so hard that the man could no longer go through them.

The ninth night the Lizard commanded a terrible rain storm to come and the night to be so dark that the man couldn't see where he was going. The man ran till midnight without once hitting a tree. Just at midnight he hit one and was thrown far back.

That moment his friend was there, and said, "Do all you can," and taking hold of his hand he led him and they went faster than the man had gone alone.

The two ran together till daylight, then the friend left and the man went on alone. He began to be very weak. The Lizard was coming nearer and its strokes on the tracks were more frequent; the man fell oftener.

Night came and the Lizard made it terribly dark. The man ran against a tree and bounded far back. The Lizard was so near that the man fell behind him. The Lizard struck the tree and was thrown back also. The man was up and running forward again. The Lizard was just upon him and was reaching out to seize him when the man fell, as it seemed to him, into a hole in the ground. He thought,

"Well, I am near my end; when I strike I shall be dashed to pieces."

He kept falling and as he fell he got sleepy. Looking up he saw the Lizard coming down on the side of the hole, winding around and around. The man fell asleep. After a time he woke up and was still falling and the Lizard was still pursuing him.

At last the man landed on his feet. He seemed to have come out of the hole. He looked around and saw a beautiful country. "My friend told me to go toward the South," thought he, and he ran on in that direction.

As the man ran he knew that the Lizard was behind him coming very fast. "Now I shall die," thought he. He closed his eyes and kept on, thinking, "I will not see when it reaches me."

He ran a long time, then opened his eyes and looked around. He didn't see the Lizard but he kept running. Soon he came to a house and going in found an old man.

The old man looked up and said, "My grandson, I am glad you have come. I have been waiting for you. You are bringing with you what I have wanted to eat. Stand back there, Lizard and I will fight alone. We will see if he is as powerful as he thinks he is."

The Lizard came to the house and asked, "Where is the man I have been chasing?"

"Here I am," answered the old man.

"You are not the man."

"I am, but if you think there is another man here, you will not hunt for him till you overpower me."

"Come outside," said the Lizard, "there isn't room in here."

"Very well," said the old man and getting up he went outside. They began to fight. The Lizard tore the old man's flesh. It came together again and healed. The old man tore off Lizard's forelegs, but Lizard didn't give up; the two fought till Lizard was torn to pieces.

When the old man convinced himself that the pieces were not alive, he hung them up in the house and called to his grandson, "Come out! I have killed the Lizard that you were afraid of. I have been wishing for this kind of meat for a long time."

The old man boiled some of the meat in a large kettle. In a small kettle he cooked bear meat for his grandson.

While the meat was cooking, he put corn in a pounder and with a few strokes it was flour. Then he made bread and began eating.

When he had eaten every bit of the great Lizard, he said, "I thank you, my grandson, this meat will last me for many years. You must stay here till you are rested and cured, for you have been poisoned by the power of the Lizard."

The old man was the oldest of the Flying Meteors. One day he said to the man, "I want you to see what I have planted."

They went a short distance from the cabin to a field where something was growing.

"This is *ones* (corn)," said the old man.

There were tall stalks with ears on them as long as the man was tall and the kernels were as large as a man's head.

The old man said, "Let us go to the other side of the field."

There the man saw a field where different kinds of corn were growing.

They went to a third field where something was growing and the old man said, "These are squashes." They were very large.

They passed the squash field and went back to the cabin.

The next day the man said good-bye to his grandfather and started for home. He traveled till he came to a village. He went to the chief's house and a woman who was there looked at him, then asked, "Have you ever heard of a man who sent his wife away in the form of vapor?"

He thought a little while, then remembered, and answered, "I have. I did that myself."

"I am your wife," said the woman.

The man had had so much trouble that he had forgotten about his wife, but he was glad to find her. They went home together and lived happily.

THE GREAT BEAR AND THE SIX HUNTERS,

OR

THE SEVEN STARS OF THE DIPPER

SIX men went out hunting, for a long time they found no game. One of their number said he was sick (he was lazy) and they had to make a litter of two poles and a blanket, and four carried him. The sixth member of the party came behind bringing the kettle. Besides this each man had his own load to carry.

At last, when the hunters were getting very hungry, they came upon bear tracks. They were so hungry that when they saw the tracks they dropped their companion and their burdens and each man ran as fast as he could after the bear.

At first the tracks looked old but they thought, "We will overtake the bear sometime."

Later they saw that the tracks couldn't be more than three days old. The farther the men went the fresher the tracks were till the men said, "To-morrow we will overtake the bear."

The man they had carried so long was not tired and when they dropped him and he knew he was going to be left he jumped up and ran on after them. As he was fresher than they were he soon passed them and killed the bear.

The men in their race after the bear didn't notice that they were going up all the time. Many people saw them in the air, as they ran along, always rising.

When they overtook the bear and the lazy man, they had reached the sky and there they have remained to this day and can be seen any starlit night. The man who carried the kettle is in the bend of the Dipper, the middle star in the handle and a small star which is the only one near any other of the Dipper stars is the kettle. The Bear is at the lower outside corner. Every Autumn, when the first frost comes, one can see on the leaves of the oak-tree drops of oil, not water, and this is the oil and blood of the Bear.

On seeing it the Indians say, "The lazy man has killed the Bear."

THE CHIPMUNK AND THE BEAR

THE Bear thought herself a very powerful creature and was always trying to exhibit her strength before other animals.

One day she got into a dispute with a Chipmunk and the Chipmunk asked, "Why do you boast so much? You have no great power."

The Bear was angry and declared that she had such power that she could, if she wished, prevent the sun from rising in the morning.

The Chipmunk said, "You cannot."

"Wait and see," replied the Bear.

The Chipmunk was not to be fooled. He declared that he would wait. "We shall have the sun at the usual time," said he.

When the sun came up the Chipmunk laughed and made fun of the Bear and her boasting, till the Bear was so terribly angry that she turned on the Chipmunk. He escaped, for his burrow was close by, but as he reached it the Bear was so nearly upon him that she stretched out her paw to clutch him, but he slipped from under it and went into the hole.

The next day the Chipmunk appeared with three marks on his back, marks of the Bear's claws. And Chipmunks carry those marks to this day.

THE WREN

A BOY was once told that he must not shoot wrens, for the wren is a strange bird, difficult to hit and mysterious in its ways. One day he went out to hunt when the sun was already beyond the middle of the sky. He soon saw a wren and although warned he determined to try his luck in killing it.

He shot arrow after arrow, but no use, he could not hit the bird. Sometimes it dodged the arrows, sometimes it flew to another tree. All his efforts were vain.

At last he hid behind a bush and waited till he had an excellent aim, then he let his arrow fly. It just grazed the top of the bird's head, scratching the skin. The wren flew away fluttering. The boy watched till it disappeared behind a log at some distance in the thicket, then he ran forward quickly.

As he got near the log he heard groans and low cries of pain, and looking over the log he saw a man lying on the ground, apparently in great pain. His scalp was gone and the whole top of his head was covered with blood.

The boy, terribly frightened, ran home and told what had happened. People hurried back with him to aid the wounded man, but they could find no trace of him; the wren had flown.

The wren is to this day called "the bird without a scalp."

It had turned itself into a man to avoid being captured while stunned by pain.

THE TWELVE STARS

TWELVE children were playing together on the grass near their fathers' cabins. They thought they would play a new game, and they invented one. They joined hands in a circle and danced, not swinging around, but standing in one place. As they danced they sang: "We are dancing. We are dancing."

Their parents were watching them and listening to their song, when all at once they noticed that their feet did not touch the ground. The parents were frightened and ran out to stop the dancing, but the children were already above their heads in the air and going higher and higher, always singing: "We are dancing. We are dancing."

They went up and up until they disappeared, still holding hands, and they were next seen as twelve stars in the heavens just above their fathers' cabins. One got a little out of the circle and therefore appears a little at one side of the others.

THE WOMAN AND DOG IN THE MOON

A WOMAN is sitting in the moon and she is busy embroidering with porcupine quills. Near her is a bright fire, and over the fire hangs a kettle with something boiling in it. By her side sits a large dog that watches her continually. Once in a while she gets up, lays aside her work and stirs whatever is boiling in the kettle. While she is doing this the dog unravels her work.

This is going on all the time. As fast as the woman embroiders, the dog unravels. If she could finish her work, or if she ever does, the end of the world will come that instant.

A MAN CONQUERS STONE COAT (ICE AND COLD)

[Told by John Armstrong]

Character

GENÓ^{n}SKWA ....Ice and Cold (Stone Coat)

ONCE there was a village in a clearing in the forest. The people of that village had been told not to go North, for in the North the Stone Coats (Ice and Cold) lived, and they were man-eaters.

One of the men said, "I am not afraid of those Stone Coats, maybe there is good hunting in their country. I'm going there. If they trouble me I'll kill them."

Getting into their canoe, the man and his wife rowed up the river till they came to the country of the Stone Coats. Then the man pulled the canoe on to the bank, made a fire, and went hunting. While he was gone, a Stone Coat woman came to the camp. When the man's wife saw her she was so frightened that she lost her senses. The Stone Coat woman pushed her around, and said, "She must have been a long time dead."

The woman came to her senses, ran to the river, pulled the canoe to the water, sprang into the canoe and rowed away. The Stone Coat followed her to the bank of the river, but couldn't go farther for she had no canoe.

When the woman came to where her husband was, she said, "You boasted that you could kill the Stone Coats, now show what you can do."

The man built a fire and sharpened his flint knife. Soon a Stone Coat man came to the opposite side of the river and called out, "You are the man who boasts that you can kill the Stone Coats. Come over and try your strength."

"I'll not go to you," said the man, "You can come to me."

After a good deal of talk, Stone Coat started to cross the river. When water covered his head, he walked under the water.

The man ran up the river to where he had seen a tree in the water. He crossed on the tree, ran along the bank and, when Stone Coat came out of the water, shouted to him, "Where are you going? You must have turned around in the river."

Stone Coat started back and while he was under the water, the man crossed again on the tree, and as Stone Coat came to the bank he shouted, "You foolish fellow! Don't you know enough to cross the river?"

After the man had fooled Stone Coat a number of times, he thought, "I'll let him come. I won't fool him again."

When Stone Coat came out of the river, he looked at the man, and asked, "What is that in your hand?"

The man gave his hatchet to Stone Coat, who looking at it, rubbed the edge of it with his hand and without knowing it, gave the hatchet such power that it was harder than anything else in the world.

"Show me what you can do with this thing," said Stone Coat.

The man struck a rock. The rock split open.

Stone Coat was terribly frightened. He thought that the power came from the man. "This man," said he in his mind, "is as strong as we are. Maybe he can kill us."

He left the man, crossed the river and went off. When he reached home and told his people what he had seen they said, "We'll go away from here. We'll go toward the West and leave this man."

The man and his wife lived, undisturbed, in the Stone Coat country till one day a Stone Coat woman came to the bark house they had built, and said, "My husband and I quarreled and I ran away. After he has looked everywhere else for me, he will come here. I will help you till he comes, then you must help me."

The next day when the man started off to hunt, the Stone Coat woman went with him, and she brought him good luck. Each day she went with him and each day he killed a great deal of game.

One morning she said, "My husband will come to-day. When we begin to fight, you must put a stick in the fire and heat it red hot, and as soon as he overpowers and throws me, you must run the firebrand into his body."

When Stone Coat came he pulled up a tree. His wife pulled up another tree, and they began to fight, using the trees as clubs. At last the woman fell. That minute the man ran the firebrand into Stone Coat's body and killed him.

When the man and his wife were ready to go back to their village, the Stone Coat woman said, "When the Stone Coats went away, one of our women left her little boy. You must take him home with you."

The man went to the place the Stone Coat indicated and found, on a high cliff, two trees, a swing hung between the trees and in the swing sat a little Stone Coat boy, swinging back and forth and singing. The man felled the trees; the swing came down and the boy too, but the boy still kept singing and swaying his body as though he were swinging.

The man took the child home and as he grew up and began to play with other boys he showed great strength. If he struck a boy, he killed him. Every child he hit, even in play, he killed. The people of the village told the man that he must send the boy back to his own people. The man sent for the Stone Coat woman and she took the boy to his mother.

"The Stone Coats are Frost, Ice and great Cold."

THE END

GLOSSARY

Awéondágon.—Name of a weed.
Dádahwât.—White beaver.
Dadyoeⁿdzadáses.—He who travels around the world (wolf).
Dagwahgweoses.—Long eyebrows.
Dagwanoeⁿyent gowa.—Whirlwind, cyclone.
Daqsídes.—Long foot (rabbit).
Deⁿdeⁿdáne.—Caterpillar.
Déoneyont.—Red hot.
Dewaqsoⁿthwûs.—Flea.
Dí'di.—Blue jay.
Digiá'goⁿ gowa.—Buffalo.
Dí'sdes.—Woodpecker.
Djeonyaik.—Robin.
Djiäyeⁿ.—Spider.
Djihoⁿsdûqgwen.—Ants.
Djisdáa.—Grasshopper.
Djisgan.—Spirit, ghost.
Djissáa.—Fire.
Djoéaga.—Coon.
Djonkdjoⁿkweⁿ.—Chickadee.
Dóeⁿdzowes.—Split the earth (earthquake).
Donoⁿgáes.—Long horns (snake).
Dónyakdane.—He who travels everywhere (inchworm).
Dónyonda.—Bald eagle.
Doseno'daia.—Flying squirrel.
Dotgehondagwe.—Half red-headed (woodpecker).
Dowisdowe.—Tip-up (a bird).
Doyadastethe.—Bright body.
Dwâauⁿhdanegeⁿ.—Two feathers (rabbit).
Dzainos gowa.—Blue lizard, ancient of lizards.
Dzodjógis.—Blackbirds.
Dzóega.—Raccoon.
Dzogéon.—Little people (fairies).
Dzohó'qwais.—Chipmunk.
Dzotháwendoⁿ.—Humming bird.
Gadjiqsa.—Husk false face.
Gaiⁿsoⁿhe'.—Daddy long legs.
Gaísgen se.—Ground-bird.

Gandewitha.—Morning star.
Ganenitha.—Corn beetle.
Ganogeshegea.—Sparrow.
Gányage gowa.—Diver (duck).
Ganyâqden hanówa.—Mud-turtle.
Ganyo gowa.—Great game (white deer).
Ganyuqdjidji.—Yellowbird.
Gáqga'.—Raven.
Gásyondetha.—Lightning lion (meteor).
Géha.—Wind.
Gendágahâdényatha.—June-bug.
Génonskwa.—Stone coat (ice and great cold).
Gwíyee.—Phebe bird.
Hadäéonis.—Net maker.
Hadentheni.—Speaker.
Hadia'des.—Black-snake.
Hadiqsadon genonskwa ganyudai.—Grave of frosts, or the so-called stone coats.
Hadjisgwâs.—Mush eater.
Hadjoqdja.—Skin man.
Háiendonis.—Woodmaker (a tree worm).
Haienthwûs.—Planter.
Hanenyowa'ne.—Big bones (mud turtle). A second name for Mud-turtle, see Ganyâqden hanówa.
Hanigongendatha.—Definer.
Hánisheonon.—Muck-worm.
Hanówa.—Turtle.
Haqgeeah.—Ragged or shabby man.
Hatdedases.—Whirlwind maker.
Hathóndes.—The listener (mink).
Háweniyo.—Great Spirit.
Henes.—Panther.
Heusdeóon.—Rocks go to the water.
Hino'.—Thunder (personified).
Hino'hoháwank.—Thunder's son.
Hodionskon.—Trickster.
Hóngâk.—Wild (Canada) goose.
Hoqua.—The cry of frogs.
Hótho.—Cold weather, winter.
I'onwe.—Wild duck.
Ne vonoes.—That is what we like.
Nohnohsot.—Heron.
Nóndza'qgwe.—Woodcock.
Nongwatgwa.—Fox.
Nosgwais.—Toad.

Nyagwaihe gowa.—Ancient of bears.
Odjie'da.—Crawfish.
Odzi'néowa.—Wasp.
Ogeⁿhwan.—Gnat.
Okteondoⁿ.—Roots, rooted ones.
Oneqsas.—Mushroom eater (a bird).
Oneo.—Corn.
Oñgwe.—Man, Indian.
Ongweias.—Man eater.
Oⁿhdagwija.—Good ear.
Onóqgoⁿt gowa.—Bumble bee.
O'nowéhda.—Angleworm.
Oⁿweⁿaunt.—Blue snake.
Onwi.—Winged snake.
O'ówa.—Horned owl.
Oshada.—Dusty vapor.
Óshonyúqda.—Corn-worm.
Otgoé.—Wampum.
Otgon.—Poison.
Otgóndaheⁿ.—Red bellied (snake).
Othägweⁿda.—Flint.
Othägweⁿdonis.—Flintmaker.
Othaioni hoyáda.—Wolf-marked.
Othwénsawénhde.—Small liver beside the large one.
Otsoon.—Turkey.
Owéeyegoⁿhdji.—Old woman swan.
Plétho.—Thunder (the sound), a Delaware word.
Pléthoak.—Thunders, a Delaware word.
Popkpéknos.—Quail, a Delaware word.
Poyeshaoⁿ.—Orphan, a Delaware word.
Sadzawíski.—Thousand legs.
Sehdoⁿhgwadᵉ.—Wood-tick.
Sganoⁿhses gowa.—One of the Thunder family.
Shagodiäqdane.—The woman in the South.
Shagodyoweg gowa.—Great One who protects us; false face, god of the air.
Shagonoges.—He torments them.
Shagowenotha.—The punisher.
Shagóyádogédas.—He drives them away.
Shagoyagentha.—He hides them.
Sigweont.—Rattlesnake.
Skada'géa.—In the mist (a bird).
Skagedi.—Half (of anything).
Sweⁿgedaigea.—Hawk, hen hawk.
Téqdooⁿhuishĕ.—Woodchuck leggings, the deceiver.

*Thago*n*hsówes.*—He splits his face.
Tondayent.—White rabbit.
*Tsodiqgwado*n.—Snake.
*Wadyo*n*yo*n*dyes.*—Wild duck people.
*Wáyo*n.—Rabbit.
Wia'á.—Call of phebe bird.
*Yenogeau*n.—Ear enter (barkworm).
*Yeo*n*ogaa.*—Shingled hair.
Yeqsínye.—Spinner.
*Yontq*n*wisas.*—Name of a song.

A CATALOG OF SELECTED
DOVER BOOKS
IN ALL FIELDS OF INTEREST

A CATALOG OF SELECTED DOVER
BOOKS IN ALL FIELDS OF INTEREST

CONCERNING THE SPIRITUAL IN ART, Wassily Kandinsky. Pioneering work by father of abstract art. Thoughts on color theory, nature of art. Analysis of earlier masters. 12 illustrations. 80pp. of text. 5⅜ x 8½.   23411-8 Pa. $4.95

ANIMALS: 1,419 Copyright-Free Illustrations of Mammals, Birds, Fish, Insects, etc., Jim Harter (ed.). Clear wood engravings present, in extremely lifelike poses, over 1,000 species of animals. One of the most extensive pictorial sourcebooks of its kind. Captions. Index. 284pp. 9 x 12.   23766-4 Pa. $14.95

CELTIC ART: The Methods of Construction, George Bain. Simple geometric techniques for making Celtic interlacements, spirals, Kells-type initials, animals, humans, etc. Over 500 illustrations. 160pp. 9 x 12. (Available in U.S. only.)   22923-8 Pa. $9.95

AN ATLAS OF ANATOMY FOR ARTISTS, Fritz Schider. Most thorough reference work on art anatomy in the world. Hundreds of illustrations, including selections from works by Vesalius, Leonardo, Goya, Ingres, Michelangelo, others. 593 illustrations. 192pp. 7⅛ x 10¼.   20241-0 Pa. $9.95

CELTIC HAND STROKE-BY-STROKE (Irish Half-Uncial from "The Book of Kells"): An Arthur Baker Calligraphy Manual, Arthur Baker. Complete guide to creating each letter of the alphabet in distinctive Celtic manner. Covers hand position, strokes, pens, inks, paper, more. Illustrated. 48pp. 8¼ x 11.   24336-2 Pa. $3.95

EASY ORIGAMI, John Montroll. Charming collection of 32 projects (hat, cup, pelican, piano, swan, many more) specially designed for the novice origami hobbyist. Clearly illustrated easy-to-follow instructions insure that even beginning papercrafters will achieve successful results. 48pp. 8¼ x 11.   27298-2 Pa. $3.50

THE COMPLETE BOOK OF BIRDHOUSE CONSTRUCTION FOR WOOD-WORKERS, Scott D. Campbell. Detailed instructions, illustrations, tables. Also data on bird habitat and instinct patterns. Bibliography. 3 tables. 63 illustrations in 15 figures. 48pp. 5¼ x 8½.   24407-5 Pa. $2.50

BLOOMINGDALE'S ILLUSTRATED 1886 CATALOG: Fashions, Dry Goods and Housewares, Bloomingdale Brothers. Famed merchants' extremely rare catalog depicting about 1,700 products: clothing, housewares, firearms, dry goods, jewelry, more. Invaluable for dating, identifying vintage items. Also, copyright-free graphics for artists, designers. Co-published with Henry Ford Museum & Greenfield Village. 160pp. 8¼ x 11.   25780-0 Pa. $10.95

HISTORIC COSTUME IN PICTURES, Braun & Schneider. Over 1,450 costumed figures in clearly detailed engravings–from dawn of civilization to end of 19th century. Captions. Many folk costumes. 256pp. 8⅜ x 11¾.   23150-X Pa. $12.95

CATALOG OF DOVER BOOKS

STICKLEY CRAFTSMAN FURNITURE CATALOGS, Gustav Stickley and L. & J. G. Stickley. Beautiful, functional furniture in two authentic catalogs from 1910. 594 illustrations, including 277 photos, show settles, rockers, armchairs, reclining chairs, bookcases, desks, tables. 183pp. 6½ x 9¼. 23838-5 Pa. $11.95

AMERICAN LOCOMOTIVES IN HISTORIC PHOTOGRAPHS: 1858 to 1949, Ron Ziel (ed.). A rare collection of 126 meticulously detailed official photographs, called "builder portraits," of American locomotives that majestically chronicle the rise of steam locomotive power in America. Introduction. Detailed captions. xi+ 129pp. 9 x 12. 27393-8 Pa. $13.95

AMERICA'S LIGHTHOUSES: An Illustrated History, Francis Ross Holland, Jr. Delightfully written, profusely illustrated fact-filled survey of over 200 American lighthouses since 1716. History, anecdotes, technological advances, more. 240pp. 8 x 10¾. 25576-X Pa. $12.95

TOWARDS A NEW ARCHITECTURE, Le Corbusier. Pioneering manifesto by founder of "International School." Technical and aesthetic theories, views of industry, economics, relation of form to function, "mass-production split" and much more. Profusely illustrated. 320pp. 6⅛ x 9¼. (Available in U.S. only.) 25023-7 Pa. $9.95

HOW THE OTHER HALF LIVES, Jacob Riis. Famous journalistic record, exposing poverty and degradation of New York slums around 1900, by major social reformer. 100 striking and influential photographs. 233pp. 10 x 7⅞. 22012-5 Pa. $11.95

FRUIT KEY AND TWIG KEY TO TREES AND SHRUBS, William M. Harlow. One of the handiest and most widely used identification aids. Fruit key covers 120 deciduous and evergreen species; twig key 160 deciduous species. Easily used. Over 300 photographs. 126pp. 5⅜ x 8½. 20511-8 Pa. $3.95

COMMON BIRD SONGS, Dr. Donald J. Borror. Songs of 60 most common U.S. birds: robins, sparrows, cardinals, bluejays, finches, more–arranged in order of increasing complexity. Up to 9 variations of songs of each species.
Cassette and manual 99911-4 $8.95

ORCHIDS AS HOUSE PLANTS, Rebecca Tyson Northen. Grow cattleyas and many other kinds of orchids–in a window, in a case, or under artificial light. 63 illustrations. 148pp. 5⅜ x 8½. 23261-1 Pa. $5.95

MONSTER MAZES, Dave Phillips. Masterful mazes at four levels of difficulty. Avoid deadly perils and evil creatures to find magical treasures. Solutions for all 32 exciting illustrated puzzles. 48pp. 8¼ x 11. 26005-4 Pa. $2.95

MOZART'S DON GIOVANNI (DOVER OPERA LIBRETTO SERIES), Wolfgang Amadeus Mozart. Introduced and translated by Ellen H. Bleiler. Standard Italian libretto, with complete English translation. Convenient and thoroughly portable–an ideal companion for reading along with a recording or the performance itself. Introduction. List of characters. Plot summary. 121pp. 5¼ x 8½. 24944-1 Pa. $3.95

TECHNICAL MANUAL AND DICTIONARY OF CLASSICAL BALLET, Gail Grant. Defines, explains, comments on steps, movements, poses and concepts. 15-page pictorial section. Basic book for student, viewer. 127pp. 5⅜ x 8½. 21843-0 Pa. $4.95

THE CLARINET AND CLARINET PLAYING, David Pino. Lively, comprehensive work features suggestions about technique, musicianship, and musical interpretation, as well as guidelines for teaching, making your own reeds, and preparing for public performance. Includes an intriguing look at clarinet history. "A godsend," *The Clarinet*, Journal of the International Clarinet Society. Appendixes. 7 illus. 320pp. 5⅜ x 8½. 40270-3 Pa. $9.95

HOLLYWOOD GLAMOR PORTRAITS, John Kobal (ed.). 145 photos from 1926-49. Harlow, Gable, Bogart, Bacall; 94 stars in all. Full background on photographers, technical aspects. 160pp. 8⅜ x 11¼. 23352-9 Pa. $12.95

THE ANNOTATED CASEY AT THE BAT: A Collection of Ballads about the Mighty Casey/Third, Revised Edition, Martin Gardner (ed.). Amusing sequels and parodies of one of America's best-loved poems: Casey's Revenge, Why Casey Whiffed, Casey's Sister at the Bat, others. 256pp. 5⅜ x 8½. 28598-7 Pa. $8.95

THE RAVEN AND OTHER FAVORITE POEMS, Edgar Allan Poe. Over 40 of the author's most memorable poems: "The Bells," "Ulalume," "Israfel," "To Helen," "The Conqueror Worm," "Eldorado," "Annabel Lee," many more. Alphabetic lists of titles and first lines. 64pp. 5$\frac{3}{16}$ x 8¼. 26685-0 Pa. $1.00

PERSONAL MEMOIRS OF U. S. GRANT, Ulysses Simpson Grant. Intelligent, deeply moving firsthand account of Civil War campaigns, considered by many the finest military memoirs ever written. Includes letters, historic photographs, maps and more. 528pp. 6⅛ x 9¼. 28587-1 Pa. $12.95

ANCIENT EGYPTIAN MATERIALS AND INDUSTRIES, A. Lucas and J. Harris. Fascinating, comprehensive, thoroughly documented text describes this ancient civilization's vast resources and the processes that incorporated them in daily life, including the use of animal products, building materials, cosmetics, perfumes and incense, fibers, glazed ware, glass and its manufacture, materials used in the mummification process, and much more. 544pp. 6⅛ x 9¼. (Available in U.S. only.) 40446-3 Pa. $16.95

RUSSIAN STORIES/PYCCKNE PACCKA3bl: A Dual-Language Book, edited by Gleb Struve. Twelve tales by such masters as Chekhov, Tolstoy, Dostoevsky, Pushkin, others. Excellent word-for-word English translations on facing pages, plus teaching and study aids, Russian/English vocabulary, biographical/critical introductions, more. 416pp. 5⅜ x 8½. 26244-8 Pa. $9.95

PHILADELPHIA THEN AND NOW: 60 Sites Photographed in the Past and Present, Kenneth Finkel and Susan Oyama. Rare photographs of City Hall, Logan Square, Independence Hall, Betsy Ross House, other landmarks juxtaposed with contemporary views. Captures changing face of historic city. Introduction. Captions. 128pp. 8¼ x 11. 25790-8 Pa. $9.95

AIA ARCHITECTURAL GUIDE TO NASSAU AND SUFFOLK COUNTIES, LONG ISLAND, The American Institute of Architects, Long Island Chapter, and the Society for the Preservation of Long Island Antiquities. Comprehensive, well-researched and generously illustrated volume brings to life over three centuries of Long Island's great architectural heritage. More than 240 photographs with authoritative, extensively detailed captions. 176pp. 8¼ x 11. 26946-9 Pa. $14.95

NORTH AMERICAN INDIAN LIFE: Customs and Traditions of 23 Tribes, Elsie Clews Parsons (ed.). 27 fictionalized essays by noted anthropologists examine religion, customs, government, additional facets of life among the Winnebago, Crow, Zuni, Eskimo, other tribes. 480pp. 6⅛ x 9¼. 27377-6 Pa. $10.95

FRANK LLOYD WRIGHT'S DANA HOUSE, Donald Hoffmann. Pictorial essay of residential masterpiece with over 160 interior and exterior photos, plans, elevations, sketches and studies. 128pp. 9¼ x 10¾. 29120-0 Pa. $12.95

THE MALE AND FEMALE FIGURE IN MOTION: 60 Classic Photographic Sequences, Eadweard Muybridge. 60 true-action photographs of men and women walking, running, climbing, bending, turning, etc., reproduced from rare 19th-century masterpiece. vi + 121pp. 9 x 12. 24745-7 Pa. $12.95

1001 QUESTIONS ANSWERED ABOUT THE SEASHORE, N. J. Berrill and Jacquelyn Berrill. Queries answered about dolphins, sea snails, sponges, starfish, fishes, shore birds, many others. Covers appearance, breeding, growth, feeding, much more. 305pp. 5¼ x 8¼. 23366-9 Pa. $9.95

ATTRACTING BIRDS TO YOUR YARD, William J. Weber. Easy-to-follow guide offers advice on how to attract the greatest diversity of birds: birdhouses, feeders, water and waterers, much more. 96pp. 5³⁄₁₆ x 8¼. 28927-3 Pa. $2.50

MEDICINAL AND OTHER USES OF NORTH AMERICAN PLANTS: A Historical Survey with Special Reference to the Eastern Indian Tribes, Charlotte Erichsen-Brown. Chronological historical citations document 500 years of usage of plants, trees, shrubs native to eastern Canada, northeastern U.S. Also complete identifying information. 343 illustrations. 544pp. 6½ x 9¼. 25951-X Pa. $12.95

STORYBOOK MAZES, Dave Phillips. 23 stories and mazes on two-page spreads: Wizard of Oz, Treasure Island, Robin Hood, etc. Solutions. 64pp. 8¼ x 11. 23628-5 Pa. $2.95

AMERICAN NEGRO SONGS: 230 Folk Songs and Spirituals, Religious and Secular, John W. Work. This authoritative study traces the African influences of songs sung and played by black Americans at work, in church, and as entertainment. The author discusses the lyric significance of such songs as "Swing Low, Sweet Chariot," "John Henry," and others and offers the words and music for 230 songs. Bibliography. Index of Song Titles. 272pp. 6½ x 9¼. 40271-1 Pa. $9.95

MOVIE-STAR PORTRAITS OF THE FORTIES, John Kobal (ed.). 163 glamor, studio photos of 106 stars of the 1940s: Rita Hayworth, Ava Gardner, Marlon Brando, Clark Gable, many more. 176pp. 8⅜ x 11¼. 23546-7 Pa. $14.95

BENCHLEY LOST AND FOUND, Robert Benchley. Finest humor from early 30s, about pet peeves, child psychologists, post office and others. Mostly unavailable elsewhere. 73 illustrations by Peter Arno and others. 183pp. 5⅜ x 8½. 22410-4 Pa. $6.95

YEKL and THE IMPORTED BRIDEGROOM AND OTHER STORIES OF YIDDISH NEW YORK, Abraham Cahan. Film Hester Street based on *Yekl* (1896). Novel, other stories among first about Jewish immigrants on N.Y.'s East Side. 240pp. 5⅜ x 8½. 22427-9 Pa. $7.95

SELECTED POEMS, Walt Whitman. Generous sampling from *Leaves of Grass*. Twenty-four poems include "I Hear America Singing," "Song of the Open Road," "I Sing the Body Electric," "When Lilacs Last in the Dooryard Bloom'd," "O Captain! My Captain!"–all reprinted from an authoritative edition. Lists of titles and first lines. 128pp. 5³⁄₁₆ x 8¼. 26878-0 Pa. $1.00

THE BEST TALES OF HOFFMANN, E. T. A. Hoffmann. 10 of Hoffmann's most important stories: "Nutcracker and the King of Mice," "The Golden Flowerpot," etc. 458pp. 5⅜ x 8½. 21793-0 Pa. $9.95

FROM FETISH TO GOD IN ANCIENT EGYPT, E. A. Wallis Budge. Rich detailed survey of Egyptian conception of "God" and gods, magic, cult of animals, Osiris, more. Also, superb English translations of hymns and legends. 240 illustrations. 545pp. 5⅜ x 8½. 25803-3 Pa. $13.95

FRENCH STORIES/CONTES FRANÇAIS: A Dual-Language Book, Wallace Fowlie. Ten stories by French masters, Voltaire to Camus: "Micromegas" by Voltaire; "The Atheist's Mass" by Balzac; "Minuet" by de Maupassant; "The Guest" by Camus, six more. Excellent English translations on facing pages. Also French-English vocabulary list, exercises, more. 352pp. 5⅜ x 8½. 26443-2 Pa. $9.95

CHICAGO AT THE TURN OF THE CENTURY IN PHOTOGRAPHS: 122 Historic Views from the Collections of the Chicago Historical Society, Larry A. Viskochil. Rare large-format prints offer detailed views of City Hall, State Street, the Loop, Hull House, Union Station, many other landmarks, circa 1904-1913. Introduction. Captions. Maps. 144pp. 9⅜ x 12¼. 24656-6 Pa. $12.95

OLD BROOKLYN IN EARLY PHOTOGRAPHS, 1865-1929, William Lee Younger. Luna Park, Gravesend race track, construction of Grand Army Plaza, moving of Hotel Brighton, etc. 157 previously unpublished photographs. 165pp. 8⅞ x 11¾. 23587-4 Pa. $13.95

THE MYTHS OF THE NORTH AMERICAN INDIANS, Lewis Spence. Rich anthology of the myths and legends of the Algonquins, Iroquois, Pawnees and Sioux, prefaced by an extensive historical and ethnological commentary. 36 illustrations. 480pp. 5⅜ x 8½. 25967-6 Pa. $10.95

AN ENCYCLOPEDIA OF BATTLES: Accounts of Over 1,560 Battles from 1479 B.C. to the Present, David Eggenberger. Essential details of every major battle in recorded history from the first battle of Megiddo in 1479 B.C. to Grenada in 1984. List of Battle Maps. New Appendix covering the years 1967-1984. Index. 99 illustrations. 544pp. 6½ x 9¼. 24913-1 Pa. $16.95

SAILING ALONE AROUND THE WORLD, Captain Joshua Slocum. First man to sail around the world, alone, in small boat. One of great feats of seamanship told in delightful manner. 67 illustrations. 294pp. 5⅜ x 8½. 20326-3 Pa. $6.95

ANARCHISM AND OTHER ESSAYS, Emma Goldman. Powerful, penetrating, prophetic essays on direct action, role of minorities, prison reform, puritan hypocrisy, violence, etc. 271pp. 5⅜ x 8½. 22484-8 Pa. $7.95

MYTHS OF THE HINDUS AND BUDDHISTS, Ananda K. Coomaraswamy and Sister Nivedita. Great stories of the epics; deeds of Krishna, Shiva, taken from puranas, Vedas, folk tales; etc. 32 illustrations. 400pp. 5⅜ x 8½. 21759-0 Pa. $12.95

THE TRAUMA OF BIRTH, Otto Rank. Rank's controversial thesis that anxiety neurosis is caused by profound psychological trauma which occurs at birth. 256pp. 5⅜ x 8½. 27974-X Pa. $7.95

A THEOLOGICO-POLITICAL TREATISE, Benedict Spinoza. Also contains unfinished Political Treatise. Great classic on religious liberty, theory of government on common consent. R. Elwes translation. Total of 421pp. 5⅜ x 8½. 20249-6 Pa. $10.95

CATALOG OF DOVER BOOKS

MY BONDAGE AND MY FREEDOM, Frederick Douglass. Born a slave, Douglass became outspoken force in antislavery movement. The best of Douglass' autobiographies. Graphic description of slave life. 464pp. 5⅜ x 8½. 22457-0 Pa. $8.95

FOLLOWING THE EQUATOR: A Journey Around the World, Mark Twain. Fascinating humorous account of 1897 voyage to Hawaii, Australia, India, New Zealand, etc. Ironic, bemused reports on peoples, customs, climate, flora and fauna, politics, much more. 197 illustrations. 720pp. 5⅜ x 8½. 26113-1 Pa. $15.95

THE PEOPLE CALLED SHAKERS, Edward D. Andrews. Definitive study of Shakers: origins, beliefs, practices, dances, social organization, furniture and crafts, etc. 33 illustrations. 351pp. 5⅜ x 8½. 21081-2 Pa. $10.95

THE MYTHS OF GREECE AND ROME, H. A. Guerber. A classic of mythology, generously illustrated, long prized for its simple, graphic, accurate retelling of the principal myths of Greece and Rome, and for its commentary on their origins and significance. With 64 illustrations by Michelangelo, Raphael, Titian, Rubens, Canova, Bernini and others. 480pp. 5⅜ x 8½. 27584-1 Pa. $9.95

PSYCHOLOGY OF MUSIC, Carl E. Seashore. Classic work discusses music as a medium from psychological viewpoint. Clear treatment of physical acoustics, auditory apparatus, sound perception, development of musical skills, nature of musical feeling, host of other topics. 88 figures. 408pp. 5⅜ x 8½. 21851-1 Pa. $11.95

THE PHILOSOPHY OF HISTORY, Georg W. Hegel. Great classic of Western thought develops concept that history is not chance but rational process, the evolution of freedom. 457pp. 5⅜ x 8½. 20112-0 Pa. $9.95

THE BOOK OF TEA, Kakuzo Okakura. Minor classic of the Orient: entertaining, charming explanation, interpretation of traditional Japanese culture in terms of tea ceremony. 94pp. 5⅜ x 8½. 20070-1 Pa. $3.95

LIFE IN ANCIENT EGYPT, Adolf Erman. Fullest, most thorough, detailed older account with much not in more recent books, domestic life, religion, magic, medicine, commerce, much more. Many illustrations reproduce tomb paintings, carvings, hieroglyphs, etc. 597pp. 5⅜ x 8½. 22632-8 Pa. $12.95

SUNDIALS, Their Theory and Construction, Albert Waugh. Far and away the best, most thorough coverage of ideas, mathematics concerned, types, construction, adjusting anywhere. Simple, nontechnical treatment allows even children to build several of these dials. Over 100 illustrations. 230pp. 5⅜ x 8½. 22947-5 Pa. $8.95

THEORETICAL HYDRODYNAMICS, L. M. Milne-Thomson. Classic exposition of the mathematical theory of fluid motion, applicable to both hydrodynamics and aerodynamics. Over 600 exercises. 768pp. 6⅛ x 9¼. 68970-0 Pa. $20.95

SONGS OF EXPERIENCE: Facsimile Reproduction with 26 Plates in Full Color, William Blake. 26 full-color plates from a rare 1826 edition. Includes "TheTyger," "London," "Holy Thursday," and other poems. Printed text of poems. 48pp. 5¼ x 7. 24636-1 Pa. $4.95

OLD-TIME VIGNETTES IN FULL COLOR, Carol Belanger Grafton (ed.). Over 390 charming, often sentimental illustrations, selected from archives of Victorian graphics—pretty women posing, children playing, food, flowers, kittens and puppies, smiling cherubs, birds and butterflies, much more. All copyright-free. 48pp. 9¼ x 12¼. 27269-9 Pa. $7.95

PERSPECTIVE FOR ARTISTS, Rex Vicat Cole. Depth, perspective of sky and sea, shadows, much more, not usually covered. 391 diagrams, 81 reproductions of drawings and paintings. 279pp. 5⅜ x 8½. 22487-2 Pa. $9.95

DRAWING THE LIVING FIGURE, Joseph Sheppard. Innovative approach to artistic anatomy focuses on specifics of surface anatomy, rather than muscles and bones. Over 170 drawings of live models in front, back and side views, and in widely varying poses. Accompanying diagrams. 177 illustrations. Introduction. Index. 144pp. 8⅜ x11¼. 26723-7 Pa. $9.95

GOTHIC AND OLD ENGLISH ALPHABETS: 100 Complete Fonts, Dan X. Solo. Add power, elegance to posters, signs, other graphics with 100 stunning copyright-free alphabets: Blackstone, Dolbey, Germania, 97 more–including many lower-case, numerals, punctuation marks. 104pp. 8⅛ x 11. 24695-7 Pa. $8.95

HOW TO DO BEADWORK, Mary White. Fundamental book on craft from simple projects to five-bead chains and woven works. 106 illustrations. 142pp. 5⅜ x 8. 20697-1 Pa. $5.95

THE BOOK OF WOOD CARVING, Charles Marshall Sayers. Finest book for beginners discusses fundamentals and offers 34 designs. "Absolutely first rate . . . well thought out and well executed."–E. J. Tangerman. 118pp. 7¾ x 10⅝. 23654-4 Pa. $7.95

ILLUSTRATED CATALOG OF CIVIL WAR MILITARY GOODS: Union Army Weapons, Insignia, Uniform Accessories, and Other Equipment, Schuyler, Hartley, and Graham. Rare, profusely illustrated 1846 catalog includes Union Army uniform and dress regulations, arms and ammunition, coats, insignia, flags, swords, rifles, etc. 226 illustrations. 160pp. 9 x 12. 24939-5 Pa. $10.95

WOMEN'S FASHIONS OF THE EARLY 1900s: An Unabridged Republication of "New York Fashions, 1909," National Cloak & Suit Co. Rare catalog of mail-order fashions documents women's and children's clothing styles shortly after the turn of the century. Captions offer full descriptions, prices. Invaluable resource for fashion, costume historians. Approximately 725 illustrations. 128pp. 8⅜ x 11¼. 27276-1 Pa. $11.95

THE 1912 AND 1915 GUSTAV STICKLEY FURNITURE CATALOGS, Gustav Stickley. With over 200 detailed illustrations and descriptions, these two catalogs are essential reading and reference materials and identification guides for Stickley furniture. Captions cite materials, dimensions and prices. 112pp. 6½ x 9¼. 26676-1 Pa. $9.95

EARLY AMERICAN LOCOMOTIVES, John H. White, Jr. Finest locomotive engravings from early 19th century: historical (1804–74), main-line (after 1870), special, foreign, etc. 147 plates. 142pp. 11⅜ x 8¼. 22772-3 Pa. $12.95

THE TALL SHIPS OF TODAY IN PHOTOGRAPHS, Frank O. Braynard. Lavishly illustrated tribute to nearly 100 majestic contemporary sailing vessels: Amerigo Vespucci, Clearwater, Constitution, Eagle, Mayflower, Sea Cloud, Victory, many more. Authoritative captions provide statistics, background on each ship. 190 black-and-white photographs and illustrations. Introduction. 128pp. 8⅞ x 11¾. 27163-3 Pa. $14.95

LITTLE BOOK OF EARLY AMERICAN CRAFTS AND TRADES, Peter Stockham (ed.). 1807 children's book explains crafts and trades: baker, hatter, cooper, potter, and many others. 23 copperplate illustrations. 140pp. 4⅝ x 6.

23336-7 Pa. $4.95

VICTORIAN FASHIONS AND COSTUMES FROM HARPER'S BAZAR, 1867–1898, Stella Blum (ed.). Day costumes, evening wear, sports clothes, shoes, hats, other accessories in over 1,000 detailed engravings. 320pp. 9⅜ x 12¼.

22990-4 Pa. $16.95

GUSTAV STICKLEY, THE CRAFTSMAN, Mary Ann Smith. Superb study surveys broad scope of Stickley's achievement, especially in architecture. Design philosophy, rise and fall of the Craftsman empire, descriptions and floor plans for many Craftsman houses, more. 86 black-and-white halftones. 31 line illustrations. Introduction 208pp. 6½ x 9¼.

27210-9 Pa. $9.95

THE LONG ISLAND RAIL ROAD IN EARLY PHOTOGRAPHS, Ron Ziel. Over 220 rare photos, informative text document origin (1844) and development of rail service on Long Island. Vintage views of early trains, locomotives, stations, passengers, crews, much more. Captions. 8⅞ x 11¾.

26301-0 Pa. $14.95

VOYAGE OF THE LIBERDADE, Joshua Slocum. Great 19th-century mariner's thrilling, first-hand account of the wreck of his ship off South America, the 35-foot boat he built from the wreckage, and its remarkable voyage home. 128pp. 5⅜ x 8½.

40022-0 Pa. $5.95

TEN BOOKS ON ARCHITECTURE, Vitruvius. The most important book ever written on architecture. Early Roman aesthetics, technology, classical orders, site selection, all other aspects. Morgan translation. 331pp. 5⅜ x 8½. 20645-9 Pa. $8.95

THE HUMAN FIGURE IN MOTION, Eadweard Muybridge. More than 4,500 stopped-action photos, in action series, showing undraped men, women, children jumping, lying down, throwing, sitting, wrestling, carrying, etc. 390pp. 7⅞ x 10⅝.

20204-6 Clothbd. $27.95

TREES OF THE EASTERN AND CENTRAL UNITED STATES AND CANADA, William M. Harlow. Best one-volume guide to 140 trees. Full descriptions, woodlore, range, etc. Over 600 illustrations. Handy size. 288pp. 4½ x 6⅜.

20395-6 Pa. $6.95

SONGS OF WESTERN BIRDS, Dr. Donald J. Borror. Complete song and call repertoire of 60 western species, including flycatchers, juncoes, cactus wrens, many more—includes fully illustrated booklet.   Cassette and manual 99913-0 $8.95

GROWING AND USING HERBS AND SPICES, Milo Miloradovich. Versatile handbook provides all the information needed for cultivation and use of all the herbs and spices available in North America. 4 illustrations. Index. Glossary. 236pp. 5⅜ x 8½.

25058-X Pa. $7.95

BIG BOOK OF MAZES AND LABYRINTHS, Walter Shepherd. 50 mazes and labyrinths in all—classical, solid, ripple, and more—in one great volume. Perfect inexpensive puzzler for clever youngsters. Full solutions. 112pp. 8⅛ x 11.

22951-3 Pa. $5.95

PIANO TUNING, J. Cree Fischer. Clearest, best book for beginner, amateur. Simple repairs, raising dropped notes, tuning by easy method of flattened fifths. No previous skills needed. 4 illustrations. 201pp. 5⅜ x 8½. 23267-0 Pa. $6.95

HINTS TO SINGERS, Lillian Nordica. Selecting the right teacher, developing confidence, overcoming stage fright, and many other important skills receive thoughtful discussion in this indispensible guide, written by a world-famous diva of four decades' experience. 96pp. 5⅜ x 8½. 40094-8 Pa. $4.95

THE COMPLETE NONSENSE OF EDWARD LEAR, Edward Lear. All nonsense limericks, zany alphabets, Owl and Pussycat, songs, nonsense botany, etc., illustrated by Lear. Total of 320pp. 5⅜ x 8½. (AVAILABLE IN U.S. ONLY.) 20167-8 Pa. $7.95

VICTORIAN PARLOUR POETRY: An Annotated Anthology, Michael R. Turner. 117 gems by Longfellow, Tennyson, Browning, many lesser-known poets. "The Village Blacksmith," "Curfew Must Not Ring Tonight," "Only a Baby Small," dozens more, often difficult to find elsewhere. Index of poets, titles, first lines. xxiii + 325pp. 5⅝ x 8¼. 27044-0 Pa. $8.95

DUBLINERS, James Joyce. Fifteen stories offer vivid, tightly focused observations of the lives of Dublin's poorer classes. At least one, "The Dead," is considered a masterpiece. Reprinted complete and unabridged from standard edition. 160pp. 5$\frac{3}{16}$ x 8¼. 26870-5 Pa. $1.00

GREAT WEIRD TALES: 14 Stories by Lovecraft, Blackwood, Machen and Others, S. T. Joshi (ed.). 14 spellbinding tales, including "The Sin Eater," by Fiona McLeod, "The Eye Above the Mantel," by Frank Belknap Long, as well as renowned works by R. H. Barlow, Lord Dunsany, Arthur Machen, W. C. Morrow and eight other masters of the genre. 256pp. 5⅜ x 8½. (Available in U.S. only.) 40436-6 Pa. $8.95

THE BOOK OF THE SACRED MAGIC OF ABRAMELIN THE MAGE, translated by S. MacGregor Mathers. Medieval manuscript of ceremonial magic. Basic document in Aleister Crowley, Golden Dawn groups. 268pp. 5⅜ x 8½. 23211-5 Pa. $9.95

NEW RUSSIAN-ENGLISH AND ENGLISH-RUSSIAN DICTIONARY, M. A. O'Brien. This is a remarkably handy Russian dictionary, containing a surprising amount of information, including over 70,000 entries. 366pp. 4½ x 6⅛. 20208-9 Pa. $10.95

HISTORIC HOMES OF THE AMERICAN PRESIDENTS, Second, Revised Edition, Irvin Haas. A traveler's guide to American Presidential homes, most open to the public, depicting and describing homes occupied by every American President from George Washington to George Bush. With visiting hours, admission charges, travel routes. 175 photographs. Index. 160pp. 8¼ x 11. 26751-2 Pa. $11.95

NEW YORK IN THE FORTIES, Andreas Feininger. 162 brilliant photographs by the well-known photographer, formerly with *Life* magazine. Commuters, shoppers, Times Square at night, much else from city at its peak. Captions by John von Hartz. 181pp. 9¼ x 10¾. 23585-8 Pa. $13.95

INDIAN SIGN LANGUAGE, William Tomkins. Over 525 signs developed by Sioux and other tribes. Written instructions and diagrams. Also 290 pictographs. 111pp. 6⅛ x 9¼. 22029-X Pa. $3.95

CATALOG OF DOVER BOOKS

ANATOMY: A Complete Guide for Artists, Joseph Sheppard. A master of figure drawing shows artists how to render human anatomy convincingly. Over 460 illustrations. 224pp. 8⅜ x 11¼.   27279-6 Pa. $11.95

MEDIEVAL CALLIGRAPHY: Its History and Technique, Marc Drogin. Spirited history, comprehensive instruction manual covers 13 styles (ca. 4th century through 15th). Excellent photographs; directions for duplicating medieval techniques with modern tools. 224pp. 8⅜ x 11¼.   26142-5 Pa. $12.95

DRIED FLOWERS: How to Prepare Them, Sarah Whitlock and Martha Rankin. Complete instructions on how to use silica gel, meal and borax, perlite aggregate, sand and borax, glycerine and water to create attractive permanent flower arrangements. 12 illustrations. 32pp. 5⅜ x 8½.   21802-3 Pa. $1.00

EASY-TO-MAKE BIRD FEEDERS FOR WOODWORKERS, Scott D. Campbell. Detailed, simple-to-use guide for designing, constructing, caring for and using feeders. Text, illustrations for 12 classic and contemporary designs. 96pp. 5⅜ x 8½.
                                                                       25847-5 Pa. $3.95

SCOTTISH WONDER TALES FROM MYTH AND LEGEND, Donald A. Mackenzie. 16 lively tales tell of giants rumbling down mountainsides, of a magic wand that turns stone pillars into warriors, of gods and goddesses, evil hags, powerful forces and more. 240pp. 5⅜ x 8½.   29677-6 Pa. $6.95

THE HISTORY OF UNDERCLOTHES, C. Willett Cunnington and Phyllis Cunnington. Fascinating, well-documented survey covering six centuries of English undergarments, enhanced with over 100 illustrations: 12th-century laced-up bodice, footed long drawers (1795), 19th-century bustles, l9th-century corsets for men, Victorian "bust improvers," much more. 272pp. 5⅜ x 8¼.   27124-2 Pa. $9.95

ARTS AND CRAFTS FURNITURE: The Complete Brooks Catalog of 1912, Brooks Manufacturing Co. Photos and detailed descriptions of more than 150 now very collectible furniture designs from the Arts and Crafts movement depict davenports, settees, buffets, desks, tables, chairs, bedsteads, dressers and more, all built of solid, quarter-sawed oak. Invaluable for students and enthusiasts of antiques, Americana and the decorative arts. 80pp. 6½ x 9¼.   27471-3 Pa. $8.95

WILBUR AND ORVILLE: A Biography of the Wright Brothers, Fred Howard. Definitive, crisply written study tells the full story of the brothers' lives and work. A vividly written biography, unparalleled in scope and color, that also captures the spirit of an extraordinary era. 560pp. 6⅛ x 9¼.   40297-5 Pa. $17.95

THE ARTS OF THE SAILOR: Knotting, Splicing and Ropework, Hervey Garrett Smith. Indispensable shipboard reference covers tools, basic knots and useful hitches; handsewing and canvas work, more. Over 100 illustrations. Delightful reading for sea lovers. 256pp. 5⅜ x 8½.   26440-8 Pa. $8.95

FRANK LLOYD WRIGHT'S FALLINGWATER: The House and Its History, Second, Revised Edition, Donald Hoffmann. A total revision–both in text and illustrations–of the standard document on Fallingwater, the boldest, most personal architectural statement of Wright's mature years, updated with valuable new material from the recently opened Frank Lloyd Wright Archives. "Fascinating"–*The New York Times*. 116 illustrations. 128pp. 9¼ x 10¾.   27430-6 Pa. $12.95

PHOTOGRAPHIC SKETCHBOOK OF THE CIVIL WAR, Alexander Gardner. 100 photos taken on field during the Civil War. Famous shots of Manassas Harper's Ferry, Lincoln, Richmond, slave pens, etc. 244pp. 10⅝ x 8¼. 22731-6 Pa. $10.95

FIVE ACRES AND INDEPENDENCE, Maurice G. Kains. Great back-to-the-land classic explains basics of self-sufficient farming. The one book to get. 95 illustrations. 397pp. 5⅜ x 8½. 20974-1 Pa. $7.95

SONGS OF EASTERN BIRDS, Dr. Donald J. Borror. Songs and calls of 60 species most common to eastern U.S.: warblers, woodpeckers, flycatchers, thrushes, larks, many more in high-quality recording. Cassette and manual 99912-2 $9.95

A MODERN HERBAL, Margaret Grieve. Much the fullest, most exact, most useful compilation of herbal material. Gigantic alphabetical encyclopedia, from aconite to zedoary, gives botanical information, medical properties, folklore, economic uses, much else. Indispensable to serious reader. 161 illustrations. 888pp. 6½ x 9¼. 2-vol. set. (Available in U.S. only.) Vol. I: 22798-7 Pa. $9.95
Vol. II: 22799-5 Pa. $9.95

HIDDEN TREASURE MAZE BOOK, Dave Phillips. Solve 34 challenging mazes accompanied by heroic tales of adventure. Evil dragons, people-eating plants, blood-thirsty giants, many more dangerous adversaries lurk at every twist and turn. 34 mazes, stories, solutions. 48pp. 8¼ x 11. 24566-7 Pa. $2.95

LETTERS OF W. A. MOZART, Wolfgang A. Mozart. Remarkable letters show bawdy wit, humor, imagination, musical insights, contemporary musical world; includes some letters from Leopold Mozart. 276pp. 5⅜ x 8½. 22859-2 Pa. $7.95

BASIC PRINCIPLES OF CLASSICAL BALLET, Agrippina Vaganova. Great Russian theoretician, teacher explains methods for teaching classical ballet. 118 illustrations. 175pp. 5⅜ x 8½. 22036-2 Pa. $6.95

THE JUMPING FROG, Mark Twain. Revenge edition. The original story of The Celebrated Jumping Frog of Calaveras County, a hapless French translation, and Twain's hilarious "retranslation" from the French. 12 illustrations. 66pp. 5⅜ x 8½. 22686-7 Pa. $3.95

BEST REMEMBERED POEMS, Martin Gardner (ed.). The 126 poems in this superb collection of 19th- and 20th-century British and American verse range from Shelley's "To a Skylark" to the impassioned "Renascence" of Edna St. Vincent Millay and to Edward Lear's whimsical "The Owl and the Pussycat." 224pp. 5⅜ x 8½. 27165-X Pa. $5.95

COMPLETE SONNETS, William Shakespeare. Over 150 exquisite poems deal with love, friendship, the tyranny of time, beauty's evanescence, death and other themes in language of remarkable power, precision and beauty. Glossary of archaic terms. 80pp. 5³⁄₁₆ x 8¼. 26686-9 Pa. $1.00

BODIES IN A BOOKSHOP, R. T. Campbell. Challenging mystery of blackmail and murder with ingenious plot and superbly drawn characters. In the best tradition of British suspense fiction. 192pp. 5⅜ x 8½. 24720-1 Pa. $6.95

THE INFLUENCE OF SEA POWER UPON HISTORY, 1660–1783, A. T. Mahan. Influential classic of naval history and tactics still used as text in war colleges. First paperback edition. 4 maps. 24 battle plans. 640pp. 5⅜ x 8½. 25509-3 Pa. $14.95

THE STORY OF THE TITANIC AS TOLD BY ITS SURVIVORS, Jack Winocour (ed.). What it was really like. Panic, despair, shocking inefficiency, and a little heroism. More thrilling than any fictional account. 26 illustrations. 320pp. 5⅜ x 8½. 20610-6 Pa. $8.95

FAIRY AND FOLK TALES OF THE IRISH PEASANTRY, William Butler Yeats (ed.). Treasury of 64 tales from the twilight world of Celtic myth and legend: "The Soul Cages," "The Kildare Pooka," "King O'Toole and his Goose," many more. Introduction and Notes by W. B. Yeats. 352pp. 5⅜ x 8½. 26941-8 Pa. $8.95

BUDDHIST MAHAYANA TEXTS, E. B. Cowell and others (eds.). Superb, accurate translations of basic documents in Mahayana Buddhism, highly important in history of religions. The Buddha-karita of Asvaghosha, Larger Sukhavativyuha, more. 448pp. 5⅜ x 8½. 25552-2 Pa. $12.95

ONE TWO THREE . . . INFINITY: Facts and Speculations of Science, George Gamow. Great physicist's fascinating, readable overview of contemporary science: number theory, relativity, fourth dimension, entropy, genes, atomic structure, much more. 128 illustrations. Index. 352pp. 5⅜ x 8½. 25664-2 Pa. $9.95

EXPERIMENTATION AND MEASUREMENT, W. J. Youden. Introductory manual explains laws of measurement in simple terms and offers tips for achieving accuracy and minimizing errors. Mathematics of measurement, use of instruments, experimenting with machines. 1994 edition. Foreword. Preface. Introduction. Epilogue. Selected Readings. Glossary. Index. Tables and figures. 128pp. 5³/₈ x 8¹/₂. 40451-X Pa. $6.95

DALÍ ON MODERN ART: The Cuckolds of Antiquated Modern Art, Salvador Dalí. Influential painter skewers modern art and its practitioners. Outrageous evaluations of Picasso, Cézanne, Turner, more. 15 renderings of paintings discussed. 44 calligraphic decorations by Dalí. 96pp. 5⅜ x 8½. (Available in U.S. only.) 29220-7 Pa. $5.95

ANTIQUE PLAYING CARDS: A Pictorial History, Henry René D'Allemagne. Over 900 elaborate, decorative images from rare playing cards (14th–20th centuries): Bacchus, death, dancing dogs, hunting scenes, royal coats of arms, players cheating, much more. 96pp. 9¼ x 12¼. 29265-7 Pa. $12.95

MAKING FURNITURE MASTERPIECES: 30 Projects with Measured Drawings, Franklin H. Gottshall. Step-by-step instructions, illustrations for constructing handsome, useful pieces, among them a Sheraton desk, Chippendale chair, Spanish desk, Queen Anne table and a William and Mary dressing mirror. 224pp. 8⅛ x 11¼. 29338-6 Pa. $13.95

THE FOSSIL BOOK: A Record of Prehistoric Life, Patricia V. Rich et al. Profusely illustrated definitive guide covers everything from single-celled organisms and dinosaurs to birds and mammals and the interplay between climate and man. Over 1,500 illustrations. 760pp. 7½ x 10⅛. 29371-8 Pa. $29.95

Prices subject to change without notice.

Available at your book dealer or write for free catalog to Dept. GI, Dover Publications, Inc., 31 East 2nd St., Mineola, N.Y. 11501. Dover publishes more than 500 books each year on science, elementary and advanced mathematics, biology, music, art, literary history, social sciences and other areas.